Analysing Identity
Cross-cultural, societal and clinical contexts

People's identities are addressed and brought into being by interaction with others. Identity processes encompass biographical experiences, historical eras and cultural norms in which the self's autonomy varies according to the flux of power relationships with others.

Identity Structure Analysis (ISA) draws upon psychological, sociological and social anthropological theory to formulate a system of concepts that help explain the notion of identity. ISA can be applied to the practical investigation of identity structure and identity development – at individual level and/or group level – in a number of clinical, societal and cross-cultural settings. The book includes studies of national and ethnic identification in multi-cultural contexts and gender identity relating to social context and the urban environment. Clinical applications that describe identity processes associated with psychological distress are also looked at. These include anorexia nervosa and vicarious traumatisation of counsellors in the aftermath of atrocity.

Analysing Identity is unique in its development of this integrative conceptualisation of self and identity, and its operationalisation in practice. This innovative book will appeal to academics and professionals in developmental, social, cross-cultural, clinical and educational psychology and psychotherapy. It will also be of interest to those involved with sociology, political science, gender studies, ethnic studies and social policy.

Professor Peter Weinreich has a Personal Chair in the School of Psychology at the University of Ulster. His integrative intellectual work engendered and facilitated the evolution of the Identity Structure Analysis conceptual framework and its operationalisation through successive prototypes of the Identity Exploration computer software.

Dr Wendy Saunderson lectures in the School of Policy Studies at the University of Ulster. Her extensive use of ISA for over a decade has included research into voluntary action, alcohol addiction, anorexia nervosa, lone motherhood, women in academia and the identity processes and politics of men and women as architects, town planners and users of cities.

Analysing Identity

Cross-cultural, societal and clinical contexts

Edited by Peter Weinreich & Wendy Saunderson

Routledge
Taylor & Francis Group

LONDON AND NEW YORK

First published 2003
by Routledge
27 Church Road, Hove, East Sussex, BN3 2FA

Simultaneously published in the USA and Canada
by Routledge
29 West 35th Street, New York, NY 10001

Routledge is an imprint of the Taylor & Francis Group

Typeset in 10/12 Times New Roman by
Newgen Imaging Systems (P) Ltd, Chennai, India
Printed and bound in Great Britain by
MPG Books Ltd, Bodmin, Cornwall
Cover design by Sandra Heath
Cover Painting: *I and the Village*, 1911, Marc Chagall (1887–1986),
Museum of Modern Art, New York, courtesy of Scala Group S.p.A
Copyright © ADAGP, Paris and DACs, London 2002

British Library Cataloguing in Publication Data
A catalogue record for this book is available from the British Library

Library of Congress Cataloging-in-Publication Data
Analysing identity : cross-cultural, societal, and clinical contexts / edited by
Peter Weinreich & Wendy Saunderson.
     p. cm.
  Includes bibliographical references and index.
  ISBN 0-415-29897-0
   1. Identity (Psychology) – Social aspects. I. Weinreich, Peter, 1939–
II. Saunderson, Wendy, 1963–
  BF697.5.S65 A53 2002
  155.2–dc21

                                   2002068328

ISBN 0-415-29897-0

To all those, especially my mother Charlotte Weinreich née Kunert, my brother Helmut Kunert, my daughter Jo, and my partner Mehroo Northover née Aibara, who have had to contend with the challenges of being migrant or offspring of migrants.

Peter Weinreich

To my parents, Norman and Lily Hanna, who resisted the Irish diaspora and gave me my roots; and to Richard Ekins, who has sustained them.

Wendy Saunderson

Contents

Figures

Tables

Biographical notes on contributors

Viera Bacova, PhD, teaches psychology at the Presov University, Slovakia. She previously worked as a researcher at the Slovak Academy of Sciences, Kosice, Slovakia. Her work has introduced ISA to the wider social science community in the Czech Republic and Slovakia. Her research interests include ethnic identity and historical change, gender issues and contemporary movements in psychology.

Selwyn Black, PhD, is an associate lecturer in counselling/social psychology at the University of Ulster. His Doctorate presented a longitudinal study with a team of trauma counsellors in which he explored the long-term impact of vicarious traumatisation on counselling identity. His research interests are in understanding the psychological impact of caring in trauma counsellors and other professionals.

Paul Harris, PhD, is Head of Clinical Psychology Services, Swansea NHS Trust, and is based at Cefn Coed Hospital, Swansea. He is also Honorary Associate Professional Tutor, School of Psychology, Cardiff University. His clinical and academic interests span adult mental health, forensic psychology, and neuro-psychology. His previous posts include that of Senior Tutor, University of Papua New Guinea.

Gabriel Horenczyk, PhD, is a senior lecturer at the School of Education and the Melton Center for Jewish Education, The Hebrew University of Jerusalem. His teaching and research areas include: the psychological study of cultural and ethnic identity; cultural identity processes during intergroup contact; accultur-ation and identity processes among immigrants.

Helen Irvine, DPhil, is a lecturer in Adult Education at the University of Ulster. She is currently Course Director of the BA/BSc (Hons) Combined Studies pro-gramme, which is geared towards the mature student. Her research interests include adult participation in higher education and the support of mature students and students in transition.

Anita MacNabb, DPhil, is a senior consultant at The Management Institute, University of Ulster, where she is responsible for the design and delivery of management development programmes for business owners, community leaders and business advisors. She has used Identity Structure Analysis in her published work and in her recently awarded DPhil, in which she examined the entrepreneurial profiles of aspiring and established business owners.

Salim Munayer, PhD, is the Academic Dean of the Bethlehem Bible College, where he also teaches theology. He is the director of *Musalaha*, an organisation dedicated to promoting reconciliation between Arab Palestinians and Israeli Jews. He has recently completed his PhD at the University of Wales; his dissertation examined the ethnic identity of Palestinian Arab Christian adolescents in Israel.

Maria O'Kane, MRCP, is a consultant psychiatrist and adult psychotherapist employed by the Homefirst Community Trust, Antrim, Northern Ireland. She has a long-standing interest and experience in the treatment of female patients with eating disorders in the NHS.

Nathalie Rougier, PhD, was born in Ussel, France, and studied psychology at The Université Blaise Pascal in Clermont-Ferrand for six years before moving to Northern Ireland to undertake ISA research into the ethno-religious identities of Irish clergy. She completed her Doctorate in psychology at the University of Ulster in 2001. Her research interests include identity development and change, ethnic and national identifications and intergroup relations.

Wendy Saunderson, PhD, lectures in the School of Policy Studies at the University of Ulster. Her main research interests embrace inequalities and social exclusion in relation to gender, disability, childhood and lone parenthood. Her extensive use of ISA for over a decade has included research into identity and voluntary action, children's education for mutual understanding in Northern Ireland, alcohol addiction, anorexia nervosa, 'new managerialism' in UK universities, the psychosocial health of lone mothers and, particularly, the identity processes and politics of women as architects, town planners and users of cities.

Karyn Stapleton, DPhil, is currently a research officer with the Institute of Ulster–Scots Studies at the University of Ulster. Her research interests include 'language and gender'; feminist theory; postmodernism; cultural/ethnic identities, and the ontology/epistemology of 'discursive identities'. She has published work on ethnic identity, gender and discourse, the construction of feminist identity, and an application of ISA to feminist and postmodern theory.

Maaret Wager, DPhil, is research fellow at the Department of Social Psychology and is involved with faculty development and educational innovations in the Faculty of Social Sciences, University of Helsinki. She is also leader of the interdisciplinary research project 'Gender and Academia'. She completed her Doctorate on academic women's identity in 1993 in Northern Ireland, where she worked for four years. She has been teaching Social Psychology for almost twenty years.

Biographical notes on contributors xv

Peter Weinreich has a Personal Chair in Psychology at the University of Ulster. He continues to be dedicated to developing the Identity Structure Analysis (ISA) conceptual framework and the Identity Exploration (IDEX) computer software for interdisciplinary research and practical application. The ISA/IDEX endeavour continues to be sustained and refined by research doctorates and by way of its increasing use in projects internationally.

John Wilson is Professor of Communication and Sociolinguistics at the University of Ulster. He is currently Director of the University's Institute of Ulster–Scots Studies. His research interests and major publication areas include pragmatics, sociolinguistics and political languages.

Foreword

How should a human being best be described? The answer to this perennial question must depend to some extent on the point of the activity to which the description is germane. There can be no general answer. Furthermore, in our culture alone there are many vocabularies from which descriptive terms can be drawn. There are words for character traits, for aspects of personality, for skills and talents, for bodily characteristics, for social relations and status, for moments in a personal history, for religious and political persuasions and commitments, for deviations in ways of thinking and acting from what are considered right and proper ways of being, and so on. Every one of these expressions can be used to describe any person to whom it seems appropriate. They delineate kinds. Yet each person is unique, an individual unlike any other. The problem to which this book is devoted is to devise a system for describing people that does justice to ways in which each person is similar to others and to ways in which each human being is unique. How are identities, in both senses, formed?

For all sorts of reasons English has become the language of psychology as an academic discipline and as a field for intervention in the lives of troubled people. Yet anthropologists have demonstrated in dozens of studies how widely the vernaculars of historically and geographically diverse cultures differ, not only in their vocabularies but also in the very categories of attributes that the resources of local languages allow as relevant to human beings as they actually live their lives. What are we to make of *purusa* (the self as it appears in the world) and *prakti* (the equilibrium of the three 'principles' of personal being), of *li* (the principle of right living) and *ch'i* (the material aspect of *hsing* or mind), the basic concepts of classical Indian and traditional Chinese psychologies respectively? The project of the series of studies reported in this book is to develop a generic system of descriptions, from a starting point in English, that will subsume the many species of person characterisations with which we are now acquainted. At this stage in the development of the techniques those involved in Identity Structure Analysis (ISA) have not yet followed all the ramifications of cross-cultural possibilities and problems.[1] Nevertheless, by opting for formal analyses of descriptive concepts they have chosen generality by abstraction rather than the more simplistic attempts by old paradigm psychologists to reach generality by induction over large populations of 'subjects'.

By giving formal definitions and algebraic expressions of key concepts in the ISA identity scheme it is hoped the cultural and linguistics particulars of English as the source language can be transcended. Raising the level of abstraction to transcend particularities of subject matter has been the major technique in the development of logic, and in such attempts as that of Wierzbicka (1999: Chapter 1, Section 8) to create a transcultural system of basic concepts.

What is it that makes an individual person unique? In English the two main variants of the concept of 'sameness' are not readily distinguished lexically. 'This is the *same* as that' and 'This is the *same* something as I encountered yesterday' use one word, '*same*', for two very different concepts of identity. The former is qualitative identity, two or more things belonging to the same category or having the same type of attribute. The latter is numerical identity, one thing being the very same entity or individual at two or more times or in two or more contexts. In other languages the distinction is marked lexically, for instance, in Spanish 'igual' generally expresses qualitative identity, while 'mismo', for the most part, expresses numerical identity. The concept of selfhood, as expressed by uses of the word 'self', is even more complex in its contemporary semantics. From being a simple reflexive pronoun used to indicate that the activities or attributes described in some utterance are those of the speaker, still in use as 'myself', it has expanded its domain to include the characteristic attributes of a human being, whether or not that person is the speaker. In this guise it has entered the domain of psychology as the 'self-concept', in phrases like 'self-esteem' and so on. How can these ambiguities in quite fundamental concepts be resolved or transcended?

Western theories of the nature of human beings as persons have been dominated by a metaphysical thesis, first formulated in the seventeenth century by René Descartes. Each human being was supposed to be a synthetic unity consisting of two radically distinct substances, a body and a mind. Human individuality lay in the alleged fact that each mind is a unique substance, while every body is made of common material stuff. One matter and many minds. Whether this theory has been accepted or rejected by subsequent theoreticians, it has had a pervasive influence on how the vocabularies of the vernacular of Western Europe have been interpreted by philosophers and psychologists. Can it be finally evaded?

Here then are some of the issues to which any attempt at a generic conceptual system for describing human beings must be answerable. How to deal with the broad range of person-oriented vocabularies, with their seemingly fundamental material and mental subdivisions, without slipping into Cartesian metaphysics. How to manage the balance between the uniqueness, the idiographic aspect of personhood, and generality, the nomothetic aspect, without eliminating either. Raising the level of abstraction of the working concepts is an essential preliminary to achieving these goals.

THE PROJECT OF IDENTITY STRUCTURE ANALYSIS

It would be a great advance, not only in psychology but in all sorts of domains, such as medicine, counselling, the law, sport and so on, if a common generic vocabulary could be devised that would not only resolve the ambiguities of the vernacular, but stand above the huge array of cultural variations in ways of talking about people. This is the project of *Identity Structure Analysis*, hereafter 'ISA'. The development of ISA has been motivated above all by the need to establish a *common* method for investigating selfhood as identity, in both its individual and its general meanings. What is *unique* about this person? What *sort* of person is this?

Only if a common method of analysis has been used can valid comparisons, generalisations and so on be made, from case to case. Of course that is just one of the necessary conditions for cross-person and cross-situational comparisons and generalisations. Another is that the method of analysis should employ a common system of categories and attributes.

The locus of ISA lies in the ways that people appraise their situations, the events in which they play a part and their own characters and roles in these events. In so far as ISA is aimed at tracking development of identities in both senses of the unique and the generic, it is tied in with biography and autobiography. A key principle of the ISA approach is this:

A person's appraisal of the social world and its significance is an expression of his or her identity.

Of course this is 'identity' in the sense of what *sort* of person it is who is making the appraisals. But the totality of such appraisals will, it is believed, have idiosyncratic aspects. It will not be just a knee-jerk response on the hypothesis that in the long run such appraisals will reveal a person's identity in the other sense – that is, what it is about that person that is unique.

The issue of the double meaning of selfhood and identity is tackled in the expository sections of this study. A useful comparison of ISA and the currently popular discursive approach, DP, in which systems of meanings and rules are immanent in local social practices of meaning-making, brings out an important difference in emphasis. Whereas DP is concerned with bringing to light the common though local resources for meaningful joint action, ISA is as much concerned with bringing to light what have been called 'subjectivities', 'how it is for me'. Once again the problem of the unique and the generic has to be faced. For many feminists 'subjectivity' referred to the generic 'take' on life and the world that was *typical* for women: 'How it is for me, *qua* woman'. The emphasis was on how this differed from the generic subjectivity of men. Subjectivities, in this sense, were important in ethnic studies, and particularly in the understanding of 'How it is for me, *qua* "minority member" '. However, any subjectivity is a unique person's take on the world. So ISA must also aim to bring to light, that is to public expression and understanding, the characteristics of a unique point of view, an individual take on the world.

A third key element in the analysis is the cluster of concepts roughly comprehended under the idea of 'identification with'. Identity formation owes a good deal to ways in which a person tries to be like or not to be like another. Sometimes this might be coolly cognitive, sometimes empathic. However, ISA is intended to follow the patterns of 'identification with (or not with)' that seem to have been important in someone's life manifested in self-construals.

The value of any such scheme and its associated technique depends to a great extent on the facility with which it can be put to use. To this end ISA has been developed in tandem with a computerised procedure for analysing the huge bulk of material that all efforts at detailed and realistic psychological studies tend to produce. There are several generic content analysing programmes available, but the ISA programme is specifically designed for use as an identity exploration tool. It makes use of bipolar constructs, which, at a fundamental level, are independent of one another.

PUTTING THE SCHEME TO WORK

The bulk of the material in this volume is devoted to specific applications of ISA to problem fields in the human sciences. They are drawn from the kinds of problems that are the downsides of life, the sources of human misery, alienation and bewilderment. Identity as ethnicity is tackled from the ISA point of view. The range of applications further includes the investigation of identities and identity formation in various matters to which gender as an aspect of the sense of self is germane, in anorexia nervosa, as revealed in clinical assessment, and in counselling for trauma. The underlying conceptual structure of each and every study is the relation between self-construal, an aspect of personal identity, and identification, perceived relationships to the kinds of persons who are other or regarded as other, in the context and in various role relationships. The results of these studies taken as a whole, show how closely tied are self-construals and perceptions of others. This strengthens the point brought out by Smith's (1995) studies in which the sibling technique of repertory grid analysis was used to track self-construals in relation to the changing array of other persons. At the same time analyses using ISA bear upon the general question of the universality of developmental processes as these are realised in specific cultural settings. The primordial is emphasised over the situational.

Ethnicity

The power of idiographic methods to break through stereotypical generalisations is illustrated vividly in the ISA studies of ethnicity. Primordial sentiment is shown to have developmental primacy, which may to an extent be supported by cultural ethos, but which may also be challenged by enlightened thought and complex autobiography, illustrated cross-culturally in Ireland and Slovakia. Further, in Israel several young Palestinian Christians used an ISA instrument for an exercise in systematic self-construal. Once again the virtues of the idiographic methodology are manifest. Behind the bland generalisations of the nomothetic design of mass study lie radically different variants of the identity/identification pattern, variants that would have been lost in the processes of induction. Yet each is a variant of a basic 'primordial' structure.

Feminist issues

The use of the ISA approach is particularly well illustrated by one of the detailed studies reported in this volume: urban identity as it is displayed by men and women. Using a distinction between urban production and consumption to manage the conceptual scheme employed in the study, the results of using ISA are striking. The polarities of personal self ('as I am now') and professional self ('as a town-planner') are revealed as interrelated through the former being 'modified' by the latter for women as urban producers, in that their sense of identity in the 'what *sort* of person' sense is partially assimilated into the existing ethos of the profession. On the other hand, women in general experience conflict between personal self and self as social actor, in that identification with aspects of the city and its planners (not identity) is conflictual with respect to much that has to do with their role as primary child carers. Here we see the two ISA concepts of identity and identification at work in teasing out a complex and dynamic sense of selfhood.

Other close order studies include work on the identity characteristics of women in business as entrepreneurs. Again the work is driven by the two ISA concepts of *'personal identity'* and *'identification with'*. Thus when motherhood is a salient feature of personal identity there is conflict in patterns of identification with other successful entrepreneurs. In a study of identity in the case of women in the academic world another aspect of ISA becomes prominent, the relation between what one takes one's selfhood actually to have been and what one takes as possible selfhoods might be. The point is well taken, as autobiography has both a retrospective and a prospective dimension. The use of ISA with its emphasis on unique identity structures within a common repertoire of identity-making resources is shown to illuminate the socio-psychological dynamics of those taking up further education as adults. Again the technique allows differences in the developing identity structure of women and men returnees to be brought out systematically.

Pathological life forms and disturbing life events

Another main group of studies concerns those areas of psychological troubles that lie just outside the boundaries of psychopathy, yet are the concern of professional carers. It has long been argued by those concerned with disorders, as locally conceived, that much is lost by jumping to generalities prematurely. This piece of wisdom is highlighted and supported by an ISA study of the life of just one person suffering from anorexia. This idiographic study is complemented by a more nomothetic use of the ISA technique to look for common features in a wide variety of problems with 'mental health'. Here the old notion of 'self-concept' is given a fillip using the past, present and future self-pattern to focus on stability and change. The results are interesting in that, in an idiographic sample case, past and present self-construals are alike, while present and future construal differ. At the same time by repeating an ISA on the same person, consistency of self-construals can be examined.

While the two predominantly idiographic studies focus on self-construal in various cases of upset people, another study uses ISA to look at self-construal and particularly the complementary process of identification in a more or less 'made to measure' group of people – counsellors themselves. Thus vicarious traumatisation, *identification*, can affect the self-construals, *identity*, of counsellors.

CONCLUSIONS

In many ways the ISA approach is sibling to the well-established methods of repertory grid analysis. It uses bipolar constructs; it is oriented towards the idiographic aspects of personhood and so towards psychological reality. It eschews premature generalisations arrived at through simplistic inductions. The complementary aim of generality can be achieved only at the conceptual level. According to the programme of ISA this is not so much a direct aim as a by-product of the use of formal modes of expression that generalise by raising the level of abstraction, rather than by increasing the raw extension of the class of persons under scrutiny. The empirical studies enrich the programme in many ways, but the ones reported in this volume have a special interest. They show how ISA can serve as the research tool *par excellence* in bringing to light the subtle interplay between self-construal and construal of others through the relation of 'identification with (or not with)'.

The team of psychologists whose work is brought together in this volume is to be congratulated on taking a significant pace towards a genuinely scientific psychology. Not only that – this work is of demonstrable and unique value to those who are faced with the upsets and miseries of our complicated form of life.

ROM HARRÉ

NOTE

1 For example: in Japan, the extreme dominance of social identity in many forms over personal identity in all public displays; in Sarawak, identity related in both senses to ancestral sources and living descendants (local Dyaks).

REFERENCES

Smith, J. A. (1995) Repertory grids: An interactive, case-study perspective. In J. A. Smith, R. Harré & L. van Langenhove (eds), *Rethinking Methods in Psychology*. London: Sage.

Wierzbicka, A. (1999) *Emotions across Languages and Cultures*. Cambridge: Cambridge UP.

Acknowledgements

The development of ISA has continued over the years and builds on the work of psychologists of various persuasions, sociologists and social anthropologists. In its practice, ISA has benefited from cohorts of undergraduate psychology students mastering basic concepts and developing a greater sense of their own identity development during practical work. Many doctoral students have contributed feedback and through their efforts demonstrated the efficacy of ISA. Their dissertations cover a wide area and are included in an Appendix. The implementation of the ISA conceptual framework would not be possible without the efforts and intellectual expertise of writers of computer software, most recently Laurence Asquith and Stephen Ewart. Many colleagues have engaged in debate that has been challenging. Brian Dean, Claire Adams and John Alderdice have provided crucial support during periods of uncertainty. We particularly wish to acknowledge our respective partners, Mehroo Northover for her inestimable contributions both intellectually and personally, and Richard Ekins for his unfailing intellectual and emotional support.

PETER WEINREICH AND WENDY SAUNDERSON

Part I

Theory and practice

INTRODUCTION

This volume presents theory and practice of an open-ended framework of theoretical concepts and process postulates about processes of identity development and redefinition, which is based on extant orientations derived in the main from the disciplines of psychology, sociology and social anthropology. The conceptual framework, Identity Structure Analysis, attempts to provide a seamless interface between psychology, sociology and social anthropology, and related subject areas such as political science, economics, social policy, education, and so on. The justification for this mission arises from observations common to the subject matter of these disciplines. Prominent among these is that individuals appraise and interpret the events in which they participate, and they identify with other people and social institutions. They experience others within a framework of institutions that are imbued with a sense of relative permanence through social representations (Moscovici & Paicheler, 1978; Farr & Moscovici, 1984; Moscovici, 1988; Billig, 1988; Jodelet, 1993; Flick, 1995). While social representations are not entirely unchanging, they are nevertheless maintained within societal structures that have symbolic meaning interpreted according to shared norms.

Identity Structure Analysis (hereafter, ISA) refers to the *structural* representation of the individual's existential experience, in which the relationships between self and other agents are organised in relatively stable structures over time, but which become further elaborated and changed on account of new experiences (Weinreich, 1979a,b, 1980, 1983a,b, 1985a,b, 1986a,b, 1989a,b, 1991a,b, 1992, 1998, 1999; Weinreich, Harris, & Doherty, 1985; Weinreich, Kelly, & Maja, 1987, 1988; Weinreich, Luk, & Bond, 1996). The structuring and restructuring of experience may be conceptualised as following Piagetian principles of assimilation and accommodation (Piaget, 1950, 1952), but with the emphasis on the sociocultural milieu (Vygotsky, 1930–1935/1978) in which self relates to other agents and institutions. For example, there may be a partial assimilation of new minor *within-range* experiences to the extant structural arrangement of previously experienced events and states of mind. There may follow a partial accommodation of existing structures of experience to new major *different-order* events, such as achieving insights and exercising novel skills, or experiencing bereavements, traumas and passionate encounters involving others. Layers of experience will become sequentially and structurally organised. However, the sequencing of structural organisation and reorganisation will not only depend on processes of cognitive development, but will also be profoundly influenced by cultural context and biographical experience. The structural representation of self and other agents constitutes the person's identity, which because of idiosyncratic personal experiences will be unique and because of normative world-views will exhibit various degrees of commonality from person to person. The evolving conceptual tools of ISA provide for modes of analysis of the person's identity structure that are operationalised for practical application, so that the distinguishing features of identity may be objectified.

ISA attempts to *objectify the subjective*: to make the subjective subject-matter of identity objectively explicit by way of transparent procedures of assessment. Discourses that represent subjective experience and concepts that address subjective states of mind are frequently regarded as peculiarly inaccessible to objective analyses. However, operationalisation of ISA concepts enables the hitherto subjective parameters of identity to be objectively assessed.

Whatever societal, economic, technological and political factors impinge on the overall well-being of communities, their significance is interpreted with varying degrees of appropriateness by individuals, be they leaders or followers, rogues or upstanding people, wise or stupid people. Individuals appraise societal scenarios, actions of others, and self's experiences for significance to self's own identity aspirations – that is, from a variety of perspectives according to the identities of the people in question. People's biographical progressions, experienced and expressed as the person's identity, provide the framework for appraisals of events by means of which society, economics, politics, history, culture, ethnicity, gender and self are partly understood or misunderstood.

Deficiency versus evolutionary problematic

One pervasive strand of conceptualisation of social and personal problems at the societal level, such as ethnic conflict, stereotyping and prejudice, implicitly assumes that people are mostly rational. Societal failures such as disadvantage, culture of racism – or cognitive deficiencies in information processing such as social categorisation, stereotyping – are viewed as being fundamental causes of problems in society. Failures within society or deficiencies within the brain compromise rational thinking and behaviour. Solutions to problems are seen to be potentially available through the correction of disadvantage and maltreatment, or by way of better modes of information processing. *Deviations from rationality* are the implicit problematics to be explained with a view to instilling corrective procedures. Explanations are sought in 'things going wrong' in society, or with 'imperfect' cognitive mechanisms so as to 'explain' personal difficulty, societal conflict, stereotyping and so on. The emphasis is on righting societal wrongs and working to overcome deficiencies.

Another strand gives evolutionary considerations more prominence, in which explanations of social evils are sought in developmental and socio-psychological processes that are not rational in the sense of rational thinking. Attention is directed to explanations of processes that are viewed as fundamental to sustaining immediate individual survival as a member of a cohesive group that continually contends with challenges to general survival in the wider material and social world. In this approach the emphasis is on explaining why many issues of human behaviour and society that cause immense grief to people, such as psychological disturbance, societal discrimination and ethnic cleansing, are fundamentally features of individual and societal processes. In this approach, rational thinking is not accepted as being the fundamental norm. Instead, the power of rational thought is more often seen to be placed in the service of greater mastery and more effective survival of the 'group' (a variable entity that may typically be immediate kin, an ethnic group, or some other historically salient community). Depending on circumstances, the effective survival of the group may be at the expense of another group. The problematic to be explained is not seen to stem from deviations from rationality but from processes that perpetuate intense social and individual 'wrongs', which may only by concerted societal effort be contained to varying degrees should the broader public so wish. In this perspective, 'wrong behaviour and evil events' have their origins in fundamental ongoing psychological and societal processes that are omnipresent and these processes are the problematics to be explained.

The emphasis in ISA is towards contributing to the explication of the latter kind of problematic. It attempts to provide a broad conceptual framework within which fundamental omnipresent psychological and societal processes may be conceptualised, while not diminishing the simultaneous and crucial significance of the contribution of societal and individual deficiencies to the overall explanation of individual and societal affairs.

In other words, ISA assumes that fundamental universal processes generate prejudice, stereotyping, discrimination, ethnic conflict, and intolerance for deviations from pervasive societal and cultural norms of gendered behaviour and sexual orientation. The processes that result in 'ills of society' are not just breakdowns or deficiencies in properly functioning societies and persons, but are engaged in by all people of any culture though moderated by societal norms. Norms of atavistic populism, characterising certain sections of a community, may promote cultural, educational and political regimes that galvanise these processes with resulting inhumane consequences for specific individuals and particular outgroups. Alternatively, hard-won and enforced norms of fair play, respect and tolerance for difference may ameliorate such processes, though with some difficulty and requiring much concerted effort on the part of 'enlightened' cultural, educational and political agencies.

Given the ever-presence of these fundamental processes, the issue of what are considered to be appropriate social norms constitutes an active arena of moral debate in society. Social norms endorsed by the populace at large tend to be instigated by way of the political dominance of specific parties that are felt to 'represent the interests of the people'. The norms vary considerably from culture to culture and from one historical era to another. 'Enlightened' moral beliefs tend currently to be concerned with the sanctity of life, individual well-being, freedom for personal expression irrespective of creed, ethnicity and religion, and justice in respect of these beliefs. Such 'enlightened beliefs' are evidently not universally shared nor implemented across the world. In many instances around the globe, norms of atavistic populism encouraged by charismatic but unprincipled leaders galvanise the universally pervasive propensities of stereotyping, intolerance of deviation, discrimination and ethnic conflict, in the 'interests of survival of the group and its identity'. As will be seen, the ISA conceptual framework encompasses explanatory process postulates of the kind referred to here, together with the significance that contending social norms have in respect of variations in identification with individual agents and societal agencies. For example, Chapter 3 presents a theoretical analysis and an empirical investigation of the interplay of normative cultural ethos with the psychology of basic primordialist sentiments and acquired situationalist perspectives towards ethnicity and nationality.

ISA is a conceptual tool and, aided by the accessible Identity Exploration (IDEX) computer software (Weinreich & Ewart, 1999a,b), a methodological resource. The aims of this volume are to present the ISA conceptualisation and its capacity for bringing diverse topics, ranging from clinical, through societal to cross-cultural, into a coherent framework. ISA presents an orientation to identity processes by means of which our conscious experiences of the world may be elucidated. Central to consciousness is the process by which people appraise the world in which they live and themselves in it. People's self-appraisal and their appraisal of others are fundamentally related to the identifications they have made with others throughout childhood and beyond, hence to processes of identity development and redefinition of identity.

Appraisal, in general terms, involves awareness and effort after meaning, or making sense of oneself in the circumstances of the moment. It is the central process by which people assess circumstances for the potential fulfilment of their identity aspirations during the current period of their lifecycle. In particular, appraisal involves people's assessment of the viability of situations – often involving other agents – in relation to their behavioural intentions, which influences and orients their actual behaviour. In the process they use discourses to communicate with others and reflect on themselves. Such discourses are manifest expressions of their identities from moment to moment. Appraisal is necessary for psychological survival, in which people's propensity is to appraise the social world in a manner biased strongly towards the positive, that is, a positivity bias predominates in which people are preferably accorded more positive than negative qualities. Perceived negative acts and negative qualities stand out all the more by contrast. This positivity bias is evident in the studies reported in this volume, as well as in all ISA studies completed to date.

The ISA conceptualisation enables social realities to be related to identity processes. Examples include certain people's propensities towards primordialist sentiments about nationality and ethnicity (Chapter 3), extreme clinical disturbances such as anorexia nervosa (Chapter 11) and clinical depression (Fox, 1996), or the more everyday concerns of gender identity (Chapter 6), identity in the context of urban place (Chapter 7), occupational stress (Reid, 1990), or entrepreneurial identity aspirations when promoting business enterprises (Chapter 9). These diverse issues may be elucidated within the same conceptual framework, which in principle can be applied to many pressing salient contemporary issues such as religious fundamentalism or ethnic cleansing. In practice ISA may be regarded as an open-ended metatheoretical framework for deriving explanations in terms of theoretical propositions that constitute intercommunicating 'theories' about the phenomena under consideration – intercommunicating because they share the same framework of concepts.

At various episodes during their lifecycles people encounter individuals, social organisations and other agents that have especial significance, with whom they may form further identifications. By so identifying, they may acquire new modes of thinking about the social and material world that are partly expressed in terms of discourses derived from the others. ISA conceptualises people's broadening of identifications and elaboration of discourses in a manner that can be naturally and effectively operationalised in follow-up studies of individuals over time.

An integrative approach to human and social being

Everyone experiences the desire to make suitable sense of the particular world one engages in from moment to moment. A fundamental aspect of this process is the striving to make sense of oneself: to comprehend who one is, where one has come from, and the kind of person one aspires to be in the future. This issue of identity and one's location within the complex world is central to everyone's being. The quest for meaning to one's existence is true of most people, even when, as behaviourists or certain kinds of experimental psychologists, they hold a personal ideology that denies the validity of the subjective, subscribing to the belief that only external observations of human behaviour are deemed to have validity. Making some measure of sense of the world and oneself in it is a prerequisite to negotiating one's lifestyle in relation to people with whom one must interact and social institutions to which one must relate. A person's appraisal of the social world and its significance is an expression of his or her identity. People's different interpretations of some action such as abortion, or the significance they assign to a scientific theory such as Darwinian evolutionary theory, depend on their appraisals of the social world, which express their identities in all their idiosyncrasies. Aspirations to be rational and follow scientific methods of investigation may be core dimensions of a person's identity, but this does not mean that in practice the person's science is pursued for wholly rational reasons and without strong individual values and beliefs.

This text aims to provide concepts the use of which may explicate the manner by which individuals appraise everyday interactions with people in complex and evolving contexts. Appraisal is set within the biographical development of individual identity within the socio-historical context of the era in question.

1 Identity structure analysis

Peter Weinreich

THEORETICAL UNDERPINNINGS OF IDENTITY STRUCTURE ANALYSIS

The literature on identity presents many approaches subsumed by the term 'identity' which emphasise differing identity processes. Those presented here reflect a wide range. In so far as each approach has validity in conceptualising identity processes, it must be capable of being integrated into a unified conceptualisation. The following thumbnail sketches provide only synoptic accounts of distinguishing features. Their purpose is no more than to highlight their contributions to underpinning or informing the ISA conceptualisation.

Psychodynamic approaches

Psychodynamic approaches strongly emphasise developmental issues in the formation of identity in which a person's identity is grounded in childhood and subsequent experiences. They also emphasise the 'incorporation' of the experience of the other into one's identity, the other being in various guises – parent, peer, admired or despised person, and many others. A person's identity is to a significant extent grounded in identifications and transactions with others.

E. H. Erikson

The Psychodynamic (PD) approach of E. H. Erikson (Erikson, 1950, 1959a,b, 1968) is life-span developmental from a predominantly psychodynamic viewpoint, but conceptualised within cultural context. Erikson's definition of identity spans one's past sense of self, what one is currently in the eyes of oneself and for others, and one's expectations for the future.

Distinguishing features: The process of forming a viable sense of identity for the culture is conceptualised as an adolescent task, during which the child has to resynthesise earlier identifications for contemporary requirements of being recognised as a worthy member of the community to which he or she belongs. Initial attachment to and identification with 'primary' caretakers provide the grounding for subsequent development. Erikson emphasises that identifications with others are partial rather than total. Those persons who do not master a resynthesis of childhood identifications remain in a state of 'identity diffusion'. Those who retain their initially given identities unquestioned have 'foreclosed identities'. Others who are searching in a productive manner without having settled on an identity are in 'moratorium'. Those who cannot make an acceptable identity deemed worthy by society might adopt a negative identity in preference to having no identity at all. An 'identity crisis' in the developmental context of relinquishing childhood dependencies and confronting imminent adulthood provides the initial impetus to the individual questioning issues of identity. This most sophisticated and influential conceptualisation of identity emphasises that identity formation is a process that begins with partial identifications with influential others in early childhood. The process comes to prominence with greater cognitive awareness during adolescence as the maturing child masters skills, becomes aware of rapid bodily changes and sexuality, and deals with developing greater personal autonomy and diminishing dependency on parental figures. Erikson's formulation conceptualises the individual as an active agent, identifying with others, seeking meaning and working at tasks. These tasks include developmental ones set within the entire life-span, which may or may not have successful outcomes.

Potential elaboration: Erikson's conceptualisation is based in acute clinical observation of symptomology of identity disturbances. Nevertheless, conceptualisation of identification processes at an analytical level would have the promise of greatly increasing our potential understanding of the myriad identity states that represent the array of individual experiences. The crucial matter of the resynthesis of childhood identifications with others is clearly stated, yet the underlying psychological processes are not explicitly conceptualised. Erikson's evocative writings on identity do not immediately lend themselves to formulating agreed empirical procedures for the systematic investigation of identity processes. Marcia and his colleagues (see next) take one route to operationalising Erikson's conception of identity processes. ISA takes another route, summarised later on in this chapter, which conceptualises resynthesising childhood identifications in terms of resolving accumulated conflicts in identification with others. The ISA elaboration gives close attention to the underlying concept of 'identification', and to the processes involved in forming additional identifications with newly encountered people and re-experiencing existing ones. Erikson's stage-specific adolescent task of achieving identity – versus being in a state of identity diffusion – can be recast as being representative of identity processes at any 'transitional phase', a major one being adolescence.

The Identity Status approach

The Identity Status (IS) approach (Marcia, 1980, 1987; Marcia, Waterman, Matteson, Archer, & Orlofsky, 1993) is an interpretation of Erikson's work on identity, in which the person is classified into 'identity statuses'.

Distinguishing features: The primary identity process is seen to be one of achieving an identity through questioning – the crisis of identity – and making commitments. Having thought through one's position to that of achieving an identity, one's status is 'identity achievement'. If one has not, but continues a given identity without questioning, one's status is 'identity foreclosure'. Being in a state of confusion over one's identity is to be in 'identity diffusion', or if thinking about one's identity but putting off definite commitments this is to be in 'identity moratorium'. IS is a popular operationalisation of Erikson's theorising about identity, in which identity statuses are shown as having empirically distinctive consequences. It has been prolific in generating research.

Potential elaboration: Working at the level of reports on self-questioning and whether or not self has made commitments, Marcia's conceptualisation of and work derived from his identity status paradigm (e.g., applied to ethnic identity awareness by Phinney, 1989; Phinney & Rosenthal, 1992), shares with Erikson's exposition a lack of attention to underlying processes. As a result, the operationalisation of identity statuses is problematic, so that empirical studies using the approach can give rise to contradictory findings: someone who has earlier been classified as being in the 'identity achievement' status is later designated as having an 'identity foreclosure' status, a theoretical contradiction. As stated in respect of Erikson's original formulation, ISA conceptualises the underlying processes of identification and their resynthesis.

R. D. Laing

The Social Psychiatry (SP) approach of R. D. Laing (Laing, 1960, 1961; Laing & Esterson, 1964) involves a definition of identity that closely follows Erikson's in emphasising past, current and future components of the experienced self.

Distinguishing features: Various processes of social interaction and family dynamics are postulated to result in 'psychiatric' disorders, as when people make demands on each other that can be psychologically destructive in coercing a person to be other than what they are. Such experiences of self are located primarily within a context of collaborative processes within dysfunctional families that convey demeaning and contradictory messages to the 'victim' of family 'alliances'. The concept of 'metaperspective of self', that is, self's perception of the other's view of self (Laing, Phillipson, & Lee, 1966), is well elaborated and effectively operationalised for empirical investigation.

Potential elaboration: The interpretative observations of dysfunctional family dynamics are groundbreaking. They would further benefit from detailed assessment of the identities of principal family members in terms of identification processes and pertinent metaperspectives as operationalised in ISA (see later). A study of anorexic daughters and their mothers and fathers using ISA (Connor, 1991) established a typical enmeshment of the daughter within a particular mother–father relationship, wherein both judged the world to high conventional moral standards and had high expectations of their daughter. With a judgemental mother and a colluding but aloof father, the daughter's metaperspective of self – based primarily in her mother's view but also in her father's view of herself – was derogatory and undermined her sense of autonomy. Leaving little space to exert a valued independence, the daughter takes excessive control over her body weight, and monitors her eating to maintain an idealised slim figure that represents discipline, self-control and achievement.

The Transactional Analysis approach

The Transactional Analysis (TA) approach was described by Berne (1961, 1964) and Steiner (1974).

Distinguishing features: The residual foundation of one's childhood experiences, such as helplessness or playfulness – the 'child' of self – is structured together with one's adult-like thinking, problem-solving and skilful self – the 'adult' of self – and one's parental caring and judgemental self – the 'parent' of self – derived from the experience of one's own parents or caretakers. Transactions with other people may 'hook' into one or other of self's child, adult or parent states, which may be comfortable though not necessarily productive *parallel* transactions when they are reciprocal, or uncomfortable *cross*-transactions when they are at crossed purposes. People may form various life scripts, such as ones that invite and accumulate putdowns from others, generating miserable experiences and depression. The apparently simple basic model is capable of considerable differentiation to represent complex childhood experiences. A prominent emphasis of the approach is an elucidation of the different self states (helpless child, assertive adult) that may be activated by others or by circumstances, or put into action by self (overbearing adult, professional expert). The approach effectively conceptualises the psychological bases of typical transactions that take place between people which have as much to do with 'playing games' as with rational purposeful action.

Potential elaboration: The approach relies on close observation and intuitive interpretation, which may be formalised within ISA in terms of explicitly defined self states or situated selves. Thus, in an ISA study during the South African apartheid era (Weinreich, Kelly, & Maja, 1987, 1988), black youth relinquished their normally expressed adult state when freely themselves for a helpless child state when cued into, or hooked by, an Afrikaner context of paternalistic coercion. Although some of these youth maintained their well-adjusted adult state throughout, the majority cued into a very vulnerable state of identity when situated with Afrikaners.

Symbolic interactionist approaches

Symbolic interactionism emphasises the human skill in the use of language and symbols in communication with others. It is deeply concerned with the symbolic modes of expression of self to others, and the stratagems people use to present themselves and influence others. The significance of the other person and the societal context of self-expression feature prominently in approaches informed by symbolic interactionism. Developmental aspects such as the acquisition of language and discourse emphasise learning within a symbolic universe created and expressed by significant others in society. Early steps in taking the role of the other though childhood games provide the basis for the adoption of, and the expression of, self in terms of role identities based in roles for which 'appropriate behaviours' assigned by society are expected. These roles may be domestic-based such as being mother, father, daughter, or son; workplace-based such as entrepreneur, production line worker, or professional; or societal-based such as politician, media star, Mafia; or whatever. A conceptual overlap may be noted between the psychodynamic view that identity is grounded in identifications and transactions with others and the symbolic interactionist perspective of the adoption and expression of self in terms of role identities.

Symbolic interactionism

The Symbolic Interaction Role Identity (SIRI) approach has a long history (Mead, 1934; Cooley, 1953; Sullivan, 1953; Stryker, 1980; Weigert, 1983). Symbolic interactionism conceptualises self as a process continually elaborated and defined in interaction with others, such that one's self-conception is viewed as being a reflected or mirror image of self constituted over time by way of the accumulated perceptions of self by the many others encountered.

Distinguishing features: In this very influential approach, the 'looking glass self' is conceptualised as being a consensus about self's typical characteristics as reflected by the 'generalised other' that represents an amalgamation of others who view self's enduring ways. *Self* is thereby firmly situated within a nexus of others without which there would be no notion of 'self'. Identities are given by the roles people occupy as defined by society – one's identity as 'father', 'bus-driver', 'immigrant', and so on. Low-status roles defined by society accrue to the individual's own self-concept. From this conception the ubiquitous discrimination/self-devaluation proposition follows, for example, women as second-class citizens would have diminished self-concepts, denigrated minority ethnic groups likewise would exhibit damaged self-concepts, and women of such ethnic groups would be doubly disadvantaged in self-conception. However, empirical evidence indicates that this conceptualisation is overstated as a generalisation (Shrauger & Schoenman, 1979). Comparative studies of different ethnic minority youth using ISA indicate that, despite derogatory views of themselves by their fellow students, they do not devalue themselves (Weinreich, 1983a; Kelly, 1989).

Potential elaboration: Updated conceptualisations emphasise the person as an active agent, who presents self in certain ways so as to influence the other's perception of self, such that self is not merely equivalent to a 'reflected self' by the generalised other (see next, 'Dramaturgical World as a Stage'; and 'Self as a Story or Theory/Narratology'; and 'Social Constructionism/Discourse Analysis'). Evidently, the *metaperspective* concept, so well elaborated by Laing *et al.* (1966), has immediate relevance particularly in distinguishing between the other's view of self and one's interpretation of that other's perspective on self. This feature of self's interpretation of other people's views on self – self's metaperspective of the other towards self – is also incorporated within the ISA conceptualisation and operationalised for empirical investigation.

The Dramaturgical World as a Stage

The Dramaturgical World as a Stage (DWAAS) approach was described by Goffman (1959, 1963, 1981).

Distinguishing features: DWAAS conceptualises the presentation of the self according to well-defined scripts readily recognised by others for ease of routine social interaction, in which 'back stage' realities are hidden from view. It presents a powerful metaphor for the way that individuals negotiate their identities with others, involving such devices as 'saving face' and participating in 'repair work' to re-establish acceptable identities. It delineates the subtle ways in which discourses may be used to position one's identity in relation to others in various social contexts.

The Self as a Story or Theory

The Self as a Story or Theory (SAST) approach is contemporarily known as the Narratology approach (Lecky, 1945; Shotter & Gergen, 1989; Rosenwald & Ochberg, 1992; McAdams, 1997).

Distinguishing features: In this approach two major themes predominate. One is the appeal to an informal story that is a theory of self, which self uses to 'explain' to self and others why one is and acts the way one does – self's reiterated story of disadvantage and abuse 'explains' one's proneness to being victimised. Another is the elaboration of a story of 'explanation' of, moral justification for, or coming to terms with untoward deeds – murder, rape, corruption – committed by self. The approach draws attention to the notion that certain individuals express a dominant view of themselves and the world in terms of their story to which all else is relegated. An example might be a story in which one is a victim of circumstances that are continually recalled as being the reason for all subsequent experiences – 'poor me'.

Potential elaboration: In so far as the person has formulated a 'story' that amounts to a kind of theory of self's existence, that story becomes a core reference point. Self will tend to judge encounters with the social worlds in accordance with it: whether self's activities are consistent with, and whether other agents' activities confirm, one's story. In TA terms (see earlier) the story is a 'script', ultimately with an endpoint to be fulfilled. For Personal Construct Theory (see later) it functions as an all-encompassing 'superordinate construct', to which other constructs are subsumed. In terms of the operationalisation of ISA, the story might well be empirically assessed as being a profound 'core evaluative dimension of identity', a dominant identity aspiration against which activities of self and others are evaluated, or perhaps only as a contributing feature of one's identity.

Social Constructionism/Discourse Analysis

The Social Constructionism/Discourse Analysis (SC/DA) approach (Harré, 1979, 1983; Shotter, 1984; Potter & Wetherell, 1987; Billig, 1987, 1991;

Reicher & Hopkins, 2001) includes the socio-historical perspective of Gergen (1991; Gergen & Gergen, 1984, 1991).

Distinguishing features: This approach attends to the agentic quality of self, especially in the use of language in all its complexity to present self and to communicate or hide the person's intentions in interactions with others. It emphasises the symbolic aspects of language and thereby the social construction of the material and social world. Processes typically used to express one's identity include stratagems and devices to persuade, mislead, and give moral accounts of one's behaviour. These may be empirically delineated by way of sophisticated analyses of texts and accounts. Human behaviour and thought, generated by the self as agency, are conceptualised as being intentional, located in a nexus of others, and subject to being expressed within shared normative moral universes.

Potential elaboration: The general approach takes a perspective of rational behaviour in the agentic pursuit of self's intentions. With a focus on each encounter with another being situated in newly evolving contexts, the approach presents one's identity as being always newly created and expressed in the current context, ultimately an ephemeral sense of identity. Consideration of underlying psychological dynamics in the development and expression of identity, and the manner in which self's identity is in part the outcome of a biographical history of past experiences would attend to stable features of identity. While identities are situated in varying social contexts, and hence expressed anew on every occasion, the currently situated self, as agent, expresses the continuity between self's biographical experiences and long-term future aspirations. Such continuity is conceptualised in Erikson's and Laing's definition of identity (see earlier), which is adopted with modification to include the notion of *construal* by the ISA conceptualisation. Thus current expressions of identity are anchored to one's past biographical experiences, even as these may be presently reappraised, and to one's future aspirations even as these may also be redefined in the longer term. With the operationalisation of ISA, discourses that express the longer-term relatively stable features of one's identity can be empirically differentiated from the more ephemeral and vacillating presentations from moment to moment (see Chapter 5).

An interesting arena for linguistically based social constructionism is the use by bilinguals of two languages to alternatively express self. As language codifies culture and different languages codify alternative cultures, the possibility of a person expressing dual linguistic personalities has to be contemplated. Following Ervin-Tripp (1973), Northover (1988b) used ISA to investigate the manner of expression of self in Gujerati–English bilinguals in England. The results demonstrated the systematic but slight modulation of identity according to language used. In addition, they indicated profound modulations between being situated in Gujerati and English contexts according to 'orthodox' or 'progressive' identity aspirations in respect of the ethnic culture of origin, which differed by gender. 'Progressive' females modulated their expressions of identity the most, while 'orthodox' females maintained a resolute sameness of expression firmly located within their own culture. Of the males, modulation by 'progressives' was considerable, while the 'orthodox' modulated to a lesser extent and with discomfort.

Self-concept, social identity and self-esteem approaches

These approaches attend to more detailed conceptualisations and investigations of the central core of identity, namely the self, and emphasise the significance of self-esteem both in conceptions of self and extending to one's group. Self may be conceptualised as being differentiated between aspects considered in personal terms – *personal identity* – and aspects derived from group membership – *social identity*. While the personal self-concept approach attends to individual processes of maintaining and enhancing self-esteem, the social identity approach conceptualises processes that focus on the individual as member of the group.

The Self-Concept and Self-Esteem approach

First, we examine the Self-Concept and Self-Esteem (SCSE) approach (Rosenberg, 1965, 1981; Coopersmith, 1967; Rosenberg & Simmons, 1972; Harter, 1982, 1990; Harter & Monsour 1992; Hoyle, Kernis, Leary, & Baldwin, 1999).

Distinguishing features: Earlier research concentrated on societal and family contributions to self-worth and self-esteem. More recent research has attended to partitioning self into multiple self-concepts, such as academic self-concept, sporting self-concept, etc., and developing self-esteem with respect to each. The approach acknowledges that self-esteem has societal and familial antecedents. It conceptualises associated dynamic processes as instigated by self-motives. Thus the 'self-enhancement' motive is formulated as a psychological drive to maintain, protect and enhance people's self-esteem; the 'self-consistency' motive likewise to maintain a consistent image of themselves and seek valid information about themselves; the 'self-assessment' motive to perceive themselves accurately; and the 'self-improvement' motive to seek opportunities to better themselves, developing new competencies and pursuing new activities and roles (Hoyle *et al.*, 1999).

Potential elaboration: What are here conceptualised as motives may be reconceptualised as progress made by the agentic self towards fulfilling one's identity aspirations. For example, at a phase in the lifecycle, self may aspire to emulate certain moral values, hold down a job successfully, live in accordance with a particular world-view, marry and have children, earn sufficient income to maintain a home for one's family to a standard, and so on. However, in reality one may have morally compromised oneself by two-timing one's partner, jeopardised one's job by poor time-keeping, been incapable of behaving according to one's world-view, and found oneself far from earning the desired income. If so, then one's appraisal of where one is at – as judged against one's identity aspirations – is a miserable self-assessment with attendant poor self-esteem, in line with James's (1890) famous expression: *Self-esteem = Success/Pretensions*. If one does not countenance a change in self's aspirations, one will continue to strive towards them: to reform morally, keep time better, pursue the world-view, and work for better qualifications and career prospects to earn a better income. ISA replaces the motive concept by conceptualising self-evaluation as self's appraisal of where one is at in relation to one's identity aspirations, when situated in a particular social context. Whether or not issues of self-consistency, self-assessment and self-improvement are important will evidently depend on whether being consistent, perceiving oneself accurately, and bettering oneself beyond current aspirations are predominant identity aspirations for the individual in question. The individual's earlier identifications, biographical experiences and current thinking provide the backdrop for these aspirations, hence considerable differences would be expected both at a personal level and across cultures, where differing norms may predominate concerning consistency of behaviour, accuracy of self-perception and opportunities for betterment.

Social Identity Theory

We move on to the Social Identity Theory (SIT) perspective (Tajfel, 1981a; Turner, Hogg, Oakes, Reicher, & Wetherell, 1987; Hogg & Abrams, 1988; Abrams & Hogg, 1999).

Distinguishing features: SIT established the importance of the process whereby the individual categorises others as being members of a group, instigating processes of maintaining a positive social identity for the ingroup, thereby discriminating against outgroups. When the societal status of the ingroup is low, alternative strategies of creating newly defined positive distinctiveness for the ingroup, passing as a member of another valued group, or migrating elsewhere may be pursued. By introducing the significance of the act of overt categorisation as member of a group or a class (compared with being unaware of such putative group membership) SIT emphasises the location of group identities within societal contexts. The 'self-categorisation' elaboration of SIT by Turner (Turner *et al.*, 1987) reconceptualises what is known as the 'depersonalisation' condition in a group context as being one of a 'transformation' of identity, not a loss of identity.

Potential elaboration: There would be merit in conceptually integrating the group 'categorisation' processes within a theoretical formulation of the person's appraisal of self and others. A person's current appraisal occurs not within a vacuum, but within a context of biographical experiences in a socio-historical context. The ambiguous notion of 'positive social identity' would benefit from distinguishing between a societal definition of a social identity (alter-ascribed) and the individual member's perspective from within the group (ego-recognised). Elaborating the term 'social identification' to recognise differing modes of identification would greatly clarify the complexity of ingroup and outgroup identification. One may *aspirationally* identify to a degree with an honoured outgroup – to be emulated – and *empathetically* identify with it too in certain respects – *de facto* sharing of attributes – while continuing to *empathetically* identity with the ingroup. In a study of Hong Kong Chinese students using ISA, those who empathetically identified more with the favoured Western groups – British, American and Americanised Chinese – expressed higher self-evaluation (Weinreich *et al.*, 1996). Within the socio-historical circumstances of Hong Kong and given the biographical experiences of the students, closer identification with esteemed out-groups fostered self-esteem, not so much ingroup identification. With the ISA elaboration of these concepts, the manifestation of the many kinds of ingroup/outgroup identification processes can be understood with considerable clarity.

Construal and appraisal, cognition and affect

Inevitably with progress in conceptualising the complex of self and identity processes, new conceptual issues become salient. One such issue concerns self's interpretation of a situation engaging self's activities, which is as much an expression of self as an assessment of the situation. Central to the significance of the present moment for the person, is the person's *construal* of self and the others present by means of individualised personal constructs. Personal constructs function as templates for assessing and anticipating the thoughts, actions and feelings of oneself and the others in the present circumstances. *Appraisal* is closely associated with construal, but conceptualises how present construals of self, others, events and activities are appraised in emotive terms by reference to the person's well-being and integrity of identity.

G. A. Kelly

In the Personal Construct Theory (PCT) of G. A. Kelly (Kelly, 1955; Fransella & Thomas, 1988; Fransella & Dalton, 1990), Kelly's fundamental postulate and corollaries focus on the manner by which the individual construes self's social world.

Distinguishing features: The fundamental postulate and a series of corollaries to this postulate elaborate the notion of the person's construal as being central to interpreting thoughts and activities involving self in interaction with others. At the core of PCT is the powerful conception of the discrete 'bipolar personal construct', which refers to a personally individualised template for anticipating and interpreting people and events. An example of a bipolar construct might be: ... *gives priority to needs for oneself* contrasted with ... *attends to obligations to the family*. PCT's elaboration of the properties of constructs provides important conceptual tools for investigating the individualised meanings of activities pursued within the social world. One such property is the range of convenience of specific constructs, when some may be used for construing characteristics of a narrow range of people and others for a more inclusive range. Another property is the structural organisation of constructs. For example, this may be hierarchical when certain constructs are subordinated to a hierarchy where the meaning of the one is conditional on the meaning of the superordinate construct, or monolithic when all constructs of a set imply the same essential meaning as do the others. A prominent feature of the approach is the specification of empirical methods of assessment. One procedure is the use of 'triadic sorts' when eliciting constructs for ascertaining what characteristic self might construe two people as having in common – *emergent* pole – which distinguishes them from a third person by way of a contrasting characteristic – *contrast* pole. Another is the use of a 'repertory grid' of bipolar constructs against people, agents and objects – collectively *elements* – for systematically obtaining an individual's construal of these elements.

Potential elaboration: The powerful notion – the bipolar personal construct – points to the potential for elaborating the individual's process of appraisal of the social world within a developmental perspective of identity formation and change as conceptualised by Erikson. Integrating aspects of PCT with features of other approaches to self and identity would enhance the conceptualisation of identity processes. ISA takes steps along such lines as detailed later in this chapter, when the notion of the discrete bipolar construct plays a fundamental role in the conceptualisation of identity. The ISA definitions of identity and component aspects such as ethnic and gender identity reference the centrality of construal in formulations that are directly derived from Erikson's and Laing's earlier definitions.

The Appraisal Process

We now examine the Appraisal Process (Arnold, 1960a,b; Lazarus, 1966, 1991; Lazarus & Folkman, 1984; Shweder, 1991).

Distinguishing features: Stress and emotion are conceptualised as processes arising from the nature of the interaction of the person with situations, in which self's emotional responses depend on appraisals of a situation that vary according to the 'personality' of the person. Both the personality and the context of the situation contribute in interaction to stress and emotional arousal. One person may appraise an unbearable emotionally draining workload as a failure of self's professional competence and become depressed, whereas another may appraise the same circumstances as unrealistic managerial demands and become angry with the policies implemented by management. Coping with the experienced stress of this same situation would evidently differ between the two people.

Potential elaboration: The psychological concept of personality tends to be conceptualised in trait terms, which are relatively fixed characteristics of the person. Conceptualising the process of appraisal is difficult with this perspective on individual personality. However, the overall appraisal process may be conceptualised as being a function of a number of constituent processes as follows. The person *cues* into the reference for self's present intentional activity – carrying out work-related tasks – that is, into self as situated in a work context. Self *construes* the meaning of the situation – as consisting of a lack of resources. Self *evaluates* the perceived consequences of the construal such that potential failure with the tasks – when interpreted as self's fault – would result in depression, or – as management's fault – in anger. This elaboration builds upon the notion of personal construct, but pays attention to cueing into contexts specified by present intentions, and evaluation of the situation for the integrity of one's intentions. This formulation of self's appraisal of current circumstances is detailed within the ISA conceptualisation given in this chapter and operationalised in the next.

Cognitive–affective dissonances

The appraisal process depends on both construal and evaluation, and entails experienced emotional states that accompany one's appraisal of satisfying or distressing circumstances. Construal emphasises cognition with attributions to and interpretations of people's activities. However, the actors in the situation are also evaluated in terms of affective qualities such being liked and loved or disliked and hated. Cognitions are what one can say about a person, while affects refer to what one feels about the person, a conceptually important distinction about closely interrelated features of appraisal. In practice, cognitions are rarely devoid of affective connotations: what is happening cognitively speaking tends to imply distinctive affective feelings. The interrelationships between cognition and affect, and cognition and behaviour, have been thoroughly researched during an exhaustive period of experimental investigation. This body of research dealt with processes that are inherent during the appraisal process, when self's cognitions of others and their activities may conflict with self's affects towards them – a good friend engaging in despicable gossip about oneself. Cognitive–affective incompatibilities are ubiquitous features of everyday appraisals of a social world that is far from perfect.

Cognitive–Affective Consistency theories

There are various Cognitive–Affective Consistency theories (Osgood & Tannenbaum, 1955; Festinger, 1957; Heider, 1958; Rosenberg & Abelson, 1960; Ableson *et al.*, 1968; Weinreich, 1969, 1989a; Wickland & Brehm, 1976; Aronson, 1992).

Distinguishing features: Much earlier research in the experimental social psychology of attitude formation and change was devoted to elucidating processes bringing into balance cognition and affect or behaviour when these were experienced as being discrepant. The generic name given to theorising about discrepancies in cognition and affect or behaviour is cognitive–affective consistency theory, within which there are subtle differences in approach. Festinger's (1957) theory of cognitive dissonance, for example, concentrates on circumstances when one's cognitions are incompatible with one's behaviour. Empirical evidence demonstrates strong tendencies to realign one's attitudes and cognitions so as to decrease dissonances. The approach elucidates the powerful processes by which one strives for a state of compatibility, balance and consonance between one's cognitions and one's affects. So strong is the preference to believe good things about an admired person – being consonant – that one may reject or distort contrary evidence about that person – being dissonant.

Potential elaboration: The earlier research focus on beliefs, cognitions and behaviour as disembodied elements of investigation, provided a stimulus to creative experimental investigations of consonance and dissonance. However, an essential progression is to incorporate this understanding of dissonance processes into the conceptualisation of the person, whose appraisals of self and others in relation to strongly held beliefs frequently result in cognitive–affective disso-nances. An earlier ISA exposition of appraisal and dissonance processes (Weinreich, 1969) is further elaborated in this chapter, for which assessment procedures are presented in Chapter 2.

Social anthropology and indigenous psychologies

The meaning that self and identity have for people from different cultures varies considerably, so any conceptualisation of identity processes has to be able to incorporate these different meanings. Social anthropology has a long tradition of investigating the meanings of existence and the organisation of communities within specific cultural contexts. The term 'indigenous psychology' refers to psy-chological understanding within a cultural perspective that is indigenous to the people in question. The contemporary insistence on investigating psychological states and processes within the framework of an indigenous psychology stems from the realisation that evidence from Western investigations may merely reflect normative features of Western societies. Non-Western social scientists in particu-lar were concerned with the imposition of Western findings – as supposed uni-versals – on other societies when it would be incorrect and inappropriate to do so.

The Social Anthropological and Ethnographic approach

The Social Anthropological and Ethnographic (SAE) approach is more recent (Carrithers, Collins, & Lukes, 1985; Shweder, 1991; Pasternak, Ember, & Ember, 1997; Valsiner, 2000).

Distinguishing features: The varieties of kinship structures that organise human reproduction in differing cultures are associated with differing forms of gender rela-tions which depend in part on the scarcity or profundity of basic economic resources. Rites of passage and appeals to cultural world-views are analysed as processes that maintain kin structures and the continuity of the community. Social anthropological studies reveal an understanding of the many alternative forms of indigenous psy-chologies (Heelas & Lock, 1981) that provide meaning to life in the cultures of dif-fering ethnic groups. Ethnographic methods can effectively demystify alien cultures.

Potential elaboration: The approach depends strongly on the communicative and observational skills of the investigator participating in an unfamiliar culture. Informants may have their own agendas and may not be wholly reliable go-betweens for the social anthropologist stranger in the midst of their people. In-depth investigations of self and identity processes informed by ethnographic analyses might be implemented using procedures that operationalise the common open-ended conceptual framework provided by ISA.

The foregoing synoptic survey of influential orientations to self and identity outlines a series of conceptualisations, aspects of which are to be integrated within ISA. In sum, these orientations include in broad terms psychodynamic approaches to processes of identification and states of identity, symbolic

interactionist perspectives on self situated in social context, and detailed considerations of self-concept, social identity and self-esteem. They are augmented by
conceptualisations of construal and appraisal processes, and cognitive–affective
considerations. Ultimately they have to contend with ethnographic representations of different cultural world-views and indigenous psychologies.

IDENTITY STRUCTURE ANALYSIS

This text outlines preliminary conceptual and methodological tools for the
science and art of analysing identity in its myriad manifestations. ISA attends to
the issues raised by the extant approaches just described, by way of integrating
concepts derived from them. The task of integration requires work on clarifying
ambiguities and formulating explicit definitions. In the process familiar notions
come to have differing connotations. For example, the ubiquitous notion of *identity conflict*, associated with being the victim of *prejudice* or *culture conflict* and
having low self-esteem, is reformulated in terms of patterns of *conflicted identifications with* specific people and institutions, which by no means is to be equated
with low self-esteem. In respect of *identity diffusion*, the explicit unambiguous
definitions of ISA concepts open the way to understanding that identity diffusion
is not necessarily an indication of poor self-concept, but instead may be associated with identity states that range from despairing *identity crisis* to cheerful *diffuse high self-regard*. In the ISA formulation, while high self-esteem will often be
an indication of confidence in one's identity, it may in some be associated with
defensive identity states and in others with diffuse states, these being vulnerabilities of a different kind.

As outlined earlier, the main precursors to ISA include features of Eriksonian
psychodynamic developmental theorising, symbolic interactionism and social
constructionism, personal construct psychology, appraisal theory, and cognitive–affective consistency principles. The ISA conceptualisation has to be able to
incorporate and represent indigenous psychologies within an open-ended and
extendable framework. Concepts derived from these approaches are fundamental
to the integrated conceptualisation that ISA offers, but they are necessarily
reworked. Erikson's concept of identity diffusion is reformulated as a dispersion
of the person's conflicted identifications with others. The reflected self of symbolic interactionism is recast in terms of a metaperspective of self. Use of the
term 'personal construct' is generalised beyond Kelly's emphasis on the anticipation of events to include all manners of discourses used by people to interpret
their social worlds as experienced in the past and currently, as well as anticipated
into the future.

ISA conceptualises one's appraisal of social situations as involving one's interpretation of their significance to self's identity aspirations and one's judgements
of the opportunities provided for expressing one's identity from moment to
moment. Appraisal provides and records experiences of situations and events.
Each new experience engenders the potential for both a reappraisal of earlier

viewpoints and an elaboration of identity. The process by which the individual appraises self and others draws on the formulation of the 'agentic self' who is intentional and emotive, as well as being cognitive. Stress experienced as a consequence of one's appraisal of particular situations is conceptualised both in terms of direct affective arousal and incompatible cognitive and affective assessments of events.

SECTION 1: AGENCY, SELF AND IDENTITY

Two major arenas of interrelated processes guide the presentation of the ISA conceptual framework. These are *appraisal and the current expression of identity* and *identification and the formation and development of identity*. Roughly these distinguish between present activities in expressions of identity and origins of identity in preceding biographical experiences. The theoretical exposition of the processes of appraisal considers the manner in which self construes and evaluates the social and material world for its significance to one's world-view and the implementation of one's identity aspirations. Self's appraisal of other agents' characteristics and activities in context and contingent appraisal of one's own success or otherwise in pursuing one's intentions engage with the many different scenarios encountered, both expected and unexpected. Self's appraisals of ongoing situations in the here and now are interpretations from the perspective of self's identity. Self's contingent activities and gestures, including covert commentaries to self, are expressions of self's identity. However, the here and now of self's expression of identity is set within the complex of formative biographical experiences. The theoretical exposition of the processes of identification attends to the formation and development of identity in biographical and socio-historical context.

Fundamental to the exposition is the notion that self is an active agent who in the main acts in accordance with one's intentions implemented with greater or less autonomy according to personal and societal circumstances. The issue of autonomy receives more detailed consideration after clarification of the distinction between the terms 'self' and 'identity'.

Distinction between the concepts of self and identity

The concept of *self* may be elusive, but Harré's elucidation and discussion of the singular agentic self (Harré, 1998) adds considerable clarification to be detailed later in 'Section 2: The Singular Self'. However, the ISA conceptual framework distinguishes between self and identity. ISA reserves the term 'self' for the immediate referent of self's actions, remembered and reconstructed features of self contextually located in past experiences, and anticipated and fantasised notions of self yet to be encountered. 'Identity' refers to the totality of self's experiences of being-in-the-world, including experiences of numerous other agents in socio-historical context, such that self's presentation of identity at any moment is the expression of the continuity between past biography and future aspiration. 'Identity', expressed by the agentic self in the present, incorporates the individual's past experiences as foundations for the intended future as anticipated from time to time, whereby self is experienced as located in a changing nexus of other agents. *Self* is the singular agent, whereas one's *identity* incorporates experiences in interaction with other people and representative agents.

Leaving aside discussion of the subtleties of conceptualising the agentic self for the moment, the following passages elaborate on the structure and organisation of identity. After these preliminary considerations, the formal ISA definition of 'identity' leads readily to definitions of various features of identity such as *ethnic identity, gender identity, occupational identity* and so on.

Biographical experiences: Continuity in identity

A fundamental defining characteristic of identity is the *continuity* of oneself experiencing the social world and one's activities, such that during various biographical episodes, experiences are codified incompletely and with various biases and inaccuracies. Construals of significant biographical phases in the past are reconstructions in the present, which are typically elicited by cueing into emotional residues of past experiences.

Although representing the unique self, continuity in identity is constructed out of imperfect, selected, and distorted memories. Identity is not sameness, but refers to the continuity of self in relation to biographical episodes, changing situational contexts – public, private, with friends, undergoing trauma – and mood-states – depressed, anxious, cheerful. Continuity generally represents some degree of greater or lesser change. In practice, when dealing with identity, it is the extent and nature of the continuity that requires explication – that is, the manner whereby the person in question continues as a particular human being.

One's experience of identity for self is not synonymous with one's identity for others, who may have a variety of views about oneself. Self will often be confronted with disjunctions over one's identity in interactions with others. Others rarely have access to one's own conception of identity – an *ego-recognised* identity (Weinreich, 1983b). However, others may ascribe an identity to oneself – an *alter-ascribed* identity – often at variance with one's ego-recognised identity. One may relate to these disjunctions in a variety of ways. If one thinks that the other's view of self may have validity, self may accept it, revise one's sense of identity and reappraise the nature of continuity in one's identity. More likely, however, self rejects the alter-ascribed identity, defends one's ego-recognised version and makes appropriate effort to express it to the other. When considering membership in categories or groups – gender, class, occupation – the pervasiveness of stereotyping often results in people being subjected to alter-ascribed social identities that are considered unwarranted. Rather than accept these as being proper appraisals of self, one is likely to privately if not publicly reject them.

People are confronted with a certain difficulty when appraising another's view of oneself, given that the other may not be explicit or may wish to enter into a little deception. One has to interpret how the other views self, given whatever information in terms of discourses and gestures the other provides about oneself. Self does not have direct access to the other's perspective on oneself and can form only an interpretation of that perspective, the technical term for which is a 'meta-perspective' of self as based in the other (Laing *et al.*, 1966). One generates meta-perspectives of self as located with the various others of one's acquaintance.

Identity aspirations and the ideal self

The term 'ideal self' (sometimes 'ego-ideal') requires careful attention. Unfortunately, the term tends to be reified as 'the ideal self', whereas it references one's aspirations towards being the kind of person one would like to be. What one would wish for oneself will vary from person to person, from culture to culture, and from one biographical period to another. One's identity aspirations when growing up in a subsistence economy compared to a technological economy would differ substantially. In any culture they would change from childhood to adulthood and beyond.

In contradistinction to positive aspirations directed towards achieving desired objectives, one also has negative aspirations directed towards avoiding distressful outcomes in the future or dissociating from these when already experienced. Negative aspirations have to do with shameful or distressing incidents involving oneself in the past, one's currently unacceptable characteristics and behaviours, and one's anticipation of future unpalatable possibilities. Some individuals are more certain about those things they wish to avoid, their negative aspirations, than those they desire, their positive ones. In ISA the term 'aspirational self' is becoming used more often in preference to 'ideal self', because it both guards against reification and expresses the negative 'wish not to be like this' as well as the positive 'desire to be like that'.

Indigenous psychologies and social representations

Identity aspirations, indigenous psychologies[1] and discourses

Individuals express their identity aspirations by way of discourses that they use to define goals and objectives they would like to achieve for themselves, contrasted with reprehensible characteristics from which they would like to dissociate. These aspirations will vary greatly from person to person, from culture to culture and from one historical era to another. They could include wanting to live with a partner or companion for love, companionship, sexual fulfilment, and having children. Other aspirations may be to pursue a career, have a particular job and be independent in thought and action. Further ones may focus on spiritual beliefs, sharing in and showing solidarity with the lifestyle of a particular ethnicity, and implementing the corresponding moral code.

The foregoing name just a few typical and broadly stated identity aspirations. Many will be much more particular. Each will be contrasted with reprehensible possibilities that may feature in people's lives as disfavoured actualities, from which they wish to dissociate but are often unable to do so. Clinically disturbed states may arise when, in appraising their own circumstances, people form distressing assessments in relation to their identity aspirations.

Living within a particular culture, say, Christian, Judaic, Islamic, or Confucian, one will meet prototypical norms for spiritual rituals, icons and symbols, for morality, for sexual congress and procreation, for useful jobs, prestigious careers and rational thinking, and for expression of emotions. The prototypical norms provide reference points for the accumulated wisdom of the culture, the indigenous psychology for contemporary times, being the manner of comprehending people's thoughts, feelings and actions within cultural context. Much of our knowledge of indigenous psychologies, as represented in folklore, history, and spiritual and philosophical discourses, derives from the work of social anthropologists and ethnographers, although 'indigenous' psychologists are latterly making systematic scientific contributions (Kim & Berry, 1993a).

Thus, indigenous psychologies represent the differing wisdoms about human affairs enshrined within alternative cultures. They provide for meaning in human affairs as locally understood, and govern judgements of standards of behaviour for those within a culture. They impose constraints on debates about changing standards. For example, on a significant issue such as abortion, technological advances enhancing the viability of the foetus at an ever-earlier age modify the nature of the debate. However, the debate remains within the confines of an indigenous psychology that may hold the sanctity of life to be a fundamental moral principle, but against which is pitted notions of personal autonomy and the viability of the putative infant and its child care. 'Personal autonomy' may be expressed as women's control over their bodies and choice about having a wanted as opposed to an unwanted child, considerations that are heightened when conception results from rape. Associated with such debates in different cultures are differing moral standards concerning the organisation of sexual relations, moral transgressions and the perceived status of males and females, these being aspects of the received wisdoms of particular indigenous psychologies (Pasternak *et al.*, 1997). Cultures where female infanticide is to a degree countenanced have alternative behavioural standards in which technological advances may be used to facilitate the abortion of female foetuses.

Indigenous psychologies change through time and space as peoples update their differing understandings of the world in line with contemporary developments as they witness them. In some respects cultures have monolithic connotations, but in reality they cannot be all-encompassing nor are they static. There will be many subcultures, such as delinquent and Mafia; aristocratic and plebeian; urban and rural; straight, gay, and lesbian. Each generation tends to challenge certain themes of previous generations, nevertheless using features of the prevailing indigenous psychology as reference points that are not completely superseded. The manifestation of clinical distress accompanying a person's inability to live up to certain identity aspirations will differ in imagery and behaviour from one predominant indigenous psychology to another (Littlewood & Lipsedge, 1982).

In ISA terms, these indigenous psychologies (mostly 'lay' but informed by 'scientific' psychology) form the immediate context for people's individual identity aspirations. As people's identity aspirations constitute the basic meaningfulness of people's lives into the future, they provide the primary reference points in ISA for fundamental parameters of identity. Chapter 2 presents procedures for implementing these reference points in practice. While it is evident that people's identity aspirations – varying as they do – cannot be synonymous with indigenous psychologies, the discourses by means of which they are expressed will be contextualised by them. In ISA the *emic* or culturally specific features of indigenous psychologies, as interpreted by the individual, are incorporated centrally within the conceptual framework.

No one could possibly know and comprehend every representation, thought and activity that would make up the set of interrelated manifestations that form an indigenous psychology. However, shorthand expressions and symbols that stand in for whole sets of complex ideas, feelings and behaviours are continually being reiterated within a culture, such that, for example, 'the nuclear family' in the West, or '*baradari*' in the Indian subcontinent, is immediately understood in all its complexities. The Western 'nuclear family' refers to the freely entered marriage of man and woman, who take on a particular set of responsibilities for the welfare of their children, within a loose set of obligations and feelings towards parents and prospective grandchildren. The Indian *baradari* connotes the close-knit extended clan or sub-caste within which reciprocal responsibilities are duty bound in terms of arranged marriages where man and woman are largely subordinate to the clan. In practice, depending on the awareness of people, a relatively small number of discourses and texts can articulate the most salient features of an indigenous psychology. It remains for the professional folklorist, historian, moral philosopher and psychologist to express the detail of indigenous psychologies in their full intricacy. In the meantime, people get along well enough with their shorthand discourses, a factor that assists the practical implementation of the ISA conceptualisation in the field.

Thus, what would be the daunting task of elaborating all of the discourses that would more or less represent an indigenous psychology, is not in practice necessary when dealing with the identity aspirations of participants in the field. Sensitivity to salient shorthand discourses used in everyday expressions will elicit the dominant themes of a person's principal identity aspirations, contextualised within an indigenous psychology. To be sure, given their daily concerns, people will have more focused aspirations that are expressed by way of more fluent discourses about their jobs, mates, politics, families and manifestations of particular lifestyles.

Identity aspirations, discourses and bipolar constructs

Ethnographic fieldwork or clinical-type interviews may provide the discourses typically used by individuals to express themselves interrelated to the social world within which they habitually move. Such discourses may be quite simple observations about aspirations, current activities and past experiences, in which encounters with others may similarly be expressed. Or they may be quite complex and indicate observations of, for example, a conditional nature: *if these people were to give some support, then the following outcomes would be possible*. In general people's discourses will relate to their identity aspirations. They judge others in terms of whether or not they fit in with their own agendas for the kind of world in which they might fulfil their aspirations. Implicit in a text used approvingly is some other text that expresses a psychological contrast to what is desired, for example, the text *has a deep concern for others* may have as its psychological contrast *puts the pursuit of commercial success before other considerations*. Someone with entrepreneurial aspirations may endorse the pursuit of commercial success rather than a deep concern for others.

In the terminology of personal construct psychology, the two contrasting texts just quoted would constitute the two poles of a bipolar construct. From the perspective of ISA either the one or the other pole of this construct might be endorsed as an identity aspiration, depending on whether the person aspires primarily to a deep concern for others or to commercial success. Some people may veer towards a preference for the one pole over the other, but feel themselves to be in a dilemma, wanting to express concern and achieve commercial success simultaneously.

ISA conceptualises the person's aspirational self as constituting a set of positive and negative identity aspirations, expressed in discourses denoting ways and means towards their implementation. In effect, discourses express the individual's values, beliefs and intentions, as these are bound up in locating both self and others of the moment in relation to these aspirations. Some discourses will denote core evaluative dimensions of identity while others will be hesitant expressions of conflicted dimensions. Procedures delineated in Chapter 2 may establish which of a person's discourses express core or conflicted dimensions of identity.

However, people's identities are more than identity aspirations. Their identities have foundations in past experiences. People contend with their current circumstances. *Continuity* from past experiences through current episodes towards future aspirations links together the component parts of one's identity, which is emphasised in the following definition.

Definition of identity

> *A person's identity is defined as the totality of one's self-construal, in which how one construes oneself in the present expresses the **continuity** between how one construes oneself as one was in the past and how one construes oneself as one aspires to be in the future.*
>
> (Weinreich, 1969, 1980, 1983a,b, 1986a,b, 1989a)

This definition is an inclusive one and directs attention to the totality of one's identity at a given phase in time. The definition applies to the young child, the adolescent, the young adult, and the older adult in various phases of the lifecycle.

Clearly, depending on whether one is a young child or an adult at the height of one's powers, how one construes oneself as one was in the past will refer to very different salient experiential markers. These might be 'being a baby' in the former case, or 'childhood experiences' or 'first work opportunities' in the latter. Likewise, how one construes oneself as one aspires to be in the future will differ considerably according to one's age and accumulated experiences.

The inclusiveness of this definition assists in elucidating component aspects of one's total identity, such as one's gender identity, ethnic identity, occupational identity and so on. These are not separate identities, but components of the totality of a person's identity, a fact that is obscured by research studies that concentrate only on one or other component of identity, such as gender identity, to the exclusion of other components.

The ISA definitions of component aspects of identity highlight the peculiarly salient features of each component. They draw attention to the commonality of experience in respect of each aspect of identity when located within a particular community in a specific historical era. Thus, for example, the child incorporates societal norms that emphasise particular kinds of close relationships with one's blood mother and father as standard features of one's identity. So the adopted or donor-inseminated (AID) child, on discovery of the fact, finds a fundamental lacuna at the core of identity – the lack of the blood parent that would normatively be integral to mainstream versions of identity. The discovery is invariably experienced as a sense of loss accompanied by feelings of uncertainty of personal origins, experiences that become significant components of the adopted or AID person's identity (see later: 'yearning identity'). However, in time populations may establish a variety of norms about blood parents and provide alternative notions of 'parentage' normatively incorporated into distinctive identities, such that adoptive and AID versions stand in their own right. These kinds of changes are seen in contemporary times in respect of gender identity towards more egalitarian versions and familial identity towards a variety that includes single parent, gay and lesbian, and traditional nuclear.

The conception of identity in its totality that incorporates component aspects guards against a prevalent kind of reification in which aspects of identity are treated as being discrete objects separated from other aspects of identity. For example, 'ethnic identity' is still often thought about as a given entity or a given set of inevitable prescriptions for a particular ethnic group. With such reification, talk about ethnic identity is frequently divorced from considerations of other aspects of the totality of identity, such as gender. Furthermore, investigations that reify ethnic identity (wishing to portray what this is) retreat from engaging in the cultural debates that ensue over the many differing complex expressions of ethnicity, gender and other aspects of identity that members of an ethnicity will display.

Ethnic identity: Definition

The greater proportion of people, who are born into and experience their childhood within a well-defined peoplehood with a shared socio-cultural history, has the ethnic identity of that peoplehood. Often the term 'nation' or 'ethnic group' is used to refer to a peoplehood of this kind (see Hutchinson & Smith, 1996, for a comprehensive set of readings on ethnicity and ethnic groups). Those who belong to the nation or ethnic group in this manner manifest in various ways an ethnic identity that spans ancestral origins and future progeny. Ethnic identity for those who know they belong to a coherent peoplehood constitutes a pre-eminent feature of the totality of their identity because it is based in a time-span continuity of generations that tends to eclipse all other aspects of identity. Expressions of one's gender identity, for example, are formulated within the context of the cultural discourses of the particular ethnic group and in this sense are subordinate to that normative ethnic context.

Gender identity does not have the time-span of the intergenerational continuity of ethnicity, except in so far as its modes of expression are situated within an ethnicity. A definition of ethnic identity follows:

> *One's ethnic identity is defined as that part of the totality of one's self-construal made up of those dimensions that express the continuity between one's construal of past ancestry and one's future aspirations in relation to ethnicity.*

(Weinreich, 1986a)

The salient features of ethnic identity are the individual's interpretation of ancestral heritage and aspirations for one's actual or imagined progeny, a complex of constructions located in socio-historical context spanning the generations and including at differing phases in the lifecycle awareness of grandparents and grandchildren. The existence of ancestors and progeny subsumes the biological facts of procreation as socially constrained within the moral codes of the ethnicities in question, with implications for the expression of gender identity (see later under 'Gender identity').

In practice, the delineation of a person's expression of ethnic identity must include assessment of self's views and beliefs about past ancestral manifestations of the ethnicity in question, and self's anticipations for the future for ethnic progeny, to which self's personal ancestry and progeny belong. Because of its continuity over generations, ethnic identity will have the quality of social representation indicated by folklore, ethnic interpretations of historical events and cultural institutions that together constitute the ethnicity. However, depending on self's status and position within the ethnic group, individual construals of ethnicity will vary immensely according to historical era and self's time and place within the era.

Although overlapping and common elements of social representation will be evident, there will be no completely homogeneous 'reified' ethnic identity, but many different variations in interpretation of an ethnicity, for example in respect of religious doctrine associated with an ethnicity this may be orthodox, reformed or progressive. A cultural or ethnic icon is an artefact that successfully represents and captures the emotive connotations of the ethnicity and is instantly recognised as such by members of the community. Nevertheless, those who recognise an icon in this manner do not necessarily concur in the social representation of the ethnicity to which it refers.

An investigation of ethnic identity using ISA has demonstrated intergenerational continuities and discontinuities in definitions of ethnic identity in a context of multi-ethnic influences. Hong Kong Chinese students identifying themselves as ethnic Hong Kongese identified to varying degrees with mainland Chinese, a notion of 'traditional Chinese', the Taiwanese, the Japanese, the British, the Americans, American-born Chinese, and Vietnamese boat-people (Weinreich *et al.*, 1996). *Continuity in parental–peer identification* characterised dominant mainstream and alternative modern versions of the Hong Kong ethnic identity, with a greater emphasis on peer identification or parental identification respectively for the two versions. *Parental–peer discontinuity in identification* was the hallmark of two contrasting cases. In one, a greater degree of identification with prestigious outgroups as self-defined – the Western groups – tended to accompany peer identification but not parental identification. In the other, identification with traditionally defined ancestry was aligned with parental – specifically maternal – identification but not peer identification.

Other ISA studies of ethnic identity have demonstrated different kinds of modulation in the expression of ethnic identity according to context when situated with one's own or a different ethnic group – Pakistanis in Birmingham and Greek Cypriots in London, with own group and with the English (Kelly, 1989); rural and urban youth in South Africa, with own group, with English-speaking whites and with the Afrikaners (Weinreich *et al.*, 1988). Further marked differences in the expression of one's ethnic identity according to 'progressive' or 'orthodox' cultural orientations (Kelly, 1989) and use of English-language or Gujerati-language in Gujerati–English bilinguals have been established (Northover, 1988a,b). An investigation of migrant Kashmiris to Britain found that the versions of Kashmiri ethnic identity expressed by offspring in Britain, while updated to represent the experience of growing up in a radically different context from their parents' origins, remained resolutely Kashmiri (Ali & Northover, 1999).

These empirical studies demonstrate that any ethnic identity is invariably expressed in a variety of ways, which may represent disputed differences in orientation to the ethnicity in question. Continuity and discontinuity of intergenerational identification contribute to alternative expressions. The kinds of modulation in expression of identity when situated with one's own or another ethnic group crucially reflect the socio-historical relationships between the groups. Language as the means of codification alters one's expression of identity.

Chapter 2 presents procedures that enable a person's ethnic identity to be assessed in relation to ancestral origins and future aspirations for progeny, as well as to contextual alternatives – with one's own and another ethnic group. Chapter 3 postulates on theoretical grounds the developmental primacy of primordial perspectives on ethnicity and reports a cross-cultural study of antecedents and consequences of people's varying primordialist and situationalist sentiments about ethnic and national identity. The subject of Chapter 4 is an investigation of ethnic identity in an ethno-religious minority within a group that is itself a minority ethnic group with subordinate status.

Racial identity: Definition

Ethnic identity is to be clearly distinguished from racial identity, the definition of which now follows:

> *One's racial identity is defined as that part of the totality of one's self-construal made up of those dimensions that express the continuity between one's construal of past racial features and one's future aspirations in relation to racial characteristics.*

As examples of the kinds of cases this definition might encompass, consider an instance when 'one's construal of past racial features' may be 'Caucasian', but 'one's future aspiration in relation to race' may be for the irrelevance of one's racial designation. Another instance has one's past construal as 'abject Oriental', but future aspiration as 'proud Vietnamese'.

'Race' as a genetically determined variation of humankind with biologically distinctive features has been used politically and pseudo-scientifically with appallingly devastating consequences, such that in informed contemporary discourse the concept is regarded as suspect in respect of any explanatory power it may have. However, although few peoples retain thoroughly homogeneous racially typed genes given intermixing, there remain some relatively homogeneous groupings with a degree of racial distinctiveness. Discernible racial categories include the Negroid with black skin colour and black tight curly hair, and the North African/Mediterranean Arab/Semitic with brown skin colour and black hair. Others are the Caucasian with white skin colour and varied hair and eye colour, and the Mongoloid with white to yellow skin colour, smooth black hair, brown eyes and a general lack of facial hair.

The perceived salience of defining physical features that are genetic in origin is largely socially and personally constructed, as represented in the earlier definition of racial identity. One mixed-race person's 'construal of past racial features' may include *passing for white*, but with a newly expressed solidarity with blacks this person's 'construal of future aspirations in relation to racial characteristics' may be realigned to *black*.

While there remains widespread confusion over the concepts of race and ethnicity, the definitions of ethnic and racial identity given here indicate that the basic elements are quite distinct. Although ethnicity and race are both socially constructed, the markers are different. The markers for ethnicity are cultural manifestations of ancestry and those for race are physical features from genetic inheritance. The Hutus and Tutsis of Rwanda and Burundi represent a common Negroid racial identity, but are of culturally distinctive ethnic identities with an antagonistic history of dominance and subordination. Confusion between *ethnic* and *racial* identity may arise when cultural ancestry appears to be indistinguishable from genetic inheritance (Helms, 1990; Harris, Blue, & Griffith, 1995; Thompson & Carter, 1997).

Gender identity: Definition

> *One's gender identity is defined as that part of the totality of one's self-construal made up of those dimensions that express the continuity between one's construal of one's past gender and one's future aspirations in relation to gender.*

(Weinreich, 1986a)

The obtrusiveness of gender identity arises from the centrality of procreation to the reproduction of humankind and with it the sensitivity to sexual matters, biological manifestations of gender, and social constraints impinging on gender relations. Included in one's gender identity are experiences of forms of sexual arousal from childhood through puberty and adolescence into adult phases of the lifecycle. Gender identity also encompasses biological differences in body and build according to sex, and in particular the potential for the female to give birth to infants. It incorporates diverse social norms governing the usually acceptable conduct between the genders, which vary according to culture and subcultures, including gay and lesbian. Valsiner (2000) reviews cultural variations in family/ kinship groups and marriage forms, and interpretations of adolescent girls' and boys' cultural adaptation to maturation. Maccoby (1998) discusses, from a predominantly Western perspective, evidence and explanation for gender asymmetry in male and female relationships and gender identity as contributing to gender segregation in young people. Contributors to a volume edited by Bell, Caplan, and Karim (1993) amply illustrate the obtrusiveness of gender identity in ethnographic fieldwork. Golombok and Fivush (1994) provide a critically informed perspective of gender development from the vantage of Western cultures. The volume edited by Anselmi and Law (1998) provides a comprehensive set of readings on questions of gender. Studies to be reported here in Chapters 5 to 9 indicate the obtrusiveness of gender identity in a variety of arenas, and for females the significance of procreation and motherhood for their gender identity.

Socio-economic class or occupational identity: Definition

> *One's socio-economic class identity is defined as that part of the totality of one's self-construal made up of those dimensions that express the continuity between one's construal of one's past position and one's future aspirations in relation to class.*

(Weinreich, 1986a)

Everyday efforts towards providing sustenance and shelter for survival are highly organised and co-ordinated in contemporary times, and can be generally conceptualised as 'work'. Work is another central activity of everyday being-in-the-world, hence the importance of occupational identity as another salient component of the totality of one's identity. Social resources, education, aptitude, application and opportunity contribute to the class of work that may be undertaken, with ramifications for one's lifestyle.

Familial identity: Definition

One's familial identity is defined as that part of the totality of one's self-construal made up of those dimensions that express the continuity between one's construal of one's past position and one's future aspirations in relation to familial status.

(Weinreich, 1986a)

Debates down the centuries about the family, embedded in the various subcultures of differing ethnicities, demonstrate a significant but changing arena for the familial component of identity. The child's experience of growing up in an extended, or close-knit nuclear, or a single-parent family is a formative feature of one's identity. Later in adulthood, familial identity may embrace the experience of exercising responsibility for the welfare of dependent children within whatever family form one participates.

These explicit definitions of different aspects of the totality of one's identity make wholly manifest that they are not independent of one another. Aspects of identity are intertwined according to vastly different biographical experiences within a variety of socio-historical contexts from country to country. Qualities such as one's ethnicity, gender, socio-economic class and occupation, familial circumstances and race are not simply social variables that have set contributions to make to one's sense of identity. They are experienced in complex interrelationship in accordance with one's biography in socio-historical context.

The aspects of identity defined so far do not constitute all of the 'social identities' available in any community (for example, in respect of generation, religion, language, career and so on), but they are significant in contemporary times. Two further aspects of identity feature only for a much smaller set of people, whose mixed ancestral origins or lack of explicit parental origin makes them of special interest. The first of these is termed 'hybrid identity' in which a person's parents are of different ethnic ancestry or racial origin. The other is called 'yearning identity' in which one's parental origins are unknown, as is often the case with adoption or when conception has been by way of in vitro fertilisation.

Hybrid identity: Definition

One's identity is termed 'hybrid' when one's origins are construed as dimensions derived from different ethnic or racial parental constituents, and continue to be construed as future aspirations expressing multiple distinctive origins.

Yearning identity: Definition

One's identity is termed 'yearning' when one's origins are construed as dimensions without known parental antecedents, and continue to be construed in terms of future aspirations expressing yearned-for resolution about origins.

The yearning to discover who are their blood parents is well known among adopted children and statutory measures are in place in some societies to assist the adopted child in finding them. In more recent times as a result of technical advances in donor insemination, individuals born as a result of anonymously donated sperm are experiencing acute difficulties over their parental origins, when their yearning remains unfulfilled (Turner & Coyle, 2000). On discovering the truth as adults they may suffer crises of identity accompanying feelings of abandonment and loss.

Establishing parental 'antecedents' of identity provides intergenerational continuity and locates one's identity in the wider scheme of humanity when the community promotes norms of close relationships with one's blood mother and father.

Another two prevalent kinds of identity are of significance in contemporary times for people whose presence in the community represents age-old patterns of historical processes and events, namely migration for various reasons and displacement of indigenous peoples by colonial conquest. 'Migrant ancestral identity' references those individuals whose parental origins reside in another land. 'Displaced indigenous identity' refers to the state of an indigenous peoplehood that has been subjugated by conquest and has had its cultural integrity severely compromised.

Migrant ancestral identity: Definition

One's identity is termed 'migrant ancestral' when one's origins are construed as derived from a migrant ethnic ancestry, and continue to be construed as future aspirations to express a distinctive ethnic origin.

Offspring of migrant parents to a country that has a dominant culture markedly different from that of the country of origin, are neither everyday participants in the life of the parental country nor fully-fledged kinship members of the mainstream culture of their current country of abode. Offspring of the many migrant ethnic groups in contemporary nation states across the world experience their identities as being informed in important respects by the domestic culture of their ancestral heritage, while simultaneously identifying with selective aspects of the mainstream public culture within which they currently participate. While the subsequent generation to a migrating group is likely to wish to retain its ethnicity, the disjunction in experience of the countries of origin and abode between migrants and their offspring makes for a distinctive feature of migrant offspring identity (Weinreich, 1979b, 1983a; Liebkind, 1989; Ali & Northover, 1999).

Displaced indigenous identity: Definition

> *One's identity is termed 'displaced indigenous' when one's origins are construed as derived from an indigenous ethnic ancestry displaced by conquest, and continue to be construed as aspirations to express a distinctive indigenous origin.*

In recent times Aboriginals in Australia, Maoris in New Zealand, indigenous peoples in the Americas, black tribes in Africa during colonialism, and many other peoples throughout history all over the world, have been subjugated to foreign rule, and their cultural manifestations subordinated and desecrated by conquest. Concerted attempts to diminish and destroy the indigenous cultures are generally nevertheless resisted by the vanquished. Generally speaking, a displaced indigenous identity also references an ethnic identity, but one contending with forced usurpation from its territorial heritage.

The foregoing elucidation of aspects of people's identities demonstrates a mistaken conception when investigators refer to the 'multiple identities' of a person. A person has only the one identity, but experiences multiple aspects of identity that relate to gender, ethnicity, socio-economic class and so on. Depending on circumstances, this identity may be hybrid in terms of parentage, or yearning in the absence of known parentage, or migrant ancestral, or displaced indigenous, or simply mainstream, but always singular and unique in terms of biographical experience.

SECTION 2: THE SINGULAR SELF

Having now established the distinction between the core, but delimited, concept of self and the inclusive concept of identity, the elusive 'self' receives considerable clarification by way of Harré's (1998) elucidation and discussion of the 'singular agentic self'. Particular themes in his discussion are elaborated here. These are: Self's location in arrays of other beings; Human intentionality and normativity; The necessity of appreciating that psychology is a metaphysical and methodological *double science*; Personhood being the unique person that comprises self in three aspects – the *singular agentic*, the *reflective* and the *publicly expressive*.

Harré (1998: 4) emphasises that 'To have a sense of self is to have a sense of one's location, as a person, in each of several arrays of other beings, relevant to personhood.' One's location in the here and now, or as remembered at some moment in the past, or as anticipated in various future scenarios, varies in often spectacular ways, and can have very different personal ramifications for self's intentions, all contributing to the person's sense of self. When celebrating the birth of a relative's child, one's relationships with family members contribute to a sense of personal location in the world in certain ways, whereas one's involvement with other people encountered say at school, work, or leisure contributes differently. The ramifications of self situated in differing contexts is expressly conceptualised in ISA (see later under 'Cueing of identity states and situated selves' and Chapter 2).

This perspective on the sense of self makes clear that self is not a material entity that is subjected to natural forces, but is an experiential location in continually changing successive social contexts of arrays of others. As such, the science of conceptual and methodological investigation of personhood cannot be subsumed within that of traditional natural science. Harré (1998) significantly clarifies a number of fundamental issues about conceptualising the human sciences in respect to the ontology of human behaviour and personhood. He emphasises the thoroughgoing distinction between the natural and the human sciences, the latter being distinguished by human intentionality and normativity. Humans have intentions and appraise their behaviours for appropriateness against normative societal criteria that may alter historically and differ culturally:

> Underlying most of the arguments for a radical distinction in methods of enquiry in the natural and human sciences lie two features of human behaviour which have no counterpart in the behaviour of inorganic materials. Human behaviour displays or seems to display intentionality, that is, human actions are what they are by virtue of their meaning, point or aim. And human behaviour also displays normativity, that is it is generally subject to appraisal as correct, proper, appropriate or as incorrect, improper, inappropriate. It can be right or wrong.
>
> (Harré, 1998: 33)

For analyses of narrative conventions, which can be expressed according to normative rules, Harré (1998: 32) appeals to Bruner's (1991, 1993) work emphasising the important part played by shared narrative conventions in the shaping of people's actions.

Psychology may be approached from either or both of the natural and human science perspectives depending on the phenomena being investigated. That is, psychology is a 'double science'. Thus, in respect of investigating the biochemical changes associated with neuro-psychological processes, a natural science perspective would be appropriate, but establishing in a court of law the psychology of effective prosecution or defence would be more appropriately approached from the human science perspective. Taking psychology as a discipline, Harré points to 'the rediscovery of Wundt's insight that psychology is a metaphysical and methodological double science' (Harré, 1998: 30). However, investigating the psychology of personhood requires the adoption of the human science approach, elaborated and clarified by Harré. Attempting to formulate intentional human behaviour in natural science terms is simply inappropriate and is to fail to comprehend the distinction between natural and human science. To be sure, on occasion in psychological investigation both natural and human science approaches are required, as for issues such as personhood following brain damage or the psycho-pharmacological effects of drugs.

Harré spells out the case for the human science approach to personhood. Appealing to Vygotsky (1962) he first draws the distinction between thought and language in respect of the origins of each of these activities, then emphasises that the human mind develops through acquiring skills in interaction with others, assisted by the acquisition and use of language. Conversation is crucial:

> 1. For each individual person thought and language have independent origins. Thought begins in the native activity of the nervous system, while language begins in social interaction. 2. The structure of the developed human mind comes about through the acquisition of skills in psychological symbiosis with others.
>
> (Harré, 1998: 27)

Harré (1998: 39) presents an analysis and elaboration of Wittgenstein's (1953) private language argument that distinguishes between expressive and descriptive uses of language. Words for private feelings, such as pain, are learned as alternatives to natural ways of expressing feelings, being involuntary groans and other inarticulate expressions of pain. These self-expressive uses of language (how I feel) differ from descriptive uses that describe things (observable characteristics of entities). The pronoun 'I' is used to express oneself as a singular responsible being, that feels, thinks and acts. 'Wittgenstein's distinction between descriptive and expressive uses of words suggests that we research the private sense of self by studying the public expression of selfhood in such devices as the personal pronoun' (Harré, 1998: 43).

Conceptual designation of agentic self, self-concept and public self

Harré conceptualises the psychology of personhood as a human science, using social constructionism and emphasising the human capacity for language and conversation. He distinguishes the approach as 'discursive psychology'. Drawing on conceptual analyses by Vygotsky (1962, 1978), Wittgenstein (1953, 1969), Bruner (1991, 1993), Mead (1934) and Goffman (1959, 1963, 1981), he presents a formulation of personhood in which the unique person ('Person') comprises the self in three aspects ('Self 1', 'Self 2' and 'Self 3'). In the first instance the singularity of the self is located in time and space, being the agent who intentionally acts, interacts with others and appraises the circumstances of the person's being in relation to others by means of linguistic discourses and conversations. This singular agentic self is designated 'Self 1'.

However, the person, in agentic mode 'Self 1', reflects upon his or her characteristics and has an awareness of a constellation of beliefs, including beliefs about or conceptions of oneself. This reflexive self, which includes what is summarily often referred to as the self-concept, is distinguished from the singular agentic 'Self 1' and is conceptualised as 'Self 2'. 'Self 2' is the person's reflection on the capacities, skills, beliefs and autobiographical events of the person and may have many aspects: '... the sense one has of oneself as possessing a unique set of attributes which, though they change nevertheless remain as a whole distinctive of just one person' (Harré, 1998: 4).

In addition, the public self expressed by agentic self in interaction with others – the presentation of self in everyday life (Goffman, 1959) – together with this public self as perceived by others, is demarcated as 'Self 3'. 'Self 3 has aspects: There is the persona as the person intends to present it, in ways of speaking and acting, and then there [are] the ways such displays are interpreted by others, when they attribute personality or character to someone' (Harré, 1998: 78). Personhood is symbolically represented as 'Person {Self 1, Self 2, Self 3}, where Person is the robust existent and the three bracketed concepts refer to aspects of and conditions for the flow of personal action' (Harré, 1998: 9). Summarising his conceptual clarification, Harré writes (1998: 148):

> In my tidied up 'grammar' of discourses of the self ... there are four main concepts in play: 'person' (the unique being I am to myself and others); 'Self 1', the centre or 'origin' of relational properties that make up my field of perception and action; 'Self 2', the totality of attributes both ephemeral and enduring of the person that I am, including my self-concept, the beliefs I have about the characteristics I have as a person including my life history, and 'Self 3', the personal characteristics I display to others. ... while 'person' is a genuine substantive ... the three 'selves' are ontologically quite different. ... As entities, Self 1, Self 2 and Self 3 are fictions, though indispensable fictions.

The conceptual clarification that Harré achieves is by way of demonstrating the confusions that abound in the literature on the psychology of the self when these three meanings of the same word *self* elide. For example, he demonstrates (1998: 152–6) that in multiple personality disorder (MPD) the disorder can only be understood as the singular Self 1 formulating multiple Selves 2, and not separate multiple personalities (that is, not multiple agentic selves, Self 1s). Likewise, in an illuminating discussion of 'self-deception', Harré shows (1998: 169–75) that, while a person can deliberately deceive others, the notion of deceiving self is impossible. In order to deceive self the singular agentic self (Self 1) would need to know what characteristic of self (Self 2) the agentic self would wish to deny. Although the person may present self (Self 3) in such a manner as intentionally not to disclose this characteristic to others, to do so would be for self (Self 1) to recognise its existence for Self 2. The analysis concludes that the agentic self cannot intentionally deceive self, since self would have to know this in order to deceive, hence cannot do so without being aware of that about which self wishes to deceive self, so is not deceived.

The common use of 'self-deception' may be more appropriately interpreted as self's former inattention to an unpalatable truth about which the person becomes uncomfortably aware. The person thought that self was talented but is confronted with events indicating the contrary, and on reflection speaks of self-deception: *I deceived myself about my lack of talent*. One's lack of awareness, however, is not equivalent to 'oneself intentionally deceiving self'.

Agency, autonomy and control

In respect of human agency, a person's sense of autonomy and being in control is a variable characteristic from situation to situation, with modulation between identity states. In some situations one has a fair degree of autonomy and may have a good degree of control over one's own activities, with perhaps some influence over another's activities. Thus a teacher may have some autonomy with regard to the manner of teaching a syllabus without having much autonomy in respect of its content. The teacher may be in good control of the class and hence teaching activities, and thereby influence students' learning. If all is well when cueing into classroom activities the teacher's identity state is one of well-being. However, cueing into a different context when intimacy and trust are sought, the same person, being at the mercy of another's whims, may feel little control over matters and experience an identity state of anguish. Just how variable people's autonomy might be from one context to another is evident from a study of South African black youth during the apartheid era (Weinreich *et al.*, 1988). When free-standing with little constraint on autonomy, only 7.5% exhibited a 'very vulnerable' identity state, but this became a substantial 35.9% when situated with English-speaking whites and a massive 71.0% when situated with Afrikaners, the latter context representing a very much diminished sense of autonomy.

Irrespective of variable degrees of autonomy from situation to situation, some individuals strive to maintain control over their own activities and other people to a far greater extent than do others. Such individuals may in contemporary common parlance be referred to as 'control freaks'. Overall, the salient feature of autonomy as a fundamental characteristic of human agency is the variable nature of its expression, both situationally and in terms of individual propensity. Variations in career-women's personal autonomy as an individual propensity and differing constraints of domesticity or workplace on expressions of autonomy are well demonstrated by Wager's study of academic women at the University of Helsinki (see Chapter 6).

Conceptualising agency and autonomy evidently requires close attention. By emphasising the quality of agency in personhood and human affairs, the impression abounds that autonomy is the key to all human behaviour. This is clearly not the case and agency is not synonymous with autonomy. The autonomy of the agentic self may sometimes be maximal, but although agentic the self may be unable to act with autonomy when overwhelmed by external constraints (prevented by others) or by internal factors (conflicting moral imperatives in a dilemma). Autonomy experienced as a sense of being in control is compromised to some extent *when I have a headache*, to a greater extent *when I'm in a panic*, and altogether *when I'm losing consciousness*. In practice, the intentions of the agentic self tend to be compromised in various ways.

The principal ramification of this clarification of agentic self's variable autonomy and compromised intention is that purported explanations solely in terms of intention – *uncompromised* – cannot be sustained. Other psychological processes about which the person has little awareness will be significant in explicating agentic behaviour. The following is a simple symbolic exposition of compromised intentions, using Harré's *Self 1* and *Self 2* distinction, so that the fundamental issue of the agentic self's variable autonomy can be formally and explicitly conceptualised. The processes of cueing, both externally and internally, and appraisal of circumstances for implementing one's intentions and assessing potential outcomes for one's identity aspirations are central to the procedures for assessing parameters and states of identity.

Thinking, innovation, and compromised intentionality of agentic self

Assessing identity requires clarification of what the participant to an investigation is doing when expressing identity by way of discourses used to appraise self and others. 'Self appraises oneself' is a beguilingly simple notion, but the distinctions between agentic self, *Self 1*, self-conceptions, *Self 2*, and public self-presentations, *Self 3*, give warning that the agentic self is not itself assessed or appraised. In respect of oneself only self-conceptions and public self-expressions are available for appraisal: the agentic self is the agent that appraises, who appraises self 'as experienced', and appraises self 'through expression', *Self 2* and *Self 3*. Self-conceptions and public self-presentations are of course not the immediate agentic self of the here and now, the agent of the doing and thinking. What some commentators refer to as the 'authentic self' is not amenable to assessment, only the experienced and expressed aspects of self, *Self 2* and *Self 3*, are available. This is the case whether assessment is by agentic self directly, or by way of observations of oneself by others.

Symbolic representation of compromised intentionality

Before presenting the first instance of symbolic representation of compromised intentions, the power of thought – a characteristically human feature – requires acknowledgement. The singular agentic self, *Self 1*, is intentional as typically expressed through language and action, but the intentions so exhibited are already modified from pre-conscious cerebral thinking by way of previously existing schemata. Thought depends on sets of skills, current cues and immediate recall and, while at times misconceived, it is potentially extraordinarily and powerfully innovative.

The first instance to be considered is the implementation of innovative thought (say, about the plot and characters of a novel) as a new intention (to write the story). The person's new intention translates into a trial expression (smatterings of written text), the outcome being appraised for its merits, whereby the person forms a conception of self's aptitude (say, promising or inadequate) in respect of this new intention. This self-appraisal is a reflexive attribution and an elaboration of *Self 2*. Subsequent expressions of the 'new intention' are filtered through the previously experienced appraised aptitude and modified accordingly [the symbol $\rightarrow$ denotes *results in*]:

(i)   *Person {Innovative thought}*
(ii) $\rightarrow$ *Self 1: new intention*

(iii)   → *Self 1: trial expression*
(iv)   → *{Self 1: trial expression}*{appraised consequences}*
(v)   → *Self 2: new intention*

That is, (i) the person has an innovative thought at a cerebral level, which (ii) the agentic self *Self 1* translates into a new intention for action, (iii) gives it a trial expression, and (iv) appraises the consequences for self and others, which (v) are reflexively experienced by self giving rise to a self-conception *Self 2* in respect of pursuing this new intention.

On subsequent occasions pursuing this 'new intention' is represented thus:

(i)   *Self 1*Q{Self 2: new intention}*
(ii)   → *Self 1*{cued Self 2: new intention}*
(iii)   → *Self 1:{pertaining to Self 2: new intention}*

Here, (i) the process *Q* reactivates the particular *Self 2: new intention* and (ii) re-cues the original intentionality of *Self 1*, but modulated in accordance with (iii) appraised consequences *pertaining to Self 2: new intention*.

This analysis concludes that the biographical experiences of consequences of pursuing intentions invariably involve constructions of *Self 2* that arise from the person's appraisal of self's experiences in view of consequences. Moments of innovative thought as such are rare, while the pursuit of new intentions arising from them is modulated by the experience of their attempted implementation: *Self 1*Q{Self 2: new intention}*. For innovative thoughts that are abandoned, when for example appraised consequences of their attempted implementation are unsuccessful, *Q{Self 2: new intention}* loses any intentionality and becomes a void. The singular agentic *Self 1* under these circumstances, when the person attempts to re-pursue this 'new intention', would then experience the zero autonomy of 'being blocked'.

However, as the appraisal of consequences depends on how the person appraises the totality of factors affecting the situation being appraised, sufficient ambiguity about such factors is frequently present for 'apparent' lack of success to be put down to circumstances that could be changed on future occasions. 'If you don't succeed at first, try again.' If the guy's 'innovative thought' about the new girl in the neighbourhood becomes his intention to chat her up for a date, and his mode of expressing this is rebuffed by her, there is likely to be ample ambiguity in his appraisal of the situation for him to continue with his intention, but now taking into account perhaps a critical view of his earlier expression and revising it, and hoping also for a change of heart in her.

If being 'in character' denotes a person who is fully agentic and acting wholly in accordance with intentionality, that is with maximal personal autonomy, then all instances of *compromised* agency represent states of diminished personal autonomy. When one has 'lost control' (through anger or because situational odds are stacked up against one), then the sense of personal autonomy is very much reduced. While there will be individual differences between people in their ability to control events, all people will experience variable degrees of personal autonomy from time to time. The sense of personal autonomy, a characteristic feature of human behaviour and experience, is not constant but fluctuates enormously.

Given that new intentions tend to become compromised, the more representative case of the agentic self is one of intentional expression (IE) in the light of previous experience. Replacing *new intention* by *intentional expression* in the previous symbolic formulation, the general symbolic representation of the agentic self pursuing an intention is of the form:

$$Self\ 1*Q\{Self\ 2:\ IE\}$$
$$\rightarrow Self\ 1*\{cued\ Self\ 2:\ IE\}$$
$$\rightarrow Self\ 1:\{pertaining\ to\ Self\ 2:\ IE\}$$

where Q refers to the process that cues the aspect of self associated with the expression of the intention *{cued Self 2: IE}* and re-cues the earlier characterised mode of expressing the intention *{pertaining to Self 2: IE}*, which is the compromised intentionality of Self 1.

Commentary: The ISA conceptual framework in relation to Harré's discursive psychology

ISA adopts the same emphasis on the agentic person and the singularity of *Self 1* as conceptualised by Harré. It is also concerned with the grammar of expression, particularly in relation to the person's appraisal of self and others as agents communicating with one another by means of discourses. It follows the fundamental distinction between the singularity of the agentic self and the multiplicity of aspects of the reflexive self, *Self 2*, and self's personas variously witnessed by others, *Self 3*. Likewise, ISA warns against the dangers of reification. For example, it insists that the *ideal self* is understood in terms of the person's aspirations denoted semantically by the English phrase *me as I would like to be* (or the equivalent of 'personal aspiration' in other languages), but not as being some identifiable thing. When the term 'entity' is used generically within the ISA conceptualisation it is to be understood not as a materially substantive thing or object, but as a personally constructed entity or state of being. In this respect ISA shares the concerns of social constructionism. The semantic meanings of discourses as expressed and understood in time and place by different persons and differing peoplehoods form integral features of the ISA conceptual framework.

However, ISA conceptualises identity processes as occurring throughout the person's life-history, during which self appraises and reappraises other agents and agencies within historically changing cultural milieus. Commensurate with this perspective, the conceptualisation of identity necessarily incorporates the other people with whom the person relates, either directly in person or symbolically through myth and media, as understood and interpreted by self. Identity is, as emphasised before, an inclusive concept, inclusive of self's experiences and representations of other people and the social and material world encountered by self. Identity is more than the self is. Self is the central agency expressing intention, appraising the day-to-day social and material world, experiencing it emotionally in respect of its relevance to self's aspirations. The agentic self formulates the sense of identity over biographical time, which includes representations of other agents and agencies[2] beyond that of the self. The inclusion of representations of other agents and agencies in the conceptualisation of the person's identity, recognising the location of self within the nexus of others, is what distinguishes the concept of *identity* from that of *self*.

What one has experienced during episodes of the past, the manner of one's being and self presentation currently, and one's aspirations for oneself in the future, as delineated aspects of *Self 2*, are features of one's temporal continuity of identity, as construed and appraised by the agentic self, *Self 1*. In line with Erikson's writings, ISA views the formation and redefinition of identity during these episodes in the past, present and anticipating the future as being contingent on the partial identifications the person forms with influential others. Self's *identification with others*, self's *presentation to others* and self's *interpretation of others' views of self* represent complex intersections of various aspects of self-concept, *Self 2*, and public self, *Self 3*. In ISA the rationale for the explicit definition of further concepts is to provide for the practical empirical delineation of such complexities.

In addition, ISA adopts Harré's elucidation of the fundamental agentic character of the singular self, but allows that the person operates with limited and variable autonomy. At certain times and in certain contexts, the person may express considerable autonomy in thought and action, successfully pursuing a particular intention (for example, solving a difficult problem in an innovative fashion). At other times the person is so constrained by circumstances beyond self's control that one's autonomy is all but eliminated.

An added feature of psychological processes is that their operation occurs mostly without personal awareness. But through enquiry and reflection the individual may from time to time understand their nature and achieve awareness of them. People can develop personal insight through a variety of methods ranging from informal discussions with others to professional procedures. The agentic self remains the centre of action, but not everything about the person's pursuit of intentions is rational and autonomous. Non-rational processes, of which the person may have only the haziest of intimations, often influence the person's appraisal of circumstances and interfere with the priorities of intentions that the person wishes to pursue.

ISA attempts to provide a conceptual framework within which non-rational processes (such as identifying with others, appraising social situations, cueing into alternative identity states) may be better understood and integrated with the 'agentic singular self' conception. Discursive psychology requires elaboration in recognition of the person not being wholly autonomous, subject only to social constraints and natural forces. The facts of variable autonomy and non-rational processes make for unexpected kinds of complexity in 'human science' psychology.

The human capacity for utterly unpredictable innovation is a further consideration, as this can rapidly lead to unforeseen but widespread alterations in social norms such that contemporary understanding in terms of normative behaviour becomes suddenly redundant. Previously widespread normative aspects of identity endorsed by one generation are superseded by innovative updates evolved by a subsequent generation (such as the contemporary revolution in what gender identity entails for different communities or the rapid reformulation of ethnic identities in many parts of the world).

SECTION 3: THE APPRAISAL PROCESS

Person–situation interaction: Cueing, construal and evaluation

The appraisal process may be conceptualised as having three major distinguishable features. The first, *cueing*, when self cues into and focuses on a specific context – say, as a bystander to a brutal killing – is a precursor to the second, *construal* of the cued situation, followed by the third, *evaluation* of the situation in respect of self's intentions and identity aspirations.

During *construal*, self (*Self 1*) attributes characteristics to the other agents acting to the cued context – defencelessness to the victim, thuggery to the assailants. Self also construes self's behaviour in terms of perceived outcomes the killing, the escape of the assailants and one's own inaction – construing *Self 2* as helpless and cowardly.

Self *evaluates* the attributions made to other agents and to self. Here, self evaluates the victim's defencelessness negatively (pitifully) and the assailants' thuggery negatively (angrily). Self evaluates the attributions of self's helplessness and cowardliness as falling short of self's identity aspirations to be effective and brave.

A person's appraisal of a situation, as just described, consists of self-appraisal as well as appraisal of the other agents and agencies. As conceptualised here, one's appraisal consists of a focused cueing into the context of prevailing activities, construing the characteristics of the agents and of oneself, and evaluating these attributes by reference to one's identity aspirations. Self-appraisals may vary rapidly from one situation to another.

Depending on the nature of self-appraisal when cued into differently appraised contexts, self's empathetic identification with other agents may modulate (Weinreich *et al.*, 1987; Northover, 1988a,b; Kelly, 1989). Thus, if cued into a context when self experiences oneself as victim, then self will tend to empathetically identify more closely with other victims. If, however, when cued into another context one sees oneself as masterful, then one's empathetic identification will more likely be with other masterful people and less with victims.

Cueing, whether self or other initiated, primes self's initial orientation to context, which may subsequently alter due to the nature of present interactions and aroused memories. Cues may be non-verbal such as gesture, facial expression in people and like expression in animals, body language, smell, place, artefact, weather condition, symbol and so on. Or they may be verbal and include various linguistic devices used consciously by people to draw attention to specific circumstances. Some cues may be innate, as in the nipple of the breast to the feeding infant, but many will have been learnt and used with considerable deliberation, as with rhetorical stratagems intended to achieve specific outcomes during argumentation. As well as modes of self-cueing, other agents will also use strategies for cueing self into paying attention to them, their activities and their agendas. Others may hook into presumed biographical experiences of self and activate an established biographical script in order to elicit desired ends for themselves (Berne, 1961, 1964; Steiner, 1974).

The process of cueing, as the precursor to the full appraisal process, incorporates self's cueing into states of identity experienced as a matter of biographical history and categorising other agents into relevant classes. States of identity may vary from intentional and proactive to victimised and passive, from depressed to buoyant, and so on. Relevant classes into which others may be categorised could be of any kind – fat cats or paupers, facilitators of self's aspirations or detractors, Afro-Caribbeans or Chicanos, males or females, and so on, all *as classes* being stereotypes of one kind or another.

Cueing is of course selective. One cannot cue into all of one's past history of biographical experiences at once. Cueing cannot be to all identity states – present, past and anticipated – simultaneously. It can only be to specific contexts; whether primarily induced by other agents coercing self to be witness to activities beyond one's control, or by self pursuing specific intentions and identity aspirations. Likewise, categorisation of other agents into classes is selective and depends on the salience of specific cues. When categorising agents into classes relevant to cued contexts (Tajfel, 1981b; Brown, 1995), stereotyping in terms of normative attributions and evaluations invariably follows, but in varying forms as engendered by context. Thus, women as nurses in a hospital context may be stereotyped emphasising caring attributes, whereas women as bosses in commercial enterprises may be stereotyped as go-getting and power-dressing.

Given space and time, a person may reflect on past and current experiences. In assessing them for their significance to one's aspirations, self may clarify or forge links between selected biographical contexts and identity states in order to better maintain and maximise feelings of autonomy in the present (Weinreich *et al.*, 1988). Ultimately, however, self's appraisal of situations, their construal and evaluation whether in actuality or in imagination, depends on cueing, which may be internal as when deliberately guided by self or external as when induced by factors over which self has no control.

Cueing of identity states and situated selves

Individuals will vary in respect of what exactly might be the circumstances that cue specific identity states and differing manifestations of self situated in a variety of contexts. In the South African study (Weinreich *et al.*, 1988), *being with Afrikaners*, *being with English-speaking whites*, or *being simply oneself* provided powerful cues. The circumstances that cue identity states of depression and anxiety, or well-being and confidence can in many cases be readily cited, although sometimes more in-depth exploration may be required to delineate them. The cues that alert individuals to instigate malicious behaviour that is out of character, or suggest to self that deception might be efficacious in the short term, are more likely to be consequences of individual biographical experience.

Situated in differing contexts and in relation to differing events and identity states, the person may instigate a presentation of self (*Self 3*) *not being true to myself and behaving out of character* or *posing for effect in order to impress*. Such situated selves, though not in accordance with one's aspirational or ideal self, are nevertheless very much aspects and expressions of one's identity, as is evident from the following:

Situation identity: Definition

> *One's identity as situated in a specific context is defined as that part of the totality of one's self construal, in which how one construes oneself in the situated present expresses the continuity between how one construes oneself as one was in the past and how one construes oneself as one aspires to be in the future.*
> (Weinreich *et al.*, 1988)

One's past biographical self and one's aspirational self, however much the situated self may be at variance with one's ideal, ensure the continuity of identity, recognised as being characteristic of the same person. Whereas too great an emphasis on the disembodied situational self in the symbolic interactionist perspective suggests a chameleon-like ephemeral view of identity, the ISA definition just given firmly locates the situated expressions of identity within a biographical continuity.

Trauma and cueing into differing identity states

People directly involved with radical trauma are affected by the experience, which becomes part of their identities. Traumatic scenarios can range from being caught up in catastrophic events such as earthquakes, floods, crashes and sinkings, to experiencing a disruptive and abusive childhood, to rape and threats to personal life, to being engaged in warfare, and to being a survivor of genocide. The emotions of dread, fear, and anxiety, associated with intense traumas that continue over minutes, days, weeks, months and possibly years, are likely to be of such accumulated intensity that they form irredeemably 'unforgettable' biographical features of identity formation. The possibility remains that specific cues in contemporary times institute reverberations with the past experienced traumatised states of identity, however much they may have been successfully reappraised and put into the broader context of one's contemporary life (Black & Weinreich, 2000a,b). Chapter 12 reports a study of the identity processes of professional counsellors who worked intensively with survivors of a major traumatic occurrence, and who were themselves prone to vicarious traumatisation.

In the case of trauma, cueing into the reappraised experience of it will most likely result in a marked modulation of the state of one's identity currently, sensed as anxiety, dread and loss of control over one's emotional state. However, in the course of life events, people will experience other states of identity, accompanied by a sense of well-being when accomplishing important identity aspirations, which may be obtaining a desired job, forming a new intimate relationship, or achieving some crucial objective. Cueing into different identity states (sensed as anxiety, sadness, well-being, etc.) is a common feature of the daily experiencing of one's identity. On a day-to-day basis, one's identity state is not a constant, but may modulate during the day from one state (anxiety) to another (well-being).

Appraisal, discourses and structural pressures

People's intentions, though of the here and now, often express the longer-term aims of implementing their identity aspirations, or defending against activities inimical to these aspirations. As such, some personal intentions are imbued with affect of life–death intensities if their symbolic significance to the integrity of one's identity is overwhelming. Other agents may be appraised as directly threatening, as in fights and times of war, or symbolically threatening to one's integrity, as by acts of humiliation, disparaging judgements, or more extremely, rape.

The discourses that the person uses to express self and to construe and evaluate others' activities in respect of self's intentions, are generated in current time. In this sense they are forever 'newly expressed' and gauged, however well or badly, to suit the purposes and activities of the moment. However, the meanings of the components of discourses are already codified, through informal and formal learning initially in the home, then in the wider community. While denotative meanings of vocabularies are generally shared in normative fashion, their affective connotations are private to the individual and can be labelled only by reference to imagined affective states in others. Normative consensus will generally extend to denotative meanings, but affective connotations will vary greatly from person to person for the same component of vocabulary or syntactical form. Thus, discourses about abortion, meanings of which are agreed denotatively, will vary substantially from person to person in their affective connotations according to pro-choice or anti-abortion stances. Discourses that justify abortion under specific circumstances will tend to be acceptable to and have positive connotations for pro-choice people, but be unacceptable to and have negative ones for anti-abortionists. Evidence abounds in ISA studies for the very different affective connotations people attach to the same cognitions, texts and discourses (see Chapter 3 in respect of primordialist and situationalist sentiments about ethnicity). Two people, attributing the same characteristics to another but with alternative affective connotations, evaluate that other differently.

Evaluation of another: Definition

A formal definition[3] of a person's evaluation of another takes into account the specific evaluative connotations that the person's discourses have when construing the other:

> *One's evaluation of another is defined as one's overall assessment of the other in terms of the positive and negative evaluative connotations of the attributes one construes in that other, in accordance with one's value system.*
> (Weinreich, 1980/86/88)

Evaluation of current (past) self: Definition

Self has the capacity for reflexive appraisals of self, so an explicit definition of self-evaluation,[4] in respect of current or past self-image, in like format follows:

> *One's evaluation of one's current (past) self is defined as one's overall self-assessment in terms of the positive and negative evaluative connotations of the attributes one construes as making up one's current (past) self-image, in accordance with one's value system.*
> (Weinreich, 1980/86/88)

This definition of self-evaluation is generic, but in reality self (*Self 1*) is continually monitoring and appraising oneself (*Self 2*) from moment to moment, from one social context to another and from one mood-state to another. In effect, the generic current or past self in this definition is to be replaced with self situated in context when one's overall self-assessment is likely to fluctuate considerably (e.g., academic and sporting self; Harter, 1982, 1990).

Self-esteem: Definition

Although self-evaluation as just defined has a clear-cut sense, the notion of self-esteem is more complex in that it implies a continuity over time, with past experiences contributing as well as current appraisals of self. Thus, someone who currently appraises self as competent and progressing well towards fulfilling self's identity aspiration, but has experienced gross failings in the past, will have a different sense of self-esteem compared with another person whose current successes continue in line with past accomplishments. Both of these persons' experience of self-esteem will differ from that of a person who was used to a high past self-evaluation, but currently is in an anti-developmental trough of despair as is witnessed in those suffering from anorexia nervosa (Weinreich *et al.*, 1985; Connor, 1991). Self-esteem is predicated both on past as well as current self-evaluation:

> *One's self-esteem is defined as one's overall self-assessment in evaluative terms of the continuing relationship between one's past and current self-images, in accordance with one's value system.*
> (Weinreich, 1980/86/88)

Self-esteem by itself is a poor indicator of identity processes. The *self-esteem* parameter should always be considered in relation to instances of enduring, increasing, or decreasing *self-evaluation*. Self-evaluation should also be viewed in conjunction with other features of identity. For instance, expressions of high self-esteem such as *defensive high self-regard* and *diffuse high self-regard* denote different kinds of 'vulnerable' identity (see the *identity variant* classification later, under 'Identity variants'). This analysis – detailed further in Chapter 2 – demonstrates that the popular notion of the self-esteem 'motive' is a fiction. *Self-evaluation*, from which is derived *self-esteem*, is shorthand for indicating self's judgement of progress towards implementing one's identity aspirations (James, 1890).

Ego-involvement with entities: Definition

The parameter *evaluation* assesses whether the person or agent is appraised positively or negatively. But it is unable by itself to designate the intensity of one's involvement with other agents or the force of their impact as experienced by self. Another parameter *ego-involvement with other agents or entities* (Sherif and Cantril, 1947) represents this intensity of involvement with people, institutions, emblems, or whatever agents, and is defined here.

> *One's ego-involvement with another is defined as one's overall responsiveness to the other in terms of the extensiveness both in quantity and strength of the attributes one construes the other as possessing.*
>
> (Weinreich, 1980/86/88)

Again, by token of self-reflection, self (*Self 1*) may be ego-involved with oneself (*Self 2*) to varying degrees when appraised as situated in various past and present contexts. Some people are very self-involved while others are more highly ego-involved with other people. Cross-culturally, Western societies are deemed to be strongly individualist and self-involved, whereas in other communities the individual may be self-effacing and more involved with extended kin or community obligations.

The practical operationalisation of the parameters *evaluation of entities*, *self-evaluation* and *self-esteem* in various contexts, and *ego-involvement* is outlined in Chapter 2. The procedures incorporate the person's usage of discourses to interpret and judge the activities of agents and agencies.

Appraisal: Cognitive–affective incompatibilities

Discourses that are understood by people to have the same cognitive sense – *has a cat that jumps onto people's laps* – may nevertheless vary in their affective connotations from person to person – positive for cat-lovers, negative for cat-phobics! As bipolar constructs, texts with their often-implicit psychological contrasts have affective associations that are specific to the individual. Self as singular agent (*Self 1*) appraises reflexive self (*Self 2*) and other agents using constructs available to oneself, which may express circumstances that might be neutral about, or facilitating of, or threatening to, one's identity aspirations.

A person's discourses expressing the trustworthy nature of various agents appraised in terms of self's identity aspirations will be imbued with positive emotional overtones. The activities of these trustworthy agents will have been judged as representing desirable qualities from self's perspective. When such an agent engages in a further activity that is also appraised as desirable for self, this is entirely compatible with the agent's trustworthiness for self – cognitive–affective consonance between a new cognition with positive affect and the existing cognition with positive affect. However, should the agent follow a course of action appraised as detrimental to self's aspirations, then the negative affect accompanying this appraisal is incompatible with the positive affect of trustworthiness experienced to date – cognitive–affective dissonance between a new cognition with negative affect and the existing cognition with positive affect. An attempted resolution of cognitive–affective dissonance would be to reappraise the earlier judged desirable qualities to become disfavoured ones – in the light of present knowledge one must have been mistaken. Empirical investigations of such cognitive–affective incompatibilities have had a long tradition among experimental social psychologists (Osgood & Tannenbaum, 1955; Festinger, 1957; Heider, 1958; Rosenberg & Abelson, 1960; Ableson *et al.*, 1968; Weinreich, 1969). The evidence of many studies demonstrated that people much prefer harmonious appraisals and are strongly inclined to change their attitudes, opinions and beliefs about self and other agents in their attempts to achieve such harmony, balance and consonance.

The constellation of agents encountered during one's life will have been attributed characteristics such that self evaluates them as more or less favourable or unfavourable 'gestalts'. While self may have a preference for cognitive–affective consonance, realistic appraisals acknowledge the disjunctions in people's activities and it is rare for any person to be appraised in wholly favourable terms.

The affective connotations of discourses are not automatic givens, but exist in the present as continually maintained by cognitive–affective pressures deriving from the person's attributions to others. When previous encounters have been experienced in cognitive–affective compatible manner, the pressures are harmonious and positive, maintaining the existing affective connotations of the discourses in question. However, when they entail cognitive–affective incompatibilities the pressures are distressful and negative, and undermine previously existing affective connotations – what had earlier seemed straightforward and desirable no longer feels so good, and is maybe ripe for reinterpretation as undesirable.

Structural pressures on constructs: Process postulates

The stability of the affective connotations expressed by discourses depends on the positive (sustaining) and negative (undermining) pressures that derive from structures of cognitive–affective consonances and dissonances with which the discourses are associated as a result of their use during past encounters with the social and material world. The greater the positive pressure for sustaining compatible affective associations the more stable will be the evaluative connotations of the bipolar construct and the discourses subsumed by it. The more the construct and corresponding discourses are associated with cognitive–affective incompatibilities, the more the stability of the construct's affective associations is undermined to the limit of vacillation from positive to negative affect or vice versa.

Structural pressure on a construct: Definition

A term, 'structural pressure on a construct', is introduced to reference the pressures that arise from the structures of cognitive–affective consonances and dissonances associated with the use of the construct:

> *The structural pressure on a person's construct is defined as the overall strength of the excess of compatibilities over incompatibilities between the evaluative connotations of attributions one makes to each entity by way of the one construct and one's overall evaluation of each entity.*
>
> (Weinreich, 1980/86/88)

As an identity parameter, how the quality 'structural pressure on a construct' may be operationalised is given in Chapter 2. Here, the preceding analysis is formalised into postulates about the person's processes when using discourses to express self and appraise the material and social world in terms of self's values and beliefs (Weinreich, 1989a). Sure affective tone – of certain approval or disdain – would accompany the usage of particular discourses when stability of affective connotations derives from experienced cognitive–affective compatibilities. The structure of experienced consonances generates positive structural pressures that dynamically sustain stable affective connotations. The discourses in question designate core evaluative dimensions of identity, for which endorsed elements express secure identity aspirations.

However, ambivalent and vacillating emotional modalities may characterise the person's usage of other discourses when having experienced cognitive–affective incompatibilities, generating negative pressures that undermine stabilising positive ones. These discourses would represent conflicted evaluative dimensions of identity that signify 'emotionally confused' identity aspirations, qualities towards which one might aspire in some frames of mind and from which one might wish to dissociate at other times.

Postulate 1. Core evaluative dimensions of identity
When the net structural pressure on one of a person's constructs is high and positive, the evaluative connotations associated with it are stably bound (Weinreich, 1989a).

Postulate 2. Conflicted evaluative dimensions of identity
When the net structural pressure on a construct is low, or negative, as a result of strong negative pressures counteracting positive ones, the evaluative connotations

associated with the construct are conflicted: the construct in question is an arena of stress (Weinreich, 1989a).

Postulate 3. Unevaluative dimensions of identity
When the net structural pressure on a construct is low as a result of weak positive and negative pressures, the construct in question is without strong evaluative connotations (Weinreich, 1989a).

With these postulates ISA retrieves social constructivism and discourse analysis from extreme relativism. By locating the characteristics of the individual's discourses within the nexus of self's experienced relationships with others, ISA demonstrates that each new encounter and discursive expression has a biographical history that in many instances provides for continuity of interpretation and emotional tone. ISA posits other instances when self uses discourses in unstable and volatile manner. ISA operationalises the *structural pressure* parameter so that empirical assessment may be made of these differing usages of discourse.

Contrary to the extreme relativistic position that one newly creates and expresses one's identity afresh on every encounter with another, empirical evidence demonstrates that one uses certain discourses with stable evaluative connotations to express core features of one's identity repeatedly. One's repeated self-presentation by spontaneous use of characteristic modes of expression is what characterises oneself in the eyes of others. Furthermore, one may well use other discourses in contradictory ways that are also characteristic features of one's identity. The individual may of course resort to novel expressions when challenged by other agents or when wishing to challenge them, or when intent on developing a new persona with changed identity aspirations.

Symbolic formulation of the appraisal process

The formulation that follows is a first-approximation codification of the appraisal process in relation to the development, elaboration and redefinition of the person's identity. It translates to ready operationalisation for empirical investigations, procedures for which are detailed in Chapter 2. The agentic quality of self (*Self 1*) is emphasised and self's appraisal of particular persons and events in particular contexts is codified, the analytic framework being one that acknowledges a reflexive mode of self appraisal (engendering *Self 2*) and the incorporation of elaboration and innovation over time. In the following, the device $f(\dots \text{'agent'} \dots \text{'process'} \dots)$ refers to 'is a function of the specified agent engaged in the specified process'.

Appraisal = f *(agentic self involving interpretation and judgement)*

By 'interpretation' is meant the meaning attributed to the situation with which a person is engaged. By 'judgement' is meant the evaluation of that interpretation with respect to the personal aspirations of that person (i.e., in respect of the person's aspirational or ideal self) from the vantage-point of the current self situated in social contexts and within variable identity states.

That is, in general, a person's appraisal of a specific situation is made by way of construing, or attributing meaning to, agents and events in context, within the limitations of one's constructs as cued by the situation, and evaluating or judging this construal in relation to one's aspirations. Generally, the person's appraisal is expressed by means of appropriate discourses and pragmatic devices. Appraisal may be briefly represented as:

Appraisal = cued construal (attribution) and evaluation (judgement), expressed using discourses and pragmatic devices

Consider appraisal to be an ongoing effort by the individual to interpret the social world from moment to moment, from day to day, from one biographical phase to another. The person's appraisal of situations from moment to moment will depend on both one's characteristic self-attributions (say, *unsure*) when cued by a specific context (say, *new challenge*) or a particular mood state (say, *anxious*) and the others' actions in that context (say, *aggressive*). Thus, in a study of black South African youth (Weinreich *et al.*, 1987), specific contexts in which self is situated are *with Afrikaners, with English speaking people, me now*. In an investigation of Gujarati/English bilinguals (Northover, 1988a,b) situated contexts are *with Gujaratis* and *with the English*. In a study of ethnic identification (Kelly, 1989) specified contexts are *with Pakistanis, with English people* for Pakistani offspring, and *with Greek Cypriots, with English people* for Greek Cypriot offspring. An exploration of identity in an urban environment (Saunderson, 1995; see Chapter 7 here) examined the situated contexts of town planners *as users of the built environment* and *as producers of the built environment*. A study of vicarious traumatisation experienced by counsellors dealing with victims of the Omagh bomb (Black & Weinreich, 2000b; see Chapter 12 here) delineated contexts such as *before the Omagh bomb, in the short-term aftermath of the Omagh bomb, facing the long-term consequences of the Omagh bomb*. In each study, self-attributions differed substantially according to the context of situated self or identity state.

Representing self's judgement of oneself as a function of the situation or mood state $f(situated\ self,\ identity\ state)$ and self's interpretation of others present as a function of these entities and their actions, self's appraisal of self in relation to the other entities in the situation may then be expressed as:

Appraisal = f*(cued situated self or identity state)* · f*(cued entities/actions)*

where

f*(cued situated self or identity state)*
= f*(context of appraisal: cued self)*
· f*(construal and evaluation of cued self in the context)* (1)

and

> f*(cued entities/actions)*
>> = f*(context of appraisal: cued entities/actions**)*
>>> · f*(construal and evaluation of cued*
>>>> *entities/actions in the context)* (2)

***at the moment in terms of people, events, institutions, etc. of significance in the context in question, and their actions.*

In expression (1) f*(context of appraisal: cued self)* refers to the compromised agentic self in respect of intentional expression, IE, where Q refers to the cueing process that cues aspect 'cued Self 2: IE' (see earlier under 'Symbolic representation of compromised intentionality'):

> *Self 1*Q{Self 2: IE}*
>> → *Self 1*{cued Self 2: IE}*
>> → *Self 1:{pertaining to Self 2: IE}*

or agentic self compromised by *Self 2 at the moment as cued by specific social contexts or current mood states*, for example, as cued by a context of trust when being with a close friend, or being in a state of anxiety over the fulfilment of exacting obligations.

Further, in expression (1):

> f*(construal and evaluation of cued self in the context)*
>> = f*(aspirations)*
>>> · f*(self assessment in terms of implementation of aspirations*
>>> *in the context)*

where f*(aspirations)* refers to *aspirations both positive – intending to implement self's desires – and negative – to avoid states that are repugnant to self*, that is, in terms of discourses or constructs delineating the aspirational self

> = f*(constructs)* · f*(aspirational or ideal self)*

In expression (2):

> f*(construal and evaluation of cued entities/actions in the context)*
>> = f*(attributions to each entity)*
>>> · f*(assessment of attributions to each entity)*

where

> f*(attributions to each entity)* = f*(constructs: entity)*
>>> · f*(aspirational or ideal self)*

in which entities/actions, constructs and aspirational self are themselves continually being elaborated or curtailed on each new expression, i.e., the interpretative and evaluative meanings of discourses are likely to change from social context to context, from one mood state to another, and over time.

However, further consideration avoids taking an unduly relativistic stand by analysing the processes by which certain features of identity and supporting discourses will be sustained in stable configurations over lengthy periods. The operations represented in the foregoing symbolic formulation of the appraisal process form the basis of the operationalisation of ISA outlined in Chapter 2.

SECTION 4: IDENTIFICATION PROCESSES

Benign and defensive identification: Process postulates

The concept of identification (S. Freud, 1923; A. Freud, 1936; Bettelheim, 1958; Bronfenbrenner, 1960; Bandura, 1969) is ambiguous and in need of clarification. To date the processes of identification are not well understood, although there have been some remarkable illustrations of the outcomes of such processes. One ubiquitous outcome is the intensity of identification with one's ethnic or national group to the extent of giving up one's life for it in warfare. Another more extraordinary outcome is the kind of identification with one's persecutors as witnessed by Bettelheim (1958) who observed longer-term prisoners in a German concentration camp copying the verbal and bodily forms of aggression of the Gestapo, often behaving worse than the Gestapo when in charge of other prisoners.

The term 'identification' may refer to *process* or *outcome*. The *process* of self forming an identification with another establishes an aspirational stance in respect of the other – perhaps, wishing to emulate the stand taken by the other on an important issue. The *outcome* of this process is self's subsequently established and continuing 'identification with the other'. This exposition continues with formulating postulates about processes and then attends to clarifying identification outcomes.

Self's identification processes are complex, as self may form identifications with significant others who have intimate impact on one's well-being – one's parents – or with others who are not intimates, but are nevertheless appraised with admiration or abhorrence – a media star or a corrupt politician. Extant patterns of aspirational identifications with others are the outcomes of biographical experiences and successive part identifications formed with these others either *intimately* during previous direct encounters, or *remotely* by witnessing their impact on the world at large. The following formulation distinguishes between intimate and remote contexts.

Forming an *intimate* aspirational identification with another is a process predicated on the power the other possesses to impact for good or ill on self's well-being. Without power to impact on one's experiences, the other would have no relevance to self and would be insignificant. Power over self may be experienced as *benign*, protecting self's well-being and sustaining self's existence, in which case the other is in essence a powerful 'benefactor' for the time being. Contrariwise, power may be experienced as *malign* when self feels coerced to engage in activities appraised as detrimental to oneself and threatening to one's dignity – for the moment, the other is a powerful 'aggressor' (see Anna Freud, 1936: identification with the aggressor).[5] The same person may be experienced alternately as benevolent or malevolent, as in the case of a parent experienced by the child as benign and supportive, or aggressive and demeaning, according to circumstances.

During the process of aspirational identification with another, the other is perceived to be agentic and intentional in thought and action. The resultant *outcome of identification* is that, when absent, the other in question is remembered as being an active intentional agent distinguishable from inanimate objects. For oneself the other *though absent* continues to have the qualities of being able to manipulate outcomes, good or bad, for self's well-being.

The following postulates specify two broad kinds of identification processes under circumstances when the other's impact on self is *intimate* and direct, according to whether power over self is appraised as benign or malign. The first considers benign circumstances:

Postulate 1. Process of intimate benign identification
When an individual experiences *supportive* use of power over oneself by another, a process of *intimate benign*[6] *identification* with that other occurs.

In the process of benignly identifying with another, one appraises the other's power as bringing about fulfilment of self's needs. One forms an attachment of warmth with the supportive person who provides the benign environment for oneself – the infant benignly identifying with and forming a secure attachment with the mother caring for her offspring. One's benign identification is with attributes of that other as perceived by self. During a process of intimate benign identification, the agentic self (*Self 1*) incorporates as a part of self (*Self 2*) the experience of *the benign other in relation to oneself*. In order to demonstrate in turn one's own mastery of *beneficent power* towards others, self imitates the benign behaviour of the other, wishing to emulate it more fully. The resultant 'wish to emulate' the other is, as defined later, designated *idealistic–identification* with that other.

The second postulate considers threatening conditions and a process of *defensive*[7] identification with another:

Postulate 2. Process of intimate defensive identification
When an individual experiences *threatening* use of power over oneself by another, a process of *defensive* identification with that other occurs.

An example of this process would be a child subjected to threats to body and soul defensively identifying with the perpetrator of these threats, the aggressor. 'Aggression' may take many forms: it may be symbolically demeaning as in ridicule, denigration, and defamation, or directly physical as in acts of sexual abuse, rape, injury, or threat to life. Consequent upon the habitual and inescapable proximity of the threatening other, the child forms an attachment of dread. Self may attempt to diminish the aggressor's violence by momentarily finding favour with the aggressor and, experiencing the relief of *symbolically* defusing the aggression, self may defensively identify with the perceived characteristics of the other. To be on the side of – *to identify with* – the aggressor during the attack is to experience a psychological diminution of threat by adopting an ersatz mastery over the aggression, in which self as recipient (*Self 2*) is symbolically dissociated from the agentic self (*Self 1*). Self acquiesces and 'accepts' the threatening stance of the other, though wishing to dissociate from the other's behaviour towards self. During a process of intimate defensive identification, the agentic self (*Self 1*) incorporates within one's conception of self (*Self 2*) the experience of *the coercive other in relation to oneself*. Because the coercive context of the aggression allows no escape, identification is with the stance of the other, even while wishing to dissociate from that stance. The resultant 'wish to dissociate' from the (stance of the) other is, as defined later, termed *contra-identification* with the other.

Through contra-identification with the threatening person and adopting a threatening stance as one's own characteristic, self discovers another way to exert power over others – not benignly, but using coercive power to subordinate them. As a consequence, one may at times engage in thoughts and actions recognised as being harmful to both self and others, but feel impelled to engage in them and furthermore experience relief in so doing. At the extreme, without some form of amelioration the sexually abused child may all too effectively contra-identify with the coercive perpetrator, subsequently incorporate the sexual stance into self's repertoire, and in time sexually abuse others. Alternatively, the violently accosted and terrorised child may contra-identify with the aggressors and subsequently, when older and stronger, flaunt acts of aggression, as in hooliganism, attempting to terrorise others into subordination. In these cases, using coercive power over others is thought by the perpetrators to be indicative of themselves 'winning' and demonstrating 'prowess', their satisfaction being spiked by a loathing that accompanies the underlying wish to dissociate from these acts that one feels 'compelled', through defensive identification, to carry out.

Whether or not people act in terms of benign and defensive identifications at any particular moment will depend on their intentional states and the cues for elicitation of the identifications in question. To have these identifications does not mean that they will be continually acted upon, but only when social contexts cue them. In so far as situational cues or internal thoughts evoke self to switch between positive and negative aspirational identifications, self has the capacity for 'good' and 'evil'.

Not all processes of identification occur in circumstances of intimate events. The following postulates consider circumstances when one may form aspirational identifications with remote others, who do not impinge on oneself in a direct and intimate manner. The identification processes are in these instances predicated on the power the other has to impact on self by means of an appraised resonance of well-being or abhorrence. Postulate 3 considers the benign form and postulate 4 the defensive form of non-intimate identification:

Postulate 3. Process of non-intimate benign identification
When an individual appraises a non-intimate other as having admirable qualities with the power to induce potent experiences of well-being, a process of non-intimate *benign* identification with that other occurs.

The agentic self, appraising various circumstances, may actively view them with a combination of thoughtfulness and spontaneous response – when listening to an impressive speaker, seeing a brilliant performer – that contributes to an experience of well-being.

Postulate 4. Process of non-intimate defensive identification
When an individual appraises a non-intimate other as having abhorrent qualities with the power to induce potent experiences of apprehension, a process of non-intimate *defensive* identification with that other occurs.

In instances of abhorrent acts committed by others that do not directly involve self – corruption, rape, 'ethnic cleansing' of a community – the experience of apprehension is by way of comprehending their impact on people with whom one shares a common humanity. In socio-historical circumstances of aggression against one's own group when self is powerless, non-intimate defensive identification with the aggressors subsequently tends to translate, when the power differential reverses, into self's 'principled' intention to take revenge against the other in ways that mirror those earlier used by the former aggressors. Such principled intentions of revenge are pursued with passionate moral fervour, as ethnic cleansing around the world testifies.

These process postulates attempt to specify the circumstances in which people form partial identifications with others, the outcomes of which are enduring aspirational identifications with these others. However, many of the day-to-day features that currently characterise self at any moment do not conform to one's aspirations, and some may be distressing features resulting from experiences instigated by *coercive others*. The *outcomes* of processes of identification receive attention next, although these may well be transformed in due course by the agentic self working at them.

Identification with others: Aspirational and empathetic modes

People's many differing extant patterns of identifications with others are outcomes of biographical experiences and successive part identifications formed with these others during previous encounters, moderated by the agentic self contending with their accumulative meaning. ISA delineates two distinctive modes of identification outcomes, the *aspirational* and the *empathetic*, which may be operationalised by empirical assessment procedures as outlined in Chapter 2.

The *aspirational* mode refers to self's wish either to emulate an admired individual or to dissociate from a despised person, as appraised by oneself. One's wish to emulate another denotes a propensity towards implementing an ideal and is termed *idealistic-identification* – self idealistically identifies with the admired individual. Contrariwise, one's wish to dissociate from another refers to a propensity towards rejecting the abhorrent, and is designated *contra-identification* – self contra-identifies with the abhorred individual. Formal definitions follow.

Idealistic-identification with another or group: Definition

> *The extent of one's idealistic-identification with another is defined as the similarity between the qualities one attributes to the other and those one would like to possess as part of one's ideal self-image.*

(Weinreich, 1980/86/88)

Contra-identification with another or group: Definition

> *The extent of one's contra-identification with another is defined as the similarity between the qualities one attributes to the other and those from which one would wish to dissociate.*

(Weinreich, 1980/86/88)

Some elaboration of the process of defensive identification will clarify what a person's contra-identification with another may entail. The person engaging in benign and defensive identification processes forms aspirational (idealistic- and contra-) identifications with others, and expresses corresponding imitative behaviours whether desired or not. Thus, following defensive identification with her father, a young girl admonishes her doll for 'bad behaviour'. She wishes to dissociate from the aggressive stance of her angry father towards herself, that is, she contra-identifies with this elemental characteristic of him, but she imitates his behaviour, expressing it towards her doll.

The term 'contra-identify with another' and the form of words 'wish to dissociate from the other' require further attention. Identifying with another, whether in a positive or negative sense, requires *knowledge* of the characteristic of the other in question. Identification is with a feature of the other as interpreted and understood by the person. Conversely, with no significant occurrence impinging on self, there is nothing with which to identify. The threatening stance of the other, when experienced by self, is a matter for potential identification, being understood and incorporated into self's knowledge. But such identification with threat carries with it the sense of wishing to dissociate from the negative affective state activated by threat: *contra-identifying constituting a wish to dissociate from this power to induce such emotion.*

What is the rationale for the process of defensive identification to incorporate that from which one wishes to dissociate? The girl *knows* the feature of her father's behaviour from which she wishes to dissociate. As he exerts his power over her, she (*Self 1*) cannot in practice dissociate from this feature which she appraises as characterising *herself*, that is, *her experience of her father in relation to herself* (*Self 2*). Being agentic, but not in control, she incorporates this knowledge of herself – *this aggressive feature of her father in relation to herself* (*Self 2*) – as an element of identification under coercive circumstances, from which she would wish to dissociate but cannot. As stated earlier, for agentic self (*Self 1*) to defensively identify with the coercive agent is to psychologically diminish the threat, symbolically dissociating the self as recipient (*Self 2*) from the agentic self (*Self 1*). The outcome is the girl's contra-identification with this feature of her father.

Totalistic, partial and elemental identification with characteristics of another

In referring to *an element of identification*, the foregoing analysis highlights the elemental aspects that contribute to varying extents of identification with another. In early childhood, when dependency on one, two or a few adults only is likely, the process of identification with a constant powerful adult may be total. However, subsequent encounters with other adults who impinge upon one's welfare are more likely to result in partial identifications, some of these being elements of idealistic-identification, others being elements of contra-identification. At a conceptual level, the term *elemental identification* will be used in order to denote that most processes of identification are partial, rather than total. These processes involve elemental identifications with specific characteristics of others that are salient at the time of the most powerful encounter, benign power in the case of idealistic-identification and coercive or symbolically threatening power in the case of contra-identification.

An *elemental identification* is defined *as being an identity of a characteristic attributed to the other and experienced in oneself* (Weinreich, 1989b). Attributed characteristics may of course be based in hopelessly inaccurate perceptions of the other, as in cases of children's distorted perception of parents or many people's stereotypical attributions to members of ethnic or racial groups. As other people can exercise benign and coercive power in relation to oneself over a period of time, one may form both elemental idealistic- and contra-identifications with them – idealistically-identifying with these others in some respects and contra-identifying with them in other ways.

Empathetic identification with others: De facto *states of recognition and closeness*

The earlier process postulates about benign and defensive identification focus on the person's aspirational orientations of wishing to emulate and wishing to dissociate from the other. Definitions of *idealistic- and contra-identifications* make explicit these continuing aspirational modes. The conceptual analysis here continues with attention to the *empathetic* mode of identification, which refers to self's sense of an identity existing between self and the other in actuality – of having characteristics in common irrespective of whether these might be for emulation or dissociation.

What people manage to be at any moment tends to be less than the models they wish to emulate and sometimes too near those from which they wish to dissociate. They nevertheless meet others in everyday walks of life whose characteristics match their own, including shared failings and disconcerting lapses. They *empathetically* identify with these others, feeling close to them. The formal definition of empathetic identification, operationalised in Chapter 2, follows:

Empathic identification with another: Definition

> *The extent of one's current empathetic identification with another is defined as the degree of similarity between the qualities one attributes to the other, whether 'good' or 'bad', and those of one's current self-image.*
> (Weinreich, 1980/86/88)

The earlier analysis of benign and defensive identification suggests that a person may engage in behaviours that may vary between being generally admirable and sometimes questionable depending on context. In one context (*at work*), self may express particular characteristics, which differ from those more saliently evident in another context (*at home*). Accordingly, self's empathetic identification with another will modulate from one context to another, being closer in some contexts and more distant in others. With self's elemental identifications with various others invariably differing in pattern, self's empathetic identification with each other person modulates with context differently – closer to one person in a particular context, but closer to another in an alternative context. ISA procedures can provide assessment of modulations in people's empathetic identifications according to specified contexts (see Chapter 2).

Conflicted identifications with others

The foregoing exposition points the way to an explicit awareness of self's conflicts in identification with others. When being close to another (*empathetic identification*) but wanting to dissociate from the other's characteristics (*contra-identification*), self's identification with that other is conflicted. Self experiences a tension in so far as the other represents a recognisable state of oneself that does not accord with one's identity aspirations. Thus, if one empathetically identifies with another, while simultaneously contra-identifying with that person, one's identification with the person in question is conflicted. In other words, one has a conflicted identification with another when one is as the other in various respects, while wishing not to be so in certain of these and other respects – *one is represented in the other, while wishing not to be.*

With the likelihood over an extensive period that one engages in both benign and defensive identification with various people, the chances are high that one simultaneously empathetically and contra-identifies with others to varying degrees. People's identifications with various others are conflicted in ways that depend on their biographical experiences. The formal definition of a person's conflicted identification with another is given here:

Identification conflict with another: Definition

> *In terms of one's current self-image the extent of one's identification conflict with another is defined as a multiplicative function of one's current empathetic identification and contra-identification with that other.*
>
> (Weinreich, 1980/86/88)

Reappraisal of self and others in respect of conflicted identification and new identifications: Process postulates

One's personal development of identity evolves in large part through one's successive part identifications with others during all manner of biographical episodes to date, as conceptualised by the foregoing postulates concerning processes of benign and defensive identification in circumstances of intimate or non-intimate involvement. Two postulates contend with the processes with which the person may engage consequent upon these biographical developments. One refers to the person attempting to resolve *identification conflicts* with others by way of reappraising self and others. The other refers to the person establishing new values and beliefs in accordance with one's *additional identifications* with hitherto unknown people and perspectives, which then provide a newly elaborated context for one's reappraisal of self and others.

Postulate 1. Resolution of conflicted identifications
When one's identifications with others are conflicted, one attempts to resolve the conflicts, thereby inducing re-evaluations of self in relation to others within the limitations of one's currently existing value system (Weinreich, 1989a).

The explanatory implications of this postulate are far reaching. Recall that one's conflicted identification with another agent or agency refers to the state of affairs when one both empathetically identifies and contra-identifies with that other. That is, by sharing much in common one 'is there' with the other, while in certain respects one 'wishes not to be there'. The tension is of course a matter of one's own identity. Thus, in a normative kind of loving heterosexual relationship one empathetically identifies closely, sharing a lot in common, with one's much-loved partner. But one draws the line at being entirely the same as one's partner in respect of gender and important gender-related attributes, distinctly wishing not to be the other gender with these particular attributes. Ultimately, the closer that one empathetically identifies with the other agent – *when one cannot be and does not wish to be the other* – so does the identification conflict with the other become more acute. One's conflicted identification with the other – *a matter of one's own identity* – becomes greater the closer to the other one becomes.

In striving to diminish one's conflicted identification with another, a person has several options. One is to review the attributes in the other that one wishes not to possess and reappraise them as being desired, which may not be altogether possible in the case of the heterosexual relationship. Another is to diminish one's empathetic identification with the other, that is, to generate differences between the other and self in a process of some degree of dissociation from that other through greater differentiation ('giving oneself space'). Further options involve a mixture of these two, that is, to diminish elements of both empathetic and contra-identification with the other.

In Tajfelian Social Identity Theory, a central proposition concerns group members achieving 'distinctiveness' from another group. The present analysis provides a cogent explanation for the process of differentiation in terms of striving to resolve a conflicted identification with the other group through diminishing empathetic identification with it – *lessening commonalities, thereby necessarily increasing distinctiveness*. It also explicitly focuses attention on the particular elemental identifications of relevance to the context in question. This process of dissociation from the other group appears to be significant in maintaining sectarianism between members of Protestant British and Catholic Irish communities in Northern Ireland, who in both instances have their greatest conflicted identifications with the other group (Weinreich, 1983b). The greater the empathetic identification they have with the other group, the greater will be their conflicted identification with them based in those features of the other from which they wish to dissociate – faith, nationality and culture. Striving to resolve the greater identification conflict with the other group, means either to identify with the other faith, nationality and culture – a total change of allegiance and citizenship – or to return to diminishing empathetic identification by further exaggerating differences – generating greater distinctiveness.

The second postulate has especial significance in the light of possible outcomes indicated here in respect of the first postulate. It encompasses the earlier postulates about processes of benign and defensive identification, but directs attention to the elaboration of one's value and belief system, being a reappraisal of one's world-view.

Postulate 2. Formation of new identifications
When one forms new identifications with newly encountered individuals, one broadens one's value system and establishes a new context for one's self-definition, thereby initiating a reappraisal of self and others which is dependent on fundamental changes in one's value system (Weinreich, 1989a).

In Sherif's classic field experiment at a summer camp for youth, the reconciliation of warring factions was achieved by the staff engineering major mishaps affecting all at the camp – *the fault of external agencies* – for which new camp-wide aspirations to pull together to resolve the mishaps were formulated (Sherif *et al.*, 1961; Sherif, 1966). These new aspirations represented fundamental changes in value system associated with newly formed contra-identifications with the disruptive external agencies.

The preceding analysis of the agentic quality of the person forming identification with others indicates that these others, by adoption and imitation, are the origins of significant values, beliefs and orientations to the world. But identification with others does not account for all of one's viewpoints, as self – being agentic – thinks innovative thoughts and independently works out understandings of many matters. To varying degrees self generates one's own values and beliefs, within a context of initial orientations to the world derived from identifications with others. Self's idealistic- and contra-identifications with others may be crucially reformulated by reference to criteria independently generated by oneself.

Resynthesising identifications: Identity diffusion

Erikson (1959a, 1968) graphically portrayed in his writings the potentially difficult phase that adolescents experience when making sense of themselves and the contemporary world into which they are being inducted by powerful figures who represent the cultural norms of society. Many of these people are generally well respected and may also earn the respect of adolescents. However, some figures respected by society may offend adolescents because of outmoded practices, personal animosity or perhaps abuse. On the other hand, others deemed unacceptable to 'establishment' agencies may appeal to adolescents.

The world of adolescence is one of transition from an arena where, as child, primary carers had largely provided the rules of conduct to one where, as adulthood beckons, peers provide contesting rules and self takes greater responsibility for one's conduct. While certain sections of the community continue to insist on established norms of conduct and others proffer alternative norms, self in alliance with peers may progressively formulate differing aspirations, the implementation of which would entail modifying the previous generation's priorities. Questioning of established rules of conduct and formulating contemporary viewpoints require the adolescent to resynthesise childhood identifications with noteworthy adults, siblings and peers so as to forge an updated sense of identity oriented towards adult tasks (Erikson, 1959a). Self's reformulated sense of identity, if successfully negotiated with significant peers and adults, enables the adolescent to leave childhood behind and move on to adulthood in a manner that accords with integrity for oneself and acceptance by one's immediate community.

During the child-to-adult identity transition, adolescents contend with newly developing sexual awareness and profound bodily changes that induce them to reflect on their sense of identify and forge new identifications. They also have access to thought processes of increasing complexity and sophistication with which to handle such imperatives. With societal norms for guidance and rites of passage, thoughtful reflection, trial and error, and comparing notes with peers,

most adolescents effect a sufficiently effective resynthesis of childhood identifications to achieve a reformulated sense of identity recognised and accepted by society. Alternatively, adolescents may be confronted with hostility and, despite best
efforts to resynthesise earlier identifications and negotiate acceptable viewpoints,
remain confused about their place in society and their meaning to themselves.

Erikson's term 'identity diffusion' refers to the state of affairs when a person is
unable to effectively resynthesise earlier identifications. A phase of self-
questioning and reflection on one's role in society, termed 'identity crisis', is a
usual precursor to forging coherent identity aspirations with well-formulated
commitments. However, adolescents who do not proceed to such a phase, but
remain with an unchanging 'given' identity without questioning, have 'foreclosed
identities'. Those who are still in the questioning phase without having made
identity commitments are in a state of 'psychosocial moratorium'.

Erikson describes the clinical symptomology of being in a state of identity diffusion – anxiety and confusion about the person one is, one's roles, beliefs, and
commitments. However, he does not elaborate on the underlying processes
involved in resynthesising earlier identifications nor conceptualise identity diffusion in terms of explicit identifications with specific others. ISA contends that the
individual strives to resynthesise identifications because they have become in various ways incompatible with one another, since without such incompatibilities the
person would have no reason to reflect upon them as being problematic and in need
of resynthesis. Using a level of analysis that appeals to the elemental identifications and conflicted identifications considered earlier, ISA interprets the resynthesis process as one in which the individual strives to resolve the incompatibilities of
conflicted identifications with others. *Identity diffusion* is considered to be the dispersion of conflicted identifications with others, where the greater the magnitude
of identification conflicts and the more extensive their dispersion across others, the
more severe the diffusion. A formal definition of overall identity diffusion is:

Identity diffusion: Definition

> *The degree of one's identity diffusion is defined as the overall dispersion and
> magnitude of one's identification conflicts with others.*

(Weinreich, 1980/86/88)

Identity diffusion in the foregoing analysis is an inevitable concomitant of any
identity transition, not only the adolescent one. Further, in interpreting identity
diffusion as the dispersion of a person's identification conflicts with others, ISA
presents an important shift in emphasis concerning the process of resynthesis of
identifications. Whereas a complete resolution may be possible in respect of a
person's conflicted identification with just *one* other, simultaneous resolutions of
conflicted identifications with *many* others are not feasible. As the person strives
to resolve one identification conflict, the likelihood is that others will increase or
new ones emerge. In practice, a person without any degree of conflicted identification would be someone who does not realistically differentiate other agents in

respect of the usual complexities of attributes, desirable and undesirable. The best that one could hope to achieve when remaining in touch with social realities would be to *optimise* one's conflicted identifications overall. With regard to resythesising identifications and resolving the spread of conflicted identifications constituting identity diffusion, ISA postulates that:

Postulate: Optimisation of identity diffusion
The individual strives to maintain an optimal level of identity diffusion.

The optimal level is neither so low as to demonstrate a lack of acceptance of usual residual identification conflicts with others, nor so high as to be acutely problematic. The acceptable degree of tolerance of conflicted identifications is likely to vary from person to person, so that to some extent the optimal level of identity diffusion may differ from person to person. From a cross-cultural perspective, people working to societal norms of differing cultures will tolerate varying forms of identification conflicts and to varying intensities, so that cultures will vary concerning typical ranges of optimal identity diffusion in their members. What may be a moderate optimal level for members of one culture may be excessively high for another.

Identity variants

The conceptualisation of identity processes so far has been at the molecular level formalised in concepts such as elemental identifications, aspirations, values and beliefs, bipolar constructs and discourses. ISA defines higher-order concepts, such as empathetic identification, aspirational identification, structural pressures on constructs, and identity diffusion. The conceptual framework includes postulates about processes, which apply to all individuals, but given individual biographical histories will be manifested with great variety and greatly varying outcomes, as will be demonstrated in the evidence reported in this volume. In most investigations information at the molecular level will be necessary to achieve a useful understanding of the particular constellation of processes within the individual. However, global representations of states of identity can provide rapid overviews of certain major propensities. In Marcia's interpretation of Erikson's writings, his conceptualisation is primarily at the global level of 'identity statuses' (Marcia *et al.*, 1993).

The ISA conceptualisation presents an interpretation of Erikson's formulation seeking to comprehend the underlying processes that result in identity diffusion, that is, at the molecular level. The current analysis maintains that people in general contend with optimal levels of identity diffusion. If people hold to realistically differentiated views of their fellow beings having complex combinations of desired and shunned qualities, they cannot simultaneously resolve all of their conflicted identification with others. Having conflicted identification with certain others is the norm. At a global level, commensurate with Marcia's (1980, 1987) 'identity statuses', ISA distinguishes between people with levels of identity diffusion *much higher* and *much lower* than the norm. The highly diffused individuals are classified as being in *diffused* states of identity. Those with very low levels, who do not acknowledge a differentiated appraisal of the social world, are classified as being in *foreclosed* or *defensive* states of identity. *Diffused* and *foreclosed* states of identity have similar connotations to Marcia's typology of like-named identity statuses, except that underlying processes of conflicted identifications explicitly provide the basis for the ISA formulation.

By taking the parameter of *self-evaluation* in conjunction with that of *identity diffusion*, ISA achieves a classification of identity variants elucidating myriad states of identity that accords with Erikson's original emphasis on the individual's resynthesis of earlier identification, which is missing from Marcia's typology. Accepting that most people have moderately positive self-evaluation, some individuals' self-evaluation is much higher and others' much lower than the norm. Those high in self-evaluation, or low, respectively judge themselves to be either close to fulfilling their identity aspirations, or unsuccessful in achieving them. Those individuals classed as having *high self-evaluation* may variously exhibit a diffused identity state – designated as *diffuse high self-regard* – or a foreclosed one – classified as *defensive high self-regard*. Those with *low self-evaluation*, when in a diffused state are designated as being in *identity crisis*, or when foreclosed as being in a *defensive negative* identity state. The full ISA classification of identity variants is presented in Chapter 2.

Marcia's typology has no equivalents to the identity variants of *diffuse* and *defensive high self-regard*. Marcia's 'moratorium' status may be equivalent to the *identity crisis* variant and Marcia's negative interpretation of 'identity diffusion' is most nearly represented in ISA by the *crisis* variant. In ISA the connotations of 'identity diffusion' are such that people with moderate levels constitute the norm, and those with high levels may be in a state of diffuse high self-regard, neither of these corresponding to Marcia's blanket negative interpretation of his diffusion status. In cases of identity foreclosure, Marcia's typology makes no distinction between positive states – *defensive high self-regard* – and negative states – *defensive negative*.

The ISA conceptualisation of identity processes clarifies the nature of possible dynamics at various transitional phases in an individual's biographical history of experiences. Changes in underlying identifications and identity aspirations, elaborations and updatings of values, beliefs and world-views, reappraisals of self's competencies and judgements of one's behaviour situated in differing contexts, all may well result in the person experiencing differing identity states in time. While to be in a *confident* state of identity is most desirable, ISA posits no end-point for identity formation, such as Marcia's 'identity achievement' status. One thinks through and develops all kinds of previously unforeseen identity aspirations and goes through many transitions and periods of doubt and uncertainty. The empirical evidence from ISA studies reported in this volume and elsewhere demonstrates some of the variety of states of identity that indicate potential for changes in fortune.

The ISA conceptualisation attempts to escape the moral overtones evident in the terminology of 'status' with its implications of a hierarchy from good ('achievement') to bad ('diffusion'). The ISA approach is basically morally agnostic in respect of identity variants. Although the experience of being in identity crisis will be an unhappy state of affairs and being in a state of identity diffusion is likely to be uncomfortable, such circumstances provide the impetus for the person to contemplate alternative ways of regarding self. The impetus for change in and development of one's identity follows from the process postulate concerning one's striving to resolve identification conflicts with other agents and agencies. Given the propensity for survival, the individual will in due course strive to readjust aspirations and resolve conflicted identifications, and by so doing will reappraise possibilities for one's future life course and develop further competencies. Even 'defensive' modes can be usefully adaptive at times, as is found with first-time mothers who did not develop 'maternity blues'. Unlike those with high identity diffusion during pregnancy, who subsequently developed 'maternity blues' and even higher identity diffusion after the birth of the child, well-adjusted mothers were defensive and with lowered identity diffusion during pregnancy, but following the birth readjusted to quite usual extents of identity diffusion (Needham, 1984). In periods of rapid development and change, identity diffusion may be a characteristic of acknowledging flux, thereby adding a further impetus to the opening up towards new potentialities.

Likewise, the negative moral overtones of such notions as 'culture conflict', 'identity conflict', 'conflicted identifications with others' should be carefully examined (Weinreich, 1983a; Kelly, 1989). In most cases, the negative connotations are misplaced, when such circumstances are the stuff of ordinary day-to-day living. What becomes imperative therefore is the delineation of the particular circumstances of such problematic instances when the conflicted feature becomes of unbearable magnitude.

Vulnerable and threatened identities

From the foregoing commentary on identity variants, identity vulnerabilities that are apparently readily distinctive require careful portrayal. First, vulnerable identities are of different kinds. Diffuse identities are likely to be over-receptive to varieties of beliefs and values potentially reinforcing or adding to the vulnerability of existing confusions, uncertainties and vacillations. Defensive identities will tend to be rigid and unreceptive to alternative perspectives, the vulnerability then being a lack of adaptability and flexibility in changing circumstances. Negative versions of identity have the added vulnerability of hopelessness in respect of extant identity aspirations. However, as emphasised earlier, each of these kinds of vulnerability has, in the short term, potentially adaptive merits. Diffusion engenders thought and effort to redefine one's circumstances in more comprehensively differentiated terms as one strives to resolve conflicted identifications in a complex social world. Change in, and further elaboration of, one's identity are the likely consequences of identity diffusion. Defensiveness, or foreclosing on self's identity definition for the time being, can be an effective strategy for concentrating on matters in hand, such as pregnancy in first-time mothers who do not subsequently experience 'maternity blues', or people in general single-mindedly pursuing an important goal and putting off distracting matters. The hopelessness or demoralisation of negative identity states may provide the impetus to reassess out-of-reach identity aspirations to accord more realistically with one's skills and the social circumstances of the moment.

Threats to identity are fundamentally different from vulnerabilities in identity (Weinreich *et al.*, 1988). Identity vulnerabilities are located within people's identity structures, whereas threats to identity derive externally from other people and agencies:

Threatened identity: Definition

One's social identity is threatened when other people view oneself as a member of a social group in ways that are grossly discrepant from one's own view of self as member of that group.

(Weinreich, 1986)

A discrepant *alter-ascribed* social identity is a threat to one's *ego-recognised* social identity. People whose identities are not vulnerable are likely to recognise threats to their identities for what they are and take appropriate action to defend their integrity. However, people with vulnerable identities are likely to have problems when their identities are threatened. If defensive, they may either ignore the threat, as when they remain unaware of it, or they may defensively overreact and misjudge the extent of threat, either way they would be unable to respond to the threat effectively. If diffuse, they may incorporate the threatening view as yet another conflicted facet of self, further contributing to confusion and uncertainty. If demoralised, without defensiveness or diffusion, they may recognise the threat but remain apathetic and unresponsive, and not defend their integrity. Thus, the nature of threat to identity may be the same – as in racism or sectarianism – but reactions will differ according to people's identity states and kinds of vulnerability. People with secure identities will find strategies to preserve the integrity of their lifestyles. Derogatory stereotypes, racist, sexist, or sectarian attacks, while disconcerting and possibly life-threatening, nevertheless do not undermine secure identities, but are judged as being the expressions of unthinking, prejudiced, inadequate, brutal and self-serving people.

CODA: Psychological–societal interface in changing cultural and historical contexts

The conundrum of whether explanations are of the psychological reductionist or the social structural variety can be readily resolved by way of investigating the nature of people's *aspirational* and *empathetic* identification with the salient social institutions of a community, as experienced and interpreted by the actors. Established social institutions and contemporary social structures are entities that are experienced as having agentic power and intent. Individuals interpret them for their significance – *often incorrectly* – and act in accordance with their interpretations. In the context of societal institutions, individual behaviour may then be understood by reference to one's identification with and appraisal of them. However, individuals are also agents who may influence and redefine the nature of existing social organisations. In collaboration with others, they may reinterpret social structures and create new institutions in the service of pursuing their own contemporary identity aspirations. They are able to harness the power of innovative thought to pursue these contemporary aspirations.

The earlier commentary on psychology as a double science reminds us that the *natural science* perspective centring on deterministic cause–effect explanation cannot explicate issues of self and identity, and that this most characteristically human feature – innovative thought – cannot in principle be predicted. From a *human science* perspective, the stance of ISA is that the capacity for innovation is manifested relatively strongly only from time to time in particular individuals and within particular socio-historical contexts. Major thinkers, whose innovative thoughts had profound consequences for changing human conceptions of living in the world, are relatively few – Galileo, Newton, Einstein among physicists; Bell, Brunel, Turing among technologists; Valasquez, Picasso, Moore among artists; Abraham, Christ, Mohammed among religious and moral thinkers; Shakespeare, Shaw, Ibsen among playwrights, et cetera. Although such innovators exist within any age and express the quintessential human spirit, in the course of any mainstream era much continues for the time being to be predictable in normative terms until societal movements revolutionise the parameters of social debate and engender newly emerging lifestyles and belief systems. To this extent, explanations may for periods be normatively determinist. However, the human scientific enterprise of investigating self and identity requires an open-ended conceptualisation that can, in principle, encompass unpredictable innovations and their consequences. The conceptualisation should be able to encompass major transformations in social structures and social norms, as well as holding for normative eras. Chapter 2 outlines the algorithms for the operational procedures for elucidating parameters of self and identity, and provides schema for elucidating major personal transitions in identity and major transformations in society located in socio-historical context (summarised in Figure 2.4).

Applications of the ISA theoretical framework and its operationalisation to cross-cultural, societal and clinical studies follow. Chapter 3 derives a theoretical explication of primordialist and situationalist perspectives on national and ethnic identity and details cross-cultural research on it. Chapter 4 investigates ethnic identity of a minority within a minority.

Societal studies range from one that integrates contemporary discourse analysis with the ISA conceptual framework (Chapter 5) to considerations of gender identity in professional academics (Chapter 6), urban identity in producers and consumers of the city environment (Chapter 7), identity processes over time of returnees to higher education (Chapter 8) and entrepreneurial identity in relation to small business enterprises (Chapter 9).

Application of ISA to clinical studies provides the subject matter of Chapter 10 on clinical patients. Chapter 11 details the identity processes of a young anorexic woman. Chapter 12 focuses on identity changes of professional counsellors who attend to the many traumatised victims of high-profile disasters and who may thereby themselves experience 'vicarious traumatisation'.

NOTES

1 The term 'indigenous psychologies' (Heelas & Lock, 1981; Kim & Berry, 1993a) is used in two ways to refer to: (1) the scientific study of human behaviour (or the mind) that is native, that is not transported from other regions, and that is designed for its people (Kim & Berry, 1993b), likewise the national or cultural specificity of scientific psychologies in various cultures (Boski, 1993); (2) 'folk' or 'lay' psychology held by ordinary people in a given culture (Heelas & Lock, 1981; Boski, 1993). In practice, while there is clear merit in distinguishing a scientifically rigorous conceptual and systematic empirical mode of investigation from intuitive speculation, nevertheless, the psychology of people is also informed by world-views, moral values, and pervasive but implicit agendas that suggest that 'scientific' psychology is imbued with much 'lay' psychology and vice-versa (Jodelet, 1993). In the current text, 'indigenous psychologies' refers to the indigenous 'lay' psychologies as may be informed by the cultural specificities of indigenous scientific psychologies. The ISA conceptual framework is conceptually rigorous and systematically operationalised for empirical investigations, and can be used both to elucidate 'lay' indigenous psychologies and to contribute to 'scientific' indigenous psychologies.
2 Agencies are of the material and social world encountered by the person, hence the significance of 'the soil' and the known place, seascape, urban landscape, etc. (see Chapter 7).
3 In considering appraisal the agentic *Self 1* construes and evaluates the other. This is to be understood in the following definitions.
4 Formal definitions of self-evaluation refer to *Self 2*, *Self 1* being the construing and evaluating agent.
5 The term 'identification with the aggressor' has unfortunate connotations if taken literally. For example, when applied to a parent it suggests that the parent is in all respects an aggressor, which is unlikely except in exceptional cases. The parent is more likely to be a caring and concerned person who, from the child's perspective, will on occasion be felt to be coercive. An aggressor would be someone who systematically and continually abuses another.
6 This process of identification is roughly equivalent to S. Freud's *anaclitic* identification (the Latin term *anaclitic* means 'leans on').
7 '*Defensive*' refers to the attempt to defend the integrity of the self from coercion against one's will.

REFERENCES

Ableson, P. A., Aronson, E., McGuire, W. J., Newcomb, T. M., Rosenberg, M. J., and Tannenbaum, P. H. (eds.) (1968) *Theories of Cognitive Consistency: A Sourcebook*, Chicago: Rand McNally & Company.
Abrams, D., and Hogg, M. A. (eds.) (1999) *Social Identity and Social Cognition*, Oxford: Blackwell.
Ali, N., and Northover, M. (1999) 'Distinct identities: South Asian youth in Britain', in J.-C. M. Lasry, J. G. Adair and K. L. Dion (eds.) *Latest Contributions to Cross-Cultural Psychology*, Lisse, Netherlands: Swets & Zeitlinger.

Anselmi, D. L., and Law, A. L. (1998) *Questions of Gender: Perspectives and Paradoxes*, New York: McGraw-Hill.

Arnold, M. B. (1960a) *Emotion and Personality: Psychological Aspects (Vol.1)*, New York: Columbia University Press.

Arnold, M. B. (1960b) *Emotion and Personality: Neurological and Physiological Aspects (Vol.2)*, New York: Columbia University Press.

Aronson, E. (1992) 'The return of the repressed: Dissonance theory makes a comeback', *Psychological Inquiry*, 3: 303–311.

Bandura, A. (1969) 'Social-learning theory of identificatory processes', in D. A. Goslin (ed.) *Handbook of Socialization Theory and Research*, Chicago: Rand McNally.

Bell, D., Caplan, P., and Karim, W. J. (eds.) (1993) *Gendered Fields: Women, Men and Ethnography*, London: Routledge.

Berne, E. (1961) *Transactional Analysis in Psychotherapy*, London: Souvenir Press.

Berne, E. (1964) *Games People Play*, New York: Grove Press.

Bettelheim, B. (1958) 'Individual and mass behavior in extreme situations', in E. E. Maccoby, T. M. Newcomb and E. L. Hartley (eds.) *Readings in Social Psychology* (3rd edn), New York: Holt, Rinehart & Winston.

Billig, M. (1987) *Arguing and Thinking: A Rhetorical Approach to Social Psychology*, Cambridge: Cambridge University Press.

Billig, M. (1988) 'Social representations, objectification and anchoring: A theoretical analysis', *Social Behaviour*, 3: 1–16.

Billig, M. (1991) *Ideology and Opinions: Studies in Rhetorical Psychology*, London: Sage.

Black, W. R. S., and Weinreich, P. (2000a) 'Exploring the issue of identity in trauma counsellors', *Eisteach: Journal of Counselling and Therapy for the Irish Association for Counselling and Therapy*, 2: 27–32.

Black, W. R. S., and Weinreich, P. (2000b) 'An exploration of counselling identity in counsellors who deal with trauma', *Traumatology*, Online Journal: www.fsu.edu/~trauma 6, 1.

Boski, P. (1993) 'Between West and East: Humanistic values and concerns in Polish psychology', in U. Kim and J. W. Berry (eds.) *Indigenous Psychologies: Research and Experience in Cultural Context*, Newbury Park, CA: Sage.

Bronfenbrenner, U. (1960) 'Freudian theories of identification and their derivatives', *Child Development*, 31: 15–40.

Brown, R. (1995) *Prejudice: Its Social Psychology*, Oxford: Blackwell.

Bruner, J. S. (1991) 'The narrative construction of reality', *Critical Inquiry*, Autumn: 1–21.

Bruner, J. S. (1993) 'The autobiographical process', in R. Folkenflik (ed.) *The Culture of Autobiography*, Stanford, CA: Stanford University Press.

Carrithers, M., Collins, S., and Lukes, S. (1985) *The Category of the Person: Anthropology, Philosophy and History*, Cambridge: Cambridge University Press.

Connor, T. (1991) *An Identity Exploration of Anorexia Nervosa within a Family Context*, DPhil dissertation, University of Ulster.

Cooley, C. H. (1953) *Human Nature and the Social Order*, Glencoe: Free Press. [Original publication: New York: Scribner's 1902.]

Coopersmith, S. (1967) *The Antecedents of Self-esteem*, New York: W. H. Freeman.

Erikson, E. H. (1950) *Childhood and Society*, New York: Norton.

Erikson, E. H. (1959a) *Identity and the Life Cycle*, Selected papers, New York: International Universities Press.

Erikson, E. H. (1959b) *Psychological Issues (Vol.1)*: 101–166.

Erikson, E. H. (1968) *Identity, Youth and Crisis*, New York: Norton.

Ervin-Tripp, S. (1973) *Language Acquisition and Communicative Choice: Essays by S. Ervin-Tripp*, Stanford, CA: Stanford University Press.

Farr, R. M., and Moscovici, S. (eds.) (1984) *Social Representations*, Cambridge: Cambridge University Press.

Festinger, L. (1957) *A Theory of Cognitive Dissonance*, Evanston Row, IL: Peterson.

Flick, U. (1995) 'Social representations', in J. A. Smith, R. Harré and L. Van Langenhove (eds.) *Rethinking Psychology*, London: Sage.

Fox, M. (1996) *An Exploration of the Depressed Identity using Identity Structure Analysis*, MSc Applied Psychology dissertation, University of Ulster.

Fransella, F., and Dalton, P. (1990) *Personal Construct Counselling in Action*, London: Sage.

Fransella, F., and Thomas, L. (eds.) (1988) *Experimenting with Personal Construct Psychology*, London: Routledge & Kegan Paul.

Freud, A. (1936) *The Ego and the Mechanisms of Defense*, New York: International Universities Press, 1946.

Freud, S. (1923) *The Ego and the Id*, New York: Norton, 1960.

Gergen, K. J. (1991) *The Saturated Self*, New York: Basic Books.

Gergen, K. J., and Gergen M. M. (eds.) (1984) *Historical Social Psychology*, Hillsdale, NJ: Lawrence Erlbaum Associates Inc.

Gergen, K. J., and Gergen M. M. (1991) 'Tales that wag the dog: Globalisation and the emergence of postmodern psychology', in M. H. Bond (ed.) *Working at the Interface of Cultures*, London: Routledge.

Goffman, E. (1959) *The Presentation of Self in Everyday Life*, New York: Doubleday Anchor.

Goffman, E. (1963) *Stigma*, Englewood Cliffs, NJ: Prentice Hall.

Goffman, E. (1981) *Forms of Talk*, Philadelphia: University of Pennsylvania Press.

Golombok, S., and Fivush, R. (1994) *Gender Development*, Cambridge: Cambridge University Press.

Harré, R. (1979) *Social Being: A Theory for Individual Psychology*, Oxford: Blackwell.

Harré, R. (1983) *Personal Being*, Oxford: Blackwell.

Harré, R. (1998) *The Singular Self*, London: Sage.

Harris, H. W., Blue, H. C., and Griffith, E. E. H. (eds.) (1995) *Racial and Ethnic Identity: Psychological Development and Creative Expression*, New York: Routledge.

Harter, S. (1982) 'The perceived competence scale for children', *Child Development*, 53: 87–97.

Harter, S. (1990) 'Issues in the assessment of the self-concept of children in adolescence', in A. M. La Greca (ed.) *Through the Eyes of the Child: Obtaining Self Reports from Children in Adolescence*, Boston: Allyn & Bacon.

Harter, S., and Monsour, A. (1992) 'Developmental analysis of conflict caused by opposing attributes in the adolescent self-portrait', *Developmental Psychology*, 28: 251–260.

Heelas, P., and Lock, A. (eds.) (1981) *Indigenous Psychologies: The Anthropology of the Self*, London: Academic Press.

Heider, F. (1958) *The Psychology of Interpersonal Relations*, New York: Wiley.

Helms, J. E. (1990) *Black and White Racial Identity: Theory and Research*, Westport, CT: Greenwood.

Hogg, M. A., and Abrams, D. (1988) *Social Identifications: A Social Psychology of Intergroup Relations and Group Process*, London: Routledge.

Hoyle, R. H., Kernis, M. H., Leary, M. R., and Baldwin, M. W. (1999) *Selfhood: Identity, Esteem, Regulation*, Boulder, CO: Westview.

Hutchinson, J., and Smith, A. D. (eds.) (1996) *Ethnicity*, Oxford: Oxford University Press.

James, W. (1890) *Principles of Psychology*, New York: Holt, Rinehart & Winston.

Jodelet, D. (1993) 'Indigenous psychologies and social representations of the body and self', in U. Kim and J. W. Berry (eds.) *Indigenous Psychologies: Research and Experience in Cultural Context*, Newbury Park, CA: Sage.

Kelly, A. J. D. (1989) 'Ethnic identification, association and redefinition: Muslim Pakistanis and Greek Cypriots in Britain', in K. Liebkind (ed.) *New Identities in Europe: Immigrant Ancestry and the Ethnic Identity of Youth*, Volume 3 of the European Science Foundation series: 'Studies in European Migration', London: Gower.

Kelly, G. A. (1955) *The Psychology of Personal Constructs*, New York: Norton.

Kim, U., and Berry, J. W. (eds.) (1993a) *Indigenous Psychologies: Research and Experience in Cultural Context*, Newbury Park, CA: Sage.

Kim, U., and Berry, J. W. (1993b) 'Introduction', in U. Kim and J. W. Berry (eds.) *Indigenous Psychologies: Research and Experience in Cultural Context*, Newbury Park, CA: Sage.

Laing, R. D. (1960) *The Divided Self*, London: Tavistock.

Laing, R. D. (1961) *The Self and Others*, London: Tavistock.

Laing, R. D., and Esterson, A. (1964) *Sanity, Madness, and the Family*, London: Tavistock.

Laing, R. D., Phillipson, H., and Lee, A. R. (1966) *Interpersonal Perception*, London: Tavistock.

Lazarus, R. S. (1966) *Psychological Stress and the Coping Process*, New York: McGraw-Hill.

Lazarus, R. S. (1991) *Emotion and Adaptation*, New York: Oxford University Press.

Lazarus, R. S., and Folkman, S. (1984) *Stress, Appraisal and Coping*, New York: Springer.

Lecky, P. (1945) *Self Consistency: A Theory of Personality*, New York: Island Press.

Liebkind, K. (ed.) (1989) *New Identities in Europe: Immigrant Ancestry and the Ethnic Identity of Youth*, Volume 3 of the European Science Foundation series: 'Studies in European Migration', London: Gower.

Littlewood, R., and Lipsedge, M. (1982) *Aliens and Alienists: Ethnic Minorities and Psychiatry*, Harmondsworth: Penguin.

McAdams, D. P. (1997) *The Stories we Live By* (2nd edn), New York: Guilford Press.

Maccoby, E. E. (1998) *The Two Sexes: Growing Up Apart, Coming Together*, Cambridge, MA: Harvard University Press.

Marcia, J. (1980) 'Identity in adolescence', in J. Adelson (ed.) *Handbook of Adolescent Psychology*, New York: Wiley.

Marcia, J. (1987) 'The identity status approach to the study of ego identity development', in T. Honess and K. Yardley (eds.) *Self and Identity: Perspectives Across the Lifespan*, London: Routledge & Kegan Paul.

Marcia, J., Waterman, A. S., Matteson, D. R., Archer, S. L., and Orlofsky, J. L. (1993) *Ego Identity: A Handbook for Social Research*, New York: Springer-Verlag.

Mead, G. H. (1934) *Mind, Self and Society*, Chicago: University of Chicago Press.

Moscovici, S. (1988) 'Notes towards a description of social representation', *European Journal of Social Psychology*, 18: 211–250.

Moscovici, S., and Paicheler, G. (1978) 'Social comparison and social recognition: Two complementary processes of identification', in H. Tajfel (ed.) *Differentiation Between Social Groups: The Social Psychology of Intergroup Relations: European Monographs in Social Psychology, No 14*, London: Academic Press.

74   *Weinreich*

Needham, S. (1984) *Maternity Blues and Personal Identity Development in First-Time Mothers: An Exploratory Study*, BPS Diploma in Clinical Psychology dissertation, British Psychological Society.

Northover, M. (1988a) 'Bilinguals and linguistic identities', in J. N. Jorgensen, E. Hansen, A. Holmen, and J. Gimbel (eds.) *Bilingualism in Society and School*, Copenhagen Studies in Bilingualism, Vol. 5. Clevedon: Multilingual Matters.

Northover, M. (1988b) 'Bilinguals or "dual linguistic identities"?' in J. W. Berry and R. C. Annis (eds.) *Ethnic Psychology* (International Association for Cross-Cultural Psychology), Lisse, Netherlands: Swets & Zeitlinger.

Osgood, C. E., and Tannenbaum, P. H. (1955) 'The principle of congruity in the prediction of attitude change', *Psychological Review*, 62: 42–55.

Pasternak, B., Ember, C. R., and Ember, M. (1997) *Sex, Gender, and Kinship: A Cross-Cultural Perspective*, Upper Saddle River, NJ: Prentice Hall.

Phinney, J. S. (1989) 'Stages of ethnic identity development in minority group adolescents', *Journal of Early Adolescence*, 9: 34–49.

Phinney, J. S., and Rosenthal, D.A. (1992) 'Ethnic identity in adolescence: process, context and outcome', in G. R. Adams, T. P. Gullotta, and R. Montemayor (eds.) *Advances in Adolescent Development (Vol. 4) Adolescent Identity Formation*, Newbury Park, CA: Sage.

Piaget, J. (1950) *The Psychology of Intelligence*, San Diego, CA: Harcourt Brace Jovanovich.

Piaget, J. (1952) *The Origins of Intelligence in Children*, New York: International Universities Press.

Potter, J., and Wetherell, M. (1987) *Discourse and Social Psychology*, London: Sage.

Reicher, S., and Hopkins, N. (2001) *Self and Nation*, London: Sage.

Reid, H. (1990) *Stress in Residential Social Work: A Study of Organisational and Individual Factors*, DPhil dissertation, University of Ulster.

Rosenberg, M. (1965) *Society and the Adolescent Self-image*, Princeton, NJ: Princeton University Press.

Rosenberg, M. (1981) 'The self-concept: social product and social force', in M. Rosenberg and R. H. Turner (eds.) *Social Psychology: Sociological Perspectives*, New York: Basic Books.

Rosenberg, M., and Simmons, R. G. (1972) *Black and White Self-Esteem: The Urban School Child*, Washington, DC: American Sociological Association.

Rosenberg, M. J., and Abelson, R. P. (1960) 'An analysis of cognitive balancing', in C. I. Hovland and M. J. Rosenberg (eds.) *Attitude, Organisation and Change*, New Haven, CT: Yale University Press.

Rosenwald, G. C., and Ochberg, R. L. (1992) *Storied Lives: The Cultural Politics of Self-understanding*, New Haven, CT: Yale University Press.

Saunderson, W. (1995) *Theoretical and Empirical Investigation of Gender and Urban Space: The Production and Consumption of the Built Environment*, DPhil dissertation: University of Ulster.

Sherif, M. (1966) *Group Conflict and Cooperation: Their Social Psychology*, London: Routledge & Kegan Paul.

Sherif, M., and Cantril, H. (1947) *The Psychology of Ego-Involvements*, New York: Wiley.

Sherif, M., Harvey, O. J., White, B. J., Hood, W. R., and Sherif, C. W. (1961) *Intergroup Conflict and Cooperation: The Robber's Cave Experiment*, Norman, OK: University of Oklahoma.

Shotter, J. (1984) *Social Accountability and Selfhood*, Oxford: Blackwell.

Shotter, J., and Gergen, K. J. (eds.) (1989) *Texts of Identity*, London: Sage.

Shrauger, J. S., and Schoenman, T. J. (1979) 'Symbolic interactionist view of self-concept: Through the looking glass darkly', *Psychological Bulletin*, 86: 549–573.

Shweder, R. A. (1991) *Thinking Through Cultures: Expeditions in Cultural Psychology*, Cambridge, MA: Harvard University Press.

Steiner, C. M. (1974) *Scripts People Live: Transactional Analysis Life Scripts*, New York: Grove Press.

Stryker, S. (1980) *Symbolic Interactionism: A Social Structure Version*, Menlo Park, CA: Benjamin-Cummings.

Sullivan, H. S. (1953) *The Inter-Personal Theory of Psychiatry*, New York: Norton.

Tajfel, H. (1981a) *Human Groups and Social Categories*, Cambridge: Cambridge University Press.

Tajfel, H. (1981b) 'Social stereotypes and social groups', in J. Turner and H. Giles (eds.) *Intergroup Behaviour*, Oxford: Blackwell.

Thompson, C. E., and Carter, R. T. (eds.) (1997) *Racial Identity Theory: Applications to Individual, Group and Organisational Interventions*, Mahwah, NJ: Lawrence Elrbaum Associates Inc.

Turner, A. J., and Coyle, A. (2000) 'What does it mean to be a donor offspring? The identity experiences of adults conceived by donor insemination and the implications for counselling and therapy', *Human Reproduction*, 15: 2041–2051.

Turner, J. C., Hogg, M. A., Oakes, P. J., Reicher, S., and Wetherell, M. (1987) *Rediscovering the Social Group: A Self-Categorization Theory*, Oxford: Blackwell.

Valsiner, J. (2000) *Culture and Human Development*, London: Sage.

Vygotsky, L. S. (1962) *Thought and Language*, Cambridge, MA: MIT Press.

Vygotsky, L. S. (1978) *Mind in Society: The Development of Higher Mental Processes*, [M. Cole, V. John-Steiner, S. Scribner, and E. Souberman, (eds.)], Cambridge, MA: Harvard University Press. [Original work published 1930, 1933, 1935]

Weigert, A. J. (1983) 'Identity: Its emergence within sociological psychology', *Symbolic Interaction*, 6: 183–206.

Weinreich, P. (1969) *Theoretical and Experimental Evaluation of Dissonance Processes*, PhD thesis, University of London.

Weinreich, P. (1979a) 'Cross-ethnic identification and self-rejection in a black adolescent', in G. Verma and C. Bagley (eds.) *Race, Education and Identity*, London: Macmillan.

Weinreich, P. (1979b) 'Ethnicity and adolescent identity conflict', in V. Saifullah Khan (ed.) *Minority Families in Britain*, London: Macmillan.

Weinreich, P. (1980/86/88) *Manual for Identity Exploration using Personal Constructs* (2nd edn), Coventry: University of Warwick, Economic and Social Research Council, Centre for Research in Ethnic Relations.

Weinreich, P. (1983a) 'Emerging from threatened identities: Ethnicity and gender in redefinitions of ethnic identity', in G. M. Breakwell (ed.) *Threatened Identities*, Chichester: Wiley.

Weinreich, P. (1983b) 'Psychodynamics of personal and social identity: Theoretical concepts and their measurement', in A. Jacobson-Widding (ed.) *Identity: Personal and Socio-cultural*, Stockholm: Almqvist & Wiksell International.

Weinreich, P. (1985a) 'Identity exploration in adolescence', *International Journal of Adolescent Medicine and Health*, 1: 51–71.

Weinreich, P. (1985b) 'Rationality and irrationality in racial and ethnic relations: A metatheoretical framework', *Ethnic and Racial Studies*, 8: 500–515.

Weinreich, P. (1986a) 'The operationalisation of identity theory in racial and ethnic relations', in J. Rex and D. Mason (eds.) *Theories of Race and Ethnic Relations*, Cambridge: Cambridge University Press.

Weinreich, P. (1986b) 'Identity development in migrant offspring: Theory and practice', in L. H. Ekstrand (ed.) *Ethnic Minorities and Immigrants in a Cross-Cultural Perspective*, (International Association for Cross-Cultural Psychology), Lisse, The Netherlands: Swets & Zeitlinger.

Weinreich, P. (1989a) 'Variations in ethnic identity: Identity Structure Analysis', in K. Liebkind (ed.) *New Identities in Europe: Immigrant Ancestry and the Ethnic Identity of Youth*, Aldershot: Gower.

Weinreich, P. (1989b) 'Conflicted identifications: A commentary on identity structure analysis concepts', in K. Liebkind (ed.) *New identities in Europe: Immigrant Ancestry and the Ethnic Identity of Youth*, Aldershot: Gower.

Weinreich, P. (1991a) 'Ethnic identities and indigenous psychologies in pluralist societies', *Psychology and Developing Societies*, 3: 73–92.

Weinreich, P. (1991b) 'National and ethnic identities: Theoretical concepts in practice', *Innovation in Social Science Research*, 4: 9–29.

Weinreich, P. (1992) 'Socio-psychological maintenance of ethnicity in Northern Ireland – A commentary', *The Psychologist*, 5: 345–346.

Weinreich, P. (1998) 'Social exclusion and multiple identities', *Soundings: A Journal of Politics and Culture*, 9: 139–144.

Weinreich, P. (1999) 'Ethnic identity and enculturation/acculturation', in J.-C. M. Lasry, J. G. Adair, and K. L. Dion (eds.) *Latest Contributions to Cross-Cultural Psychology*, Lisse, The Netherlands: Swets & Zeitlinger.

Weinreich, P., and Ewart, S. (1999a) *IDEXbasic for Windows Version 3.0: Identity Exploration computer software for idiographic, basic case studies.* Jordanstown: University of Ulster School of Psychology.

Weinreich, P., and Ewart, S. (1999b) *IDEXnomo for Windows Version 3.0: Identity Exploration computer software for nomothetic, comparative studies.* Jordanstown: University of Ulster School of Psychology.

Weinreich, P., Harris, P., and Doherty, J. (1985) 'Empirical assessment of identity in anorexia and bulimia nervosa', *Journal of Psychiatric Research*, 19: 297–302.

Weinreich, P., Kelly, A. J. D., and Maja, C. (1987) 'Situated identities, conflicts in identification and own group preference: Rural and urban youth in South Africa', in C. Kagitcibasi (ed.) *Growth and Progress in Cross-Cultural Psychology*, 321–335, (International Association for Cross-Cultural Psychology), Lisse, The Netherlands: Swets & Zeitlinger.

Weinreich, P., Kelly. A. J. D., and Maja, C. (1988) 'Black Youth in South Africa: Situated identities and patterns of ethnic identification', in D. Canter, C. Jesuino, L. Soczka, and G. Stephenson (eds.) *Environmental Social Psychology*, (NATO Advanced Research Workshop), Dordrecht, The Netherlands: Kluwer Academic.

Weinreich, P., Luk, C. L., and Bond, M. (1996) 'Ethnic stereotyping and identification in a multicultural context: "Acculturation", self-esteem and identity diffusion in Hong Kong Chinese university students', *Psychology and Developing Societies*, 8: 107–169.

Wickland, R., and Brehm, J. (1976) *Perspectives on Cognitive Dissonance*, Hillsdale, NJ: Lawrence Erlbaum Associates Inc.

Wittgenstein, L. (1953) *Philosophical Investigations* (Trans. G. E. M. Anscombe), Oxford: Blackwell.

Wittgenstein, L. (1969) *On Certainty* (Trans. D. Paul and G. E. M. Auscombe), Oxford: Blackwell.

2 Identity exploration: Theory into practice

Peter Weinreich

OPERATIONALISATION OF IDENTITY STRUCTURE ANALYSIS

Two assessment dilemmas: *stasis/flux* and *etic/emic*

Chapter 1 introduced the theoretical underpinnings of the ISA conceptual framework and its core concepts. In practice, when empirically investigating the identity structures of individuals, these concepts have to be operationalised to become accessible parameters of identity. This chapter presents algorithms that are isomorphic representations of the formal definitions of concepts, which translate into explicit and publicly verifiable methods of assessment of the corresponding identity parameters. Theoretical concepts dictate the operationalisation so that empirical assessments are always of explicitly defined parameters.

Procedures for the assessment of parameters of identity have to contend with two profound dilemmas. The first, termed here the *stasis/flux* dilemma, concerns assessment by means of psychometric scales. The dilemma arises from the observation that one does not form or ever achieve a totally fixed notion of one's identity, yet the psychometric method of assessment is predicated on fixed items. Through appraisals and reappraisals contingent on biographical experience and reflection over time, one elaborates, refines, expands and contracts one's perspectives on life, people and self. As a consequence, one's identity is open-ended and continues in flux, ranging from gradual updatings when self merely keeps in touch with contemporary times, to major transitions when self makes life-changing decisions. The social constructionist approach to the contextual presentation of self is sensitive to such changing expressions of identity. But standard psychometric procedures do not countenance radically differing expressions of self, because their rationale stems from statistical refinements to establish the 'best' sets of items to assess the parameters in question. Once established these items are fixed and static. Typical elaborations of identity in belief and thought remain outside the scope of standard psychometric assessment.[1] The dilemma for standard psychometric assessments is that of representing the *open-ended flux* of identity by way of *static* sets of items constituting psychometric scales.

The parameter *identification* is an example where there exists no common set of items – elemental identifications being based in varying sets of values and beliefs – for assessing degrees of self's identification with the other, which holds universally across individuals and cultures. No scale of identification constructed according to psychometric principles is therefore possible, except at the surface level of asking directly in a number of guises 'how much self identifies with the other' – which does not access the varying elemental features of people's identifications.

ISA achieves resolution of the stasis/flux dilemma through the direct operationalisation of definitions of concepts into procedures for assessing identity parameters that integrally incorporate the participant's perspectives at any current moment. ISA's philosophical point of departure proposes that self will reinterpret the past and elaborate perspectives as a matter of theoretical principle – the fundamental basis of operational procedures directly arising from the ISA conceptualisation of identity processes.

The second dilemma is the familiar *etic/emic* one concerning the assessment of psychological dimensions postulated as being cross-cultural universals – *etics* – given that culturally specific interpretations characterise the indigenous psychologies of local cultures – *emics*. Evidently, the psychometric scale features of the stasis/flux dilemma are more daunting when transposed across cultures. Not only will the meanings of the items of a psychometric scale not translate readily across cultures, but the conception of any psychological issue will also be expressed differently in another culture. Although having recognisable features across cultures, different conceptions of psychological issues – anorexia nervosa, gender and professional identity, primordial sentiments about ethnicity and nationality – will be expressed in alternative discourses that are peculiar to the respective indigenous psychologies and may not have any immediately translatable equivalents across cultures.

No amount of care with putative psychometric scale items by checking translation against back-translation across languages will generate psychological equivalence, when the matter to be assessed is conceptualised differently in accordance with distinctive indigenous psychologies. Instead, the appropriate task is to ascertain as accurately as possible the emic meanings of local discourses used to conceptualise the issue in question. Conveniently this task falls within the scope of the foregoing procedures for resolving the stasis/flux dilemma by way of direct operationalisation of ISA definitions of identity concepts, but only in respect of emic concerns. The requirement for etic assessments of identity parameters that incorporate emic considerations remains outstanding.

When assessing psychological concepts, ISA uses the person's own discourses in the vernacular – as expressed and interpreted by oneself – in accordance with the emic requirement. Achievement of the etic status of cross-cultural, as well as person-to-person, comparability follows by using standardisation procedures that are internal to each person and predicated on one's own usage of discourses. *Internal standardisation* establishes scalar limits to identity parameters. These limits to a parameter – *none* to *maximum* – have equivalent analytical meanings for each person, while the emic characterisation of the parameter differs from person to person. The algorithms for standardisation and the procedures for empirical assessment are given in the following sections dealing with each identity parameter.

Internal standardisation achieves two objectives. First, the relative extents of parameters – such as *identification with others* – are standardised to the same scalar limits for the individual – *none* to *maximum* – that hold across all people everywhere, thereby implementing the etic requirement for cross-individual and cross-cultural comparison. ISA etic parameters of identity require no translation across languages and cultures. Second, the idiosyncratic meanings that individuals use in appraising themselves and the world are in every case incorporated, so that emic meanings feature within these etic parameters of identity. Investigators have to be keenly aware of the emic qualities of the discourses that are incorporated within the etic parameters. In Chapter 3 emic qualities associated with etic comparisons are demonstrated in a Slovakia/Northern Ireland cross-cultural investigation of usage of primordialist sentiments about nationality and ethnicity.

In sum, the emic/etic dilemma is resolved by integrating emic perspectives with etic scalar standardisation procedures internal to each individual. Its resolution is simultaneously the resolution of the stasis/flux dilemma, since the implementation of internal standardisation procedures applies in the same manner when a person's values and beliefs change, and identifications become further elaborated – as in identities in flux.

ISA is not merely technique. Being theoretically based, the operationalisation of ISA requires full comprehension of the relevant definitions of psychological concepts. *Ad hoc* paraphrasing of the concepts serves only to re-introduce the kinds of confusions and ambiguities that ISA strives to overcome. Consideration of the two assessment dilemmas just described emphasises that ISA cannot be adopted for investigations in the manner of psychometric scales. Each investigation requires preliminary ethnographic-style groundwork to elicit discourses in the vernacular, which will form the basis for creating customised identity instruments. Given its integrative open-ended conceptualisation, ISA functions well in connection with related approaches when conceptual links are rigorously made.

This chapter outlines the manner of elicitation of data using customised identity instruments. It continues with the algorithms that direct the computational procedures for assessing ISA parameters of identity. The text draws on the original presentation of the ISA definitions and their algorithms in the *Manual for Identity Exploration Using Personal Constructs* (Weinreich, 1980/86/88). Further guidance notes about constructing identity instruments and interpreting the results of ISA investigations are available (Weinreich, 1992).

A cautionary note should be sounded concerning the use of algebraic notation and quantification. Some practitioners and theorists of identity processes pit qualitative analyses – such as discourse analyses – against quantitative ones – such as inferential statistics – and suggest that the latter are sterile while the former are humane and sensitive. But quantification can be either sterile or sensitive, just as qualitative analyses can be banal or sophisticated. Furthermore, as used in ISA, algebra is simply an abbreviated form of discourse used for effective communication about psychological concepts that embody qualitative emic perspectives. Because of its formal symbolic syntax the language of algebra communicates efficiently and elegantly an enormous variety of instances of general propositions.

Person, singular agentic self and identity

Harré's formulation of the person P in terms of the singular agentic self S_1, reflexive self S_2 (self-concept) and public self S_3 (persona for others) $P\{S_1, S_2, S_3\}$ is expressed in ISA terms in the form $P\{S_1, Identity\}$ where $[Identity] = [S_2, S_3]$. The interrelationship between S_2 and S_3 receives explicit attention, for example, the formulations by self of *metaperspectives of self* (self for others) based in various other people are the representations of the conjunctions and disjunctions between self-concepts, S_2, and other agents' appraisals of the public expressions of self, S_3. The person's identity is a continuing process that involves a complex elaboration of experiences of interactions with others over time, with a past biography and a future orientation located within a contemporary socio-historical context. The starting point for formal procedures of operationalisation of identity parameters is the fundamental definition of identity, formulated in Chapter 1 and given again here:

Definition of identity[2]
*A person's identity is defined as the totality of one's self-construal, in which how one construes oneself in the present expresses the **continuity** between how one construes oneself as one was in the past and how one construes oneself as one aspires to be in the future.*

Ethnic, gender, occupational identity, familial identity, and other features of identity have been conceptualised as component aspects of the totality of one's identity (Chapter 1), such as:

One's ethnic identity is defined as that part of the totality of one's self-construal made up of those dimensions that express the continuity between one's construal of past ancestry and one's future aspirations in relation to ethnicity.

Ideal self-image and values: Identity aspirations

As noted in Chapter 1, users of the ISA conceptual framework are increasingly using the term *aspirational self* in place of the *ideal self-image*. This preference is partly to avoid the widespread tendency towards reification, in which the ideal self-image takes on a thing-like presence, and partly to emphasise that what is being referenced is self's identity aspirations, which generally are not yet actualities. However, for consistency with the original ISA definitions (Weinreich, 1980/86/88), the form *ideal self-image* continues to be used here.

Ideal self-image (aspirational self, or ego ideal): I

A person's ideal self-image is defined as one's construal of 'me as I would like to be'.

Entities: E_i

An entity E_i is a generic concept that may refer to anybody or anything in the field of the person's awareness at any time, as in the here and now, or recalled from past encounters, or imagined into the future. Such entities are often perceived to have agentic qualities, that is, to display intentional actions even when they are objects of the material world or mythical beings.

Self 1 as singular agent is variously aware of self displaying differing context-cued mood states and characteristics in the past, the present and in the anticipated future. Such reconstructions and reflections feature as *differing aspects* of the entity *Self 2* with agentic qualities. Sometimes *Self 1* may construe distinctive *Self 2*s, such that *Self 2* in one context – *achieving praise* – is experienced as empathetically identifying closely with one person, and in a different context – *involved in some major trauma* – closely with another quite different person. Such alternatively experienced *Self 2*s may be experienced as somewhat differing entities, albeit aspects of the complex that is the person's identity.

Bipolar constructs: c_j

Constructs are codifications that the person uses to differentiate one meaning from another and may be of all varieties, ranging from simple non-verbal gestures and expressions to complex texts, statements or discourses. Each bipolar[3] construct – representing an endorsed expression and a contrasting one – is designated c_j. As an example, consider texts that a person might use to construe the actions of self and others in respect of pitting ideals of acting ethically as a matter of principle against endorsing pragmatic decisions for the sake of efficiency. These may be in the form '. . . *puts ethics first*' contrasted with '. . . *is pragmatic and efficient*', which is designated c_j, where 'j' refers to any bipolar construct ($j = 1, 2, 3 \ldots$).

A particular person's identity aspiration may be to always consider ethics first, indicating that this is the kind of person he or she would like to be. In actuality this aspiration may not be possible in all instances. However, in construing 'me as I would like to be' using the construct c_j ('. . . *puts ethics first*'/ '. . . *is pragmatic and efficient*'), the person's identity aspiration, *or endorsed pole of the bipolar construct*, is represented as c_j^+ ('. . . *puts ethics first*') and the contrast pole as c_j^- ('. . . *is pragmatic and efficient*'). As a first approximation, c_j^+ represents an identity aspiration. In this representation, a person's aspirational self or ideal self-image is in effect the total set of identity aspirations.

Let 'I' represent the ideal self-image, constituting the sum of the person's identity aspirations, then 'I' is made up of the set of c_j^+, that is, c_j^+ belongs to I. In reality, some expressions of identity aspirations may not be articulated in spoken language, but be represented by imagery (a picture of an idyllic family home, or attractive body image, etc.) and gestures. These non-verbal constructs may be regarded as a subset of all constructs and in the generality still represented as c_js.

Positive values: c_j^+

A person's positive values are defined as those personal characteristics and guidelines for behaviour, which one aspires to implement for oneself in accordance with one's ideal self-image.

Positive values are represented by the set of c_j^+.

Negative (or contra) values: c_j^-

> *A person's negative values are defined as the contrasts of one's positive values,*
> *that is, those characteristics and patterns of behaviour from which one would*
> *wish to dissociate.*

These are represented by the set of c_j^-.

In this conceptualisation, the ideal self, or the totality of a person's identity aspirations, *I*, represents the fundamental reference point for designating positive and negative values. By referencing identity aspirations as anchoring the value system of the individual, the emic characteristics of cultures and subcultures are centrally incorporated into the ISA conceptual framework. By appeal to clinical-style interview or ethnographic work, the discourses of indigenous psychologies can be fully represented.

In the foregoing text, emphasis is placed on identity aspirations and the semantics of aspiration designated in the form of words 'me as I would like to be', or equivalent. This is in recognition of the likelihood that over time such aspirations will change. The aspirations of an 11-year-old will no longer suffice for a 20-year-old and an incautious use of the term *ideal self-image* may be to reify this as a fixed entity. Paying attention to the semantics of identity aspirations will obviate the tendency to reify the ideal self. The adoption of the term *aspirational self* in its stead may also assist against reification.

Some constructs, c_j, represent core evaluative dimensions of identity, but others may be conflicted, as might be established by reference to the parameter 'structural pressure on a construct' defined later (expressions 19 and 20). Core evaluative dimensions designate clear-cut positive and negative values defined by the bipolar texts in question.

Conflicted dimensions refer to bipolar texts that designate contentious arenas of discourse, where the value dimensions are not clear cut, but denote problematic incompatibilities when used to appraise what self and others stand for. Corresponding identity aspirations, located in the social context of positive and negative role models or reference groups, are conflicted.

Thus, in respect of the manner by which the individual's positive and negative values are here represented, note that the identification of the c_j^+ and the c_j^- provide first approximations only to the person's value system. Knowing whether these values constitute core evaluative or conflicted dimensions of the person's identity should augment their designation as positive and negative values, since their status and usage in appraising the social world will differ accordingly.

The specific c_j^+ and c_j^- as expressed and revealed in words, discourses, imagery, or gestures refer to aspirational features of a person's identity. For example, the c_j^+ and c_j^- that express discourses centred on gender identity may be about one's positive and negative sexual experiences, or favoured and disfavoured perceptions of one's body-build, or one's acceptance or rejection of prevailing cultural and subcultural norms. One's aspirations would be towards sustaining, reinvigorating and implementing the favoured expressions and dissociating from the disfavoured ones. Just as one such set of discourses refers to notions associated with one's gender identity, so further sets encompass other aspects of identity, such as ethnic, occupational, or familial identity in personalised manner.

Self-images: Situated contexts and identity mood states

The following formal exposition derives directly from the theoretical conceptualisation presented in Chapter 1. In all instances the agentic self (*Self 1*) construes aspects of self-conception (*Self 2*) or public self (*Self 3*) or other entities beyond self. The agentic self is the agency that construes and evaluates, hence none of the aspects of self here designated refers to the agentic self but to reflections on self.

Current self-image: E_c

> A person's current self-image is defined as one's construal of 'me as I am now'.

Alternative currently situated selves and identity states are represented as $E_{c1,c2,c3}\ldots$ and relate to the definition of *situated identity* (Chapter 1), where the latter emphasises the continuity of identity from past experiences to future aspirations.

Past self-image: E_p

> A person's past self-image is defined as one's construal of 'me as I used to be'.

Likewise $E_{p1,p2,p3}\ldots$ refer to alternative past biographical/situated selves and identity states, *me as I used to be when . . .*

Ego-recognised and alter-ascribed personal and social identities

Ego-recognised self-images and expressions of self $E_{c1,c2,c3}\ldots$ are distinguishable from *alter-ascribed* social identities – *self as a member of a societal category or social group* – and *alter-ascribed* personal identities – *of one's personal self* – held by alter A of $E_{c1,c2,c3}\ldots$

Metaperspectives of self: $E_{m1,m2,m3}$

Metaperspectives of self both personal and social are denoted symbolically as: $E_{m1,m2,m3}\ldots$, which refer to *self's interpretations of alter-ascribed identities*, that is, those held by A of $E_{c1,c2,c3}\ldots$ These are interpreted impressions of self's public face for others – *Self 3 – me as the other sees me*.

Positive and negative role models and reference groups

Positive role model (and reference group):

> *A person's positive role model (reference group) is defined as some other person (group) construed as possessing many of the attributes and values to which one aspires, that is, ones associated with one's ideal self-image.*

Negative role model (and reference group):

> *A person's negative role model (reference group) is defined as some other person (group) construed as possessing many of the attributes and contra values from which one wishes to dissociate, that is, ones aligned with one's contra value system.*

At this juncture, presenting the outline format of a *customised identity instrument*[4] designed to elicit an individual's appraisal of self and others, will clarify the conceptual issues that arise in operationalising the definitions of ISA concepts. The example given here is restricted to just one bipolar construct, but it indicates the fundamental feature of anchoring the concepts in the identity aspirations of the individual, which are empirically determined. This feature, together with elicitation of constructs with ethnographic sensitivity, incorporates directly the emic characteristics of the individual. This is the basis of all of the ISA procedures that provide the estimates of parameters of identity in etic form, such that the emic is integrated with the etic, as will become evident in the following exposition.

In practice, the person will generally express an appraisal of people and events in context by way of several discourses attributing various characteristics to differing entities. The algorithms of the identity parameters incorporate the many possible discourses, as bipolar constructs (c_j), as they may be used in appraising self and others, and as individually represented as in the example.

BASIC FORMAT FOR FORMAL APPRAISAL OF SELF AND OTHER AGENTS USING AN IDENTITY INSTRUMENT

In properly conducted identity investigations, ethnographic knowledge of the participants is necessary in order to elucidate the kind of discourses, in the vernacular, the person uses in interacting with others and reflecting on self and the wider material and social world. The procedure for formalising the person's construal and appraisal of self and other agents uses an *identity instrument* by means of which one appraises segments of self's social and material world. The identity instrument incorporates the *domain of self*: facets of self minimally in accordance with the fundamental definition of identity – *past self, current self, aspirational self* – but extended in accordance with appropriate contexts and mood states – *self at work, self when anxious* – and metaperspectives of self – *me as my colleagues see me*. It further includes significant *domains of others*: the nexus of other agents and agencies in self's social and material world. These facets of self – *Self 2 and*

Self 3 – and the nexus of others constitute the *designated entities* for appraisal using the customised instrument. They are presented together with discourses in *bipolar-construct format* so that agentic self – *Self 1* – may characterise each entity in turn using a specific construct, then systematically continuing to do so using successive constructs one at a time. The constructs may be discourses of any degree of complexity and should reflect the opinions and world-view of the participant to the study, as well as being informed by the focal concerns of the investigation. For the moment and by way of illustration only, a simple example will provide the basis for the formal logic of the assessment of parameters of identity (Figure 2.1).

Designation of a person's value system: Identity aspirations

The *polarity* of each of self's constructs is determined by how self rates one's ideal self-image or aspirational self in respect of it. Those poles one uses to describe one's ideal self-image are defined as positive. In the example in Figure 2.1, . . . *fights back* is defined as the positive pole of the construct and defines an identity aspiration whereby one would ideally *fight back* rather than *think this would not help*. The alternative poles are assumed to represent contra-values, namely, ones that contrast with one's ideal self-image (. . . *doesn't think it helps*) and designate aspirations not to be like these.

On the few occasions when self does not overtly apply a construct to one's ideal self-image, proxies such as *a good friend* or *a bad person* are used to define its polarity. In such cases, the discourses so identified may be regarded variously as *pseudo*, *hidden* or *surreptitious* aspirations. As a total set, the polarities of a person's construct are assumed to define that person's positive and contra value system. Constructs without evaluative connotations are excluded from this set.

Conversion of a person's basic rating scale data to 'scores' used in computations ($s_{i,j}$)

The rating a person gives to an entity on a centre-zero construct scale cannot be converted to a *score* to be used in computations, until the polarity of the construct for that particular person is known.

For any construct there are two possible polarities, depending on whether the ideal self-image – *or proxy* – is rated to the left or right of the zero-point. When the ideal self-image is rated to the left of zero, the polarity is defined as $P = 1$. In this case, the conversion of a rating for an entity E_i on the jth construct proceeds as follows:

For polarity $P = 1$

Construct scale j	$\overline{4}$	$\overline{3}$	$\overline{2}$	$\overline{1}$	0	1	2	3	$\overline{4}$
scores ($s_{i,j}$)	4	3	2	1	0	−1	−2	−3	−4

(x above the 3 on construct scale)

For example, a person construes entity E_i at point 3 to the right of the zero point using his or her jth construct with polarity 1. This rating becomes a negative score: $s_{i,j} = -3$.

EXAMPLE: A nine-point centre-zero scale used to obtain a person's construal of entities

[Construct c_j]

	fights back	4	3	2	1	0	1	2	3	4	doesn't think it helps
[Entity E_j] mum						0			x		
dad						0		x			
sister						0			x		
friend			x			0					
English White boys		x				0					
Caribbean Black girls						0		x			
me as I am now*						0	x				
me as I used to be**						0			x		
me as I would like to be***	x					0					
apprentices					x	0					
etc.						0					

*   current self-image *[Entity E_c]*
**   past self-image *[Entity E_p]*
*** ideal self-image *[Entity I]*

In this example, one has used the bipolar construct *fights back/doesn't think it helps* to appraise others in terms of the strength to which one perceives them as possessing the contrasting qualities, also to appraise oneself *currently* and in the *past*, and crucially *as one aspires to be* ('me as I would like to be', the ideal self-image). The centre-zero scale itself provides no indication of the favourable or unfavourable evaluative connotations of one's construct, the latter being determined by reference to one's aspiration as indicated by one's rating of one's ideal self-image. In this case, *fights back* is the characteristic one aspires to possess, having the favourable or positive evaluative connotation (**polarity 1**), although self is *currently* appraised as tending towards *doesn't think it helps* and self in the *past* much more so.

Another person, thinking perhaps that there is too much gratuitous confrontation in the world generally, may aspire instead towards *doesn't think it helps (to fight back)* for whom this quality would have positive connotations (**polarity −1**).

The *polarity* of a construct denotes whether its left- or right-hand pole has favourable connotations for the person. **Polarity 1** denotes a favourable left-hand pole, **polarity −1** a favourable right-hand pole.

In practice, of course, people's use of constructs often tends to be complex and conditional on circumstances, and the polarity of a construct as ascertained here is only a first approximation concerning a single element of a person's value and belief system. Examples of the complexities and the apparent 'inconsistencies' in using constructs are elaborated further in Weinreich (1980/86/88) and research evidence is provided in other texts referenced in this volume.

Figure 2.1 Formal systematic construal and appraisal of entities: an example of a 'page' of an identity instrument. (Original figure from Weinreich, 1986, Appendix p. A2.)

The second polarity, defined as $P = -1$, arises when the ideal self-image is rated to the right of the zero mid-point. Conversion of ratings to scores is then as follows:

For polarity $P = -1$

						x			
Construct scale j	$\bar{4}$	$\bar{3}$	$\bar{2}$	$\bar{1}$	0	$\bar{1}$	$\bar{2}$	$\bar{3}$	$\bar{4}$
scores $(s_{i,j})$	-4	-3	-2	-1	0	1	2	3	4

In this instance, a person's rating of an entity E_i at point 3 to the right of the zero point becomes a positive score: $s_{i,j} = 3$, for the jth construct with polarity $P = -1$.

The process of eliciting meaningful and relevant constructs for individuals is not always successful, nor may the individual use each construct when appraising every entity. The respondent has the clear option of using the mid-point zero of the scale, which corresponds to *no score* and has no part in the computation of identity parameters.

Ego-ratings of constructs (α_j)

A further precaution against assuming that all constructs are equally important uses the person's *ego-rating* of each construct ranked on a five-point scale, from the least important ($\alpha = 1$) to the most important ($\alpha = 5$). In cases of no information about a person's *ego-ratings*, mid-point ratings ($\alpha = 3$) contribute to the computations.

PARAMETERS OF IDENTITY

The following sections outline the parameters of identity that derive from the consideration of the person's biographical history in which self successively identifies with agents of the social and material world. Postulates about the processes of identification are given in Chapter 1. The concern of the elaboration here is with the estimated outcomes and implications of such processes for the individual. The snapshot of the moment provides a co-ordinated set of empirical estimates of outcome parameters derived from the information gleaned from the participant's construal and appraisal of self and others.

In each case the explicit definition of the psychological concept is presented together with the algorithm that directly corresponds to the definition, the algorithm being the basis for the computational procedures for gaining empirical estimates of the parameter in question. Although the empirical estimates are *quantitative*, the *qualitative* characteristics of self's appraisal of self and other agents together with the *qualitative* nature of discourses used by self remain explicit. The resultant analyses are emic, albeit with parameters that are etic for comparison across individuals and across cultures.

The first parameter considered, *ego-involvement*, is the person's degree of involvement with others or their impact on self. This is followed by the parameter designating the person's relative positive or negative *evaluation* of these others and of self in various contexts. Further parameters concern extents of a person's *aspirational* and *empathetic identification with agents* in respect of specified biographical contexts and mood states. From these are derived the parameters detailing extents of the person's *conflicted identification with others* being based in various contexts, past and present. The parameter *identity diffusion* designates the extent of dispersal and magnitude of conflicted identifications across others. Together, the parameters *identity diffusion* and *self-evaluation* define the *identity variant* classification of the person for a specified social and biographical context. A further parameter designates the extent of possible *splitting* of construed attributions between others or self in different aspects. Another one represents the degree of the person's *remote-idealisation* of another.

Discourses remain qualitatively discrete and evident in their linguistic (denotative) meaning. However, a powerfully diagnostic parameter, *structural pressure on a construct*, taps into the affective connotations of a discourse and assesses the extent and nature of cognitive–affective dissonances in the person's use of the construct in appraising self and others.

Ego-involvement with the other

Self is usually much involved with those agents that impinge daily on one's life and whom one knows well, who tend as a consequence to impact on oneself whether self likes them or not. One tends to attribute many qualities and characteristics to these accustomed personas, and by contrast few to remote passers-by. However, some agents have unusually powerful impact despite being quite removed from the person's daily encounters. As appraised by the person, they engage in activities and represent scenarios exemplifying or threatening a wider humanity, such as entertainers, artists and thinkers on the one hand, or terrorists, abusers and warmongers on the other. The parameter that represents such impact is *ego-involvement with an entity*.

Ego-involvement with entities (G_i)

> One's ego-involvement with another is defined as one's overall responsiveness to the other in terms of the extensiveness both in quantity and strength of the attributes one construes the other as possessing.

The extensiveness of one's response to another (E_i) depends on the number of characteristics one attributes to the other, one's ego-ratings (α_j) of the constructs one uses, and the magnitude (without sign) of the scores ($s_{i,j}$) on these characteristics, that is,

Extensiveness of a person's response to E_i:
$$\sigma_i = \frac{\sum_j |\alpha_j s_{i,j}|}{\sum_j \alpha_j} \tag{1}$$

People's characteristic response patterns vary substantially, for example, between narrow and broad responders about the centre-zero point on the identity instrument scales. *Internal standardisation* proceeds by establishing the maximum value (max σ) for extensiveness of response to any entity, which provides an estimate of the person's strongest responsiveness to, or greatest involvement with, any one of a set of entities. One's *ego-involvement with* each entity is then defined relatively to the maximum.

$$\text{Ego-involvement with entity } E_i: \quad G_i = 5\left(\frac{\sigma_i}{\max \sigma}\right) \tag{2}$$

where σ_i is given by expression 1 and the value of 5 is used so that estimates of G_i may be directly compared with self-reported ratings of importance on a five-point scale.

The parameter G_i represents the intensity of involvement with the entity E_i and can range from zero to 5, where ego-involvement of 5 with an entity represents the entity with which or whom the person is most highly ego-involved: the parameter is thereby standardised for comparison across individuals. As with all ISA parameters, this one integrates emic content with etic cross-individual and cross-cultural standardisation in terms of scale magnitude, thereby resolving the *emic/etic* assessment dilemma.

Evaluation of the other

One may be strongly ego-involved with another such as one's much-loved partner whom one respects and likes immensely, but be also strongly ego-involved with a different distressingly hateful person. Ego-involvement with another does not designate whether the other is evaluated favourably or unfavourably. The appropriate parameter for designating the extent to which another is favoured or disfavoured is *evaluation of another*.

Evaluation of another ($\hat{R}(E_i)$)

One's evaluation of another is defined as one's overall assessment of the other in terms of the positive and negative evaluative connotations of the attributes one construes in that other, in accordance with one's value system.

In general, the evaluation of any entity E_i is given by the extent to which positive and negative characteristics are attributed to it, that is,

$$\text{Evaluation of entity } E_i: \quad R(E_i) = \frac{\sum_j \alpha_j s_{i,j}}{\sum_j \nu_j} \tag{3}$$

where, if the entity obtains a score $s_{i,j} = 0$, then $\nu_j = 0$, otherwise $\nu_j = \alpha_j$. This means that the person's evaluation of another is based only on those constructs used to appraise that other. Irrelevant ratings (zero scores) do not contribute to the computation. Compensation for characteristic differences in response style across individuals is achieved through *internally standardising* evaluations $R(E_i)$ against the maximum value (max R), irrespective of sign, obtained for the set of entities construed by the respondent, that is

$$\text{Standardised}^5 \text{ evaluation of entity } E_i: \quad \hat{R}(E_i) = \frac{R(E_i)}{|\max R|} \tag{4}$$

The index of *standardised* evaluation can range from -1.00 to $+1.00$, from a wholly unfavourable to a wholly favourable evaluation. Since the scores $(s_{i,j})$ are anchored in the individual's aspirational self – *me as I would like to be* – the standardised evaluation parameter is thereby referenced to one's aspirational self.

Self-evaluation as situated in biographical current and past social contexts and identity mood-states

Evaluation of current (past) self ($\hat{R}(E_c)$ and $\hat{R}(E_p)$)

One's evaluation of one's current (past) self is defined as one's overall self-assessment in terms of the positive and negative evaluative connotations of the attributes one construes as making up one's current (past) self-image, in accordance with one's value system.

$$\text{Standardised evaluation of current self-image:} \quad \hat{R}(E_c) = \frac{R(E_c)}{|\max R|} \tag{5}$$

where $R(E_c)$ is given by the expression for $R(E_i)$ where $i = c$ the current self-image. For alternative situated selves and identity states, each $E_{c1}, E_{c2}, E_{c3} \ldots$ is substituted for E_c in expression 5.

$$\text{Standardised evaluation of past self-image:} \quad \hat{R}(E_p) = \frac{R(E_p)}{|\max R|} \tag{6}$$

where $R(E_p)$ is given by the expression for $R(E_i)$ where $i = p$ the past self-image, and substitutions in expression 6 of $E_{p1}, E_{p2}, E_{p3} \ldots$ represent alternative past biographical/situated selves and identity states.

Self-esteem

Self-esteem (S)

One's self-esteem is defined as one's overall self-assessment in evaluative terms of the continuing relationship between one's past and current self-images, in accordance with one's value system.

One's self-esteem is interpreted as a combined assessment of one's evaluation of one's current and past self-images. It is expressed algebraically as the weighted sum of one's standardised evaluations of one's current self-image and one's past self-image, that is

$$\textit{Self-esteem:} \quad S = \frac{G_c \hat{R}(E_c) + G_p \hat{R}(E_p)}{G_c + G_p} \tag{7}$$

where the weightings are G_c and G_p, one's ego-involvement in one's current and past self-images respectively.

> The parameter of self-esteem given by the above expression ranges from -1.00 to $+1.00$, from wholly negative to wholly positive, the reference point again being the ideal self. This definition of self-esteem takes into account the notion that the individual's past self-image contributes to the ongoing self-evaluative processes as assessed in terms of one's aspirational self, and conforms to the ISA definition of *identity*. The component *past self* and *current self* evaluations will give evidence of whether these processes are progressively developmental – *more positive current than past self* – or anti-developmental – *less positive current than past self.*

As with the current and past self-images, self-esteem is also situated and represented by the presence of E_{c1}, E_{c2}, E_{c3} . . . and E_{p1}, E_{p2}, E_{p3} . . . in expression 7.

Metaperspectives of self

Self's evaluations of metaperspectives of self, both personal and social, are assessed by substituting E_{m1}, E_{m2}, E_{m3} . . . referring to self's interpretations of alter-ascribed identities – *held by A of* $E_{c1,c2,c3}$ . . . – in expression 5.

Ambivalence towards an entity

The notion of the person's evaluation of another as presented earlier is essentially one of a global assessment – *a by-and-large judgement* – ignoring the specific attributions that contribute to the judgement. This can mask considerable ambivalence when self attributes both admirable and despicable characteristics to the other. The salience of such ambivalence will depend on how strongly one is ego-involved with the other. *Ambivalence towards an entity* and *entity dissonance* are the parameters that designate ambivalence and its salience respectively. Their definitions and algorithms follow.

Ambivalence towards an entity (AMB(E_i))

> *A person's ambivalence towards an entity when evaluated on balance in positive terms is defined as the ratio of negative to positive attributions, and conversely when negatively evaluated as the ratio of positive to negative attributions.*

A person's evaluation of another E_i often masks an ambivalent construal of liked and disliked characteristics, such that both positive and negative scores $s_{i,j}$ are included in the assessment of evaluation of the other (expression 3). Ambivalence is a function of the balance between disliked and liked attributions. If the assessed evaluation of E_i is positive, any negative characteristics – *or scores* – will have evaluative connotations – *signs* – incompatible with that positive evaluation. By comparing the signs of each product $a_j s_{i,j}$ with the sign of the evaluation $R(E_i)$, ambivalence can be defined as a ratio of the incompatible (dissonant) to the compatible (consonant) characteristics, i.e.,

Ambivalence towards entity E_i:

$$AMB\,(E_i) = \frac{\sum_j(\text{dissonant elements})_{i,j}}{\sum_j(\text{consonant elements})_{i,j}} = \frac{\sum_j a_j s_{i,j}[\text{incomp'ble signs}]}{\sum_j a_j s_{i,j}[\text{compatible signs}]} \quad (8)$$

If an evaluation $R(E_i) = 0$, then $AMB(E_i) = 1$ since the dissonant and consonant elements will be equally balanced. The index for ambivalence ranges from 0.00 to 1.00, from no ambivalence to maximum.

Entity dissonance (DISS(E_i))

Ambivalence towards another may be of greater or less significance depending on the person's ego-involvement with that other. Combining ambivalence with ego-involvement results in a new variable defined as *entity dissonance*, which expresses the salience of the ambivalence, i.e.,

Entity dissonance E_i: $DISS\,(E_i) = G_i{\cdot}AMB\,(E_i)$ (9)

Since *entity dissonance* is the product of *ambivalence* and *ego-involvement* its magnitude ranges from 0.00 to 5.00 maximum.

Representation of the construct and entity/action systems

Visual representations (Figures 2.2 and 2.3, reproduced from Weinreich, 1969) represent the relationships between constructs within self's construct system and self's assessments of people and actions within self's entity/action system elaborated through experience.

Figure 2.2 represents a *surface* comprising constructs c_j, the *construct system*, and another one of entities E_i and actions as assessed to date through biographical experience, the *entity/action system*. When cued and activated through interaction with various agents or in imagination, self's constructs are generally articulated as discourses and gestures in context according to self's intentions and

Portion of identity structure

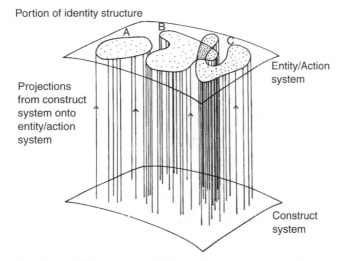

Projections from construct system onto entity/action system

Entity/Action system

Construct system

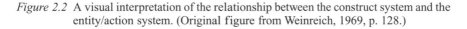

Three entities (or actions) ABC are represented. The attributed characteristics of the entities are made up of projections from the construct system. Where these projections overlap, as with B and C, the entities share similar attributes. The strength of the connections between the constructs and the entities represents the strength of beliefs concerning the attributes. Each entity which can be distinguished from another entity will have a structure of projections differing in at least one attribute.

Figure 2.2 A visual interpretation of the relationship between the construct system and the entity/action system. (Original figure from Weinreich, 1969, p. 128.)

appraisals at the time. As indicated, self (*Self 1*) attributes particular characteristics to three entities using self's available non-verbal and verbal constructs, in such a manner that self construes entity A as having a set of qualities entirely distinct from those of entities B and C. Self construes entities B and C in the main differently, excepting some small overlap of attributions. Although many of the person's constructs derive from normatively agreed cultural meanings, nevertheless their specific connotations tend to be unique and accord with the individual's biography. In this sense, the attributions a person makes to another entity are projections of self's experiential interpretations of the social and material world to date. Evidently, both the person's constructs and characterisations of entities will become further elaborated and redefined, or in respect to some arenas of discourse simplified and diminished.

However, a person's constructs are bipolar – $c_j = c_j{}^+, c_j{}^-$ – and have affective connotations here designated simply in terms of desirable and undesirable emotional significance, or positive (+) and negative (−) affect. Figure 2.3 elaborates the representation of Figure 2.2 in order to portray this bipolarity, which is designated by two *surfaces*, P and N, signifying the two related sets of evaluative poles of the bipolar constructs. *Surface P* designates the one set of evaluative poles that relate to *positive affective states* and *surface N* the other set with *negative affect*.

Portion of identity structure

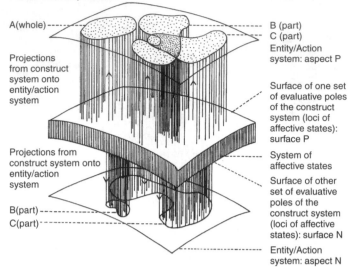

Of the three entities schematically represented here, self is least **ego-involved** with entity A and most with B (see text, expressions 1 and 2). However, self's **evaluation** of A is wholly favourable, of B is more favourable than unfavourable, and of C is more unfavourable than favourable (expressions 3 and 4).

Self's construal of A is without any **ambivalence**, of B is with a small degree of ambivalence, and of C is with considerable ambivalence (expression 8). The greatest **entity dissonance** that self has in respect of the three entities is towards C (expression 9).

Splitting in self's construal of A and B is total, as it is of A and C (expression 10). Between B and C self construes some overlap of favoured, but a complete split in disfavoured, attributes. In total, self's construal of B and C is mostly split.

Figure 2.3 A visual interpretation of the relationships between the construct system, the system of affective states and the entity/action system. (Original figure from Weinreich, 1969, p. 136.)

The representation of the person's construal of the three entities is now in terms of attributions distinguished between desirable and undesirable ones, or as projections from the two surfaces P and N. Self appraises entity A as having totally desirable characteristics and without sharing any with entities B and C. As in Figure 2.2, self attributes characteristics to entities B and C that overlap to a small extent, the shared qualities being all desirable ones, but attributes to entity C many undesirable characteristics, none of which is in common with the few attributed to entity B. The ISA conceptualisation hereby firmly incorporates the person's experienced emotional states, represented as the system of affective states, as being fundamentally integral to people's appraisal of the social and material world.

The representation in Figure 2.3 is in practice refined as indicated in the formerly presented algorithms where each construct c_j varies in relative significance to the person – α_j – and each entity E_i varies in the degree of attribution of some quality by way of any construct – $s_{i,j}$ – and in the extensiveness of attributions.

These refinements are already incorporated in expressions 1 and 2 for ego-involvement in, and expressions 3 and 4 for evaluation of, the entity.

Splitting in appraisal of entities

Often generic agents or entities are appraised at one level, without a concern for their constituent parts. So people will talk about the Smith family and how it differs from the Newton family, or they may compare the French with the Germans or British. However, the Smith family may also be seen in terms of mother, father and two daughters, and the Newton family likewise consisting of parents and their children. The French may be differentiated between urban cosmopolitans and rural farmers, the Germans between technocratic professionals and skilled workers, and British between upper/aristocratic and middle/working classes. In each case, what self (*Self 1*) may appraise at one level to be a cogent entity may at another level be split into component parts – *parents into mother and father – self-concept into aspirational self, past self and current self (all of Self 2)*. The *split* index defined here assesses the extent to which self appraises the one component entity as being split from the other:

Split in appraisal of entities ($\theta_{k,l}$)

> *The extent of splitting in a person's construal of two entities is defined as the ratio of the deficiency in actual overlap possible between their attributed characteristics to the total possible overlap, given the set of constructs one uses to construe them both.*

The index of split in a person's construal of two entities E_k and E_l may be expressed algebraically as

$$\text{Split in construal of } E_k \text{ and } E_l: \quad \theta_{k,l} = \frac{(E_k \cup E_l) - (E_k \cap E_l)}{(E_k \cup E_l)} \tag{10}$$

$\theta_{k,l}$ may range from zero (no split) to unity (total split). Since the extent of splitting may be in respect of positive or negative attributes, separate split indices designate splitting in construal for positive and negative attributes and the overall index of splitting is the weighted sum of these.

The Boolean algebraic expression of the *union* of the attributes construed in entities E_k and E_l, $(E_k \cup E_l)$, refers to all of the distinctive attributes of E_k and E_l combined, and the Boolean *intersection* of them, $(E_k \cap E_l)$, denotes those that overlap between the entities. Thus, referring to entities A and B in Figures 2.2 and 2.3, the union $(E_A \cup E_B)$ designates the attributes of A and B combined – *say, x*. The intersection $(E_A \cap E_B)$ designates those that are in common between A and B – *say, y, which in this case is none: y = 0*. Substituting in expression 10 in this instance, the split in construal of E_A and E_B is: $(x - y)/x = 1 - a$ *total split: self appraises these two entities as having nothing in common.*

Splitting in appraisal of self

The person may construe self characteristically differently in various contexts and in this sense may appraise self in the one context as being somewhat split off from self in another context. So in certain circumstances self may appraise self's past encounter with someone as being not true to oneself, a self-image split off from the more habitual expression of self. Such splitting in self-construal in differing contexts $E_{c1, c2, c3}\ldots$ or $E_{p1, p2, p3}\ldots$ can be designated by the split index $\theta_{c1, c2}$ or $\theta_{p1, p2}$, etc.

Identification with others

Chapter 1 discussed postulated conditions when self may benignly or defensively identify with other agents in circumstances of intimacy and non-intimacy. Identification processes are imperfect and only partial, being in terms of incomplete comprehension of the activities of the other as they are experienced at the time by self. The child will have rather rudimentary constructs with which to construe the activities of the other and to appraise the affective ramifications of these activities for self.

The discussion continues by distinguishing between a person's two modes of identification, *aspirational* and *de facto empathetic*, being outcomes of self's processes of successively identifying with others. *Aspirational identification* refers to self continuing to partially identify with agents and their characteristics in aspirational terms – *desiring to emulate positive features or dissociate from negative ones. Empathetic or de facto identification* denotes the extent that one acknowledges an affinity with another – *given shared qualities whether or not these are aspirational* – in particular social contexts.

As emphasised throughout the discussion, identification, whether aspirational or empathetic, is frequently only of partial extent. However, the manner of partial identification will differ in terms of qualities accruing to the other, as when one may have the *same extent* of identification with two people but in respect of *differing qualities*. The use of the notion of *elemental identification* clarifies the exposition of partial identification and assists in designating appropriate algorithms as demonstrated later.

Elemental identifications

In general terms, the likelihood of identification being partial is emphasised by attention being given to the differing elements of identification that self forms with various agents in the course of one's biographical experiences. The definition of the concept of *elemental identification* follows:

> *An elemental identification is defined as being an identity of a characteristic attributed to the other and experienced in oneself*
>
> (Weinreich, 1989b, p. 221).

All instances of identification in degree, ranging from little to considerable, can now be readily conceptualised as comprising differing configurations of elemental identifications.

Aspirational identifications with agents

Aspirational identifications with others are of two kinds, which may at first approximation be conceptualised as being with *positive* and *negative* role models – *with favoured agents whom self wishes to emulate or despised ones from whom self wishes to dissociate*. Self's elemental aspirational identification would reference a specific quality of the other for emulation if positive and for dissociation if negative.

Instances when one wishes to emulate others to a degree refer to extents of *idealistic-identification* with the others as defined in Chapter 1 and repeated here with algorithm.

Idealistic-identification with another or group (f_i^I)

> *The extent of one's idealistic-identification with another is defined as the similarity between the qualities one attributes to the other and those one would like to possess as part of one's ideal self-image.*

Let *I* represent the ideal self-image attributes and E_i those of the other, then

$$\text{Idealistic-identification with entity } E_i: \quad f_i^I = \frac{I \cap E_i}{I} \tag{11}$$

where the Boolean intersection $I \cap E_i$ – *designating overlap between I and E_i* – is represented by the positive attributes, E_i^+, since the ideal self-image, *I*, is assumed to be synonymous with the person's positive value and beliefs (that is, the positive poles of the constructs). Self's desire to emulate specific qualities of the other denotes instances of elemental idealistic-identification with that other.

> A worked example of the computational procedures for f_i^I is given in Weinreich (1980/86/88, p. A16). The range of values for a person's idealistic-identification with another is zero to unity, that is, from an absence of to complete identification with the other in question.

In Figure 2.3 the person idealistically-identifies with entity A to the extent of the proportion of elemental idealistic-identifications, $I \cap E_A$ – *aspect P*, to the total possible, *I*. Likewise, self's idealistic-identification with entities B and C is $I \cup E_B$ and $I \cup E_C$ as proportions of the total possible, *I*. Although the extents of idealistic-identification with E_A, E_B and E_C are roughly comparable, the quality of that identification differs substantially since $I \cap E_A$, $I \cap E_B$ and $I \cap E_C$ all denote quite different sets of elemental idealistic-identifications.

The contrasting instance when self wishes to dissociate from the other to a degree references the extent of contra-identification with the other:

Contra-identification with another or group (Φ_i^I)

> *The extent of one's contra-identification with another is defined as the similarity between the qualities one attributes to the other and those from which one would wish to dissociate.*

Let $\tilde{I}$ represent the contra value system – *the poles of one's constructs contrary to those designating one's ideal self-image* – then,

Contra-identification with entity E_i: $\Phi_i^I = \dfrac{\tilde{I} \cap E_i}{\tilde{I}}$ (12)

$\tilde{I} \cap E_i$ represents the negative attributes of E_i, that is E_i^-.

A worked example of the computational procedures for Φ_i^I is given in Weinreich (1980/86/88, p. A16). The range of values for a person's contra-identification with another is zero to unity, that is, from no contra-identification to complete contra-identification with the other in question.

Self's wish to dissociate from particular qualities of another denotes elemental contra-identifications with that other. In Figure 2.3 self does not contra-identify with entity A in any respect, $\tilde{I} \cap E_A = 0$ (aspect N). However, self's elemental contra-identifications with entity B are to a limited extent, $\tilde{I} \cap E_B$, whereas those with entity C are to a large extent, $\tilde{I} \cup E_C$. In addition, the quality of self's contra-identification with E_B and E_C is of a completely different kind, there being a total split in construal of negative attributes between entities B and C, $[\theta_{B, C}]^-$ (expression 10).

Empathetic identifications with agents in situated context and mood-state

Self's degree of *empathetic identification* with another tends to modulate, as it depends on self's appraisal of oneself and the other in social context. Self-appraisal will vary as cued by context – *with friends, with work colleagues* – and mood – *relaxed, stressed*. Again according to context, self may appraise the other as being supportive or threatening of self's intentions of the moment. An *elemental empathetic identification* denotes the identity of a quality characterising self by context or mood and featuring in the other, evidently depending on context. The definition for *empathetic identification* with another in relation to the current self is given again here and expressed as an algorithm:

Current empathetic identification with another or group (Ψ_i^c)

The extent of one's current empathetic identification with another is defined as the degree of similarity between the qualities one attributes to the other, whether 'good' or 'bad', and those of one's current self-image.

Current empathetic identification with entity E_i:

$$\Psi_i^c = E_c \cap E_i = \frac{(E_c^+ \cap E_i^+) + (E_c^- \cap E_i^-)}{E_c^+ + E_c^-}$$ (13)

where E_c denotes one's construal of one's current self-image, and E^+ and E^- denote the positive and negative characteristics attributed to the entity in question.

A worked example of the computational procedures for Ψ_i^c is given in Weinreich (1980/86/88, p. A14). The range of values for a person's current empathetic identification with another is zero to unity, that is, from an absence of to complete identification with the other in question.

Suppose that in Figure 2.3 entity C is the current self-image E_c, here a poor self-image given the extent of E_c^-. Suppose also that entity B is a particular E_i so that $E_i = E_B$. The person's current empathetic identification with entity B is

$$\Psi_B^c = \frac{(E_c^+ \cap E_B^+) + (E_c^- \cap E_B^-)}{E_c^+ + E_c^-} \quad \text{(from expression 13),}$$

where $E_c^+ \cap E_B^+$ are self's elemental empathetic identifications with the positive attributes of E_B, and $E_c^- \cap E_B^-$ likewise with the negative attributes – *common positive and common negative characteristics perceived by self (Self 1) in both current self (Self 2) and entity B*. In this instance, the extent of common positive attributes is small and there is no common negative attribute. The total set of characteristics that the person (*Self 1*) attributes to self (*Self 2*) is $E_c^+ + E_c^-$, which are all those belonging to entity C in both aspects of the entity/action system, P and N. In the example, the proportion of *de facto commonalities between entities C and B to the total attributes of the current self-image* is small, and the extent of current empathetic identification with entity B is limited – *entity C is not close in de facto terms to entity B*. In respect of other entities E_i self's pattern of current empathetic identifications with them will denote varying degrees of closeness in characteristics from entity to entity.

Situated selves and mood states: Modulation in empathetic identification with others

The characteristic expression of self may fluctuate from one social context to another – *professional or perhaps hard-pressed when situated with work colleagues*; *relaxed or perhaps distressed with family* – or according to mood state – *anxious, euphoric*. If $E_{c1, c2, c3 \ldots}$ designates these alternative situated selves and mood states during the current period, self's patterns of empathetic identification with others may modulate accordingly (with E_{c1}, E_{c2}, E_{c3} in expression 13).

Past biographical selves, as remembered and reconstructed at the present time, may likewise be designated as $E_{p1, p2, p3 \ldots}$. Derivative 'past' empathetic identifications with others, based in these perhaps misremembered and currently restructured past characterisations of self, will also modulate according to one or another 'past self-image' (with E_{p1}, E_{p2}, E_{p3} substituted for E_c in expression 13). This analysis suggests that the self may readily imagine 'past empathetic identification' with another, who may not have been actually known then but encountered more recently – *an 'as if' experience*. Self recognises an affinity between one's biographical past-self and the other *in present time* without this having been possible at the past time.

Conflicted identifications with agents

In a particular situation involving other agents, self may empathetically identify with them to varying degrees and also contra-identify with some of their characteristics, opinions and activities. When self *de facto* identifies with another while aspiring to dissociate from aspects of the other, self's identification with that other is conflicted: *self is 'there' in the other while wishing not to be.* The more that self empathetically identifies with another and *simultaneously* contra-identifies with that other, the greater the identification conflict. Conflicted identification with another does not arise solely from the person's contra-identification with the other, since without some degree of empathetic identification with that other there would be no identification conflict. Further, as the person's empathetic identifications with others modulate according to social context and mood, patterns of conflicted identifications will fluctuate. The formal definition of the person's identification conflict with another is repeated here followed by its algorithm:

Identification conflict with another (K_i)

> *In terms of one's current self-image the extent of one's identification conflict with another is defined as a multiplicative function of one's current empathetic identification and contra-identification with that other.*

Algebraically, a person's conflict in identification with some other or group is defined as follows:

Current conflict in identification with entity E_i:

$$K_i^c = \sqrt{((\text{empth identifn})_i(\text{contra-identifn})_i)}$$
$$= \sqrt{(\Psi_i^c \Phi_i^I)} \tag{14}$$

where Ψ_i^c and Φ_i^I are given by the expressions 13 and 12 respectively. The square root of the product is taken so that the index for identification conflict K_i^c remains in dimensional terms a measure of *identification*, not *(identification)^{squared}*.

> The characteristics of this parameter are discussed in Weinreich (1980/86/88, p. A18). The range of values for a person's conflict in identification with another is zero to unity, that is, from no conflicted identification with that other to the maximum theoretically possible, though psychologically unlikely.

As before, substitution of alternative current and past situated selves and identity states E_{c1}, E_{c2}, E_{c3} ... and E_{p1}, E_{p2}, E_{p3} ... in expressions 13 and 14 will denote modulated conflicted identifications based in alternative current and past contexts.

Identity diffusion

Erikson's (1968) introduction of the term 'identity diffusion' contrasts the successful achievement of a sense of identity during adolescence with the failure to forge a coherent identity, and remaining in a state of identity diffusion. The achievement of identity arises out of the person's effective resynthesis of earlier partial identifications, whereas the failure to generate such a resynthesis is to be in identity diffusion. Erikson's analysis is at the level of symptomology, but does not deal with the underlying psychological processes. ISA presents an analytic explanation of the process of resynthesis of identifications in terms of the person striving to resolve identification conflicts with other agents, where the state in which self has identification conflicts dispersed across such agents that remain substantial in magnitude represents *identity diffusion* (Chapter 1). Understood in this manner, identity diffusion no longer refers to a total failure in identity contrasted with the successful achievement of identity, but a parameter that may range in magnitude according to the extent and dispersion of the person's conflicted identifications. As such, rather than simply representing failure, identity diffusion provides the circumstances in which the person attempts to resolve identification conflicts, thereby providing the impetus for potential identity development. Identity diffusion points to a likely fluidity between social contexts and an identity transition between biographical phases. Conceptualised as a parameter designating the existence of widespread and generally quite usual conflicted identifications with other agents, identity diffusion is defined as follows (Chapter 1):

Overall identity diffusion (Δ_c)

The degree of one's identity diffusion is defined as the overall dispersion and magnitude of one's identification conflicts with others.

Overall current identity diffusion: $\quad \Delta_c = \dfrac{\sum_i G_i K_i^c}{\sum_i G_i}$ (15)

where K_i^c is the person's current conflict in identification with entity E_i (expression 14) and G_i is the person's *ego-involvement with* entity E_i (expression 2). Thus, the magnitude of one's identification conflict with each entity is weighted by one's degree of involvement with that entity, so that in assessing the dispersion of conflicted identifications those entities with the greater impact have greater weight.

Identity diffusion (Δ_c) can theoretically range from zero to unity, though in practice the upper limit is psychologically not a viable state of affairs.

Identity diffusion and remote-idealisation (ρ)

In certain rather extreme cases a person may construe one's self-image as split off from one's construal of others, while at the same time idealising them. One's own self-image is then remote from unrealistically idealised appraisals of the others.

A parameter *remote-idealisation* refers to this kind of circumstance and is designated as follows:

Remote-idealisation of entity E_i in relation to current self-image E_c:

$$\rho_{c,i} = \theta_{c,i} \cdot f_i^I \tag{16}$$

where $\theta_{c,i}$ (expression 10) is the extent of splitting between the current self-image E_c and the agent E_i, and f_i^I (expression 11) is the degree of self's idealistic-identification with E_i.

> The greater the split in construal between self and the other, and the greater the degree of idealistic-identification with the other, the more the remote-idealisation of the other. $\rho_{c,i}$ ranges from zero to unity, from no remote-idealisation to maximum.

The more remotely idealised the other, the less directly contingent is that other's presence in the person's field of activities.

Contingency of entity E_i in relation to current self-image E_c:

$$Z_i^c = 1 - \rho_{c,i} \tag{17}$$

> in which the greater the remote-idealisation of the other, the less contingent that other is to self. Z_i^c ranges from zero designating no contingency – *for complete remote-idealisation* – to unity at maximum contingency – *when there is no remote-idealisation.*

Considering further the salience of a person's conflicted identifications with others, the less their contingent presence, the less contribution they have to the overall identity diffusion. The above expression for identity diffusion requires this factor of contingency to be taken into account, giving the modified expression below:

Overall current identity diffusion (weighted): $$\Delta_c = \frac{\sum_i G_i Z_i^c K_i^c}{\sum_i G_i Z_i^c} \tag{18}$$

The impact of the variable Z_i^c is generally quite small. But in exceptional cases when a person remotely idealises several others, its effect is to diminish the contribution of the remotely idealised others to overall identity diffusion. This means that somewhat greater weight is given to the person's conflicted identifications with the remaining others who are not so remotely idealised.

By substituting alternative current and past situated selves and identity states E_{c1}, E_{c2}, E_{c3} ... and E_{p1}, E_{p2}, E_{p3} ... in expressions 13 to 18, the appropriate extent of identity diffusion in respect of the various biographical selves will be denoted. Identity diffusion is not a fixed feature of the person, but may modulate according to context and biographical phase. In relation to biographical past self-images, substituting past, p, for current, c, expression 18 becomes

Overall past identity diffusion (weighted): $$\Delta_p = \frac{\sum_i G_i Z_i^p K_i^p}{\sum_i G_i Z_i^p}$$

where $p = p_1, p_2, p_3$, etc.

STRUCTURAL PRESSURES ON CONSTRUCTS

Discourses, core and conflicted evaluative dimensions of identity

When people talk they use discourses with personalised connotations to express themselves and to appraise their activities and those of others in relation to the likely implementation of their identity aspirations. A person may use certain discourses to express themes and make judgements that habitually evaluate people in terms that are mostly compatible – *self's fundamental identity aspiration is to be an athlete; self favours those others who are athletic and facilitate one's own athletic performance and disfavours those who are not athletic and diminish one's performance.* What one aspires to be, being important to oneself, is in harmony with self's judgements of others that one meets when pursuing one's aspirations. Self's discourses that convey such harmonious judgements and evaluations in respect of important identity aspirations codify *core evaluative dimensions of identity* (Chapter 1).

However, one's discourses about problematic issues – *pro-choice or anti-abortion, beliefs about global warming, 'freedom fighters' or 'terrorists'* – also express one's identity. In these instances, while some people may have clear principles in accordance with those held by admired others, other people may contend with dissonant elements as they appraise complexities in others' viewpoints and as expressed by themselves. The discourses that express vacillation and discomfort over dissonant elements of appraisal codify *evaluatively conflicted dimensions of identity. Structural pressures* (Chapter 1), the definition of which is given again here, associated with the discourses indicate the extent to which evaluative dimensions of identity are core or conflicted:

Structural pressure on a construct (Ω_j)

> *The structural pressure on a person's construct is defined as the overall strength of the excess of compatibilities over incompatibilities between the evaluative connotations of attributions one makes to each entity by way of the one construct and one's overall evaluation of each entity.*

For the jth construct in question (refer back to commentary on Figures 2.2 and 2.3) the set of entities construed is separated into two groups, those for which their overall evaluations $R(E_i)$ (expression 3) have the same sign as the construct scores $s_{i,j}$ (*consonant*) and those for which they have different signs (*dissonant*). The entities in the consonant group are represented by E_{ik}, where k is a summation variable, and the entities in the dissonant group are represented by E_{il}, where l is another summation variable. The total number of consonant entities is put equal to λ, and the total number of dissonant entities to μ.

The two groups of entities consist of:

> $E_{ik}, E_{i2}, E_{i3}, \ldots, E_{i\lambda}$ – 'consonant' group, that is, those entities whose overall evaluations are *compatible* with the evaluative connotation of the characteristic attributed by the particular construct j;

$E_{i1}, E_{i2}, E_{i3}, \ldots, E_{i\mu}$ – 'dissonant' group, that is, those other entities whose overall evaluations are *incompatible* with regard to the evaluative attributions by way of construct *j*.

In Figure 2.3, the overall evaluation of entity B is quite clearly predominantly positive, whereas entity C is on the whole somewhat negative. In the person's appraisal of entities B and C positive attributions in common by way of a particular construct (say, *j*) are indicated within the overlapped portions of B and C in the positive aspect of the entity/action system. In respect of the overall *positive* evaluation of B the positive attribution by way of construct *j* is evaluatively compatible or consonant, but the same positive attribution in respect of the overall *negative* evaluation of C is evaluatively incompatible or dissonant. With regard to tendencies to possibly re-evaluate attributions by way of construct *j*, so that the formerly positive pole might come to have negative associations, the consonant attribution would be of a kind to counter such re-evaluation but the dissonant one would assist, as follows.

The structural pressure against re-evaluation of the *j*th construct is expressed algebraically:

$$\textit{Structural pressure on construct } j: \quad \Omega_j = \sum_{k=1}^{\lambda} \left| G_{i_k} s_{i_k,j} \right| - \sum_{l=1}^{\mu} \left| G_{i_l} s_{i_l,j} \right| \tag{19}$$

where the contribution to the summation is weighted by the person's ego-involvement with each entity G_i (expression 2) and there are λ consonant scores and $s_{i_k,j}$, and μ dissonant scores $s_{i_l,j}$ in respect of construct *j*. Ω_j will be positive if the construct in question is generally consonant with respect to each entity in turn, that is, if the sign of the score of each entity on that construct is generally compatible with the sign of the overall evaluation of that entity. The sums:

$$\Omega_j^+ = \sum_{k=1}^{\lambda} \left| G_{i_k} s_{i_k,j} \right|$$

and

$$\Omega_j^- = \sum_{l=1}^{\mu} \left| G_{i_l} s_{i_l,j} \right|$$

are termed *positive* and *negative* pressure respectively.

For comparison across individuals, in which compensation is made for different response styles, the expression for structural pressure requires *internal standardisation*. This is achieved as follows. For each construct the total magnitude of *pressure*, irrespective of sign, is calculated. The maximum value thus obtained provides the comparison base for *standardisation* as represented in the following algebraic expression:

Standardised structural pressure on construct j:

$$\hat{\Omega}_j = \frac{\Omega_j}{\max\left(\Omega^+ + |\Omega^-|\right)} \times 100 \tag{20}$$

This index ranges from 100 to -100, where 100 represents the case when the evaluative connotation of the construct in question is consonant with the person's overall evaluation of each entity in turn. The positive contribution Ω_j^+ for construct j arises from consonances between that construct and entities, and the negative contribution Ω_j^- from dissonances.

Discourses that express and represent core evaluative dimensions of identity are ones associated with constructs with high stabilising structural pressures. Those that espouse the person's discomforted and contested notions about identity aspirations and beliefs about the material and social world are linked to constructs with structural pressures that undermine stabilising ones, represented by resultant low structural pressures.

IDENTITY VARIANTS

The ISA classification of *identity variants* provides a global overview of a person's macro identity states situated in specified social contexts. It bears some resemblance to Marcia's *identity status* classification (Marcia, 1980), but differs in respect of ISA's analytic approach to identification processes in the development and redefinition of identity. Marcia's approach depends on self-reports of having experienced a crisis of identity or not, and having made a commitment to an occupation and an ideology or not.

The rationale for the identity variant classification arises from consideration of two fundamental global identity processes. The first is self's process of striving to implement one's identity aspirations by pursuit of various activities. The consequence of self's judgement of success or otherwise in pursuing one's aspirations is one's greater or less *self-evaluation*. The second is self's process of attempting to resynthesise one's identifications with others to date that have resulted in incompatible elemental identifications. The extent of self's *identity diffusion* marks whether one acknowledges an optimal presence of residually conflicted identifications – *optimal levels* – or defends against them – *low levels* – or exhibits extensive unresolved conflicted identifications – *high levels*.

Accordingly, Table 2.1 presents a usefully analytic classification of *identity variants*, derived from the two parameters: *self-evaluation* (expression 6) and *identity diffusion* (expression 18). The classification provides an immediately accessible summary of self's state of identity, whether defensively *foreclosed* or highly conflicted *diffused*, and whether of *high* or *low self-regard*. Contrary to general opinion, the nine-fold classification indicates that identity diffusion is not necessarily associated with self-deprecation, as the possibilities of *diffuse, or defensive, high self-regard* show. *Crisis* of identity is an uncomfortable state of affairs when substantial identity diffusion accompanies low self-evaluation. However, in the ISA classification, the experience or otherwise of *crisis* is not a *defining criterion* of identity states as it is with Marcia's 'identity statuses'.

As discussed earlier, when moving between contexts self's identity diffusion and self-evaluation may modulate in accordance with context-cued self-appraisal

Table 2.1 The identity variant classification

Self-evaluation	Identity diffusion		
	High *(diffused variants)*	Moderate	Low *(foreclosed variants)*
High	Diffuse high self-regard	Confident	Defensive high self-regard
Moderate	Diffusion	Indeterminate	Defensive
Low	Crisis	Negative	Defensive negative

and changed empathetic identifications with others, which means that identity variants are not static. ISA's identity variants are the fluid and relatively impermanent outcomes of continuing processes of identity development and redefinition in changing socio-historical contexts as experienced within uniquely biographical episodes. The person in contemporary society is likely to engage in several major identity transitions during the lifecycle – *marrying, becoming a parent, changing career, achieving promotion, acquiring a new public reputation, migrating, becoming ill or disabled*. A person's identity may be variously confident, diffused, or foreclosed according to context and circumstance but that it could be *achieved* for all time is unlikely.

This conceptualisation questions Marcia's typology, which conceives of *identity achievement* as the desirable end-state status and *diffusion* as the failed status. Diffused states of identity in ISA represent agentic activity as when self strives to resolve identification conflicts too dispersed and too great for one's well-being. In this they are the impetus for self to review and revise conceptions of self and others. The intricate processes of identity development and redefinition may be explicated in terms of the processes outlined in Chapter 1, using the operationalisation outlined in this chapter, and demonstrated by the research presented in the other chapters. The identity variant classification by itself is unable to provide evidence of such detail, but functions to alert one to the interrelationships between parameters of identity. A person in a state of high identity diffusion tends to have low structural pressures on a greater proportion of constructs than would someone with low identity diffusion. Conversely, someone in a state of identity foreclosure tends to have constructs with very high structural pressures associated with rigid black–white appraisals.

PRACTICALITIES: THE IDENTITY EXPLORATION COMPUTER SOFTWARE

The task of assessing the parameters of identity according to the algorithms presented in this chapter may be readily performed with the assistance of the Identity

Exploration (IDEX) computer software (Weinreich & Ewart, 1999a,b).[6] The idiographic component of the software enables customised identity instruments to be created that may include self designated according to situated contexts and mood-states, metaperspectives of self and entities of the material and social world as desired. Crucially, the software tags the criterion entities for the implementation of computational procedures in accordance with the algorithms for all of the parameters given here. Internal standardisation procedures are carried out for each parameter, fulfilling the etic requirement for cross-cultural comparability. Discourses of any elaboration may be entered, which always remain visible and explicit in relation to assessments about their use – *structural pressures* – fulfilling the emic quality of culturally specific world-views. The software designates *identity variants* according to specified contexts. The nomothetic component of IDEX operates with the output from the idiographic component, and under instruction systematically collates the results of idiographic analyses according to criterion groups of interest. The collated results may be held in files for export to standard packages for statistical analyses. The phase component of IDEX tracks development and elaboration in identity structure over time, from phase to phase, when new identifications may be formed and new discourses may be adopted. As before, at the idiographic level, each identity parameter is – newly – internally standardised so that all parameters continue with etic comparability while incorporating elaboration in emic perspectives.

AGENCY, INNOVATION AND THEORY BUILDING IN SOCIO-HISTORICAL CONTEXT

The nature of explication of psychological processes of identity development and redefinition is of special interest as the natural science formulation is insufficient. Certain aspects of human endeavours are inherently non-predictable. As a matter of theoretical principle, no amount of theorising and prior empirical observation can predict genuinely innovative thought and the consequences of translating such thought into action. No one could have predicted that the outcome of Einstein's thought processes would be the entirely innovative conceptualisation of space–time in his theory of special relativity. There was of course evidence of the kinds of problems in physics and astronomy that occupied him, but no one could have anticipated Einstein's solutions to them, or the manner by which he would reach them.

The agentic and autonomous self, though often constrained, may on occasion express entirely innovative scenarios – Einstein's work, Newton's theory of motion, Darwin's theory of evolution, Maxwell's electromagnetism, Shrödinger's wave mechanics, Watson and Crick's double helix, and not forgetting creative artists and moral philosophers. As a consequence, through the co-operative endeavours of others in developing new technologies and social institutions, individuals have galvanised massive changes over historical eras in the ways people think about the material and social universe and about themselves. Outcomes of agentic innovative thinking prime the non-predictable historical transitions towards what may become newly established sets of normative values and beliefs of differing communities. However, between transitions, the currently dominant discourses within an identifiable culture will tend to inform the moral ethos of influential people with whom others identify.

Thus, on the one hand, important aspects of human behaviour in the longer term are inherently non-predictable on the basis of any conceivable kind of theorising, because innovative scenarios eventually result in people altering their mind-sets and how they think about and appraise activities and events. This observation suggests that attempts to predict outcomes of identity processes and associated human experience would in principle be unrealisable. On the other hand, through identification with others extending across at least a generation, the currently dominant ethos will provide a context of relative continuity over time until further major transitions in world-views occur.

Explications of identity processes will therefore be contingent on the specific historical era and the social context. Individual biographical experiences will bear on the specific nature of identity and, except for transitional eras, the historically normative context will predominate for the group. Evidently then, individual variations tend to occur within the normative constraints of immediately salient cultures or subcultures. Theorising about identity processes may proceed by appeal to theoretical postulates, including those outlined in Chapter 1, applied to individual biographical circumstances.

Figure 2.4 schematically portrays the formal procedure, traced through by arrow from basic theoretical assumptions and postulates to operationalisation of ISA concepts in respect of data elicited by means of customised identity instruments in historical era Q and social context X. With additional biographical and societal data, empirically grounded theoretical propositions may be established for the person in socio-historical context Q,X. For common processes within groups, each person's identity parameters are assessed idiographically before being collated for nomothetic analyses. Empirically grounded theoretical propositions may then be derived for criterion groups in socio-historical context Q,X. For another era R and a different context Y, the empirically grounded theoretical propositions for both the individual and the criterion group will differ in accordance with the norms of the prevailing socio-historical context R,Y. The theoretical propositions hold for the eras in question, but cannot be expected to remain valid for all time. The role of the IDEX computer software in the operationalisation of the ISA conceptual framework is indicated in Figure 2.4, where idiographic analyses necessarily precede nomothetic analyses as shown.

The kinds and depths of awareness that individuals possess of the identity processes they engage in vary considerably from person to person and from episode to episode. Individual activities and thoughts are mixtures of rationally thought-through intentions and other psychological processes that proceed with varying degrees of unawareness. People are often unaware, on the one hand, of vacillation associated with discourses with low structural pressures and, on the other, of strongly judgemental appraisals in terms of discourses with high

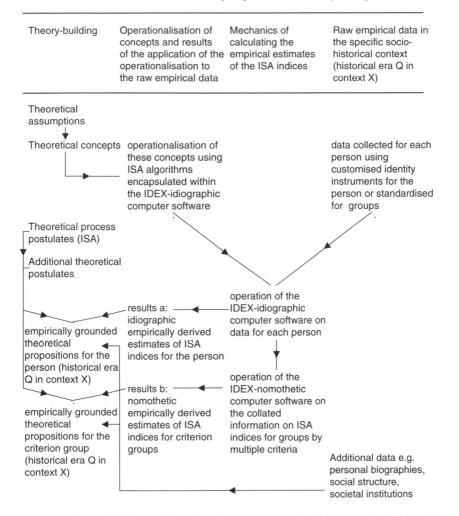

Figure 2.4 Theory-building using the ISA metatheoretical framework (Weinreich, 1989b, p. 70).

structural pressures. Wholly autonomous actions – *in the sense of choices made entirely intentionally and rationally* – are unlikely ever to exist in human affairs, given the impact of psychological processes the origins of which self is unaware. The philosophical ramifications of dealing with rational thought and intention, interrelated with psychological process of varying degrees of unawareness, pose profound problems for generating explications of human affairs based in empirical evidence. The following chapters tentatively map out explications with evidence across a number of problematic issues not usually approached using a common conceptual framework.

NOTES

1 This is not to say that the psychometric tradition has no place in empirical investigations of identity. In appropriately delimited studies, *given constancy in the meanings of items*, change in a parameter assessed by a psychometric scale is of course detectable and meaningful. However, the more formidable change that occurs in the elaboration, extension and reformulation of discourses expressing identity undermines the rationale for a psychometric scale and counters the standard notions of reliability and validity of the fixed items of the scale.

2 In the original formulation of these definitions *construal* referenced both the cognitions (constructs) and their evaluative connotations, whereas subsequently the distinction between cognition and affect became more strongly emphasised so that *appraisal* refers to *construal* and *evaluation* (Chapter 1). With the latter sense, *appraisal* – not *construal* – is the more appropriate term in these definitions. However, the difference is one of nuance, and provided that *construal* in these definitions is taken to incorporate *evaluation as well as cognition*, the original definitions suffice.

3 *Bipolar* means having two poles.

4 An *identity instrument* superficially resembles the *repertory grid* used with Kelly's personal construct theory, but differs from the latter in three fundamental respects: 1. The inclusion of mandatory facets of self in accordance with the ISA definition of identity; 2. The use of centre-zero rating scales with a genuine zero and no inference of favoured or disfavoured poles of the bipolar constructs; 3. Computational procedures for assessing identity parameters that require the mandatory facets of self and the centre-zero scales in accordance with the algorithms presented here.

5 The term *standardisation* replaces *normalisation* as used in the original text of ISA algorithms (Weinreich, 1980), because of possible confusion that may arise from the statistical connotations of *normalisation*. *Internally standardised* identity indices (etic parameters) range between specified limits for all individuals taking into account differing response characteristics and differing attributions from one person to another (emic qualities).

6 The Identity Exploration computer software has been continually updated, extended and refined in accordance with rapid developments in computer operating systems (from mainframe to personal computer). A prototype for MS-Windows is currently available from the authors.

References

Erikson, E. H. (1968) *Identity, youth and crisis*, New York: Norton.

Marcia, J. (1980) 'Identity in adolescence', in J. Adelson (ed.) *Handbook of adolescent psychology*, New York: Wiley.

Weinreich, P. (1969) *Theoretical and Experimental Evaluation of Dissonance Processes*, PhD thesis, University of London.

Weinreich, P. (1980, 1986, 1988) *Manual for identity exploration using personal constructs*, Research paper No.1 (2nd edn), Coventry: University of Warwick, Centre for Research in Ethnic Relations.

Weinreich, P. (1989b) 'Conflicted identifications: A commentary on identity structure analysis concepts', in K. Liebkind (ed.) *New identities in Europe: Immigrant ancestry and the ethnic identity of youth*, Aldershot: Gower.

Weinreich, P. (1992) *Identity exploration workshop notes*, Jordanstown: University of Ulster School of Psychology.

Weinreich, P. & Ewart, S. (1999a) *IDEXbasic of Windows Version 3.0: Identity Exploration computer software for idiographic, basic case studies*. Jordanstown: University of Ulster School of Psychology.

Weinreich, P. & Ewart, S. (1999b) *IDEXnomo for Windows Version 3.0: Identity Exploration computer software for nomothetic, comparative studies*. Jordanstown: University of Ulster School of Psychology.

The theoretical and empirical studies

Peter Weinreich

Part 1 has set forth the theoretical exposition of the ISA conceptual framework and its operationalisation in Chapters 1 and 2. The following three parts of the volume detail theoretical and empirical applications of ISA to a variety of research arenas – cross-cultural, societal and clinical. These contributions illustrate how the interdisciplinary theoretical conceptualisation and readily operationalised methodological tools of ISA clarify such fundamental issues concerning the expression of personal and social identity as these:

1 *Genetic inheritance* as an aspect of one's identity interpreted by oneself in terms of personal experiences within normative societal cultures – the most salient in these studies being one's conceptualisation of gender that gives rise to one's gender identity.
2 The longer-term *context of the socio-historical era* within which people develop their identities and redefine them throughout their life-spans – for instance, gender identity being expressed differently according to socio-historical context.
3 The shorter-term *situated context* of the person in changing situations from moment to moment – situated identities and identity states as expressed in specific social contexts of the moment.
4 The *personal biographical experience* of the individual – encouragements and abuses, and the personal events, narratives and choices that have been and continue to be expressions of one's singular self in relation to a nexus of significant others.
5 The *etic* principle in which cross-culturally universal concepts and processes are delineated – the ISA definitions of concepts and formal process postulates are conceived as being etic.
6 The *emic* principle in which culturally specific manifestations are demonstrated – the ISA conceptualisation integrates emic manifestations with etic formulations, in which the emic includes variations according to cultures within socio-historical eras and interpreted personally according to biographical experiences.

Theoretical issues inform Chapter 3 – explaining the primacy of primordialist sentiments in respect of expressions of nationality and ethnicity – and

Chapter 5 – integrating contemporary discourse analysis with ISA. In addition, theoretical concerns provide the groundwork for most other contributions, where the primary focus is a practical one concerning people's expression of identity in a range of contemporary contexts of everyday import.

Following the principles of theory building outlined in Chapter 2 and schematically summarised in Figure 2.4, the theoretical groundwork of these studies is in most instances formally presented in theoretical postulates. In line with the often exploratory nature of identity investigation, empirically derived theoretical propositions may also be formulated. Ambiguous and uninformative notions of *identity conflict* are replaced by designating *patterns of conflicted identifications with specific others*. Instead of simply designating a person's values and beliefs, the manner by which self appraises the social world of others and self in respect of specific discourses is assessed for evaluative compatibilities – *consonances* – and incompatibilities – *dissonances* – by structural pressures on the underlying bipolar constructs. No fixed *identity status* is designated, but where relevant a person's *contextually situated identity variant* is delineated.

Part II
Cross-cultural issues

INTRODUCTION

One's ethnic identity is defined as that part of the totality of one's self-construal made up of those dimensions that express the continuity between one's construal of past ancestry and one's future aspirations in relation to ethnicity.

Chapter 3 by Weinreich, Bacova and Rougier examines the notions of primordialism and situationalism when applied to national and ethnic identity. Using the principles and concepts of the ISA conceptual framework, it presents in etic terms a theoretical explanation of the primacy of primordialist sentiments about nationality that provides for emic biographical and socio-historical contexts to be incorporated. The explanation of primordialist and situationalist perspectives is formally elaborated in terms of theoretical postulates. Empirical results from a cross-cultural investigation in Northern Ireland and Slovakia – regions dominated by issues of national identity – established the mutuality of etic and emic considerations, both being necessary features of explication of psychological processes in societal context. The initial theoretical postulates are further elaborated by empirically derived theoretical propositions, which explicitly codify etic and emic (including biographical and socio-historical) factors in an integrated explanatory fashion.

In Chapter 4 Horenczyk and Munayer detail another study in which cross-cultural themes were investigated. The subject matter, within a socio-historical context of violent conflict, is the expression of ethnic identity by a minority people within a grouping that itself constitutes a minority within the wider community, namely Palestinian Arab Christians in Israel. Strong commonalities in ethnic identification indicated that, in a divided and troubled region, religious–ethnic definitions were powerful and pre-emptive. Yet idiographic analyses based in contrasting 'identity variants' revealed extraordinary diversity in individual expressions of ethnic identity. This is another example of variation in the expression of ethnic identity, a variation that is continually emphasised in the ISA approach (see Chapter 1). The authors point to one respondent as a highly nationalistic Arab with strong ideological and cultural views, characterised by the identity variant of 'defensive high self-regard'. Other studies where ethnicity is salient echo this finding that strongly nationalistic and dichotomous thinking characterises defensive high self-regard states (e.g., the strongly nationalistic and religious fundamentalist Free Presbyterians in Ulster – see Rougier, N. 2000, Ethno-religious identities: An identity structure analysis of clergy in Ireland, North and South, PhD thesis, Jordanstown, University of Ulster).

3 Basic primordialism in ethnic and national identity

Peter Weinreich, Viera Bacova and Nathalie Rougier

EVERYDAY PRIMORDIALIST AND SITUATIONALIST PERSPECTIVES ON ETHNICITY AND NATIONALITY

Contemporary communities throughout the world currently confront issues of ethnic conflict or questioning about established sovereignties. Many researchers have commented on the tenacity of people's sense of nationality or ethnicity, which, when felt to be challenged, is often accompanied by violent emotions that can have deadly consequences. Much research demonstrates that ethnicity and ethnic identity are not fixed, but can be redefined over time and can be newly constructed. If ethnicity were situational and changeable, and its construction and reconstruction the result of political manipulation for economic gain or other political interests, an explanation for the spasmodic use of ethnicity would be found in rational behaviour for economic or political advantage. However, some writers have been perplexed by the persistence of ethnicity in the absence of obvious gain, and by the affect that is associated with it.

Two stances on ethnicity and ethnic identity have been clearly delineated (Glazer & Moynihan, 1975). One emphasises the issue of ethnic persistence – a seemingly unchanging aspect of ethnicity, which persists down the generations. The other highlights the situational features of ethnic revivalism – when a dormant forgotten ethnicity is apparently manipulated for instrumental gain. The purported explanatory principles for these contrasting phenomena are the concepts of *primordialism* (Shils, 1957; Geertz, 1963; Greely, 1974; Isaacs, 1975; Connor, 1978; Smith, 1981) and *situationalism* (Hechter, 1974; Mitchell, 1974; Nagata, 1974; Epstein, 1978; Halsey, 1978; Okamura, 1981).

The problematic nature of such explanatory schemas has been debated by many contributors (for example: Okamura, 1981; McKay, 1982; Scott, 1990; Eller & Coughan, 1993). More recently attempts have been made to synthesise both principles on the grounds that either kind of representation is inadequate on its own. McKay (1982) developed a descriptive typology using both principles, which he suggests delineates the characteristics of *ethnic traditionalists, ethnic militants, ethnic manipulators, pseudo ethnics*, and *symbolic ethnics*. For example, *ethnic traditionalists* and *ethnic militants* both express to a high degree 'ethnic manifestations [that] tend to be based on primordial interests', but differ from low to high

respectively in 'ethnic manifestations [that] tend to be based on political and economic interests' (p. 404), that is, in respect of situational aspects. However, in this
typology the nature of the underlying mechanism of primordialism remains unexplained and situational features are unspecified political and economic interests.

Lange and Westin (1985, p. 22) state that both of these positions, *primordial* and
situational, are 'an example of an unnecessary polarisation of inherently complementary aspects of human life'. Scott (1990) undertakes an attempt at an
explanatory model citing the *degree of opposition to the group* (interpreted as *situationalism*) as the *independent* variable, *primordialism* as an *intervening* variable
and the *strength of ethnic identity* as the *dependant* variable, but this is found wanting in a number of respects. He confuses a heightened and reactive salience of ethnicity, when opposition to the group is manifested, with a sense of one's ethnic
identity. Ethnic identity as defined within the ISA conceptualisation is an experiential aspect of the totality of one's identity, whether conceived in situationalist or primordialist terms. The *strength* of ethnic identity, as an aspect of one's total identity,
derives from the nexus of one's identifications with ethnically located others, such
as ancestors and kin, just as one's particular sense of gender identity and occupational identity relates to specific gender and occupational identifications. Only its
experienced *salience*, cued from moment to moment and from time to time, modulates according to its relevance in interaction with others (see Chapter 1). Further,
'primordialism' in Scott's exposition is again an unexplained factor, and in view of
its essentialist connotations it makes no sense as an 'intervening variable'.

Eller and Coughan (1993) are rightly disenchanted with the lack of genuine
explanatory power of the concept of primordialism. They wish to jettison it, and ban-
ish 'primordialism' from the sociological lexicon. Instead, they appeal to the
explanatory power of the psychological theory and research on attachment and bonding, as providing a way forward for dealing with the affect associated with family and
kith and kin, thence with ethnicity. Although a useful pointer to the necessity for a
psychological input into a genuinely explanatory model for ethnic bonding and the
affect associated with it, their approach is limited in its immediate application to ethnic politics. Their dismissal of the concept of primordialism is unwarranted.

The fault in conceptualising 'primordialism' is that its essentialist connotations
have led investigators to latch onto the notion of an innate propensity, that is, it is
itself viewed as the explanatory principle for the pervasive and long-lasting nature
of ethnic identity. However, with a shift in the burden of explanation a different
perspective altogether becomes apparent. Instead of attempting to use 'primordialism' as an explanatory principle, an appropriate redefinition of the concept
emphasises an important human propensity that itself requires explanation.
Primordialist sentiments are frequently expressed in people's everyday discourses
about nationality and ethnicity. What needs to be explained is why such sentiments are manifested and, when they are, why with such intensity and affect as is
so often evident. In other words, the refocused problematic is the human propensity to think about ethnicity or nationality in primordialist terms, when historical
evidence provides many counter examples of fluidity and change, as when
national state boundaries emerge anew, alter or disappear altogether, and likewise

ethnicities become newly created and redefined. Furthermore, the relationship between primordialism and situationalism also demands attention.

The following exposition therefore attempts to explain why people hold sentiments of primordialism, and how such sentiments may be relinquished in favour of beliefs in situationalism. The explanatory analysis helps to clarify the meanings of *primordialism* and *situationalism* and proffers modified definitions of these concepts. The new definition of *primordialism* releases the concept from its formerly mystical and essentialist character, while still referencing the quality of seeming always to have existed.

Research evidence to be presented here from a comparative study of university students in Northern Ireland and academic staff at the Slovak Academy of Sciences corroborates the analysis and demonstrates differential degrees of identification by primordialists and situationalists with political parties and national groups in contemporary Ulster and Slovakia. Both Northern Ireland and Slovakia are important examples of contemporary ethnic and national politics. In the case of Northern Ireland this is because of the long-standing Catholic Irish versus Protestant British sectarian conflict, and the challenge to UK sovereignty by Irish nationalists. Slovakia's importance stems from the conjunction of ethno-national politics and the introduction of a market economy following the Czecho-Slovak break with totalitarian communism, in which the subsequent movement towards an independent Republic of Slovakia aroused suspicion in the ethnic Hungarian minority. The long-term persistence of ethnic conflict characterises Northern Ireland, whereas ethnicity has waxed and waned in its apparent significance in Slovakia. The two territories exemplify the interplay of 'primordial' with 'situational' factors, but in differing combinations, for which the specific histories of the respective ethnic and national groups, interwoven with their cultures, traditions and folklore, provide the unique evolving contexts in which contemporary events are situated.

PRIMACY OF THE SENSE OF PRIMORDIALISM TO SITUATIONALISM IN EVERYDAY PERSPECTIVES ON NATIONAL OR ETHNIC IDENTITY

Recognising the two discernible perspectives on nationality and ethnicity is not sufficient. What requires explanation is why such intensely emotional passions are aroused by appeals to the rhetoric of primordialism. This propensity towards primordialist thinking is here explained as being the outcome of the socio-developmental psychology of the child's early identifications with kith and kin. As outlined in the Identity Structure Analysis (ISA) conceptualisation, young children's early identifications with others close to them, such as parents and kin, are assumed to be emotionally intense and unquestioned (Chapter 1). The analysis by Eller and Coughan (1993) of ethnic bonding in terms of attachment theory is commensurate with the ISA approach. The child perceives the environment in which these identifications occur as being naturally given. Thus, the child initially develops cognitions about the individual's ties with social and material surroundings as being of the essence of human existence imbued with strong affect. Such ties are experienced as being representative of those between kin and community within the locality – *the soil* – and having continuity in time down the generations, that is, they are interpreted as being primordial. More often than not, key adults in the community reinforce this viewpoint. If, then, 'nationality' is understood as referring to the larger community in respect of such ties, then nationality is thereby also experienced as being primordial. *Primordialism* is in this analysis the basic and initial lay perspective on nationality or ethnicity as representing the cohesiveness of a peoplehood. It is an emotive 'gut feeling' sense of affinity with the people in question.

However, on reflection and questioning of what is initially regarded as being the natural order of things, some people will develop more of a situationalist perspective. They will appreciate that nations are not given entities for all time, but that they are socially situated, constructed and reconstructed in historical time in accordance with a complex of instrumental reasons. Nation building by conquest, or the development of spheres of influence, may secure economic advantage, foster commerce and trade, and develop cultural hegemonies that provide ideological justification for what constitutes 'national identity'. Such situationalist or instrumental viewpoints emphasise the flux of nation states in historical time.

Yet, without reason or incentive for questioning the nature of nationality, people's basic propensity remains an unchanging primordialist perspective. Nevertheless, because of their questioning of the status quo in a changing world, and their developing awareness of migrations and the historical fluidity of national boundaries, many people relinquish thinking wholly in terms of primordial givens. They tentatively develop a situationalist or constructionist perspective on nationality, wherein individual reappraisals towards situationalist viewpoints may result from personal biographical experiences, changing historical contexts, educational curricula that analyse social change, or openness to alternative perspectives, and so on.

This analysis views those people who begin to adopt a more situationalist perspective as developing an understanding of the historical complexities of nationality through their reappraisal of their initially held primordialist perspective. In addition, it contends that, given the developmental primacy of primordialist thinking – *being only modulated by subsequent questionings* – people will rarely hold to either wholly consistent situationalist beliefs or thoroughgoing primordialist sentiments. Furthermore, in eras of turmoil when events threaten to overwhelm established orders, many people may retreat to a more wholly primordialist perspective in an attempt to retain a sense of core stability to their identities. In such circumstances, rhetoric couched in the language of primordialism is expected to have a ready emotive resonance.

Given the primacy and intensity of initial identifications, except for those individuals who hold situationalism as a consciously articulated ideology, even situationalists are unlikely to be entirely free of all primordialist sentiments. On the other hand, those with a predominantly primordialist perspective may, for reasons of first-hand biographical experience, social desirability or political correctness, incorporate certain situationalist notions – *tolerance towards different peoples* – but the latter will generally not be core dimensions of identity for them. Many people might be better described as being of *mixed* primordialist and situationalist orientation, in which they hold situationalist beliefs alongside primordialist sentiments. Given the developmental primacy of primordialism as an orientation overlaid by varying biographical experiences and questionings, people will rarely hold either wholly consistent situationalist beliefs or thoroughgoing primordialist sentiments.

In historical eras of turmoil, situational flux threatens to overwhelm established orders that are seemingly imbued with a 'primordial existence' – *of having always been there in one's lifetime and beyond.* In such circumstances, people who confront intolerable uncertainties in respect of presently trying to implement their identity aspirations formed during an earlier era, are prone to reinstate a familiar earlier-held primordialist perspective promising certainty, albeit ersatz, in an attempt to recapture a sense of core stability of identity. In such cases of a reinstatement of primordialist sentiment, the retreat to primordialism will be in terms of updated and contemporary discourses. Primordialism as an orientation may be expressed in a variety of ways that suit contemporary experiences.

REVISED DEFINITIONS: PRIMORDIALIST AND SITUATIONALIST PERSPECTIVES

To avoid potential misunderstandings, observe that the current exposition does not appeal to a reified notion of *primordialism* as itself an explanation for ethnicity. Instead:

> *Primordialism is defined as a sentiment, or affect laden set of beliefs and discourses, about a perceived essential continuity from group ancestry to progeny (perceived kith and kin), located symbolically in a specific territory or place (which may or may not be the current place of the people concerned).*
> (Weinreich, Bacova & Rougier, 1997; Weinreich, 1998)

The group in question may varyingly be thought of as an ethnic or a national group – *a peoplehood.* The set of beliefs and discourses making up primordialist sentiments is not preordained. It may vary from person to person and from culture to culture, but certain of these beliefs and discourses will express the perceived essential ancestral continuity – in terms of language, tradition and custom; the inevitability of the ethnicity or nationality; the necessary relationship to the land, or whatever.

> *Situationalism is defined* as *a set of beliefs or discourses about the instrumental and socially constructed nature of the group, in which interpretations and reinterpretations of history provide rationales justifying the legitimacy of a peoplehood.*
> (Weinreich *et al.*, 1997; Weinreich, 1998)

Again, the particular beliefs will vary in detail from person to person, as individuals may be aware of differing kinds of instrumental devices and social constructions in establishing or consolidating an ethnic group or a nation according to particular socio-historical contexts.

These definitions of *primordialism* and *situationalism* allow that any one individual may simultaneously hold beliefs and use discourses that reference aspects of both primordialism and situationalism. The person who is wholly a primordialist or wholly a situationalist may well be a rarity. Someone who is wholeheartedly the one or the other may be a gut unquestioning primordialist on the one hand, or a very ideologically committed social constructionist on the other.

Within the ISA conceptualisation identity is conceived as follows:

> *One's identity is defined as the totality of one's self-construal, in which how one construes oneself in the present expresses the continuity between how one construes oneself as one was in the past and how one construes oneself as one aspires to be in the future.*
>
> (Weinreich, 1980, 1983a,b, 1986b)

This overall definition of identity provides an explanation of why ethnic identity is generally a fundamental feature of the totality of a person's identity. Consider ethnic identity as *part* of the totality of identity (Chapter 1), that is:

> *One's ethnic identity is defined as that part of the totality of one's self-construal made up of those dimensions that express the continuity between one's construal of past ancestry and one's future aspirations in relation to ethnicity.*
>
> (Weinreich, 1986b)

The peculiar importance of ethnic identity lies in its emotional bonds with ancestry and progeny, primarily through the 'family', or any symbolic notion of 'kith and kin'. The bond with ancestry – *parents and grandparents* – accentuates past dimensions of time through knowledge of personalised accounts of earlier life events, while the bond with progeny – *children and grandchildren* – projects forwards in time with the growing awareness of future potential life-courses. Hence, ethnic identity in practice denotes that part of one's total identity which encompasses a consciousness of continuity in historical time over generations, and continuity of localised spaces by reason of periods during childhood shared with parents and during parenthood shared with offspring, however curtailed such periods may be. One's bonding with ancestry and progeny constitutes strongly affective elements within one's ethnic identity.

While other aspects of identity are also peculiarly important in the totality of identity, such as *occupational* or *gender* identity, one's ethnic identity has generally a far wider encompass than these have. This is exemplified by the vastly expanded time-spans of inter-generational continuities. In addition, children form bonds and identifications with mythical or semi-mythical personas who symbolically represent continuities in shared ethnic experiences of the imagination, through involvement with the specific histories, religions, literatures, arts, pop-cultures and other traditions that make up the distinctive continuing and evolving cultures of ethnic groups.

Talk of earlier times by grandparents on the one hand, and listening to children's utterly different aspirations for the future on the other, can induce a profoundly evocative sense of personalised linkages to the history of ethnic and national groups. This may be particularly so when ethnic lines are crossed through mixed marriage, migration and colonisation, in which the disjunctive features of different cultural heritages are brought into personal consciousness.

ISA, as an open-ended metatheoretical framework of concepts and process postulates pertaining to the formation and redefinition of identity, has been applied in several studies of ethnic identity (Kelly, 1989; Liebkind, 1989; Northover, 1988a,b, 2000; Weinreich, 1979a,b, 1983a,b, 1999, 2000; Ali & Northover, 1999; Weinreich *et al.*, 1997; Weinreich, Luk & Bond, 1996; Weinreich, Kelly & Maja, 1987, 1988; Kirch, Kirch, Rimm & Tuisk, 1997). As its theoretical and methodological orientation combines *etic* with *emic* concerns, ISA is widely applicable across radically different ethnic and national world-views, as well as to subcultures of alternative belief systems. It requires ethnographic knowledge of the peoples participating in ISA studies, for whom identity issues are represented in the vernacular. As indicated in Chapter 2, the procedures and analyses of identity structure are facilitated by way of the Identity Exploration (IDEX) computer software (Weinreich & Ewart, 1999a,b).[1]

POSTULATES DERIVED FROM THE DEVELOPMENTAL PRIMACY OF PRIMORDIALIST SENTIMENTS TO SITUATIONALIST BELIEFS

Various deductions follow from the foregoing analysis of primordialism and situationalism and from the conceptualisation of ethnic identity presented here, which will be formalised in nine theoretical postulates.

Postulate 1: Primordialists' and situationalists' political identifications

First, *in circumstances where issues of nationality are highly salient, situationalists compared with primordialists will identify to a lesser extent with political groupings espousing intransigent conceptions of nationhood – the more intransigent the conception, the greater the difference* (Postulate 1).

The salience of issues of nationality will be a function of socio-historical context. Though for differing socio-historical reasons, nationality issues are highly salient in both Ulster and Slovakia.

ISA distinguishes between *aspirational* and *de facto* modes of identification (Chapter 1). The aspirational mode has two aspects: the *wish to emulate* the favoured characteristics of another – *idealistic-identification with the other* – and the *wish to dissociate from* the despised qualities of some other – *contra-identification with the other*. The de facto mode of identification refers to the actuality of identification in a defined context – *empathetic identification with the other as it is in that context*.

De facto identification contrasts with that which remains an aspiration – *idealistic-* or *contra-identification with another* – which may or may not in time be fully achieved. In the case under consideration here, situationalists will identify, both *idealistically* and *empathetically*, less with nationalist political parties than will the primordialists. As an extension to this postulate, consider also that situationalists will wish to dissociate from the primordialist rhetoric of nationalist political parties: situationalists will *contra-identify* with such parties to a greater extent than will primordialists. Individual differences between people's aspirational and de facto empathetic identification with political parties will reflect disparities in self's actual adherence compared with self's aspiration to fulfil the doctrines and principles of the parties in question. For example, sympathetic supporters of Sinn Fein, idealistically-identifying with Sinn Fein doctrines that include the espousal of the use of democratic procedures of representation coupled with coercive use of terror – 'the Armalite and the ballot box' – may baulk in practice at actually using terror themselves. Their empathetic identification, diminished in respect of their own disinclination to engage with terror, would therefore be somewhat less than their idealistic-identification with Sinn Fein.

Postulate 2: Diversified socio-cultural ethos, individual cosmopolitanism and situationalism

A second consideration is that circumstances of history and cultural difference will affect the status and extent of primordialist versus situationalist perspectives that pervade a community.

> Broadly speaking, *those historical, cultural and personal circumstances that stimulate people to think of the complexities of nationhood – acknowledging fluidity and diversity – will generate a greater propensity towards situationalism* (Postulate 2).

The significance of socio-historical contexts to psychological process is directly implicated in this postulate.

In respect of the cultural and historical contexts of the present comparative study, public discourse about a possible diversity of peoples *within* nations that grapples with the nature of peoplehood and nationhood, differs both in extent of debate and the issues debated. The cultural homogeneity of the people of Catholic Ireland generally curtails public discussion about such matters, which are largely beyond first-hand experience. With the exception in Northern Ireland of the Ulster 'Protestant British', who despite permanent settlement over a period of three centuries are regarded by many locally as a foreign occupying people, other ethnic peoples are foreigners or aliens, welcome as tourists, otherwise insignificant to date as settlers.

The position of Protestant British Ulster in this respect is interesting, because the contested claims of national sovereignty and the debates over nationality in that part of Ireland emphasise for the 'Protestant British' there that these matters are no longer simply preordained. In addition, it may be that Protestants in Ulster continue to subscribe to remnants of a 'Protestant ethic' (Weber, 1948) that tends to emphasise a greater degree of questioning and independence of thought than does Catholicism with its apparently greater emphasis on the canonical directives. These historical and cultural factors suggest that the Catholic Irish remain more prone to primordialist perspectives than the Protestant British in Ulster, who in turn will tend more strongly towards situationalism.

Slovakia provides a contrasting case to the homogeneity of Catholic Ireland and to the long-settled Ulster Protestant British community. Within living memory of some of their oldest people, the Czech and Slovak lands were part of the Austro-Hungarian Empire, when German and Hungarian minorities were in the ascendancy. Settled Hungarians in Slovakia were then the elite community. In 1918, the new democratic state of Czechoslovakia was formed from the Czech lands, Bohemia and Moravia, and Slovakia. This fledgling state was then dismembered 20 years later by the Munich Agreement of 1938, the plight of dispossessed German and Hungarian ethnic minorities providing the pretext. Slovakia gained limited autonomy under the influence of Nazi Germany, though losing the southern portion to fascist Hungary, until liberation in 1945 and the return of the Czechoslovak government from exile. A short time afterwards in 1948 and under the influence of the Soviet Union, Czechoslovakia became governed by a system of monolithic state communism and was transformed into the Czechoslovak Socialist Republic.

Within the Slovak portion of the state, attempts were made to induce the remaining Hungarian minority to assimilate to Slovak ethnicity, ultimately with only limited success. After the short-lived Prague Spring of 1968 and the Russian occupation of the state, the Velvet Revolution of 1989 eventually led to a rapid dismantling of the communist state, the introduction of a market economy, and the transformation into the Czech and Slovak Federal Republic.

After the initial excitement and sense of liberation, the ensuing economic turmoil and political confusion accompanied the commitment to democracy, coupled with popular notions of liberation and freedom. However, these sentiments were at first without stable democratic institutions and political parties. Using the rhetoric of national determination and democracy, the political leadership of the Slovak people gained sufficient popular support from Slovaks to justify an agreed and peaceful separation of the Republic of Slovakia from the Czecho-Slovak Federal Republic in 1993.

Thus, over the longer period the Slovak people have experienced several changes in ruling nationalities and, more recently and in rapid succession, they have lived through the turmoil of two further major transitions, to a market economy and to a newly acquired self-governing statehood. In the recent past, the biographies of the peoples of Slovakia, including a disconcerted Hungarian minority, have witnessed a reformulation of Slovak ethnicity from being second class under a perceived Czech hegemony based in Prague to being sovereign within an independent state. At the same time, they have also experienced the structural uncertainties of large-scale unemployment and economic instability. The Slovak intelligentsia, contending with such experiences, would generally be likely to develop strongly situationalist perspectives. Probable exceptions will be those for whom a return to primordialist sentiments would provide a core sense of stability in a threateningly uncertain world.

In terms of personal biographies, those individuals who have cause to question issues of given nationality and ethnicity will demonstrate a greater propensity towards situationalism. Such cause may be the experience of mixed nationality and kinship links, for example, by way of ethnically mixed marriages, or the result of certain educational and intellectual pursuits stressing the historically situated contexts of nationality and ethnicity. The current study reports results from the Northern Ireland sample for those of mixed ancestry, or with crossed religious and national allegiances 'Catholic British' and 'Protestant Irish', and from the Slovak sample for those with 'relevant intellectual expertise' on ethnic matters.

Postulate 3: Conflicted identification with cultural ethos

The third and fourth deductions follow from clarification of what is involved in *identity conflict*. The ISA conceptualisation of individuals forming aspirational identifications with others, and developing varying degrees of empathetic identifications with them, enables the following analysis to be made. Inevitably, during all people's biographical development, they are prone to form partial *empathetic* identifications with several others, with some of whom they simultaneously *contra*-identify to a degree. Such identifications are *conflicted* (Chapter 1). ISA comprehends *identity conflict*, an amorphous general concept, to be more precisely conceptualised as being located in the person's specific conflicted identifications with particular people and other entities.

The current analysis of the socio-developmental aspects of situationalism arising out of a pervasive initial primordialist orientation makes salient the inevitability of identification conflicts. Thus, for example, a person who empathetically identifies to a degree with a political party, with which he or she also contra-identifies in some respects, instances a specific conflicted identification with that particular entity. A primordialist who empathetically identifies with a primordialist political party that advocates 'ethnic cohesiveness', while contra-identifying with its policy of 'ethnic cleansing' will experience identification conflict with that party. From this analysis follows a centrally important derivation.

> *When individuals' empathetic identification with the ethos of a salient community within their social context is to a degree close whilst their contra-identification with it is considerable, the resultant conflicted identification with representatives of that ethos is problematic* (Postulate 3).

Postulate 4: Unproblematic congruity with cultural ethos

However, if one's empathetic identification with the party is close while one's contra-identification with it is small, the degree of one's identification conflict will be limited.

> *The more that individuals are without qualm in tune with the ethos of their social contexts – as represented by salient agents and agencies – the less will be their identification conflicts with these agents and agencies* (Postulate 4).

The current study examines the nature of identity conflicts in terms of specific conflicted identifications with particular entities. One of the fundamental process postulates of ISA posits that individuals strive to resolve strong identification conflicts to more optimal levels, thereby inducing redefinitions of oneself and of others (Chapter 1). While many such attempts will be unremarkable in their outcomes, certain patterns of resolution shared by people across a community are likely to have pathological societal consequences, as in sectarian conflict (Weinreich, 1983b), and other attempts by individuals with vulnerable identities may have distressing psychological ramifications (Weinreich, 1979a).

Postulate 5: Situationalists' enhanced developmental change in identity

A fifth deduction is that, *given their developing questioning stance on 'nationality', situationalists compared with primordialists will show greater perceived change in the ethnic or national aspect of their identities over time and greater modulation in their empathetic identifications with others who represent primordialist or situationalist perspectives on 'nationality'* (Postulate 5).

Postulate 6: Primordialists' primacy of parental identification

A sixth deduction is that *primordialists will generally affirm the primacy of parental or quasi-parental identifications, whereas situationalists will more likely relinquish some parental primacy – this is likely to be particularly the case when the parents express unquestioning attitudes* (Postulate 6).

Postulate 7: Consonant discourses as core evaluative dimensions of identity

The question of the emotional intensity that goes with nationality and ethnicity may be further elucidated by reference to the ISA conceptualisation of people's appraisal of themselves and their social worlds (Chapter 1). ISA provides a means of assessing people's characteristic manner of talking about their own and others' nationality or ethnicity in terms of their discourses. A straightforward emotional tone or affect may be associated with specific discourses – *a person may have warmly emotive thoughts and endorse romanticised texts about the country of his or her ancestry.* Alternatively, and sometimes in addition, emotionally tinged incompatibilities and contradictions about nationality may be structured within a person's identity. These may be apparent from the person's vacillating or ambivalent use of other discourses – *concerning the unwelcome economically competitive position of migrants in the labour force, when talking about a close friend who is a migrant and economically successful.*

ISA delineates the affective components of people's cognitions and discourses. It assesses the compatibility or incompatibility of conjunctions of affect arising from people's appraisal of themselves and others engaged in the social world. In other words, ISA purports to assess the cognitive–affective aspects of appraisal, and the intensity and turmoil of affect that may arise when people attempt to comprehend social events in terms of the discourses at their disposal. The pertinent measure is that of *structural pressure* associated with the person's use of a construct or portion of discourse. When using a particular discourse, the person's appraisal of self and others in terms of it may consistently arouse compatible emotional responses – *hatred of despicable people and admiration of loved ones*. The high level of cognitive–affective compatibility is posited to result in a high structural pressure maintaining the stability of the evaluative connotations associated with the discourse. High structural pressures indicate discourses that represent *core evaluative dimensions of identity*. Low or negative structural pressures indicate *ambivalent or conflicted dimensions*, when vacillation or distress is implicated through the undermining of positive – *stabilising* – pressures by negative – *destabilising* – ones.[2]

University students and established academics in contemporary democracies are unlikely to hold either extremely primordialist or situationalist perspectives, but the following postulates about pertinent discourses apply to those who do, and they are expected to apply in moderated form for the students and academics of the current study.

> *For the more strident primordialists, ISA postulates that they will endorse and express primordialist discourses as core evaluative dimensions of identity with high structural pressures when appraising national or ethnic agencies in their social world.* Likewise, *for the more ideologically committed situationalists, ISA postulates that they will use situationalist discourses with high structural pressures* (Postulate 7).

Postulate 8: Discourses representing conflicted arenas of identity

> In addition, *primordialists who subscribe to one or other situationalist discourses will tend to use them ambivalently, accompanied by low or negative structural pressure.* Similarly, *should situationalists subscribe to any primordialist sentiments they will tend to do so ambivalently and with low structural pressure* (Postulate 8).

Postulate 9: Developmental primacy of and situationalists' residual resonance with primordialist sentiments

A fundamental feature of people's developmental primacy of primordialist sentiments will be – in some – their unquestioning endorsement of primordial sentiments based in lineage, or – in others – their residual tendency to espouse such sentiments although they hold to situationalist interpretations. Even when situationalists have formed elaborated conceptions of nationality in consideration of historically placed migration, conquest, colonisation and settlement, some part of their initial identifications will continue to obtrude with primordialist resonance in contemporary time.

A further postulate representing this theoretical analysis is that, *given the developmental primacy of primordialist thinking, situationalists will continue to residually express and respond to primordialist sentiments* (Postulate 9).

These nine theoretical postulates formalise the overt expressive characteristics of people according to a theory positing the primacy of primordialist sentiment about nationality and ethnicity formed in initial identification with kin, upon which awareness of situationalist perspectives may subsequently become established. They guide the presentation of results from the comparative study of Ulster University students and Slovak Academy staff, which investigated the cultural context for, and the ramifications of, primordialist and situationalist modes of thinking about nationality and ethnicity. These postulates may be confirmed, amended or discarded according to the available empirical evidence. They will also be expected to provide the theoretical bases upon which further empirically derived theoretical propositions, as yet unanticipated, may be formulated in augmentation of theory building and explication in socio-historical context as outlined in the final section of Chapter 2 and Figure 2.4.

THE STUDY

The ISA framework of psychological concepts operationalised by way of the Identity Exploration computer software provided the methodological orientation of the study (see Chapters 1 and 2). In ISA *qualitative features* of the discourses used by people to appraise their social worlds, including self, remain explicit while *quantitative parameters* of identity can simultaneously be estimated. The discourses of interest here are in the first place about primordialist and situationalist perspectives on nationality and ethnicity, and are given later in the description of the identity instruments completed by the participants in the study.

Participants in the study

This comparative study involved participants from the University of Ulster and the Slovak Academy of Sciences. The Ulster contingent consisted of 107 (85 female and 22 male) undergraduate students of psychology (mean age 23 years, range 18–43). Of these, 53 (44 females and 9 males) described themselves as unambiguously Catholic Irish and 33 (25 females and 8 males) as Protestant British; 21 (16 females and 5 males) were either of mixed allegiances such as Irish/British Catholic and Irish/British Protestant or foreign-born students (3 people: Bermudan Protestant, Srilankan Hindu, and Netherlands Dutch Reformed). The Slovaks comprised 64 (29 male and 35 female) faculty at the Academy (mean age 37 years, range 24–64). Of these, 21 stated in a personal questionnaire an interest in the study of ethnic issues, whereas 43 had never been involved in this kind of research.

Identity instruments

An *identity instrument* constructed within the ISA conceptualisation consists of *entities* – components of the self-image, other people, social institutions and emblems, etc. – and *bipolar constructs* – discourses that the participants use to talk about, describe and interpret themselves and their social environment. In conformity with the expression of continuity in identity between one's biographical past-self experiences and one's aspirational self – *ISA definition of identity* – mandatory components of the self-image include the aspirational or ideal self, one or more designated past self-images, and one or more currently situated selves. In practice, participants appraise the entities using one bipolar construct at a time by way of centre-zero bipolar rating scales (see Chapter 2). The analysis of the ISA data for each participant proceeds in two steps assisted by the Identity Exploration (IDEX) computer software. In the first instance, data are analysed *idiographically*, that is, at the case study level, giving the various ISA indices of identity for the person. In a second stage, these indices of identity are then collated across individuals, who fall within criterion groups of interest, ready for nomothetic analyses.

Entities

Incorporated within both the Ulster and Slovak versions of the identity instrument were components of the self-image, including the mandatory ones for ISA – *ideal self, current self* and *past self*; and the mandatory proxies and validity checks – *an admired person* and *a disliked person*. Ideal self was represented by 'me as I would like to be', *current self* by 'me as I am now' and *past self* by 'me when I was about fifteen'. Further entities consisted of *parents, national groups* and *political parties* (Table 3.1). The Slovak instrument was written in the Slovak language, the English translation of its text being given here.

Mid-adolescence, around 15 years, was taken as an appropriate period for designating *past self*, when one's biographical experiences remained largely located within the narrowly domestic confines of family of origin and the restricted ethos of school and immediate peers. The mean ages of the Ulster University students at 23 years and the Slovak academics at 37 years would ensure that *current self* represented adulthood with a distancing from the immediacy of ongoing formative domestic interactions and school influences of old. This distancing would, of course, be on average of a much greater extent for the older Slovak academics. Discrepancies between one's appraisal of oneself at about 15 and oneself currently would provide evidence of the ongoing nature of reappraisals of self. They would also indicate the manner of ongoing modulations in one's empathetic identifications with others from one's past self, as currently appraised, to one's mature self now, and corresponding processes in respect of conflicted identifications and overall extent of identity diffusion.

Table 3.1 Identity instrument entities: Ulster and Slovak versions

Common entities
Me as I am now
Me as I would like to be
Me when I was about fifteen ⎫
A person I admire   ⎬   Mandatory entities
A person I dislike   ⎭
My parents
My children as I might think of
  them grown up
My partner/friend/spouse
University students
The people of Eastern European countries
West European people

Specific entities

Ulster version	Slovak version
Most of my friends	My colleagues
Irish people	Slovaks
British people	Romanies (Gypsies)
Chinese people living in Ulster	Hungarians living in Slovakia
Muslims in Britain	Hungarians living in Hungary
Greenpeace	Slovak National Party supporters
Sinn Fein	Christian-Democratic Party supporters
The Social Democratic and	Együttélés (Coexistence) supporters
Labour Party (SDLP)	
The Democratic Unionist Party (DUP)	The Slovak Government
The Official Unionist Party (OUP)	The Green Party supporters
The Royal Ulster Constabulary (RUC)	

Ulster University students: Political parties

The entities incorporated in the Ulster version of the identity instrument included the four most salient political parties in Ulster. Two of these were, on the British unionist side, the Official Unionist Party (OUP) and the militant Democratic Unionist Party (DUP). The other two were, on the Irish nationalist side, the moderate constitutional nationalist party, the Social and Democratic Labour Party (SDLP), and the intransigent nationalist party and front for the IRA, Sinn Fein.

Slovak Academy faculty: Political parties

The Slovak instrument incorporated entities relating to Slovak political parties. The Slovak government at the time of the study was made up of the ruling political party 'Movement for Democratic Slovakia' (HDS) in coalition with two minor satellite partners, of which the Slovak National Party supporters are radically nationalist. Other political entities were Christian-Democratic Party supporters, 'Coexistence' supporters representing the most radically nationalist of the ethnic Hungarian minority, and Green Party supporters.

Constructs

Discourses used by people and analysts about nationality and ethnicity provided the major portion of the bipolar constructs incorporated within both the Ulster and Slovak versions of the identity instrument (Table 3.2). They were historically contingent to contemporary times and culturally tuned to the individuals participating in the study. As the participants were not representative of national populations, these discourses should not be regarded as definitive indicants of primordialism and situationalism in Ireland and Slovakia, but as indicative for the era (mid-1990s) and locations of the study (University of Ulster and the Slovak Academy of Sciences). Other discourses about human affairs in general constituted the remaining bipolar constructs.

Discourses pertaining to primordialist and situationalist perspectives

The operationalisation of *primordialist* viewpoints was in terms of discourses that may be used to appraise people's ties with social and material surroundings as being of the *essence* of human existence and imbued with strong affect. These were cognitions of the kind that concern kith and kin, the community and the soil, and as having continuity in time down the generations. *Situationalist* or *instrumental* world-views were embodied in discourses that emphasised nations in flux in historical time and as depending on political and economic advantage. Any identity instrument should also tap into areas of discourse that relate to general aspects of their identities. See Table 3.2 for the bipolar constructs incorporated into the Ulster and Slovak instruments, where the *primordialist (P)* and *situationalist (S)* poles of the pertinent constructs are indicated and the remaining constructs tap general identity concerns.

Criteria for designating primordialists and situationalists

Because of major cultural and historical differences, the criteria adopted for designating predominantly primordialist and situationalist perspectives differed between the Slovak academics and Ulster students. First, while constructs with corresponding meanings were used in the Ulster and Slovak versions of the instrument, language usage and radically different historical contexts demanded fine-tuning of discourses (Table 3.2). For example, after piloting in the respective languages, the English translation of the Slovak version of construct 14 is:

> . . . *think/s that national identity is a matter of choice and decision (S)*, contrasted with: . . . *think/s that national identity originates from the very soil and current territory of the land (P)*,

Table 3.2 Identity instrument constructs: Ulster and Slovak versions

Ulster version

1 – cannot be trusted // – are/is trustworthy
2 – feel/s one's most important loyalty is to one's ancestral kin group (**P**) // – feel/s loyalty to the country is more important than one's ancestry (**S**)
3 – feel/s that religion is not important // – have/has a firm faith in their religion
4 – are/is tolerant // – do/es not accept different people and different views
5 – believe/s the national language is absolutely essential to the nation (**P**) // – believe/s that a common language is not necessary for national loyalty (**S**)
6 – believe/s national ties override divisions of wealth and social position (**P**) // – believe/s that economic interests rather than national ones unite a people (**S**)
7 – see/s the future optimistically // – see/s the future as uncertain, anxious or even dangerous
8 – are/is able to adapt to being of any nationality (**S**) // – consider/s nationality is given forever (**P**)
9 – think/s each nation has its particular ancestry (**P**) // – think/s most nations descend from mixed ancestries and races (**S**)
10 – I don't understand (this person/these people) // – I understand (this person/these people)
11 – believe/s that future generations won't bother about nationality (**S**)// – know/s that their descendants will continue the national group (**P**)
12 – stress/es that only the one national people have the right to the territory (**P**)// – accept/s people of different origins in their territory (**S**)
13 – are/is not recognised as being of any significance to Ulster society // – are/is widely acknowledged for their impact on Ulster society
14 – think/s that national identity can be a matter of choice (**S**)// – think/s national identity resides in the very soil and essence of the land (**P**)
15 – think/s that national sentiment may disguise selfish motives (**S**) // – do/es not doubt the genuineness of people's national feelings (**P**)
16 – live/s in harmony with their neighbours // – are/is prone to conflicts
17 – believe/s that nations are the consequences of political decisions (**S**)// – believe/s that nations develop from common ancestral experiences (**P**)
18 – think/s that national determination has potentially dangerous consequences (**S**) // – are/is in favour of national determination whatever the consequences (**P**)

Slovak version

1 – is/are trustworthy // – cannot be trusted
2 – feel/s loyalty to the state is more important than loyalty to the nation (**S**)// – feel/s one's most important loyalty is to one's nation (**P**)
3 – have/has a firm faith in their religion // – feel/s that religion is not important
4 – are/is tolerant // – do/es not accept the other people and different views
5 – believe/s language is absolutely essential to the nation (**P**) // – believe/s a common ancestral language is not necessary for national loyalty (**S**)

Continued over

Table 3.2 (Continued)

Slovak version

6 – believe/s that economic interests rather than national ones unite a people (S) // – believe/s national ties override class divisions (P)

7 – has/have an uncertain and dangerous future // – has/have an optimistic outlook

8 – consider/s nationality is given forever (P) // – are/is able to adapt to being of any nationality (S)

9 – think/s ancestors of all nations are people of various origins (different tribes, races) (S) // – think/s nations share a common ancestry (P)

10 – is/are understandable for me // – I do not understand him/her/them

11 – believe/s the descendants should be the continuation of their nation (P)// – believe(s) the further generations do not need to bother with the national matter any more (S)

12 – accept/s people of different nationalities on their territory (S) // – stress/es the national homogeneity of their territory (P)

13 – is/are widely acknowledged // – is/are not recognised

14 – think/s national identity originates from the very soil and current territory of the nation (P) // – think/s national identity is a matter of choice and decision (S)

15 – do/es not doubt the genuineness of people's national feelings (P) // – think/s that national sentiment may disguise the selfish motives as well (S)

16 – are/is prone to conflicts // – live/s in harmony with their neighbours

17 – think/s that mankind has always lived in nations (P) // – think/s mankind started to live in nations only recently/in modern age (S)

18 – claim/s national determination has top priority regardless of political consequences (P) // – think/s the preference of national principle to state principle is dangerous (S)

P: primordialist sentiment; **S**: situationalist perspective
Discourses represented in constructs 1, 3, 4, 7, 10, 13, 16 relate to human affairs beyond primordialist and situationalist beliefs.

which compares with the Ulster version:

> ... *think/s that national identity can be a matter of choice (S)*, contrasted with: ... *know/s that national identity resides in the very soil and essence of the land (P)*.

The fine-tuning required reference to the 'current territory' in the Slovak version, as historically the boundaries of the Slovak region have been ill-defined, altered, absorbed into Hungary, joined on and off to the Czech lands and only very recently separated from them.

Second, this exposition suggests that the detail of the set of beliefs that constitutes the primordialist sentiment in Slovakia will differ from that in Ulster. This requires a pragmatic approach to categorising individuals as tending towards primordialist or situationalist perspectives, which takes into account sensitivities that are historically based. As a matter of theoretical principle, no absolutist or essentialist criteria are sought.

Primordialist^{Ulst}/Situationalist^{Ulst}

Within the ISA approach, people's aspirations in relation to each bipolar construct within the identity instrument are individually ascertained by way of their construal of their 'ideal self' – *me as I would like to be*. Operationally, the endorsed, favoured pole of each construct for each person is anchored on that person's construal of 'ideal self'. For the Ulster University sample the results of these anchorings were scrutinised – using the IDEX computer software – in respect of five primordialist/situationalist constructs (Table 3.2: Nos. 5, 8, 11, 14, 15).

The five constructs consisted of the following elements of discourse used to attribute beliefs and characterisations to people:

Construct 5
... *believe/s the national language is absolutely essential to the nation (P)*
... *believe/s that a common language is not necessary for national loyalty (S)*
Construct 8
... *are/is able to adapt to being of any nationality (S)*
... *consider/s nationality is given forever (P)*
Construct 11
... *believe/s that future generations won't bother about nationality (S)*
... *know/s that their descendants will continue the national group (P)*
Construct 14
... *think/s that national identity can be a matter of choice (S)*
... *know/s that national identity resides in the very soil and essence of the land (P)*
Construct 15
... *think/s that natural sentiment may disguise selfish motives (S)*
... *do/es not doubt the genuineness of people's national feelings (P)*

For each individual a simple majority endorsement of primordialist (P) poles over situationalist (S) poles of these five constructs, or vice versa, constituted the criterion for designating a person as being predominantly *primordialist* or *situationalist*. Of only 5 of the 107 students who could not be so designated because of a lack of endorsement of one of the five constructs, two could be classified by reference to their definitive situationalist endorsement of . . . *think/s that national identity can be a matter of choice (S)* (Construct 14). The three students who remained unclassified were Catholic Irish (5.7% of Catholic Irish).

Of the 50 classified Catholic Irish, 29 were primordialists and 21 situationalists (54.7% and 39.6% respectively of the total 53). Of the 33 Protestant British, 12 were designated primordialists and 21 situationalists (36.4% and 63.6%). Of the 21 mixed in allegiances, 5 were classified as primordialists and 16 as situationalists (23.8% and 76.2%). Overall, 46 of the 107 Ulster students or 43% were designated primordialist and 58 or 54.2% situationalist: 3 or 2.8% were unclassified.

Primordialist^{Slov}/Situationalist^{Slov}

For the Slovak sample of academics, the one most definitively primordialist/situationalist construct provided the sole criterion for designating them as primordialists or situationalists. This was construct 14: . . . *think/s that national identity is a matter of choice and decision (S)* . . . *think/s that national identity originates from the very soil and current territory of the land (P)*. Of the 64 Slovak academics, 29 endorsed the primordialist pole (45.3%) and 24 the situationalist pole (37.5%), while 11 were unclassified (17.2%). The Slovak academics were differentiated between those who professed a professional interest in ethnic issues (21) and those who did not (43). Of those with experience of ethnic issues, 7 (33.3%) were classified as primordialists, 11 (52.4%) as situationalists and 2 (18.2%) remained unclassified. Of the others 22 (51.2%) had endorsed the primordialist pole, 13 (30.2%) the situationalist pole and 8 (18.6%) were not classified.

Had the Slovak criterion been applied to the Ulster students, the small number of designated primordialists among the Protestant British would not have met the conditions for statistical comparison. Of the 107 Ulster students, only 34 (31.8%) would have been classified as predominantly primordialist, of whom only 6 would have been Protestant British (18.2% of the 33). There would have been 23 Catholic Irish (43.4% of the 53) and 5 of mixed allegiances (23.8% of the 21) classified as primordialist.

Of the Ulster students, 53 (49.5%) would have been designated as situationalists (compared with 37.5% of Slovak academics) and 20 (18.7%) would have been unclassified. These findings might suggest a greater propensity towards primordialism among the Slovak academics compared with the Ulster students. However, as subsequent results will demonstrate, this would be a premature and improper conclusion, as Slovak situationalist academics expressed the most thoroughgoing situationalism of all groups in this study. Nevertheless, as a culture a generally pervasive strong primordialist ethos of the Slovaks was substantiated.

RESULTS

Ulster University students

Postulate 1: Primordialists' and situationalists' political identifications

> In circumstances where issues of nationality are highly salient, situational-
> ists compared with primordialists will identify to a lesser extent with polit-
> ical groupings espousing intransigent conceptions of nationhood – the more
> intransigent the conception, the greater the difference.

Those students describing themselves as Catholic and Irish tend to sympathise
with Irish nationalist sentiments and those describing themselves as Protestant
and British tend to support British unionism. Because of this pervasive sectarianism, the following text presents the results separately for the Catholic Irish and
the Protestant British students. However, in both instances, their predominantly
primordialist or situationalist orientations formed the bases for statistical analyses of significance.

UU Catholic Irish students

Catholic Irish primordialist students idealistically-identified with the militant
Sinn Fein substantially more than did situationalists, who instead strongly contra-
identified with the party (Table 3.3). Although to a much lower extent than with
Sinn Fein, primordialists even idealistically-identified more with the DUP, the
strident unionist (with Britain) party, than did the situationalists. Situationalists
contra-identified with all four parties to a greater extent than did primordialists,
which was congruent with the fact that the parties' political agendas were each
dominated to varying degrees by concerns of national sovereignty. Situationalists
empathetically identified with Sinn Fein much less than did primordialists. Their
only moderate degree of empathetic identification was with the constitutional
nationalists, the SDLP.

UU Protestant British students

Protestant British situationalist students, compared with primordialists, idealistically-
identified less with all four political parties, and also contra-identified with them
more (Table 3.4). Situationalists' empathetic identification with Sinn Fein was
minimal and substantially less than that of primordialists with this party. Sinn
Fein presented a particular problem for the British Protestant primordialists,
being the locus of a substantially conflicted identification within them (see
Postulate 3 later). Situationalists' empathetic identification with the SDLP and
the DUP was also less than that of the primordialists.

The results for the UU students demonstrated that, whether Catholic Irish or
Protestant British, the situationalists had low empathetic identification with, and
generally wished to dissociate from, the four political parties which all have

Table 3.3 Catholic Irish students' identifications with and evaluation of the four political parties

	Idealistic-identification			Contra-identification			Evaluation		
	PRIM	*SIT*	*F-ratio*	*PRIM*	*SIT*	*F-ratio*	*PRIM*	*SIT*	*F-ratio*
Sinn Fein	0.58	0.33	38.5226***	0.37	0.62	35.5446****	0.26	−0.40	63.3223****
SDLP	0.61	0.51	2.4220	0.23	0.38	8.7730**	0.31	0.07	6.9351*
DUP	0.38	0.26	9.6709**	0.53	0.67	16.1107***	−0.13	−0.48	27.9300****
OUP	0.35	0.27	3.3740	0.49	0.65	17.7994***	−0.14	−0.38	10.5446**

	Empathetic identification			Conflicted identification		
	PRIM	*SIT*	*F-ratio*	*PRIM*	*SIT*	*F-ratio*
Sinn Fein	0.56	0.34	17.9042***	0.43	0.43	0.0629
SDLP	0.59	0.50	1.9684	0.35	0.38	0.8123
DUP	0.38	0.32	2.2807	0.44	0.43	0.0419
OUP	0.36	0.31	1.1307	0.40	0.43	0.8593

**** $p <= 0.0001$
*** $p <= 0.001$
** $p <= 0.01$
* $p <= 0.05$
Scale range: Identification 0.00 to 1.00; Evaluation −1.00 to +1.00
PRIM: Primordialists; SIT: Situationalists

Table 3.4 Protestant British students' identifications with and evaluation of the four political parties

	Idealistic-identification			Contra-identification			Evaluation		
	PRIM	SIT	F-ratio	PRIM	SIT	F-ratio	PRIM	SIT	F-ratio
Sinn Fein	0.37	0.22	13.5852**	0.59	0.69	3.9289	-0.18	-0.55	19.4231***
SDLP	0.48	0.31	6.1246*	0.29	0.49	8.1789**	0.19	-0.17	12.9458**
DUP	0.46	0.29	6.9531*	0.34	0.59	11.7104**	0.20	-0.32	22.3243*****
OUP	0.42	0.29	4.9284*	0.35	0.56	7.3869*	0.14	-0.23	10.6276**

	Empathetic identification			Conflicted identification		
	PRIM	SIT	F-ratio	PRIM	SIT	F-ratio
Sinn Fein	0.41	0.19	22.8738****	0.48	0.33	15.9112***
SDLP	0.47	0.32	4.8041*	0.34	0.36	0.2144
DUP	0.46	0.29	5.4501*	0.35	0.37	0.0953
OUP	0.44	0.32	3.1358	0.36	0.40	0.6028

**** $p <= 0.0001$
*** $p <= 0.001$
** $p <= 0.01$
* $p <= 0.05$
Scale range: Identification 0.00 to 1.00; Evaluation −1.00 to +1.00
PRIM: Primordialists; SIT: Situationists

nationalist agendas. The exception was for the Catholic Irish situationalists in relation to the SDLP, which espouses 'constitutional nationalism' – *to be achieved through democratic means via dialogue and persuasion* – a more conditional or circumstantial approach. Postulate 1 was clearly substantiated by these findings for both Catholic Irish and Protestant British students.

Postulate 2: Diversified socio-cultural ethos, individual cosmopolitanism and situationalism

> *Broadly speaking, those historical, cultural and personal circumstances that stimulate people to think of the complexities of nationhood – acknowledging fluidity and diversity – will generate a greater propensity towards situationalism.*

Identification with Irish and British national groups

Among the Catholic Irish students, the primordialists idealistically- and empathetically identified with the Irish people very much more than did their situationalist counterparts, who instead contra-identified with the Irish national group substantially more than did the primordialists (Table 3.5). Whereas the primordialists had a marked positive evaluation of the Irish people, the situationalists had a low evaluation of them. The nationalist orientation of the primordialist Catholic Irish students was apparent, in which the Irish people were perceived as strongly primordialist in cultural ethos. Their situationalist counterparts were evidently somewhat alienated from the primordialist ethos of the Irish people in general.

By contrast, the Protestant British students were unlike the Catholic Irish in their identification with their national group. Primordialism as a perceived cultural ethos of the British people was a muted one. The only indication of a primordialist characterisation of the British was the Protestant British primordialists', compared with situationalists', somewhat greater empathetic identification with the national group, British people (Table 3.6). Even then, and giving further corroboration of the perceived primordialist ethos of the Irish people, the Protestant British primordialists empathetically identified to a significantly greater extent with the Irish people than did the situationalists, a more marked tendency than that obtaining with the British people.

As a consequence of the match between the perceived primordialist ethos of the Irish people and the orientation of the Catholic Irish student primordialists, the latter stand out by having significantly lower conflicted identification with their national group (see Postulate 4 later) compared with their situationalist peers. The Protestant British students demonstrated no corresponding differences between primordialists and situationalists in their extent of identification conflict with the British people. Evidently, primordialist Catholic Irish students identified with their national group in the most emphatic and least conflicted manner, which their situationalist counterparts were unable to do. In sum these results clearly demonstrated that Irish culture compared with British culture was perceived to be considerably more primordialist by all of this sample of Ulster

Table 3.5 Catholic Irish students' identifications with and evaluation of the national groups

	Idealistic-identification			Contra-identification			Evaluation		
	PRIM	SIT	F-ratio	PRIM	SIT	F-ratio	PRIM	SIT	F-ratio
Irish people	0.79	0.56	37.0745****	0.18	0.40	34.6035****	0.60	0.14	44.0122****
British people	0.49	0.39	4.2411*	0.44	0.49	1.3442	0.05	−0.07	1.8825

	Empathetic identification			Conflicted identification		
	PRIM	SIT	F-ratio	PRIM	SIT	F-ratio
Irish people	0.79	0.58	22.0217***	0.35	0.46	15.8404***
British people	0.47	0.43	0.6318	0.42	0.44	0.3520

**** $p <= 0.0001$
*** $p <= 0.001$
** $p <= 0.01$
* $p <= 0.05$
Scale range: Identification 0.00 to 1.00; Evaluation −1.00 to +1.00
PRIM: Primordialists; SIT: Situationalists

Table 3.6 Protestant British students' identifications with and evaluation of the national groups

	Idealistic-identification			Contra-identification			Evaluation		
	PRIM	SIT	F-ratio	PRIM	SIT	F-ratio	PRIM	SIT	F-ratio
Irish people	0.58	0.44	6.4809*	0.37	0.46	2.2092	0.18	−0.04	5.6831*
British people	0.60	0.46	3.8689	0.31	0.42	2.0330	0.24	0.03	3.8991

	Empathetic identification			Conflicted identification		
	PRIM	SIT	F-ratio	PRIM	SIT	F-ratio
Irish people	0.63	0.44	8.6514**	0.46	0.42	1.1470
British people	0.65	0.46	6.4707*	0.41	0.39	0.0625

** $p <= 0.01$
* $p <= 0.05$
Scale range: Identification 0.00 to 1.00; Evaluation −1.00 to +1.00
PRIM: Primordialists; SIT: Situationalists

University students, whether Irish Catholic or British Protestant and whether situationalists or primordialists. In confirmation of Postulate 2 in respect of sociocultural ethos, further corroboration for the influence of the ethos of greater Irish than British primordialism was witnessed in the distribution of a higher proportion of primordialist among the Catholic Irish (54.7%) than Protestant British students (36.4%). As additional confirmation for Postulate 2 in respect of individual cosmopolitan experience of migration and mixed allegiances, among 21 cosmopolitan students only 23.8% endorsed primarily primordialist sentiments.

Slovak Academy faculty

Postulate 1: Primordialists' and situationalists' political identifications

The primordialists among the Slovak academics idealistically-identified with all the political entities to a greater extent than did their situationalist counterparts. However, in strong confirmation of Postulate 1, the most significant differences related to the government ('Movement for Democratic Slovakia'), the Slovak National Party and 'Coexistence', all being strongly nationalist in orientation, with which agencies the situationalists had little idealistic-identification (Table 3.7).

Both primordialists and situationalists idealistically identified to a substantially greater degree with the Christian-Democratic Party and the Green Party. Primordialists idealistically-identified with the Christian Democrats the most and significantly more so than did situationalists.

Situationalists strongly contra-identified with the Slovak government and the radical Slovak and ethnic Hungarian nationalist parties (Slovak National Party and 'Coexistence'), whereas primordialists did so to a much lower degree. Situationalists also contra-identified with the Christian Democrats to a greater extent than did the primordialists.

Situationalists empathetically identified the least with the nationalist orientations of the Slovak National Party, the Slovak government, and 'Coexistence', significantly less than did the primordialists. Their closest empathetic identification was with the Christian Democrats, with whom, however, their identifications were significantly more conflicted than those of the primordialists. They also empathetically identified with the Green Party.

These results demonstrated overall that the situationalists were disenchanted with the Slovak government and the nationalist parties. The primordialist academics, while generally less alienated, idealistically- and empathetically identified the most with the Christian Democrats and only moderately with the Slovak government and the Slovak National Party.

Postulate 2: Diversified socio-cultural ethos, individual cosmopolitanism and situationalism

Identification with Slovak and Hungarian national groups, and Romanies

Primordialist Slovak academics, idealistically- and empathetically, strongly identified with their national group, the Slovaks, whereas their situationalist

Table 3.7 Slovak respondents' identifications with and evaluation of the five political parties

	Idealistic-identification			Contra-identification			Evaluation		
	PRIM	SIT	F-ratio	PRIM	SIT	F-ratio	PRIM	SIT	F-ratio
Green Party	0.60	0.46	6.0581*	0.18	0.22	0.8066	0.39	0.23	4.4205*
Christian-Dem Party	0.66	0.52	4.9422*	0.14	0.35	13.3461***	0.45	0.13	3.8500***
Slovak National Party	0.43	0.19	31.9318****	0.47	0.74	30.0193*****	−0.03	−0.61	42.3376****
Coexistence Party	0.39	0.21	13.6662***	0.47	0.64	7.5788**	−0.03	−0.36	13.0872**
Slovak Government	0.45	0.24	24.9989****	0.35	0.68	47.1432*****	0.05	−0.45	29.7100****

	Empathetic identification			Conflicted identification		
	PRIM	SIT	F-ratio	PRIM	SIT	F-ratio
Green Party	0.61	0.48	5.5707*	0.29	0.29	0.0021
Christian-Dem Party	0.66	0.55	2.9491	0.24	0.36	7.7087**
Slovak National Party	0.43	0.22	21.5593*****	0.42	0.35	3.6281
Coexistence Party	0.41	0.27	8.1593**	0.37	0.39	0.0871
Slovak Government	0.46	0.26	19.4311***	0.37	0.39	0.7522

**** $p <= 0.0001$
*** $p <= 0.001$
** $p <= 0.01$
* $p <= 0.05$
Scale range: Identification 0.00 to 1.00; Evaluation −1.00 to +1.00
PRIM: Primordialists; SIT: Situationalists

colleagues did not. Whereas primordialists' contra-identification with the Slovaks was small, situationalists strongly contra-identified with them (Table 3.8). Romanies were evaluated negatively by both primordialists and situationalists.

The overall findings for this group of Slovak intelligentsia were that the situationalists among them were alienated from the nationalistic ethos of contemporary Slovakia as expressed by both the Slovak people and the ethnic Hungarians. They were alienated from the Slovak political arena in general, especially with respect to the Slovak government and the nationalist orientations of the Slovak National Party and 'Coexistence'. While Slovak Academy primordialists strongly identified with their people and with Hungarians living in Hungary, their identification with nationalist political parties, including the Slovak government – 'Movement for Democratic Slovakia' – was distinctly tempered. Instead, they leant more towards the ethos of the Christian-Democratic Party and the Green Party, both of which represented their cultural primordialist sentiments more closely.

The findings for the Slovak academics indicated a socio-cultural ethos of contemporary Slovakia as being substantially primordialist, with which primordialists strongly idealistically and empathetically identified, whereas situationalists did not. Comparing the differences between Slovak academic primordialists' and situationalists' empathetic identification with Slovaks (0.79 and 0.35) with those pertaining to Catholic Irish student primordialists and situationalists with Irish People (0.79 and 0.48), suggests that the perceived primordialism of the contemporary socio-cultural ethos of the Slovaks was as strong as that of the Irish people. Situationalist Slovak academics contra-identified with the Slovak ethos (0.51) even more than did situationalist Catholic Irish students with the Irish ethos (0.40), which suggests that the Slovak ethos was to a degree even more primordialist than the Irish. Postulate 2 again receives support in socio-cultural terms, as it does in respect of individual cosmopolitanism, given the earlier stated findings that among Slovak academics with experience of ethnic issues 52.4% were situationalists (33.3% primordialists), whereas of those without such experience only 30.2% were so classified (51.2% primordialists).

Ulster University students and Slovak Academy faculty

Postulate 3: Conflicted identification with cultural ethos

> *When individuals' empathetic identification with the ethos of a salient community within their social context is to a degree close whilst their contra-identification with it is considerable, the resultant conflicted identification with representatives of that ethos is problematic.*

Returning to the evidence of conflicted identifications with the prevalent cultural ethos as perceived locally by Ulster students and Slovak academics, the following findings firmly distinguished between primordialists and situationalists. Of the Catholic Irish students, situationalists compared with primordialists had

Table 3.8 Slovak respondents' identifications with and evaluation of the national groups

	Idealistic-identification			Contra-identification			Evaluation		
	PRIM	SIT	F-ratio	PRIM	SIT	F-ratio	PRIM	SIT	F-ratio
Slovaks	0.78	0.40	36.4391****	0.18	0.51	42.0583****	0.51	−0.07	48.9672****
Hungarians in Slovakia	0.53	0.34	11.6742**	0.32	0.53	18.1338****	0.22	−0.17	16.0984***
Hungarians in Hungary	0.64	0.37	18.3843****	0.21	0.41	11.7023**	0.41	−0.08	24.8800*****
Romanies (Gypsies)	0.27	0.21	1.7633	0.49	0.46	0.6034	−0.32	−0.39	0.3882

	Empathetic identification			Conflicted identification		
	PRIM	SIT	F-ratio	PRIM	SIT	F-ratio
Slovaks	0.79	0.48	24.8131****	0.32	0.42	7.6064**
Hungarians in Slovakia	0.55	0.39	7.7128**	0.35	0.43	4.5553*
Hungarians in Hungary	0.64	0.40	16.2561***	0.27	0.36	4.9433*
Romanies (Gypsies)	0.28	0.24	0.5673	0.35	0.28	3.3091

**** $p <= 0.0001$
*** $p <= 0.001$
** $p <= 0.01$
* $p <= 0.05$
Scale range: Identification 0.00 to 1.00; Evaluation −1.00 to +1.00
PRIM: Primordialists; SIT: Situationalists

substantially greater identification conflict with the Irish people (0.46 cf. 0.35) – *a problematic identification with the primordialist cultural ethos of the Irish*. Of the Slovak academics, again situationalists compared with primordialists had problematic conflicted identification with the Slovak primordialist ethos (0.42 cf. 0.32) and with that perceived to be expressed by the Hungarians in Slovakia (0.43 cf. 0.35). In terms of problematic identification with the perceived cultural ethos of their peoples, both Catholic Irish student and Slovak academic situationalists accord with Postulate 3. In respect of the perceived lesser primordialist ethos of the British people, both situationalist and primordialist Ulster Protestant British students had substantially conflicted identifications with the British (0.39 cf. 0.41). Both also problematically identified with the Irish people (conflicted identification 0.42 cf. 0.46), situationalists in respect of perceived Irish primordialism, and primordialists in terms of substantial empathetic identification with the primordial ethos, but contra-identification with the threatening stance of the Irish towards themselves. Attempts by Protestant British primordialists at resolution of their high identification conflict with the Irish would be expected to provide a continuing process of tending to dissociate the more from the Irish (see also Weinreich, 1983a, concerning Belfast youth).

Postulate 4: Unproblematic congruity with cultural ethos

> *The more that individuals are in tune with the ethos of their social contexts, as represented by salient agents and agencies, the less will be their identification conflicts with these agents and agencies.*

As already noted, the match between the perceived primordialist ethos of the Irish people and the orientation of the Catholic Irish student primordialists resulted in their significantly lower conflicted identification with their national group compared with their situationalist peers. With respect to the Slovak academics, the primordialists amongst them demonstrated congruence and lesser conflicted identification with the ethos of the Christian-Democratic Party (0.24) and with Hungarians in Hungary (0.27), even more so than with the Slovak people (0.32). Thus, in accord with Postulate 4, primordialist Slovak academics' least problematic congruity was with the Slovak Christian Democrat ethos and then that represented by Hungarians in their home territory. Evidently, these Slovak primordialists were not strident in their orientation, having problematic conflicted identifications with the ethos of the Slovak National Party (0.42) and notable identification conflicts with that of the Coexistence Party (0.37) and the Slovak Government (0.37). There had to be others in the wider community who held to more extreme primordialist sentiments, given the grassroots support for these agencies.

Postulate 5: Situationalists' enhanced developmental change in identity

> *Given their developing questioning stance on 'nationality', situationalists compared with primordialists will show greater perceived change in the*

ethnic or national aspect of their identities over time and greater modulation in their empathetic identifications with others who represent primordialist or situationalist perspectives on 'nationality'.

This postulate has in effect two parts, one directed to global reappraisals in respect of self-evaluation and identity diffusion and the other referencing modulations in empathetic identifications. In the first respect, evidence of ongoing processes of change in identity was obtained by comparing participants' self-evaluation based in their appraisal of self *when fifteen years old* with their *current* self-evaluation. The 'past-self' appraised in this manner is, of course, not the appraisal of self that the youngsters had when actually aged fifteen. It is based in a currently reconstructed image of self in contemplation of that past phase of one's biography. Nevertheless, the differing appraisals provide evidence of the direction of currently ongoing processes of reappraisal. The results confirmed Postulate 5 that perceived change in identity, both in terms of self-evaluation and identity diffusion, was generally greater in situationalists compared with primordialists (Table 3.9).

For situationalists, the ongoing increases in self-evaluation were for Catholic Irish students 18%, Protestant British students 20% and Slovak academics 35%. Ongoing primordialists' enhancements in self-evaluation were less, for Catholic Irish students a little less at 15% (cf. 18%), Protestant British students somewhat less at 15% (cf. 20%) and Slovak academics much less at 12% (cf. 35%). With respect to identity diffusion the results more emphatically demonstrated the far greater extent of ongoing processes of reappraisal and developmental change in identity in situationalists compared with the primordialists holding on to their primordialist perspectives. Whereas the primordialist Ulster students exhibited zero change in identity diffusion, their situationalist counterparts were in the process of

Table 3.9   Self-evaluation and identity diffusion based in past and current self-images

	Primordialists			Situationalists		
	Past	*Current*	*% diff*	*Past*	*Current*	*% diff*
CATHOLIC IRISH STUDENTS (ULSTER)						
Self-evaluation*	0.428	0.640	**+14.8**	0.359	0.608	**+18.3**
Identity diffusn	0.334	0.334	**0.0**	0.392	0.334	**−17.4**
PROTESTANT BRITISH STUDENTS (ULSTER)						
Self-evaluation*	0.321	0.516	**+14.8**	0.375	0.645	**+19.6**
Identity diffusn	0.360	0.360	**0.0**	0.374	0.328	**−12.3**
SLOVAK ACADEMICS						
Self-evaluation*	0.594	0.788	**+12.2**	0.288	0.735	**+34.7**
Identity diffusn	0.291	0.261	**−10.0**	0.406	0.310	**−31.0**

*% difference for self-evaluation takes into account the scale range for evaluation, being −1.00 to +1.00
Scale range: Identity diffusion 0.00 to 1.00; Evaluation −1.00 to +1.00

decreasing identity diffusion, the Catholic Irish by 17% and the Protestant British by 12%. Although primordialist Slovak academics were demonstrating ongoing processes of diminishing identity diffusion to an extent of 10%, their situational-ist counterparts evinced by far the greatest diminution, being 31%.

Returning to the second aspect of Postulate 5 concerning situationalists' greater ongoing modulation of empathetic identifications with representatives of nation-ality and ethnicity compared with primordialists, evidence of ongoing processes demonstrated the following (Table 3.10). In line with Postulate 5, situationalist Catholic Irish students were generally decreasing their empathetic identification with political parties in Ulster and with the Irish and British people to a mean extent of about 10%, while their primordialist counterparts were actually increas-ing theirs by about half this. However, Catholic Irish primordialist students' increasing identification with primordialist ethos was unexpected (13% with Irish

Table 3.10 Empathetic identifications based in past and current self-images with political parties and national groups

	Primordialists			Situationalists		
	Past	*Current*	*% diff*	*Past*	*Current*	*% diff*
CATHOLIC IRISH STUDENTS (ULSTER)						
Sinn Fein	0.552	0.558	+1.1	0.406	0.345	−15.0
SDLP	0.507	0.588	+16.0	0.482	0.504	+4.6
DUP	0.380	0.383	+0.8	0.386	0.321	−16.8
OUP	0.359	0.357	−0.5	0.367	0.311	−15.3
Irish people	0.697	0.787	+12.9	0.609	0.585	−3.9
British people	0.483	0.467	−3.3	0.481	0.428	−11.0
Mean % difference			**+4.5**			**−9.6**
PROTESTANT BRITISH STUDENTS (ULSTER)						
Sinn Fein	0.446	0.411	−7.8	0.300	0.188	−37.3
SDLP	0.435	0.468	+7.6	0.375	0.320	−14.7
DUP	0.449	0.455	+1.3	0.358	0.285	−20.4
OUP	0.407	0.438	+7.6	0.384	0.317	−17.4
Irish people	0.556	0.625	+12.4	0.447	0.436	−8.6
British people	0.620	0.790	+12.9	0.507	0.462	−8.8
Mean % difference			**+5.7**			**−17.9**
SLOVAK ACADEMICS						
Slov Government	0.524	0.462	−11.8	0.413	0.263	−36.3
Slov National Pty	0.541	0.431	−20.3	0.413	0.220	−46.7
Coexistence	0.493	0.407	−17.4	0.416	0.266	−36.1
Slovaks	0.759	0.794	+4.6	0.605	0.476	−21.3
Slov Hungarians	0.600	0.545	−9.2	0.535	0.390	−27.1
Hung Hungarians	0.681	0.407	−5.9	0.475	0.397	−16.4
Mean % difference			**−10.0**			**−30.7**

Scale range: Identification 0.00 to 1.00

people, compared with a decrease of 4% in their situationalist counterparts), and contrary to the notion that experience of the greater cosmopolitan culture of a university would encourage awareness of situationalist perspectives. Instead, the evidence was one of increasing elevation of primordialist sentiment in the primordialist students.

Again confirming Postulate 5, situationalist Protestant British students were decreasing their empathetic identification with these representatives to an average extent of about 18%, while their primordialist peers were increasing theirs by about 6%. These situationalists' increasing dissociation from all political parties in Northern Ireland was strongly in evidence: 37% from Sinn Fein, 20% from Democratic Unionist Party, 17% from Official Unionist Party and 15% from Social Democratic and Labour Party. The unexpected elevation of primordialist sentiment in primordialists of the Ulster British persuasion, as with the Ulster Irish primordialists, was again evident.

Further in support of Postulate 5, the situationalist Slovak academics were massively decreasing their empathetic identification with nationalist political parties and the Slovak national groups of Slovaks and Hungarians, and the Hungarians of Hungary, to an extent of 31% compared with a lesser diminution of 10% by their primordialist colleagues. The primordialist Slovak academics, unlike the Ulster primordialist students of both persuasions and more in line with expectation, were not elevating their primordialist sentiments. They showed movement towards situationalist perspectives, demonstrated most notably by their dissociating from the Slovak National Party by a substantial 20% although this was less than half of their situationalist colleagues' 47%. The greater modulation in empathetic identification with national and ethnic entities witnessed for the Slovak academics compared with the Ulster students may have arisen through a combination of experiences occurring from their mid-adolescence to their current professional adulthood. In the main the academics' post-adolescent period was substantially longer than that of the students', so that intervening personal and continuing professional experience will have been likely to contribute to a greater awareness of situationalist viewpoints. In addition, of major significance will have been the pace of societal change during a period when totalitarian communism was jettisoned followed shortly afterwards by the creation of the newly independent Slovak state. Both of these events would have emphasised to the intelligentsia the situational contexts of the nature of the nation state.

Although accentuated in the Slovak academics, these comparative cross-cultural findings demonstrated that across the three national and ethnic groups, situationalists were reappraising themselves and modulating their empathetic identification with agencies representing nationalist doctrines to a substantially greater degree than were the primordialists. In each case, primordialists were increasing their empathetic identification with their national group, while situationalists were decreasing it, albeit to notably different extents in the Slovak compared with the Ulster context. Thus the results were, comparing *primordialists* with *situationalists*: +12.9% cf. −3.9% for Catholic Irish students with the Irish;

+12.9% cf. −8.8% for Protestant British students with the British; +4.6% cf. −21.3% for Slovak academics with Slovaks.

Postulate 6: Primordialists' primacy of parental identification

> *Primordialists will generally affirm the primacy of parental or quasi-parental identifications, whereas situationalists will more likely relinquish some parental primacy.*

Primordialists compared with situationalists were increasing their empathetic identification with parents to a greater extent (Table 3.11): 11% cf. 8% for Catholic Irish and 27% cf. 5% for Protestant British Ulster students, and 9% cf. 5% for Slovak academics. Contrary to the expected *decreasing* empathetic identification with parents in situationalists, all groups demonstrated some augmentation of parental identification. However, in all three ethnic groups augmentation was more evident in primordialists than situationalists, the difference being substantial for the Ulster Protestant British students. The fact that the evidence indicated that situationalists were also affirming parental identifications, albeit less so, implied that the parents of both counterparts were perceived to be either holding to congruent primordialist sentiments or tending to express compatible situationalist perspectives respectively.

Nevertheless, primordialists were currently empathetically identifying with their parents more closely than situationalists: 0.82 cf. 0.79 for Catholic Irish and 0.79 cf. 0.74 for Protestant British students; 0.84 cf. 0.68 for Slovak academics. In total these results provided confirmation in essential respects for Postulate 6, though tempered by the added recognition that situationalists were affirming identification with parents who were perceived to also incline towards situationalist perspectives. The primordialists' elevation of parental identification denoted processes towards

Table 3.11 Empathetic identifications based in past and current self-images with parents

	Primordialists			Situationalists		
	Past	*Current*	*% diff*	*Past*	*Current*	*% diff*
CATHOLIC IRISH STUDENTS (ULSTER)						
My parents	0.736	0.816	**+10.9**	0.733	0.788	**+7.5**
PROTESTANT BRITISH STUDENTS (ULSTER)						
My parents	0.620	0.790	**+27.4**	0.702	0.740	**+5.4**
SLOVAK ACADEMICS						
My parents	0.767	0.839	**+9.4**	0.648	0.683	**+5.4**

Scale range: Identification 0.00 to 1.00

the consolidation of primordialist sentiment in contradistinction to the adoption of more situationalist perspectives – *developmentally retrogressive processes*.

A slight modification of Postulate 6 incorporates the more refined account of the processes demonstrated here by evidence from the three ethnic groups, such that:

Amended Postulate 6: Primordialists' primacy of parental identification

Primordialists will generally continue to identify with their parents more than situationalists do, tending to elevate their identifications with primordialist parents, while situationalists will tend to moderately affirm their identifications with situationalist parents.

Notwithstanding the general confirmation of the developmental analysis presented in this chapter, the amended postulate could also encompass the possibility of identification with differing parental models between primordialists and situationalists – *possibly confounded with some greater degree of genetically inherited propensity towards situational openness in situationalists compared with primordialists.*

Postulate 7: Consonant discourses as core evaluative dimensions of identity

For the more strident primordialists, ISA postulates that they will endorse and express primordialist discourses as core evaluative dimensions of identity with high structural pressures when appraising national or ethnic agencies in their social world. Likewise, for the more ideologically committed situationalists, ISA postulates that they will use situationalist discourses with high structural pressures.

The more the cognitive–affective appraisals of the social world in terms of a particular construct are compatible and consonant, the greater is the stabilising structural pressure and the more is the identity aspiration so designated a core evaluative dimension of identity. The consonant primordialist discourses across the three groups evidenced some commonality. However, although firmly primordialist in respect of these discourses, none of the three groups emerged as being stridently so, as evidenced in the following results for structural pressures (Table 3.12A,C,E).

Primordialist Catholic Irish and Protestant British students, and Slovak academics endorsed these primordialist discourses in common: . . . *consider/s nationality is given for ever* [construct 8: Structural Pressures 64, 54, 49 respectively]; . . . *know/s that their descendants will continue the national group* (Ulster version), . . . *believe/s the descendants should be the continuation of their nation* (Slovak version) [11: SP 50, 34, 64]; . . . *do/es not doubt the genuineness of people's national feelings* [15: SP 46, 34, 52]. However, discourses that most represented core evaluative dimensions, as anticipated on emic grounds, differed. For primordialist Catholic Irish students it was . . . *consider/s nationality is given forever* (SP = 64): for primordialist

Protestant British students it was also this one (SP = 54), but followed closely by ... *feel/s one's most important loyalty is to one's ancestral kin group* (SP = 52): for the Slovak academics it was ... *believe/s the descendants should be the continuation of their nation* (SP = 64).

The primordialist Slovak academics were characterised as being substantially mixed in orientation with their endorsement of several situationalist discourses (Table 3.12E). Earlier evidence had already demonstrated that these Slovak academic primordialists, who idealistically identified with the Christian-Democratic Party, were not strident in their orientation as indicated by their

Table 3.12A Catholic Irish primordialists evaluative dimensions of identity

Favoured pole	SP	N
Constructs used with primordialist consensus		
2 feel/s one's most important loyalty is to one's ancestral kin group	**50**	**23**
5 believe/s the national language is absolutely essential to the nation	40	21
6 believe/s national ties override divisions of wealth and social position	44	22
8 consider/s nationality is given forever	**64**	**26**
11 know/s that their descendants will continue the national group	**50**	**28**
14 think/s that national identity resides in the very soil and essence of the land	**50**	**22**
15 do/es not doubt the genuineness of people's national feelings	46	27
17 believe/s that nations develop from common ancestral experiences	45	22
Constructs used with situationalist consensus		
9 think/s that most nations descend from mixed ancestries and races	*14*	*17*
12 accept/s people of different origins in their territory	45	25
18 think/s that national determination has potentially dangerous consequences	*31*	*18*

See key beneath Table 3.12F

Table 3.12B Catholic Irish situationalists evaluative dimensions of identity

Favoured pole	SP	N
Constructs used with situationalist consensus		
5 believe/s that a common language is not necessary for national loyalty	46	15
8 is/are able to adapt to being of any nationality	44	14
9 think/s that most nations descend from mixed ancestries and races	45	12
11 believe/s that future generations won't bother about nationality	*34*	*11*
12 accept/s people of different origins in their territory	62	21
14 think/s that national identity can be a matter of choice	52	18
18 think/s that national determination has potentially dangerous consequences	53	17
Constructs used with primordialist consensus		
2 feel/s one's most important loyalty is to one's ancestral kin group	64	17
6 believe/s national ties override divisions of wealth and social position	*9*	*13*
15 do/es not doubt the genuineness of people's national feelings	*−2*	*12*
17 believe/s that nations develop from common ancestral experiences	*17*	*12*

Table 3.12C Protestant British primordialists evaluative dimensions of identity

Favoured pole	SP	N
Constructs used with primordialist consensus		
2 feel/s one's most important loyalty is to one's ancestral kin group	**52**	**12**
5 believe/s the national language is absolutely essential to the nation	*26*	*7*
6 believe/s national ties override divisions of wealth and social position	*29*	*11*
8 consider/s nationality is given forever	**54**	**7**
11 know/s that their descendants will continue the national group	*34*	*11*
15 do/es not doubt the genuineness of people's national feelings	*34*	*7*
17 believe/s that nations develop from common ancestral experiences	*19*	*6*
Constructs used with situationalist consensus		
9 think/s that most nations descend from mixed ancestries and races	*18*	*6*
12 accept/s people of different origins in their territory	42	12
14 think/s that national identity can be a matter of choice	*29*	*6*
18 think/s that national determination has potentially dangerous consequences	*32*	*8*

Table 3.12D Protestant British situationalists evaluative dimensions of identity

Favoured pole	SP	N
Constructs used with situationalist consensus		
5 believe/s that a common language is not necessary for national loyalty	47	18
8 is/are able to adapt to being of any nationality	**63**	**14**
9 think/s most nations descend from mixed ancestries and races	47	19
11 believe/s that future generations won't bother about nationality	**52**	**13**
12 accept/s people of different origins in their territory	**70**	**20**
14 think/s that national identity can be a matter of choice	**66**	**19**
17 believe/s that nations are the consequences of political decisions	*32*	*11*
18 think/s that national determination has potentially dangerous consequences	**61**	**16**
Constructs used with primordialist consensus		
2 feel/s one's most important loyalty is to one's ancestral kin group	48	12
6 believe/s national ties override divisions of wealth and social position	*13*	*13*
15 do/es not doubt the genuineness of people's national feelings	*−1*	*10*

notable contra-identification with more extreme primordialist agencies, namely the Slovak National Party and the Coexistence Party (both 0.47, see Table 3.7). In line with the uncertain and inconstant history of Slovakia they endorsed situationalist perspectives of *the mixed origins of nations, the acceptance of different peoples,* and *the principle of the state over narrow nationality.* In particular, these mixed primordialists endorsed the situationalist notions of: *ancestors of nations being people of various origins* [construct 9: SP = 53]; *accepting people of different nationalities on their territory* [12: 62]; *loyalty to state before loyalty to*

Table 3.12E   Slovak primordialists evaluative dimensions of identity

Favoured pole	SP	N
Constructs used with primordialist consensus		
5 believe/s language is absolutely essential to the nation	47	24
8 consider/s nationality is given forever	49	25
11 believe/s the descendants should be the continuation of their nation	**64**	**27**
14 think/s national identity originates from the very soil and territory of the nation	47	29
15 do/es not doubt the genuineness of people's national feelings	**52**	**17**
Constructs used with situationalist consensus		
2 feel/s loyalty to the state is more important than loyalty to one's nation	48	29
6 believe/s economic interests rather than national ones unite a people	48	23
9 think/s ancestors of all nations were people of various origins (different tribes)	**53**	**25**
12 accept/s people of different nationalities on their territory	**62**	**27**
17 think/s mankind started to live in nations only recently/in modern age	48	14
18 think/s the preference of national principle to state principle is dangerous	46	24

Table 3.12F   Slovak situationalists evaluative dimensions of identity

Favoured pole	SP	N
Constructs used with situationalist consensus		
2 feel/s loyalty to the state is more important than loyalty to one's nation	**72**	**21**
5 believe/s a common ancestral language is not necessary for national loyalty	**67**	**15**
6 believe/s economic interests rather than national ones unite a people	**58**	**21**
8 is/are able to adapt to being of any nationality	**63**	**14**
9 think/s ancestors of all nations were people of various origins (different tribes)	**72**	**20**
12 accept/s people of different nationalities on their territory	**73**	**24**
14 think/s national identity is a matter of choice and decision	**53**	**24**
15 think/s national feelings may disguise the selfish motives as well	**50**	**16**
17 think/s mankind started to live in nations only recently/in modern age	**65**	**20**
18 think/s the preference of national principle to state principle is dangerous	**74**	**23**
Constructs used with primordialist consensus		
11 believe/s the descendants should be the continuation of their nation	*8*	*13*

SP refers to *structural pressure*, the parameter designating cognitive–affective compatibilities and incompatibilities, ranging from +100 for wholly consonant appraisals of the social world to −100 for wholly dissonant appraisals.

N is the number of respondents who endorse the indicated pole of the bipolar construct and contribute to the mean SP.

Discourses in bold highlight those with SP of 50 and above, which represent *core evaluative dimensions of identity*.

Bold italic discourses highlight those with SP of between +35 and −35, which designate *conflicted dimensions of identity* in which dissonant appraisals of the social world counter consonant ones thereby undermining the stability of the evaluative connotation of the construct in question.

one's nation [2: 48]; *economic rather than national interests uniting a people* [6: 48], and *people's preference of national to state principle being dangerous* [18: 46].

The situationalists of the three groups – Catholic Irish and British Protestant students, and Slovak academics – were generally more committed situationalists, ranking from the least being Catholic Irish students to the most being Slovak academics (Table 3.12B,D,F). All situationalists endorsed: . . . *accept/s people of different origins in their territory* [12: SP 62, 70, 73]; . . . *think/s that national identity can be a matter of choice* [14: SP 52, 66, 53]; . . . *think/s that national determination has potentially dangerous consequences* (Ulster version), . . . *think/s the preference of national principle to state principle is dangerous* (Slovak version) [18: SP 53, 61, 74]. The situationalist Protestant British students were distinctly more firmly situationalist than their Catholic Irish counterparts and notably endorsed . . . *is/are able to adapt to being any nationality* [8: SP 63] (Table 3.12D). However, the most notable finding concerned the situationalist Slovak academics, who emerged as ideologically committed situationalists. They used ten situationalist discourses as core evaluative dimensions, with structural pressures ranging from 50 to 74 (Table 3.12F). Their very strong commitment to appraising the social world from situationalist standpoints reflected their recent experiences of the disintegration of totalitarian communism followed by national self-determination within a longer-term context of changing national and imperial forces.

Evidence in confirmation of Postulate 7 was thus overall very substantial. In addition, three further findings emerged clearly. First, people's varying expression of primordialist sentiments or commitment to situationalism was readily apparent. Second, mixed endorsement of primordialist sentiments and situationalist perspectives existed to a greater or lesser extent in all groups, which is very much in line with the developmental analysis presented here. Third, emic variation in the nature of the discourses most representing primordialism and situationalism was strongly apparent.

Postulate 8: Discourses representing conflicted arenas of identity

Primordialists who subscribe to one or other situationalist discourses will tend to use them ambivalently, accompanied by low or negative structural pressure. Similarly, should situationalists subscribe to any primordialist sentiments they will tend to do so ambivalently and with low structural pressure.

Primordialist Catholic Irish students endorsed these situationalist perspectives ambivalently, indicated by low structural pressures (Table 3.12A) . . . *thinks/s that most nations descend from mixed ancestries and races* [9: SP 14] and . . . *think/s that national determination has potentially dangerous consequences* [18: SP 31], confirming Postulate 8. One other situationalist construct endorsed by them was, however, less ambivalently used, namely, . . . *accept/s people of different origins in their territory* [12: SP 45]. An element of 'political correctness' in social norms was likely to have been operative in respect of this sentiment, as further evidence given next attested.

Some primordialist Protestant British students endorsed the following three situationalist perspectives in a conflicted manner, a small majority consensus of six to eight students in each case (Table 3.12C), . . . *think/s that most nations descend from mixed ancestries and races* [9: SP 18], . . . *think/s that national identity can be a matter of choice* [14: SP 29], . . . *thinks/s that national determination has potentially dangerous consequences* [18: SP 32]. These results also confirmed Postulate 8. That the primordialist Protestant British students endorsed these situationalist perspectives, albeit ambivalently, reflected the political context and media coverage of the two traditions – Irish and British – in Ireland, in which the latter had arisen through the long history of migratory settlement of the British in Ireland. As with the Catholic Irish students, primordialist Protestant British students' acceptance of people of different origins [12: SP 42] represented to a degree social norms of 'political correctness'. However, these primordialist Protestant British students also expressed certain primordial sentiments with ambivalence. Thus, conflicted appraisals centred on believing that *the national language is absolutely essential to the nation* [5: SP 26], *national ties override divisions of wealth and social position* [6: SP 29], *their descendants will continue the national group* [11: SP 34] and *not doubting the genuineness of people's national feelings* [15: SP 34]. The primordialist Protestant British students' endorsement of these issues was compromised – *with dissonant appraisals of the social world*. Thus, English rather than a 'national language' is the everyday communicative language of many nationalities including the Irish. Hierarchical social status is witnessed as being obtrusive and divisive. There is an awareness of migration, mobility and intermarriage of people, as well as of the changing status of the British tradition in Ireland, countering an inevitable continuing national allegiance of descendants. Some scepticism about the real motives of strident nationalists, both republican and unionist, is prevalent.

As already witnessed, the primordialist Slovak academics were substantially mixed in orientation (Table 3.12E) in a manner that very much reflected the historical circumstances of the Slovak nation and its mixed origins both in terms of ancestry and in terms of migratory settlements of others, such as Hungarians and Romanies. Thus, they endorsed with little ambivalence several situationalist perspectives: . . . *accept/s people of different nationalities on their territory* [12: SP 62], . . . *thinks/s ancestors of all nations were people of various origins (different tribes)* [9: SP 53], . . . *feel/s loyalty to the state is more important than loyalty to one's nation* [2: SP 48], . . . *believe/s economic interests rather than national ones unite a people* [6: SP 48], . . . *think/s mankind started to live in nations only recently/in modern age* [17: SP 48], . . . *think/s the preference of national principle to state principle is dangerous* [18: SP 46]. In respect to Postulate 8, these Slovak academics were evidently not strident primordialists as had already been deduced from their patterns of identification with political agencies and national groups. They held primordialist sentiments, overlaid with situationalist perspectives that were also core evaluative dimensions of identity.

156   *Weinreich, Bacova and Rougier*

In firm confirmation of Postulate 8, situationalist Catholic Irish and Protestant British students endorsed two primordialist sentiments in highly conflicted manner (Table 3.12B,D): . . . *believe/s national ties override divisions of wealth and social position* [6: SP 9, 13], . . . *do/es not doubt the genuineness of people's national feelings* [15: SP −2, −1]. Situationalist Catholic Irish students also held as a conflicted dimension the primordialist sentiment . . . *believe/s that nations develop from common ancestral experiences* [17: SP 17]. Both situationalist student groups endorsed the primordialist . . . *feel/s one's most important loyalty is to one's ancestral group* [2: SP 64, 48], reflecting the historically highly salient sectarian ethos of Northern Ireland and dominance in biographical experience of each ancestral ethnicity. Another revealing finding was that Catholic Irish situationalists expressed the situationalist perspective about *future generations not bothering about nationality* in a conflicted manner [11: SP 34], belying strong contrary appraisals about descendants continuing the national group. Also, Protestant British situationalists engendered incompatible appraisals in respect of the notion that *nations are the consequence of political decisions* [17: SP 32]. They were being confronted on a daily basis with forceful evidence of a continuing Irish 'nationality' in their midst irrespective of political decision, as witnessed in the long-term dispute over Northern Ireland being a politically endorsed British province. Despite the 'political decision' that led to the province remaining within the United Kingdom of Great Britain and Northern Ireland and separated from the Republic of Ireland, Irish 'nationality' within Ulster remains formidable and has every appearance of being primordial and not readily embraced within a situationalist perspective.

Again in confirmation of Postulate 8, among the firmly committed situationalist Slovak academics (Table 3.12F), a bare majority consensus of thirteen ambivalently endorsed the primordialist sentiment . . . *believe/s the descendants should be the continuation of their nation* [11: SP 8]. Given the significance of the historically recent achievement of Slovak national independence, even the committed situationalists among the Slovak academics reverberated to the primordialist sentiment of continuity of nationality in respect of their descendants. However, cognitive–affective incompatibilities or dissonances in appraisal of their social world were very much evident, given the almost zero structural pressure which indicated that the negative pressures of incompatible appraisals and dissonances undermined almost completely the positive structural pressures.

Another feature of these results concerning evaluative dimensions of identity supports the present developmental analysis, in which people by way of their earliest identifications establish primordialist sentiments that occur within the prevailing historical and cultural ethos of the generation in question, only subsequently to be modified by situationalist awareness. Thus the manner by which the three groups, Catholic Irish and Protestant British students and Slovak academics, expressed primordialist or situationalist modes of appraisal demonstrated that individual propensities were expressed with clear emic variation. Further, this variation reflected personal developmental experiences firmly embedded within the different socio-historical and cultural contexts of the three national or ethnic communities.

Postulate 9: Developmental primacy of and situationalists' residual resonance with primordialist sentiments

Given the developmental primacy of primordialist thinking, situationalists will continue to residually express and respond to primordialist sentiments.

As indicated earlier, the evidence from all three groups of situationalists demonstrated a propensity to acknowledge some degree of primordialist sentiment. This was most strongly the case for situationalist Catholic Irish students, who firmly endorsed the primordialist sentiment . . . *feel/s one's most important loyalty is to one's ancestral kin group* [2: 64], along with their highly conflicted endorsement of three others (Table 3.12B). The same primordialist sentiment featured in the situationalist Protestant British students [2: 48], together with conflicted endorsements of two others (Table 3.12D). Even the highly committed situationalist Slovak academics reverberated, albeit in a highly conflicted manner, to one primordialist sentiment . . . *believe/s the descendants should be the continuation of their nation* [11: 8] (Table 3.12F). In each case, the situationalists' affirmation of the most obtruding primordialist sentiment mirrored that same sentiment as being a core evaluative dimension of identity in their primordialist counterparts – Catholic Irish [2: 50], Protestant British [2: 52], Slovak [11: 64] (Table 3.12A,C,E).

Two striking features of these results are that, first, in confirmation of Postulate 9, the primacy of primordial sentiment obtrudes even in the most committed situationalists; and second, the most obtrusive primordial sentiment concerns *lineage in the most intimate sense*, either in respect of ancestors in the case of the Ulster students or descendants in the case of the Slovak academics. This evidence demonstrates the continuing power of early identification with kith and kin. How that identification with one's lineage is expressed is, however, historically and culturally modulated. Given the culturally expressed social representations of the very lengthy historical feud between the Catholic Irish and Protestant British in Ulster, the contemporary Ulster experience is emically in respect of *ancestors* (the July 12th parades celebrate the Protestant victory of the Battle of the Boyne in 1690). Whereas, the newer social representation of Slovak statehood emically shapes contemporary Slovak experience in terms of the continuation of newly established independence, that is, in respect of *descendants* as continuation of the independent nation.

Having argued for the primacy of primordial sentiments and referred to evidence demonstrating that remnants of these were obtrusively present even in committed situationalists, the counter viewpoint about situationalist perspectives being endorsed by primordialists has to be addressed. In the results given earlier, primordialists tended to endorse certain situationalist perspectives that varied in extent across the three ethnic groups, being the fewest in primordialist Catholic Irish to the most in Slovak academics. Despite this variation, one situationalist perspective stood out as being most compatibly held by primordialists of all three groups, which was . . . *accept/s people of different origins in their territory* – Catholic Irish [12: 45], Protestant British [12: 42], Slovak [12: 62] (Table 3.12A,C,E).

As expected, situationalists of the three groups endorsed this same perspective with even greater compatibility – Catholic Irish [12: 62], Protestant British [12: 70], Slovak [11: 73] (Table 3.12B,D,F). Whereas situationalists' endorsement of obtrusive primordial sentiment was mostly in terms of lineage – *indicating the developmental primacy of identification with kith and kin* – primordialists' assent to acceptance of different peoples in their territory denoted adherence only to *conventional norms of politeness and welcome to strangers*. The primordialists' acceptance of strangers was not fundamentally intrinsic and intimate to lineage, but conventionally normative. The evidence about the nature of primordialists' assent to situationalist perspectives confirmed the developmentally secondary elaboration of such perspectives.

The foregoing evidence, as well as confirming Postulate 9, suggests the following empirically derived theoretical propositions:

Derived Proposition 9.1:   Primordialist obtrusion of lineage

The developmental primacy of primordialist sentiment will obtrude most strongly in terms of the intimacy of lineage.

Derived Proposition 9.2:   Emic expression of lineage in respect of ancestors or descendants

Primacy of primordialist sentiment will be expressed emically, either in terms of ancestors when long-standing historical social representations are predominant, or in terms of descendants in the case of more newly established social representations.

This proposition directly addresses the significance of socio-historical context to the emic psychological interpretation of lineage in respect of, alternatively, vindication of nationality in past heritage, or consolidation of newly expressed nationhood by way of future endeavours.

Derived Proposition 9.3:   Primordialists' endorsement of non-intrusive situationalist social norms

Situationalist perspectives that are most endorsed by primordialists will represent pervasive contemporary social norms promoting 'polite' acceptance of other peoples in their territory without implication for intimacy and membership of lineage.

Discourses on tolerance, neighbourliness, understanding, and religious faith

Beyond the specific discourses having to do with primordialist sentiments and situationalist perspectives about nationality and ethnicity, other discourses in the identity instruments enabled respondents to express their appraisals of the designated social world in respect of other central issues. In the Ulster instrument these issues were *trustworthiness, faith in religion, tolerance of different people, optimism towards the future, understanding the agents of the designated social world, impact of the agents of the designated social world on Ulster*, and *neighbourliness* (Table 3.2, constructs 1, 3, 4, 7, 10, 13 and 16).

Differences between primordialists and situationalists in respect of these general discourses were consistent across Catholic Irish and Protestant British students. Primordialist students used . . . ***lives in harmony with neighbours*/** . . . *is prone to conflict*, less as a core evaluative dimension of identity than did situationalists (structural pressure: *primordialist* CathIrish 49, ProtBrit 53; *situationalist* CathIrish 72, ProtBrit 71). Thus, situationalist students appraised others in terms of attributes of good neighbourliness more so than did primordialists. Likewise, primordialists used . . . ***is tolerant*/**does not accept other people*, less as a core evaluative dimension (*primordialist* CathIrish 49, ProtBrit 53; *situationalist* CathIrish 72, ProtBrit 71). Again, situationalists were more prone to evaluate people within their social world in respect of tolerance towards others than were primordialists. In sum, beliefs in *good neighbourliness* and *tolerance towards others* characterised situationalists substantially more than they did primordialists.

However, primordialists were more inclined towards evaluatively compatible appraisals of agents of their social world in terms of . . . *I don't understand (the designated people)*/***I understand (the designated people)*** (*primordialist* CathIrish 60, ProtBrit 65; *situationalist* CathIrish 49, ProtBrit 52). Situationalists had lesser propensity towards requiring a clear-cut understanding of agents within their social world than did primordialists, demonstrating a somewhat greater tolerance of evaluative incompatibilities or, in the terms of 'the authoritarian personality' (Adorno, Frenkel-Brunswik, Levinson & Sanford, 1950) and 'the closed mind' (Rokeach, 1960), greater tolerance of ambiguity.

In respect of . . . *religion is not important*/ . . . ***has a firm faith in their religion***, primordialists were rather more inclined towards compatible appraisals of their social world than were situationalists (*primordialist* CathIrish 47, ProtBrit 41; *situationalist* CathIrish 27, ProtBrit 20). Evidently, given their generally low structural pressures, incompatibilities were substantially the norm for situationalists and, whereas firm faith in religion was more of a core evaluative dimension for primordialists, they too evidenced moderate degrees of incompatibility. In a province where many are religious and actively worship, appraisal in terms of religious faith – when sectarian conflict is symbolically associated with two religious denominations – inevitably involves evaluative incompatibilities. Situationalist students incorporated these incompatibilities to a greater extent than did their primordialist counterparts, demonstrating both a greater tolerance of contradiction in the overall community and a retreat from religious faith as a core dimension of identity.

Three further empirically derived theoretical propositions follow from these results. Since they have no predecessors – unlike Derived Propositions 9.1, 9.2 and 9.3 – they are simply numbered consecutively.

Derived Proposition 10:   Situationalists' fellowship and tolerance

Situationalists will endorse harmonious relationships and tolerance of different people more strongly than will primordialists.

The results for the Slovak academics also supported this proposition. Slovak primordialist academics used . . . *lives in harmony with neighbours/ . . . is prone to conflict*, somewhat less as a core evaluative dimension of identity than did situationalists (Slovak primordialists, SP 54; situationalists, SP 63), and . . . *is tolerant/does not accept other people*, substantially less so (Slovak primordialists, SP 49; situationalists, SP 70).

Derived Proposition 11:   Situationalists' acceptance of social ambivalence

Situationalists will accept ambivalence in their understanding of others and social agencies more so than will primordialists.

The Slovak results conformed to this proposition, with Slovak primordialists being more inclined towards evaluatively compatible appraisals of agents in terms of . . . *I don't understand (the designated people)/I understand (the designated people)* (Slovak primordialists, SP 60; situationalists, SP 52). Understanding for primordialists is not a question of intellectually comprehending others, but recognising like-minded thinking in others. Primordialists tend to put a greater premium on understanding like-minded others and not understanding others who think differently. Like-minded others are necessarily those who share the same perspectives on the world – the way life is lived according to their custom and doctrine, and the folklore history of their people. In the Slovak instance, the notion that *those who are widely acknowledged* conformed with *understanding them*, and *those who are not recognised* with *not understanding them* was demonstrated to characterise primordialist thinking: . . . *is widely acknowledged/ . . . is not recognised* (Slovak primordialists, SP 56; situationalists, SP 40).

Derived Proposition 12:   Situationalists' acceptance of contradictions over religious faith

Situationalists more so than primordialists will attest to the contradictions that derive from holding to a firm religious faith in a community where different faiths or denominations of faith are synonymous with sectarian or communal conflict.

In Slovakia where during the communist era religion was officially regarded as an irrelevance, two-thirds of the Slovak academics endorsed having a firm faith in their religion and, compared with Ulster students, all were more prone to conflicted appraisals. Primordialist Slovak academics were nevertheless less inclined to acknowledge such conflicted appraisals than were their situationalist colleagues (Slovak primordialists, SP 36; situationalists, SP 28), as was the case with the more religiously committed Ulster students.

Of the remaining issues represented in the identity instruments, there were only small differences between primordialists and situationalists. *Trustworthiness* was a common core evaluative dimension, designating disliked people as not to be trusted and those approved as being trustworthy (structural pressures ranging from 62 to 76 for Ulster students, 60 and 68 for Slovak academics). *Optimism towards the future* featured with evaluative incompatibilities, which would have been a reflection of the uncertain political future of the province for Ulster students (SP from 30 to 41) and a different kind of political uncertainty for Slovak academics (SP 28, 30). Finally, for Ulster students the issue of the *impact or lack of significance of the designated individuals, peoples and agencies on Ulster* was one of thoroughly conflicted appraisals (SP from − 24 to 11), representing influences alternatively perceived to be detrimental or beneficial in terms of their identity aspirations.

DISCUSSION AND CONCLUSIONS

The study investigated a theoretical formulation of the developmental primacy of primordial sentiments about nationality and ethnicity. These sentiments are conceptualised as being based in children's early identifications with immediate kith and kin, a lineage which from a child's perspective stretches over the inestimable time-scale of generations that seem to have always existed. Lineage provides the context for the experience and construction of one's ethnic identity. As well as the parental generation including uncles and aunts, and one's own generation of brothers, sisters and cousins, the notion of grandparents casts the imagination back into times long before one's own existence to a seeming continuity of ancestry for all time. As for continuity into the future, lineage for the child takes care of itself in the momentous events of new births in the immediate and extended family. Continuity of ancestry stretching back into the ever far distance and forward into the forever future, firmly established experientially by way of childhood identifications, has for the child the quality of existing for all time – *being primordially given*.

A small degree of generalisation from childhood identifications with and primordialist interpretations of the immediate extended family to one's own ethnic community generates the sense of one's ethnic identity. Given the emotional intensity of early identifications and the experienced continuity of kith and kin, children also comprehend *their* community as being emotionally dominant in day-to-day matters and as primordially given. In childhood, people's experience of their ancestral community is thus imbued with an intensely affective sense of primordialism – expressed by way of primordialist sentiments as incorporated using adult language in the Ulster and Slovak identity instruments. Subsequently, some people will develop a comprehension of the contextual and situated aspects of communities and notions of ethnicity and nationality, and give voice to expressions of situationalism – situationalist perspectives featured as contrasts to primordialist sentiments in the study's identity instruments.

Theoretical postulates derived from this conceptualisation of the developmental primacy of primordialist sentiment about ethnicity and nationality guided the Ulster–Slovak cross-cultural investigation and organisation of results. These postulates served several purposes. The first was to validate the conceptualisation of primordialism and situationalism as being pervasive sentiments and perspectives that express fundamentally important orientations to ethnic and national agencies.

Empirical evidence provided strong support for Postulate 1 – *primordialists' and situationalists' political identifications*. Catholic Irish primordialist students idealistically identified with Irish nationalist political parties, as did Protestant British primordialist students with UK unionist parties, more so than did their situationalist counterparts who evinced considerable alienation from Ulster's political parties. Likewise, Slovak primordialist academics idealistically identified with Slovak nationalist political parties more so than did their situationalist counterparts.

The second postulate focused attention on the historical, cultural and individual context of the development of situationalist thinking – *diversified socio-cultural ethos, individual cosmopolitanism and situationalism*. Results demonstrated that Irish culture compared with British culture was perceived to be considerably more primordialist by both Ulster Irish Catholic and British Protestant students, whether situationalists or primordialists. Confirmation of Postulate 2 in respect of socio-cultural ethos was found in the higher proportion of primordialists among the Catholic Irish than among the Protestant British students. The greater propensity of the Catholic Irish towards primordialist sentiments concerning nationality presumably reflected the dominant cultural and doctrinal hegemony of the Roman Catholic Church in Ireland over its community, compared with the emphasis on individual conscience and individuality conveyed by the Protestant Churches. Further confirmation for Postulate 2 was manifest in the small proportion of students endorsing primarily primordialist sentiments who experienced individual cosmopolitanism of migration and mixed allegiances. Less than a quarter of 'cosmopolitans', compared with over a third of Protestant British and over a half of Catholic Irish students, were primordialists.

In cross-cultural support of Postulate 2, the findings for the Slovak academics indicated a socio-cultural ethos of contemporary Slovakia as being substantially more primordialist than that of the Irish. Primordialist academics idealistically and empathetically identified with the overall Slovak ethos more than did situationalist academics. This Slovak ethos was even too primordialist for these moderately primordialist academics who – having noticeable elements of situationalist thinking – identified less with the extreme nationalist Slovak Government than with the Christian Democrats. One reason for this strongly primordialist ethos might be the suppression of public debate during nearly 50 years by a totalitarian regime that, not countenancing ethnic divisions, drove critical awareness underground. That over half of the academics with experience of ethnic issues were situationalists compared with less than a third of those without it demonstrated the contribution of critical awareness to moderating primordialist thinking, and provided further support for Postulate 2 in respect of individual cosmopolitanism.

Postulates 3 – *conflicted identification with cultural ethos* – and 4 – *unproblematic congruity with cultural ethos* – directed attention to the experiential aspects of membership of a cultural ethos when not wholly in tune with it compared with more wholly endorsing it. In the former case, the individual's identification with the people representing the ethos would be conflicted to a problematic degree, while not so in the latter case. Both Ulster Catholic Irish student and Slovak academic situationalists accorded with Postulate 3. Their identification with the primordial ethos of respectively the Irish and Slovak people at large was substantially more conflicted than that of their primordialist counterparts. In the case of Ulster Protestant British, both the situationalists' and primordialists' conflicted identification with the British conformed with Postulate 3 in view of the evidence that the British ethos was perceived to be a muted primordialism – still too primordialist for the situationalists, but too situationalist for the primordialists. The *unproblematic congruity* proposition of Postulate 4 found support in the primordialist Catholic Irish students' low conflicted identification with their national group, and the primordialist Slovak academics' least problematic identification with the Christian Democrat ethos. No unproblematic congruity with cultural ethos was evident for the Protestant British students, whether primordialist or situationalist – a commentary on the status of their identity in the province of Northern Ireland and the UK as a whole.

Postulates 5 – *situationalists' enhanced developmental change in identity* – and 6 – *primordialists' primacy of parental identification* – focus on situationalists' developmental change from the fundamental primacy of primordialist sentiment. Primordialists' continuing adherence to primary sentiment connotes a relatively unchanging self-appraisal and sense of identity, together with little developmental change in their empathetic identification with national and ethnic agencies, remaining instead with those expressing a primordial ethos. Their primary empathetic identification with parents would remain strong. Postulate 5 references the situationalists' evolving awareness of diversity and societal change, during which they moderate their primary primordialist sentiments and overlay them with situationalist perspectives. Postulate 6 referencing primordialists' parental primacy suggests by contrast that situationalists would grow away from empathetically identifying with parents, a proposition that required some amendment in the light of evidence.

Comparing participants' appraisal of self *when fifteen years old* with their *current* self-evaluation provided evidence of ongoing processes of change in identity. In confirmation of Postulate 5, situationalists' progressive developments as appraised from past to current self-evaluation were greater than were primordialists' – marginally so for Catholic Irish students, more so for the Protestant British students and substantially so for Slovak academics. Further confirming Postulate 5, evidence of ongoing resolution of identity diffusion demonstrated greater developmental change in identity in situationalists than primordialists. Additionally, in respect of specific identifications with strongly nationalist agencies, Catholic Irish and Protestant British situationalist students evinced decreasing, contrary to primordialists' increasing, empathetic identification with them.

And again – taking account of the propensities of members of the Slovak Academy – Slovak situationalist academics manifested strongly decreasing empathetic identification with strident nationalist agencies in contrast to their primordialist counterparts, exhibiting only moderately decreasing change.

Concerning Amended Postulate 6 – *primordialists' primacy of parental identification* – two important emphases were incorporated as a result of the findings. Primordialists, contrary to any moderate movement away from parents, increasingly empathetically identified with them, and situationalists, rather than relinquishing empathetic identification with parents, tended to affirm it. In all three ethnic groups primordialists currently empathetically identified with parents more closely than did situationalists, the most substantial difference occurring with the Protestant British students. However, the evidence indicated that parents of primordialists were perceived to be holding congruent primordialist sentiments, and those of situationalists to be expressing compatible situationalist perspectives respectively, this being more emphatically the case for primordialists.

These findings augur three deductions. First, adult primordialists tend towards consolidating primordialist sentiments – a developmentally regressive process – ultimately in a seriously fundamentalist manner if continued relentlessly. Second, parents adopting differing modes of socialisation engender one's identification with – on the one hand – primordialist parents emphasising 'primordialist truths' and – on the other – situationalist parents pursuing 'enlightened realities' about community and nation. Bearing in mind that there are two parents, there is a possibility of mixed socialisation and identification. Third, genetic inheritance of qualities such as curiosity and exploration of diversity prime those who more readily relinquish primary primordial sentiments and develop situationalist perspectives. If this were the case, genetic inheritance and parental socialisation would most likely operate in tandem. In evolutionary terms, curiosity, appreciation and exploration of diversity would have strong potential for the long-term survival of the species. However in the short term, doctrines that consolidate primordialist loyalties would provide primordialists with a basic sense of familiarity and security. This could release them from debilitating anxiety and galvanise them to pursue agendas enhancing their sense of place in the world – to the disadvantage of others who do not fit or who are in the way.

The use of discourses to express identity and appraise the social world indicated fundamental emic variation, which reflected developmental experiences firmly embedded within the different socio-historical and cultural contexts of the three national or ethnic communities. Evidence for Postulate 7 – *consonant discourses as core evaluative dimensions of identity* – validated the use of primordialist and situationalist discourses as denoting core evaluative dimensions of primordialists' and situationalists' identities respectively, when endorsed and expressed in consonance with such identities. Emic variation in the nature of the discourses most representing primordialism and situationalism was strongly apparent.

In general, evidence for Postulate 8 – *discourses representing conflicted arenas of identity* – demonstrated the conflicted nature of those dimensions of identity in instances when *primordialists* endorsed and expressed *dissonant situationalist* discourses, and likewise for instances of *situationalists* in relation to *dissonant primordialist* discourses. Consider *primordialists* first. In the Ulster context, *primordialist* Catholic Irish students endorsed two *situationalist* perspectives ambivalently and some *primordialist* Protestant British students endorsed three *situationalist* perspectives in a conflicted manner. Evidence from the Slovak academics highlighted the prevailing circumstances in Slovakia, as interpreted by the Slovak academics. *Primordialist* Slovak academics endorsed certain *situationalist* perspectives as *core evaluative dimensions of identity*, contrary to Postulate 8. However, their patterns of identification (see earlier) indicated that they were not thoroughgoing grassroots primordialists. Furthermore, the specific situationalist discourses endorsed by them concerned matters that reflected salient facts about the history of the Slovak people and the recent formation of the independent Slovak State.

Turning to consideration of *situationalists, situationalist* Catholic Irish endorsed three and Protestant British students endorsed two *primordialist* sentiments in highly conflicted manner. The firmly committed *situationalist* Slovak academics endorsed only one *primordialist* sentiment, and did so ambivalently. The one primordialist sentiment endorsed without much ambivalence by the situationalist Ulster student groups reflected the historically highly salient sectarian ethos of Northern Ireland – representing the dominant biographical experience in ancestral terms of both ethnicities.

In respect of Postulate 9 – *developmental primacy of and situationalists' residual resonance with primordialist sentiments* – situationalist Ulster students of both persuasions and Slovak academics all demonstrated a propensity to acknowledge some degree of primordialist sentiment. This was most strongly the case for Catholic Irish students, yet even the highly committed situationalist Slovak academics reverberated to one primordialist sentiment. The most obtruding primordialist sentiment affirmed by situationalists featured as a core evaluative dimension of identity in their primordialist counterparts. It concerned lineage, demonstrating the continuing primacy of early identification with kith and kin – formally codified in the derived proposition 9.1: *primordialist obtrusion of lineage*. However, expression of lineage modulated according to historical and cultural context, with dominance given to *ancestors* by Ulster students and *descendants* by Slovak academics – codified in the derived proposition 9.2: *emic expression of lineage in respect of ancestors or descendants*. Primacy of primordialist sentiment was also revealed by the nature of primordialists' adoption of situationalist perspectives such as their *situationalist* acceptance of strangers, who pose no threat to fundamentals of lineage – codified in derived proposition 9.3: *primordialists' endorsement of non-intrusive situationalist social norms*.

The formulation of *derived propositions* corresponds to theory building as outlined in Chapter 2 and Figure 2.4. Proposition 9.2 would postulate primordialist emphasis to be on *ancestors* for old nations – old European nations, China, Japan, India – but on *descendants* in new nations – new Balkan nations, newly independent states of the former Soviet Union. Admixtures of emphasis would be expected in mixed cases such as new nation/old ethnicity, for example, Israel/Judaism. Another three derived propositions further clarified the developmental progression of situationalist from primordialist sentiments. Situationalists compared with primordialists expressed greater tolerance towards different peoples – derived proposition 10: *situationalists' fellowship and tolerance*. They showed more acceptance of ambivalence in their understanding of others and social agencies – derived proposition 11: *situationalists' acceptance of social ambivalence*, and of contradictions in their appraisal of religious faiths and communities in conflict – derived proposition 12: *situationalists' acceptance of contradictions over religious faith*.

Contrary to Lange and Westin's (1985) view that both primordialist and situationalist positions amount to an unnecessary polarisation of inherently complementary aspects of human life, the present theoretical analysis and empirical evidence demonstrate that these positions are not complementary. *Primordialist* sentiments have primacy as the basic lay perspective on nationality or ethnicity deriving from unquestioned primary identifications with one's kith and kin. People may subsequently develop *situationalist* perspectives when on reflection and experience they modify their basic *primordialist* feelings by incorporating elements of *situationalist* interpretations of nation states and migrations of ethnic groups. The two positions, *primordialism* and *situationalism*, are not inherently complementary but represent the developmental primacy of primordialist sentiments subsequently overlaid with situationalist perspectives in those who are prone, or encouraged, to think reflectively about the historical fluidity of nation and migration.

Inevitably, qualities of reflection and understanding will be unevenly distributed. They could vary genetically as inherited human propensities to be curious and appreciate diversity that contribute to evolutionary survival of the species, but they will be strongly influenced by contemporary zeitgeists about ethnic difference – antagonism towards or respect for other ethnic groups and cultures. They will also depend on socialisation practices that foster intolerance or encourage open-minded thinking (Adorno *et al.*, 1950; Rokeach, 1960). Constraints on reflection and understanding will occur when access to knowledge and information is restricted through lack of resource or deliberate political process. In times of threatening social upheaval, when pressing demands of everyday survival dominate, opportunities for reflection will be curtailed. Whatever the genetically inherited propensities, people's adoption of situationalist perspectives will be substantially a function of biographical experience within socio-historical context. In instances when people have developed coherent situationalist ideologies, however, some primordialist sentiments – possibly well camouflaged – will still be likely to obtrude. In situations of great social uncertainty, stress and anxiety, people will be prone to retreat to the developmentally primary perspectives of primordialism. The foregoing analysis of the primacy of primordialist sentiments provides an explanation for the powerfully irrational processes that ensue from time to time in national and ethnic politics. The use of the rhetoric of primordialism in national determination is likely to appeal residually even to convinced situationalists, but will reverberate with emotional intensity in those who have never relinquished primordialism and are subjected to existential uncertainties concerning their place in society.

In a wider sense, the analysis of ethnic phenomena in socio-historical context demands attention to psychological, sociological and social anthropological concerns within an interdisciplinary conceptual framework sensitive to historical developments in which concepts from cognate disciplines may be integrated. Much work will be concerned with elucidating concepts that are at the interfaces between traditionally conceived disciplines. ISA attempts to provide some of the groundwork. The task requires that many established concepts will be reviewed and redefined, as has been done here with *primordialism* and *situationalism*, in order to achieve a more adequate understanding of the phenomena under investigation.

NOTES

1   The Identity Exploration computer software has been continually updated, extended and refined in accordance with rapid developments in computer operating systems (from mainframe to personal computer). A prototype for MS-Windows is currently available from the authors.
2   See Chapter 1 for the theoretical conceptualisation of, and Chapter 2 for the algorithms for, positive and negative structural pressures and summated net structural pressure on a bipolar construct.

REFERENCES

Adorno, T. W., Frenkel-Brunswik, E., Levinson, D. J. and Sanford, R. N (1950) *The Authoritarian Personality*. New York: Harper.
Ali, N. and Northover, M. (1999) 'Distinct identities: South Asian youth in Britain', in J.-C. Lasry, J. Adair and K. Dion (Eds.) *Latest Contributions to Cross-Cultural Psychology* (International Association for Cross-Cultural Psychology). Lisse, The Netherlands: Swets & Zeitlinger.
Connor, W. (1978) 'A nation is a nation, is a state, is an ethnic group, is a . . .', *Ethnic and Racial Studies*, 1: 377–400.
Eller, D. E. and Coughan, R. M. (1993) 'The poverty of primordialism: The demystification of ethnic attachments', *Ethnic and Racial Studies*, 16, 2: 183–202.
Epstein, A. (1978) *Ethos and Identity*. London: Tavistock.
Geertz, C. (1963) 'The integrative revolution: Primordial sentiments and civil politics in the new states', in C. Geertz (Ed.) *Old Societies and New States*. New York: The Free Press.
Glazer, N. and Moynihan, D. (1975) 'Introduction', in N. Glazer, and D. Moynihan (Eds.) *Ethnicity: Theory and Experience*. Cambridge, MA: Harvard University Press.
Greely, A. (1974) *Ethnicity in the United States: A Preliminary Reconnaissance*. New York: Wiley.

Halsey, A. H. (1978) 'Ethnicity: A primordial bond?', *Ethnic and Racial Studies*, 1, 1: 124–8.

Hechter, M. (1974) 'The political economy of ethnic change', *American Journal of Sociology*, 79, 5: 1151–78.

Isaacs, H. (1975) *Idols of the Tribe*. New York: Harper & Row.

Kelly, A. J. D. (1989) 'Ethnic identification, association and redefinition: Muslim Pakistanis and Greek Cypriots in Britain', in K. Liebkind (Ed.) *New Identities in Europe: Immigrant Ancestry and the Ethnic Identity of Youth*, Volume 3 of the European Science Foundation series: 'Studies in European Migration'. London: Gower.

Kirch, M., Kirch, A., Rimm, I. and Tuisk, T. (1997) 'Integration processes in Estonia, 1993–1996', in A. Kirch (Ed.) *The Integration of Non-Estonians into Estonian Society: History, Problems and Trends*. Tallinn: Estonian Academy Publishers.

Lange, A. and Westin, C. (1985) *The Generative Mode of Explanation in Social Psychological Theories of Race and Ethnic Relations*. Stockholm: Centre for Research in International Migration and Ethnicity, University of Stockholm.

Liebkind, K. (Ed.) (1989) *New Identities in Europe: Immigrant Ancestry and the Ethnic Identity of Youth*. Aldershot: Gower.

McKay, J. (1982) 'An exploratory synthesis of primordial mobilizationist approaches to ethnic phenomena', *Ethnic and Racial Studies*, 5, 4: 395–420.

Mitchell, J. C. (1974) 'Perceptions of ethnicity and ethnic behaviour: An empirical exploration', in A. Cohen (Ed.) *Urban Ethnicity*. London: Tavistock.

Nagata, J. (1974) 'What is a Malay? Situational selection of ethnic identity in a plural society', *American Ethnologist*, 1, 2: 331–50.

Northover, M. (1988a) 'Bilinguals and linguistic identities', in J. N. Jorgensen, E. Hansen, A. Holmen and J. Gimbel (Eds.) *Bilingualism in Society and School*. Copenhagen Studies in Bilingualism, Vol. 5. Clevedon: Multilingual Matters.

Northover, M. (1988b) 'Bilinguals or "dual linguistic identities"?', in J. W. Berry and R. C. Annis (Eds.) *Ethnic Psychology* (International Association for Cross-Cultural Psychology). Lisse, The Netherlands: Swets & Zeitlinger.

Northover, M. (2000) 'Bilingualism and ethnicity', in E. Olshtain and G. Horenczyk (Eds.) *Language, Identity and Immigration*. Jerusalem: Magnes Press.

Okamura, J. Y. (1981) 'Situational ethnicity', *Ethnic and Racial Studies*, 4, 4: 452–65.

Rokeach, M. (1960) *The Open and Closed Mind*. New York: Basic Books.

Scott, G. M. (1990) 'A resynthesis of the primordial and circumstantial approaches to ethnic group solidarity: Towards an explanatory model', *Ethnic and Racial Studies* 13, 2: 147–71.

Shils, E. (1957) 'Primordial, personal, sacred and civil ties', *British Journal of Sociology*, 8, 2: 130–45.

Smith, A. D. (1981) *The Ethnic Revival in the Modern World*. Cambridge: Cambridge University Press.

Weber, M. (1948) *The Protestant Ethic and the Spirit of Capitalism* (translated by Talcott Parsons). London: Allen and Unwin. [Originally published in 1930 from the German *Gesammelte Aufsätze zur Religionssozologie*, Tübingen: Mohr, 1920–21.]

Weinreich, P. (1979a) 'Cross-ethnic identification and self-rejection in a black adolescent', in G. Verma and C. Bagley (Eds.) *Race, Education and Identity*. London: Macmillan.

Weinreich, P. (1979b) 'Ethnicity and adolescent identity conflict', in V. Saifullah Khan (Ed.) *Minority Families in Britain*. London: Macmillan.

Weinreich, P. (1980/86/88) *Manual for Identity Exploration using Personal Constructs* (2nd Edn). Coventry: University of Warwick, Economic and Social Research Council, Centre for Research in Ethnic Relations.

Weinreich, P. (1983a) 'Emerging from threatened identities: ethnicity and gender in redefinitions of ethnic identity', in G. M. Breakwell (Ed.) *Threatened Identities*. Chichester: Wiley.

Weinreich, P. (1983b) 'Psychodynamics of personal and social identity: Theoretical concepts and their measurement', in A. Jacobson-Widding (Ed.) *Identity: Personal and Socio-cultural*. Stockholm: Almqvist & Wiksell International.

Weinreich, P. (1986b) 'Identity development in migrant offspring: Theory and practice', in L.II. Ekstrand (Ed.) *Ethnic Minorities and Immigrants in a Cross-Cultural Perspective* (International Association for Cross-Cultural Psychology). Lisse, The Netherlands: Swets & Zeitlinger.

Weinreich, P. (1998) 'Social exclusion and multiple identities', *Soundings: A Journal of Politics and Culture*, 9: 139–44.

Weinreich, P. (1999) 'Ethnic identity and enculturation/acculturation', in J.-C. Lasry, J. Adair and K. Dion (Eds.) *Latest Contributions to Cross-Cultural Psychology* (International Association for Cross-Cultural Psychology). Lisse, The Netherlands: Swets & Zeitlinger.

Weinreich, P. (2000) 'Ethnic identity and "acculturation": Ethnic stereotyping and identification, self-esteem and identity diffusion in a multicultural context', in E. Olshtain and G. Horenczyk (Eds.) *Language, Identity and Immigration*. Jerusalem: Magnes Press.

Weinreich, P., Bacova, V. and Rougier, N. (1997) *'Primordial and Situational Ethnic Identity: Political identification in Northern Ireland and Slovakia*. Fifth European Congress of Psychology, 6–11 July, Dublin.

Weinreich, P. and Ewart, S. (1999a) *IDEXbasic for Windows Version 3.0: Identity Exploration Computer Software for Idiographic, Basic Case Studies*. Jordanstown: University of Ulster School of Psychology.

Weinreich, P. and Ewart, S. (1999b) *IDEXnomo for Windows Version 3.0: Identity Exploration Computer Software for Nomothetic, Comparative Studies*. Jordanstown: University of Ulster School of Psychology.

Weinreich, P., Kelly, A. J. D. and Maja, C. (1987) 'Situated identities, conflicts in identification and own group preference: Rural and urban youth in South Africa', in C. Kagitcibasi (Ed.) *Growth and Progress in Cross-Cultural Psychology*, pp. 321–35 (International Association for Cross-Cultural Psychology). Lisse, The Netherlands: Swets & Zeitlinger.

Weinreich, P., Kelly, A. J. D. and Maja, C. (1988) 'Black youth in South Africa: Situated identities and patterns of ethnic identification', in D. Canter, C. Jesuino, L. Soczka and G. Stephenson (Eds.) *Environmental Social Psychology* (NATO Advanced Research Workshop). Dordrecht, The Netherlands: Kluwer Academic.

Weinreich, P., Luk, C. L. and Bond, M. (1996) 'Ethnic stereotyping and identification in a multicultural context: "Acculturation", self-esteem and identity diffusion in Hong Kong Chinese university students', *Psychology and Developing Societies*, 8: 107–69.

4 Complex patterns of cultural allegiances: The ethnic identity of Palestinian Christian Arab adolescents in Israel

Gabriel Horenczyk and Salim Munayer

M. lives in a large city in the north of Israel. He defines himself as a Palestinian Christian Arab with Israeli citizenship. As a Palestinian, he shares the fate of his people in Israel, in the West Bank, and in the Palestinian Diaspora, striving for some type of national self-determination. As a Christian, M. is historically and theologically connected to Christians all over the world, and especially to Christianity in the Western world. On the other hand, M. speaks the Arab language and considers himself part of the Arab culture, particularly of the local Arab culture, shared by Muslim and Christian Arabs. M. also holds Israeli citizenship; he has many Israeli Jewish neighbours, is quite fluent in the Hebrew language, and is attracted to many aspects of Israeli Western lifestyle. Such a combination of cultural allegiances would seem to lead almost inevitably to considerable tension and conflict. But it could also contribute to the development of a rich multicultural identity, which would provide M. with 'groundedness' (LaFromboise, Coleman, & Gerton, 1993) in multiple societies and access to a larger variety of material, cultural, and normative resources. As recently indicated by Weinreich (2000, p. 32), 'People of an ethnicity growing up in circumstances where alternative ethnic groups are salient have the opportunity to identify with elements of the alternative life-styles and world views represented by these groups. Some such partial cross-ethnic identifications may serve to generate updated confident conceptions of one's own ethnic identity, whereas other such identifications may result in conflicted ethnic identifications and identity diffusion.'

Most sociological and psychological approaches to the study of ethnic identity seem largely unequipped for the difficult task of describing and understanding the complex identity of Palestinian Christian Arabs in Israel. It has been claimed that serious conceptual and methodological problems affect the study of ethnic and national identities (Lange & Westin, 1985). Reviews of research on ethnic identity within social and developmental psychology (Liebkind, 1992; Phinney, 1990) portray a wide, rich, but often confused picture of theories, methodologies, and findings. This state of affairs has been attributed in part to insufficient interaction between the various disciplines engaged in the study of national and ethnic phenomena, and a crossing of disciplinary boundaries – mainly psychology, sociology, and anthropology – has been proposed as necessary in order to achieve a comprehensive understanding of ethnic identity processes (Liebkind, 1992).

Despite the vagueness and ambiguity of the concept, ethnic identity can be consensually conceptualised as a multidimensional construct that relates to the individual's identity, or sense of self, in ethnic terms – i.e., in terms of membership in a subgroup within the larger society that claims a common ancestry and shares one or more of the following elements: culture, race, religion, language, kinship, and place of origin (Phinney, Horenczyk, Liebkind, & Vedder, 2001). Contemporary analyses of ethnic identity stress the dynamic and contextual nature of ethnic identity and identification (Horenczyk & Bekerman, 1999; Nagel, 1994). Within these perspectives, great importance is placed on the social and individual construction of ethnicity and ethnic identity. Ferdman and Horenczyk (2000) conceptualised cultural identity as one's individual image of the behaviours, beliefs, values, and norms – in short, the cultural features – that characterise one's group(s), together with one's feelings about those features and one's understanding of how they are (or are not) reflected in oneself. This focus on the individual's construction of his or her cultural group(s) reflects the need to take into account not only between-group differences in cultural features, but also important within-group variations in cultural characteristics and perceptions.

The Identity Structure Analysis (ISA) conceptual framework developed by Weinreich (1989) also assigns central importance to construal processes and contextual influences in the definition and redefinition of self in general, and of ethnic identity in particular. It is a socio-developmental, psychological approach to people's identity formation, which emphasises the person's biographical development as it is situated in socio-historical contexts. Within this conceptualisation, 'ethnic identity is defined as that part of the totality of one's self-construal made up of those dimensions that express the continuity between one's construal of past ancestry and one's future aspirations in relation to ethnicity' (Weinreich, 1986, p. 308). This self-construal is conceived as a dynamic process, which is context-dependent: A central notion within ISA theory is that of 'situated identities' which refer to the different identity states with which people operate when social contexts change and from which they pursue different kinds of action.

In plural societies, minority individuals have to continuously define and redefine their cultural identities within the complex tapestry of ingroup and outgroup cultures. As indicated by Weinreich (1989) the make-up of their identities generally contains elements of identification that cross 'ethnic boundaries'. Considerable research in the area of acculturation (for reviews, see: Berry, 1997; Ward, 1996), has focused on the interplay between the individual's attachment to his or her minority/original culture and his or her attitude towards – and involvement with – the dominant culture (Berry, Kim, Power, Young, & Bujaki, 1989; LaFromboise et al., 1993). Within this tradition, both minority and majority cultures are usually conceived in rather monolithic ways, failing to take into account the diversity in each of them. It is not uncommon for minority individuals to be faced with demands originating from a variety of minority cultures and sets of norms. Quite often, minority individuals have also to react, and accommodate, to more than one majority society (Ferdman & Horenczyk, 2000). A more complete understanding of such types of ethnic minority identity calls for conceptualisations and methodologies designed to map and explore the intricate and at times conflicted nature of these cultural identifications. This approach is certainly needed for Christian Arabs in Israel. They are, as succinctly put by Rossing (1999), 'a double minority: Arabs in the midst of the majority Jewish population of Israel, Christians within Israel's dominantly Muslim Arab society' (p. 28).

This chapter reports findings from a study that employed Identity Structure Analysis, as part of a larger research project aimed at exploring in a multifaceted way the ethnic identity of Palestinian Arab Christian youth. First, we will provide the reader with brief historical, demographic, and socio-economic contextual information showing the unique position of Palestinian Christian Arabs within the complex tapestry of Israeli society. We will then present the main results from the studies that preceded the ISA investigation, and comprised relatively large samples of respondents. ISA was finally used in order to examine in depth the richness of the ethnic identity and to further explore issues that arose during the first stages of the research project.

PALESTINIAN CHRISTIAN ARABS IN ISRAEL

As the original wellspring of Christianity, the Holy Land has the most ancient Christian community in the world. By the time of the first Muslim conquest in AD 638, the Christian community, although divided, maintained a single Patriarch in Jerusalem (O'Mahony, 1995). In later centuries, differences between the various communities became too great, and each church developed its own institutions, and pursued its own relationship with the ruling authorities.

The Ottomans developed and established what was known as the 'millet' system of recognition (and taxation) of ethnic communities (Lewis, 1996), which provided a measure of autonomy for non-Muslim minorities. Eventually, the Ottomans granted millet status to four churches, which gave them some autonomy in terms of personal status and religious issues, but encouraged both fractiousness and corruption among Christians. At the beginning of the 19th century, Christians in the Holy Land numbered between 13,000 and 16,000 (Colbi, 1988). Four-fifths of these belonged to the Greek Orthodox church, who have traditionally viewed their main function in the Holy Land as protectors and keepers of the holy sites. Other churches that played an important role in Christian life during the last decades of Ottoman rule were the Russian Orthodox and Latin Catholic, and by the mid-1840s, the Anglican church had also gained a foothold in Palestine.

Under British rule (between the years 1917 and 1947), the Christian population, in comparison with other religious groups in Palestine, increased substantially (Al-Haj, 1998). The 1922 census reported 71,000 Christians; nine years later, their number reached 90,000 (Colbi, 1969). The British kept many elements of the Turkish millet system, as the administrative status quo, and expanded its application, so that by 1939, nine churches constituted the recognised religious communities, which maintained their own religious court systems.

The State of Israel's Declaration of Independence guaranteed freedom of religion for all denominations. However, there is no Israeli constitution and therefore no means of regulating religious law. As a result, the Turkish millet system, perpetuated during the British Mandate, was largely adopted by Israeli authorities: Ten Christian communities enjoy the official status of 'recognised community', although today its only practical significance is the right to establish a religious court with jurisdiction over the community's members in matters of personal status and family law (Rossing, 1999).

According to recent figures (*Statistical Abstract of Israel*, 1998), Christians constitute approximately 2.14% of the total population in Israel, and 11.7% of the non-Jewish population. However the growth rate of the Christian communities is significantly lower as compared both to Jews and to Muslims. This gradual decline is attributed to a variety of factors: Statistics reveal that, as a group, Christians in Israel tend to marry late, and couples have fewer children. In addition, large numbers of Christian Arabs have emigrated since the establishment of the State of Israel.

In terms of educational and socio-economic status, Palestinian Arab Christians are located somewhere between the two major populations: Jews and Muslims. The proportion of Christian youth obtaining high-school diplomas is relatively high, and even surpasses slightly the rate among Jewish Israeli pupils. This achievement does not follow into higher education: Approximately 9% of the Christian population complete some sort of academic degree, as compared to 15% in the Jewish population, and only 4.5% among Muslim Arabs. Economic indices of income and employment also show that the Christian community lags considerably behind the Jewish majority; the socio-economic situation of the Arab Christian population, however, is significantly better than that of Arab Muslims.

The ethnic identity of Palestinian Arab Christian adolescents in Israel

In the first phases of the research project (Munayer, 2000) aspects of the Palestinian Arab Christian ethnic identity were examined using a variety of instruments: questionnaires measuring acculturation attitudes (Berry *et al.*, 1989) with regard both to the Jewish and Muslim majority societies and cultures, as well as perceived acculturation expectations (Horenczyk, 1996); the Multigroup Ethnic Identity Measure (Phinney, 1992) assessing ethnic identity development; and a questionnaire designed to explore the respondents' construction of cultural groups in terms of values.

The results showed that Palestinian Arab Christian adolescents wish to maintain their minority identity: their preferred acculturation attitude vis-à-vis the Jewish society is one of integration (positive attitude towards both minority and majority culture), and separation (positive attitude towards minority and negative towards majority) with regard to the Muslim majority. They seem also to perceive both Jews and Muslims as expecting them to weaken their ethnic identity and to assimilate to majority culture. Findings also suggest that the Christian youngsters have privately a more positive identification with their ethnic group, as compared to the extent to which this cultural affiliation is expressed publicly. Multidimensional Scaling procedures performed on the data obtained from the questionnaire examining the construction of group cultures revealed that the Christian adolescents see their culture as distinct from the Jewish and Muslim cultures; they perceive the Jewish and Western cultures as highly similar, a finding that may partially explain their relatively high willingness to integrate aspects of Jewish culture in their cultural identity.

THE ISA STUDY

In the final phase of the research project, an ISA instrument was administered to a small group of respondents in order to examine in a detailed and comprehensive way the cultural identifications of Palestinian Arab Christian adolescents in Israel. Since its inception, the study of ethnic identity has been one of the central foci of ISA (Weinreich, 1983, 1989) and many studies have employed ISA conceptualisations and methodology to explore ethnic identity processes among a variety of cultural groups (e.g., Kelly, 1989; Weinreich, Luk, & Bond, 1996). Our sample included six female and four male Palestinian Arab Christians living in Israel, between the ages of 15 and 18. Questionnaires were administered individually and responses were anonymous.

The ISA identity instrument used in this study was custom-designed for this research and was based on a in-depth understanding of cultural features central to the population under study and to the major research questions addressed by our investigation. As stated by Weinreich (2000), the customisation of the instruments is aimed at allowing respondents to appraise themselves, relevant significant others, and representatives of ethnic, cultural, and national groups by means of *bipolar constructs* that are meaningful to the population from which the respondents derive (the targets of appraisal are collectively termed *entities*). The entities and constructs were selected on the basis of preliminary informal interviews with representatives of the population under study, and also following previous ISA research on issues related to ethnic identity and acculturation. Tables 4.1 and 4.2 present the lists of entities and constructs included in our identity instrument.

The identity instrument employed in our study was printed in Arabic, and consisted of 19 pages, each corresponding to a different construct. The bipolar construct appeared at the top of each page, below which were listed the 21 entities (to the right – Arabic is written from right to left) each followed by a nine-point scale. The bi-directional centre-zero rating scales (4-3-2-1-0-1-2-3-4) made no *a priori* assumptions of favourable or unfavourable connotations associated with either scale end. The evaluative connotations associated with the poles of the constructs given by each individual were determined independently with respect to the aspirational self ('Me I as would like to be' or proxies).

Identity structure analysis

We will first present results from preliminary nomothetic analyses performed on the data obtained from our ten respondents. These results show some interesting

Table 4.1 Israeli Arab Christian identity instrument: Entries

Category	No.	Entity
Mandatory entities	1	Me as I am now ('current self')
	2	Me as I would like to be ('ideal self')
	3	Someone I admire
	4	Someone I dislike
Representatives of	7	Palestinian Arab Christian in Israel
cultural groups	8	Palestinian Arab Muslim in Israel
	9	Israeli Jew in Israel
	16	Druze in Israel
	19	Arab Christian in Jordan
	20	American Christian
	10	Local church leader
	11	Local Muslim leader
	12	Local Jewish leader
	13	Christian participating in church activities
	14	Muslim participating in Islamic activities
	15	Jew participating in religious activities
Family and close friends	17	My father
	18	My mother
	21	Best friend
Metaperspectives of self	5	Me in the eyes of Palestinian Arab Muslims
	6	Me in the eyes of Israeli Jews

general patterns that provide us with preliminary valuable insights on the complexity of the ethnic and cultural identities of Palestinian Arab Christian adolescents in Israel. We will then proceed to more detailed idiographic analyses of four selected respondents, each exhibiting a different and revealing pattern of cultural identities and affiliations. All individual and group indices were computed by the IDEX (Identity Exploration) software (Weinreich & Ewart, 1999).

Table 4.3 presents the means – across the ten respondents who completed ISA instruments – of the three main indices for self and the various cultural entities (including metaperspectives on self): evaluation of the entities, empathetic identification with the entities, and idealistic-identification with each of them.

Evaluation of entities

Within ISA, a person's evaluation of a given entity is defined as one's overall assessment of that entity in terms of the positive and negative evaluative connotations of the attributes one construes in that entity, in accordance with one's value system. Theoretical ranges of evaluation indices are from -1 to $+1$, with high values reflecting positive evaluation of entity.

The evaluation patterns obtained in our sample suggest, first, that Arab Palestinian Christians in Israel hold a distinctive, clear, and positive religious identity. All Christian entities are evaluated favourably: Their means range from

Table 4.2   Israeli Arab Christian identity instrument: Constructs

Left pole	*Right pole*
Not affected by the past	Affected by the past
Not religious	Religious
Feels secure	Feels threatened
Not truthful	Truthful
Doesn't live according to spiritual values	Lives according to spiritual values
Open-minded	Closed-minded
Untrustworthy	Trustworthy
Doesn't think it is important to speak the mother tongue	Thinks it is important to speak the mother tongue
Thinks that minority members should socialise only among themselves	Doesn't think that minority members should socialise only among themselves
Humble	Arrogant
Not modern	Modern
Thinks it is important for a person to have nationalistic feelings	Doesn't think it is important for a person to have nationalistic feelings
Doesn't think it is important to have relations with people from other religions	Thinks it is important to have relations with people from other religions
Not interested in Arabic cultural values	Interested in Arabic cultural values
Doesn't respect parents and family	Respects parents and family
Loves peace	Doesn't love peace
Would like to marry someone from another religion	Believes one should marry a person from own religion only
Believes in equality between genders	Doesn't believe in equality between the genders
Doesn't believe that the minority needs to accommodate to the majority	Believes that the minority needs to accommodate to the majority

0.54 to 0.66; thus, these evaluations can be considered as 'upper moderate', according to Weinreich's (1992) suggested cut-off points. The evaluations of all Jewish and Muslim entities, on the other hand, fall in the 'low' category, following Weinreich's suggested criteria, with the Jewish entities receiving slightly lower evaluations than the Muslim ones. It should be noted that the Christian non-Israeli entities are evaluated as favourably as the Christian Israeli entities. T-tests performed on all the pairs among the evaluations of entities confirmed these patterns: (a) All the differences between Christian and non-Christian entities were found to be statistically significant (even after adopting a stringent alpha value of 0.01); (b) None of the differences among the non-Christian entities was found to be statistically significant; and (c) None of the differences among the Christian (Israeli and non-Israeli) entities was found to be significant.

In order to examine further the structure of the respondents' social and cultural worlds, as they are reflected in their evaluations of central entities within those worlds, we submitted the individual indices of evaluations of the cultural entities[1] to hierarchical cluster analysis. Cluster analysis is a statistical technique aimed at grouping respondents or variables (in our case, entities as evaluated by the respondents), such that items falling in the same cluster are much like one another

Table 4.3 Evaluation of entities, empathetic and idealistic-identification with entities

Entity	No.	Evaluation −1.00 to 1.00	Empathetic identification 0.00 to 1.00	Idealistic-identification 0.00 to 1.00
Christian entities				
Palestinian Arab Christian in Israel	7	0.61	0.84	0.82
Local church leader	10	0.63	0.78	0.79
Christian participating in church activities	13	0.59	0.76	0.75
Arab Christian in Jordan	19	0.66	0.63	0.64
American Christian	20	0.54	0.61	0.63
Muslim entities				
Palestinian Arab Muslim in Israel	8	0.20	0.59	0.58
Local Muslim leader	11	0.24	0.58	0.60
Muslim participating in Islamic activities	14	0.17	0.52	0.53
Jewish entities				
Israeli Jew in Israel	9	0.05	0.48	0.49
Local Jewish leader	12	0.15	0.56	0.58
Jew participating in Jewish activities	15	0.09	0.51	0.52
Druze in Israel	16	0.10	0.51	0.51

n = 10

and different from items in other clusters. Hierarchical cluster analysis (HCA) forms clusters in a series of stages where the entire set of items is successively divided into smaller and smaller clusters. Figure 4.1 depicts the HCA dendogram obtained for the evaluations of entities, using the agglomerative algorithm of Average Linkage between Groups. The dendogram is a tree graph; the hierarchical clustering process is reflected in the branching of the tree starting at the right, yielding the final clusters at the left of the tree.

The two dividing lines superimposed by us on the dendogram provide us with an interesting and rich picture of the intra- and inter-group categorisations among our respondents. An examination of the branching sequence reveals that the primary division is between the Christian entities (#13, #19, #10, #7, and #20 – see earlier) and all the other entities (Jews, Muslims, and Druze). As previously shown in Table 4.1, these are the highly evaluated entities. Within the Christian cluster, however, a subdivision is made between Christians in America (# 20) and all the other (Middle-Eastern) Christians.

The non-Christian large cluster can be tentatively interpreted as including all the entities evaluated as 'the others' by our Arab Christian respondents. It is clearly divided into two major subclusters: the Muslim subcluster (comprising entities # 8, #11, and #14) and the Jewish subcluster (entities #9, #12, and #15).

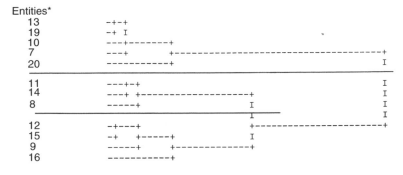

Figure 4.1 Hierarchical cluster analysis dendogram – evaluations of entities (*see Table 4.1 for corresponding entities).

Interestingly, the Druze entity (#16) is classified as part of the 'Jewish' cluster, although as a separate branch; this seems to reflect the political and rhetorical Israeli view of the Druze as 'allies' of the Jewish population in Israel (unlike most Arabs, for example, the vast majority of Druze serve in the Israeli army). It is important to note that in many other Middle-Eastern societies, Druze are not perceived (by themselves and by others) as separate from the Arab people, and that this distinct social categorisation is nowadays being challenged by many Israeli Druze (see, for example, Firro, 1999).

Identification – empathetic and idealistic

ISA conceptualisation and methodology distinguishes between two major types of identification: empathetic and idealistic. Empathetic identification indices provide measures of perceived similarity between self and the various entities, and reflect the degree of similarity between the qualities one attributes to each entity, whether 'good' or 'bad', and those of one's self-image. Idealistic-identification refers to the extent to which entities are perceived as positive role models and reference groups. Indices of idealistic-identification provide measures of aspirational identification and are defined as the degree of similarity between the qualities one attributes to each entity and those one would like to possess as part of one's ideal self-image.

The results on identification presented earlier in Table 4.3 show – at the general and undifferentiated group level – a striking similarity between the patterns and the mean scores obtained for the two types of identification – empathetic and idealistic. In other words, our respondents tend to perceive themselves as similar to representatives of those cultural groups that are perceived as positive reference groups, and dissimilar to those groups that score lower on indices of aspirational identification. Within the ISA framework, this suggests few identification conflicts among our respondents. However, as we will see later, interesting identification conflicts do emerge from the idiographic analyses of individual respondents.

We again submitted the individual scores on empathetic and idealistic-identifications with the various cultural entities to HCA. Not surprisingly, the two dendograms (Figures 4.2 and 4.3) are highly similar. We would like to stress once more that the dendograms are presented primarily as visual aids for the understanding of the complex cultural identity of our respondents.

The patterns of identification depicted in these dendograms provide us with an additional insight on the role of religion and 'locality' in the ethnic identity of Palestinian Arab Christians in Israel. As shown by the dividing lines superimposed by us on the dendogram, Christian entities (#7, #10, and #13) are clearly already separated from all the other entities at a very early branching of the trees. Unlike the evaluation of entities, the Christian identification clusters no longer include the non-local Christian entities, namely the Arab Christian in Jordan (#19) and the Christian in America (#20). These two entities are included, although as clearly separate clusters, within the 'other' large cluster in both empathetic and idealistic-identification dendograms. An examination of the identification scores

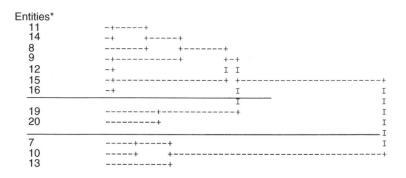

Figure 4.2 Hierarchical cluster analysis dendogram – empathetic identifications (*see Table 4.1 for corresponding entities).

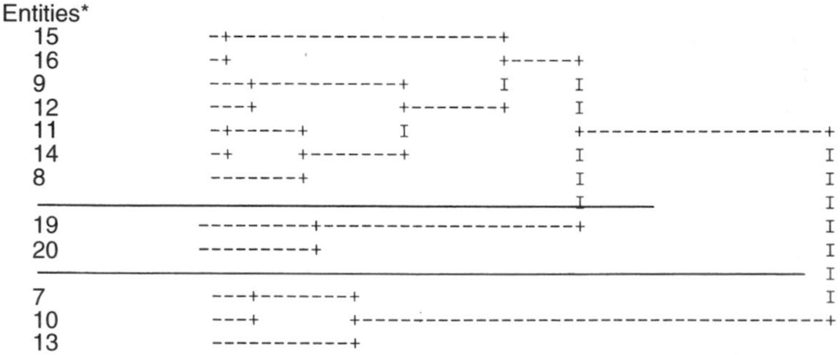

Figure 4.3   Hierarchical cluster analysis dendogram – idealistic-identifications (*see Table 4.1 for corresponding entities).

(both empathetic and idealistic) presented earlier in Table 4.3 suggests that respondents identify with Christian 'local' entities to a high degree, following Weinreich's (1992) cut-off criteria, but the identification scores of the 'non-local' Christian entities fall within the moderate range. We can tentatively suggest that whereas religion serves as the major criterion for evaluation of entities, regardless of locality, aspects related to the local scene and local culture seem to play an important role in the individual's identification with the entities (be it perceived similarity or aspirational identification), in addition to the important religious factor.

Within this 'other' major cluster, Arab Muslims entities (#8, #11, and #14) still compose a distinct subcluster. The Druze entity (#16) is, in these two dendograms, totally undifferentiated within the Israeli Jewish entities. The mean scores presented in Table 4.3 suggest that the levels of identification with all the non-Christian entities are on the low–moderate range, according to Weinreich's (1992) criteria.

An interesting additional finding emerged from the results obtained using the ISA instrument. One could predict that the respondents, who define themselves as Christian believers, would find some 'common ground' with religious representatives of the other cultural groups (Muslims and Jews). It seems, however, that religiosity, unlike religion, is not used as a criterion either for the evaluation of entities or for the identification (empathetic or idealistic) with them. This preliminary conclusion is based on the consistent pattern showing no differences between the religious representatives of the various cultural groups and those not defined as religious in the mean scores of evaluation and identification; moreover, religious and non-religious entities are not differentiated within the cluster structure in any of the three dendograms. It would seem that in this divided and ethnically troubled region, religious–ethnic definitions are so powerful and preemptive, that other cross-cutting criteria have little chance to be used for social construction and categorisation.

Idiographic analyses

We will now briefly present four idiographic analyses showing the variability as well as the complexity of cultural identity among Palestinian Arab Christian adolescents in Israel. We chose, out of the ten respondents included in our study, four adolescents (respondents 1, 4, 7, and 8) showing different 'identity variants' (a construct somewhat akin to Marcia's, 1980, identity statuses but – according to Weinreich – taken more faithfully from Erikson's original formulations), as they were computed by the IDEX software. Respondents 1, 4, and 7 are females, and respondent 8 is a male adolescent. Tables 4.4, 4.5, and 4.6 display the scores of these four respondents on indices reflecting evaluation of entities, identification (idealistic, empathetic, and identification conflicts), and structural pressure on constructs. The analysis of the emerging patterns will focus almost exclusively on those entities included in the ISA instrument related to cultural and ethnic affiliations (both in-group and out-group figures).

Table 4.4 Evaluation of entities – four selected respondents

Entities			Evaluation of entities (scale: −1.00 to +1.00)			
Respondent	No.	1	4	7	8
Christian entities						
Palestinian Arab Christian in Israel	7	0.57	0.77	0.52	0.56
Local church leader	10	0.57	0.92	0.28	0.60
Christian participating in church activities	13	0.58	0.89	0.65	0.61
Arab Christian in Jordan	19	0.64	0.78	0.76	0.61
American Christian	20	0.83	0.13	0.54	0.23
Muslim entities						
Palestinian Arab Muslim in Israel	8	−0.01	0.58	0.10	0.54
Local Muslim leader	11	−0.08	0.72	−0.24	0.23
Muslim participating in Islamic activities	14	0.19	0.30	−0.28	0.16
Jewish entities						
Israeli Jew in Israel	9	−0.30	−0.50	0.08	0.39
Local Jewish leader	12	−0.08	−0.33	−0.07	0.46
Jew participating in Jewish activities	15	−0.03	−0.45	−0.28	0.20
Druze in Israel	16	0.07	−0.73	0.04	−0.30
Metaperspectives						
Me as Palestinian Arab Muslims see me	5	0.25	0.58	−0.34	0.38
Me as Israeli Jews see me	6	0.01	−0.18	0.39	0.48

Respondent 1: A case of identity diffusion

This respondent shows relatively high positive evaluation of the Christian entities. Interestingly, her highest evaluations are of those Christian entities residing outside Israel (Jordanian Christians and American Christians). Muslim and Jewish entities are negatively evaluated (although somewhat higher evaluations were obtained for the religious Muslims).

When examining her identification scores (idealistic and empathetic), we find that the pattern slightly changes. She still exhibits high levels of identification with Christian entities, but now it is the 'local' entities who score higher as compared to the Christians outside Israel. It would seem that locality affects her identification with the figures more than her general evaluations of them. Identification with Muslim and Jewish entities is low, although somewhat higher when the out-group entity is described as participating in religious activities.

Her highest (most problematic) identification conflicts are with Palestinian Arab Muslims, Israeli Jews, local Muslim and Jewish leader, and Jews taking part in religious activities. She has also quite substantial identification conflicts with other cultural entities. She also does not empathetically identify very closely with

Table 4.5 ISA identification indices – four selected respondents

Entities	Respondent	No.	Idealistic-identification (scale: 0.00 to 1.00)				Empathetic identification (scale: 0.00 to 1.00)				Identification conflicts (scale: 0.00 to 1.00)			
			1	4	7	8	1	4	7	8	1	4	7	8
Christian entities														
Palestinian Arab Christian in Israel	7		0.78	0.89	0.78	0.89	0.89	0.89	0.89	0.89	0.44	0.23	0.44	0.31
Local church leader	10		0.72	0.83	0.44	0.89	0.72	0.83	0.56	0.89	0.35	0.00	0.35	0.31
Christian participating in church activities	13		0.78	1.00	0.72	0.89	0.78	1.00	0.83	0.89	0.36	0.00	0.30	0.31
Arab Christian in Jordan	19		0.61	0.72	0.33	0.33	0.61	0.72	0.39	0.33	0.26	0.28	0.15	0.14
American Christian	20		0.61	0.39	0.44	0.50	0.61	0.39	0.44	0.50	0.26	0.36	0.27	0.33
Muslim entities														
Palestinian Arab Muslim in Israel	8		0.44	0.67	0.56	0.78	0.56	0.67	0.56	0.78	0.56	0.38	0.47	0.41
Local Muslim leader	11		0.39	0.78	0.33	0.61	0.39	0.78	0.33	0.61	0.47	0.29	0.38	0.49
Muslim participating in Islamic activities	14		0.56	0.61	0.22	0.44	0.50	0.61	0.33	0.44	0.41	0.45	0.38	0.44
Jewish entities														
Israeli Jew in Israel	9		0.28	0.22	0.56	0.72	0.39	0.22	0.44	0.72	0.53	0.38	0.44	0.40
Local Jewish leader	12		0.39	0.33	0.50	0.83	0.39	0.33	0.39	0.83	0.47	0.45	0.41	0.38
Jew participating in Jewish activities	15		0.50	0.22	0.33	0.50	0.50	0.22	0.33	0.50	0.47	0.40	0.43	0.44
Druze in Israel	16		0.44	0.06	0.39	0.33	0.44	0.06	0.39	0.33	0.44	0.18	0.36	0.43
Metaperspectives														
Me as Palestinian Arab Muslims see me	5		0.50	0.78	0.28	0.78	0.61	0.78	0.28	0.78	0.49	0.29	0.37	0.41
Me as Israeli Jews see me	6		0.56	0.39	0.56	0.72	0.67	0.39	0.56	0.72	0.54	0.44	0.31	0.35

Table 4.6   Structural pressure on constructs – four selected respondents

Construct (left pole*)		Structural pressure (scale: −100 to +100)			
	Respondent	1	4	7	8
Not affected by the past	1	**	**	**	**
Not religious	2	−07.00	35.67	50.52	−03.55
Feels secure	3	−13.82	43.43	−01.33	72.61
Not truthful	4	68.56	88.85	34.83	58.70
Doesn't live according to spiritual values	5	55.86	75.69	51.15	61.83
Open-minded	6	53.03	52.42	61.67	48.54
Untrustworthy	7	60.29	72.20	54.87	56.75
Doesn't think it is important to speak the mother tongue	8	15.06	100.00	45.79	82.45
Thinks that minority members should socialise only among themselves	9	−04.28	76.79	33.60	86.24
Humble	10	56.47	47.09	−27.77	−09.23
Not modern	11	38.20	70.82	46.70	−06.29
Thinks it is important for a person to have nationalistic feelings	12	48.29	64.39	51.01	64.92
Doesn't think it is important to have relations with people from other religions	13	41.73	63.84	39.72	46.76
Not interested in Arabic cultural values	14	26.09	92.40	48.74	45.24
Doesn't respect parents and family	15	46.83	77.73	78.72	70.61
Loves peace	16	56.48	69.69	83.00	82.25
Would like to marry someone from another religion	17	65.04	66.51	−17.87	75.94
Believes in equality between genders	18	51.07	56.05	67.34	54.90
Doesn't believe that the minority needs to accommodate to the majority	19	39.62	54.29	24.90	78.89

* For the right pole of constructs, see Table 4.2: The polarity of each construct for each respondent is not given here, but see text for appropriate interpretations.

either the way Palestinian Muslims or Israeli Jews see her, having conflicting identifications with metaperspectives of self as derived from both Muslim and Jewish communities. These patterns contribute to her state of identity diffusion, as reflected in her identity variant calculated by IDEX.

Structural pressure on constructs relates to the manner in which the individual uses the constructs to appraise the social world of significant others and groups represented in the ISA instrument. The discourses (constructs) he or she uses to appraise self and others with a high degree of cognitive–affective compatibility are associated with high structural pressures and constitute core evaluative dimensions of identity. Others, of which his or her use entails considerable cognitive–affective incompatibilities such that structural pressures on them are low, are by contrast conflicted dimensions of identity.

Her variant of identity diffusion is also reflected in the absence of constructs with high structural pressure. Conflicted appraisals, indicated by low structural pressures, are associated with 'Feels secure–feels threatened', 'thinks/doesn't think it's important to speak the original language', and 'thinks/doesn't think that a minority should mingle only with themselves'. For this Palestinian Arab Christian in the Israeli context, these conflicted dimensions of her identity seem to reveal problematic features concerning security and minority group endorsement of remaining within the language and community boundaries of the group.

Respondent 4: A case of defensive high self-regard

This female respondent is classified by ISA as exhibiting an identity variant of 'defensive high self-regard' which, in her case, characterises her as being a highly nationalistic Arab with strong ideological and cultural views. She evaluates highly all Christian entities, except for the only non-Arab Christian figure, namely the American Christian. Muslim (also Arab) entities also receive relatively high evaluations, although the religious Muslim falls behind. Jewish and Druze entities are negatively evaluated. A similar pattern emerges from the table showing scores on identification indices: the respondent identifies highly (both idealistically and empathetically) with the Arab entities, Christian and Muslim almost alike, whereas identification with Jewish entities is low. This pattern of 'Arab unity' is also reflected in the findings regarding metaperspectives of self: The respondent identifies closely with the ways in which her Arab Muslim counterparts see her, but not with the ways in which Jewish Israelis see her. Her conflicted identification with the latter Jewish-based metaperspective is quite high. Given her rather dichotomous appraisals of strong positive role models (primarily Arab figures) and negative ones (Jews and Druze), with low empathetic identification with the latter, she has few conflicted identifications.

The findings related to structural pressures on constructs reinforce our view of this respondent as strongly 'Arab'. The two primary discourses she uses as core evaluative dimensions of identity, which underpin her pattern of identifications, are 'thinks/doesn't think it is important to speak the original language' [in this case, Arabic] and 'interested/not interested in Arabic values'.

Respondent 7: Indeterminate identity

Within the ISA framework, this is the identity state of the majority of people and is regarded as the most usual identity state to be in, hence the notion of it being indeterminate in terms of saying anything remarkable about the individual.

This respondent also exhibits strong in-group preference. She exhibits relatively high positive evaluations of the Christian entities, both Arab and non-Arab. An idiosyncratic problematic relationship with her pastor seems to underlie the low evaluation of the 'local Church leader'. Muslim and Jewish entities are evaluated quite negatively, especially when these are leaders or religious figures. Evaluation of the Druze entity is also low.

Whereas no differentiation was observed in the respondent's evaluation of local and non-local Christian Arab entities, she seems to identify (empathetically and idealistically) more strongly with the local entities as compared to the Jordanian and American Christians. Identification with the latter figures is at the (low) level of the identification with most Muslim, Jewish, and Druze entities.

Structural pressures on constructs are generally low. The relatively high value of the structural pressure associated to the 'loves/doesn't love peace' construct suggests that for this respondent the concern for peace is a central dimension in the construction of her socio-cultural world. This doesn't necessarily imply any particular stance towards the current peace process between Arabs and Jews in the region; as we saw earlier, her attitudes towards the Jewish out-group are far from being favourable.

Respondent 8: A case of confident identity

According to Weinreich, this identity variant can be roughly equated with Marcia's (1980) 'identity achievement', a developmental status to which we referred in an earlier section. ISA theory, however, implies that the identity state is only confident for the particular self-context examined – in our case, the individual's ethnic and cultural context – and may differ in another context.

The respondent's patterns of cultural and inter-cultural evaluations reflect a considerable openness to various groups (in-group and out-groups). Except for the evaluation of the Druze, none of the evaluation values is negative. However, he does not seem to hold a completely egalitarian and universalist approach: Christian entities are still evaluated more favourably than the others, except for the American Christian who is evaluated even less favourably than some Muslim and Jewish entities. This points again to the importance of examining the role of locality in the ethnic identity of Palestinian Christian Arabs in Israel. Locality sometimes seems to overshadow religion as a criterion for social categorisation; but it is important to note that the meaning of locality also tends to vary – whereas for some respondents locality is confined to the Christian Arab society within Israel (excluding the American as well as the Jordanian Christian), for other respondents locality is more pan-Arabic (including within its boundaries the Jordanian Christian).

The respondent's identification patterns reinforce our view of him as an individual who feels secure in his cultural group, but also holds a positive attitude towards other cultural groups. Almost all identification indices yield high values; the respondent seems to identify very closely with the Christian Arab entities in Israel. One again, locality seems to affect identification (both empathetic and idealistic), but – unlike evaluation of entities – here the Jordanian Christian is left out of the local context. The sense of group and inter-group security is also reflected in the high values of identification with the metaperspectives on self: The respondent seems to feel comfortable with his image in the eyes of both Muslim and Jews. Consistent with the general pattern, values of identification conflicts are relatively low.

Culture and inter-group relations seem to play an important role in the respondent's construction of his social world. The most central discourses he uses as core evaluative dimensions of identity are related to cultural maintenance (in-group socialising) on the one hand and to the pursuit of peace on the other.

Concluding notes

The idiographic analyses of four selected, although not necessarily unrepresentative, respondents provide us with fascinating portraits of the diversity and richness of the cultural identification among Palestinian Arab Christian adolescents in Israel. The vivid images emerging from the ISA analyses reflect very different ways in which members of this 'multiple minority' construe their cultural identities within highly complex and delicate intergroup relations. The ethnic identity of Respondent 4, for example, seems not to fit the general group pattern – showing a distinct Christian identity – obtained in the large-scale studies preceding this ISA investigation. Her primary, and largely preemptive, cultural self-categorisation appears to be national, namely Arabic; her Christian identity tends to play a rather minor role in her intragroup and intergroup evaluations and identifications. Although perhaps untypical, this identity configuration deserves serious attention, particularly when exploring political, societal, and educational implications of our findings.

Two of the respondents, on the other hand, exhibit strong Christian identity. Their patterns of evaluations and identifications clearly differentiate between the Christian and non-Christian entities, and reflect strong in-group preference. However, out of the idiographic ISA analyses (and also the preliminary nomothetic exploration) emerges an additional ethnic categorisation which has been largely overlooked by theory and research dealing with an already highly complex and multifaceted ethnic identity, namely locality: Both respondents tend to identify less with Christians living outside Israel, as compared to the other Christian entities. It is important to note that it is not a combined 'Arab Christian' category that is activated for intergroup differentiation, as the Arab Christian in Jordan is not included among the in-group members.

The ethnic identity pattern of the last respondent can serve as an encouraging example for the development of authentic pluralistic and multicultural identities, even within highly troubled and volatile intergroup contexts. It shows that true openness to the 'other' does not require the weakening of one's own cultural identity; it may even be the case that long-lasting intergroup tolerance can only be achieved by individuals who feel confident and secure in their own cultural groups.

NOTE

1 We could have submitted the original raw data obtained from the ISA instruments to hierarchical cluster analysis, as reported, for example, by Weinreich *et al.* (1996). The main purpose of these analyses, however, was to provide us and the readers with graphic

188   *Horenczyk and Munayer*

representations summarising the general patterns observed in the IDEX analyses using the various useful ISA measures.

REFERENCES

Al-Haj, M. (1998). The sociopolitical structure of Arabs in Israel: External vs. internal orientation. In J. E. Hofman (Ed.), *Arab–Jewish relations in Israel: A quest in human understanding*. Bristol, IN: Wyndham Hall Press.

Berry, J. W. (1997). Immigration, acculturation, and adaptation. *Applied Psychology: An International Review*, 46, 5–68.

Berry, J. W., Kim, U., Power, S., Young, M., & Bujaki, M. (1989). Acculturation attitudes in plural societies. *Applied Psychology: An International Review*, 38, 185–206.

Colbi, S. P. (1969). *Christianity in the Holy Land, past and present*. Tel Aviv: Am Hassefer.

Colbi, S. P. (1988). *A history of the Christian presence in the Holy Land*. Landham, MD: University Press of America.

Ferdman, B. M., & Horenczyk, G. (2000). Cultural identity and immigration: Reconstructing the group during cultural transition. In E. Olshtain & G. Horenczyk (Eds.), *Language, identity, and immigration*. Jerusalem: Magnes Press.

Firro, K. (1999). *The Druzes in the Jewish state*. Leiden: Brill.

Horenczyk, G. (1996). Migrating selves in conflict. In G. Breakwell & E. Lyons (Eds.), *Changing European identities* (pp. 241–250). Oxford: Butterworth Heinemann.

Horenczyk, G., & Bekerman, Z. (1999). A social constructivist approach to Jewish identity. In S. M. Cohen & G. Horenczyk (Eds.), *National and cultural variations in Jewish identity* (pp. 281–297). Albany: SUNY Press.

Kelly, A. J. D. (1989). Ethnic identification, association and redefinition: Muslim Pakistanis and Greek Cypriots in Britain. In K. Liebkind (Ed.), *New identities in Europe: Immigrant ancestry and the ethnic identity of youth*. London: Gower.

LaFromboise, T., Coleman, H. L. K., & Gerton, J. (1993). Psychological impact of biculturalism: Evidence and theory. *Psychological Bulletin*, 114, 395–412.

Lange, A., & Westin, C. (1985). *The generative mode of explanation in social psychological theories of race and ethnic relations*. Stockholm: Center for Research in International Migration and Ethnic Relations.

Lewis, B. (1996). *The Middle East: 2000 years of history from the rise of Christianity to the present day*. London: Phoenix.

Liebkind, K. (1992). Ethnic identity – challenging the boundaries of social psychology. In G. M. Breakwell (Ed.), *Social psychology of identity and the self-concept* (pp. 147–185). London: Surrey University Press.

Marcia, J. (1980). Identity in adolescence. In J. Adelson (Ed.), *Handbook of adolescent psychology* (pp. 159–187). New York: Wiley.

Munayer, S. (2000). *The ethnic identity of Palestinian Arab Christians in Israel*. Doctoral dissertation, University of Wales.

Nagel, J. (1994). Constructing ethnicity: Creating and recreating ethnic identity and culture. *Social Problems*, 41, 152–176.

O'Mahony, A. (1995). *The Christian heritage in the Holy land*. London: Scorpion Cavniesh.

Phinney, J. S. (1990). Ethnic identity in adolescents and adults: Review of research. *Psychological Bulletin*, 108, 499–515.

Phinney, J. S. (1992). The Multigroup Ethnic Identity Measure: A new scale for use with diverse groups. *Journal of Adolescent Research*, 7, 156–176.

Phinney, J.S., Horenczyk, G., Liebkind, K., & Vedder, P. (2001). Ethnic identity, immigration and well-being: An interactional perspective. *Journal of Social Issues*, 57, 493–510.

Rossing, D. (1999). Microcosm and multiple minorities: The Christian communities in Israel. *Israel Yearbook and Almanac*, 28–45.

Statistical Abstract of Israel (1998). [Number 49.] Jerusalem: Central Bureau of Statistics.

Ward, C. (1996). Acculturation. In D. Landis & R. S. Bhagat (Eds.), *Handbook of intercultural training* (2nd Edn., pp. 124–147). Thousand Oaks, CA: Sage.

Weinreich, P. (1983). Emerging from threatened identities: Ethnicity and gender in redefinitions of ethnic identity. In G. Breakwell (Ed.), *Threatened identities* (pp. 149–185). Chichester: John Wiley & Sons.

Weinreich, P. (1986). Operationalization of identity theory in racial and ethnic relations. In J. Rex & D. Mason (Eds.), *Theories of race and ethnic relations* (pp. 299–320). Cambridge: Cambridge University Press.

Weinreich, P. (1989). Variations in ethnic identity: Identity Structure Analysis. In K. Liebkind (Ed.), *New identities in Europe* (pp. 41–76). London: Gower.

Weinreich, P. (1992). *Identity exploration workshop notes*. Newtownabbey, Northern Ireland: University of Ulster at Jordanstown.

Weinreich, P. (2000). Ethnic identity and acculturation: Ethnic stereotyping and identification, self-esteem and identity diffusion in a multicultural context. In E. Olshtain & G. Horenczyk (Eds.), *Language, identity, and immigration* (pp. 31–63). Jerusalem: Magnes Press.

Weinreich, P., & Ewart, S. (1999). *IDEX basic for Windows, Version 3.O: Identity Exploration Computer Software for idiographic, basic case studies*. Jordanstown: University of Ulster School of Psychology.

Weinreich, P., Luk, C. L., & Bond, M. H. (1996). Ethnic stereotypes and identification in a multicultural context: Acculturation, self-esteem and identity diffusion in Hong Kong Chinese university students. *Psychology and Developing Societies*, 8, 107–169.

Part III

Societal issues

INTRODUCTION

One's gender identity is defined as that part of the totality of one's self-construal made up of those dimensions that express the continuity between one's construal of one's past gender and one's future aspirations in relation to gender.

Gender identity issues, especially female ones, form a common thread linking Chapters 5–9. The significance of socio-historical contexts and biographical experiences across the reported studies is clearly evident. Where studies incorporate male–female comparisons, male–female expressions of (genetically based) gender identity clearly differ in significant respects, but with cultural connotations according to socio-historical era that also modulate with specific social contexts. Together these chapters demonstrate the fallacy of placing too great an emphasis on the search for the authentic or intrinsic gender identity. These studies present evidence of distinctive variations in people's expression of personally authentic identities, which are in accordance with their gender.

In Chapter 5, with a focus on theoretical issues, Stapleton and Wilson use the ISA conceptual framework to consolidate and adduce further explication of discourse analysis in which contemporary discourse analysis is integrated with ISA. Their integrated approach with one female participant demonstrates the singular self's positioning of identity, within the nexus of others, in terms of continuity of core expressions of identity projects. ISA provided a means for establishing an individual's characteristic use of discourses, contingent upon patterns of identification with personally meaningful others, that was not evident from discourse analysis alone. Although modulated and negotiated in encounters with others, core expressions of the individual's identity were sustained by high structural pressures, which were contingent upon her patterns of identification with others. Her own gender identity emerged as being based on a specific version rather than a general concept of femininity, a finding strongly adduced in the subsequent chapter by Wager.

In Chapter 6 Wager presents theoretical postulates about gender identity of professional academic women in a contemporary socio-historical context – specifically Helsinki. Empirical findings demonstrated commonalities of professional identity development in men and women, but also differences. In the women, major variations occurred according to academic subject studied and being a mother or childless, illustrating the significance of biographical decisions – choice of subject – and experiences – motherhood. In terms of their own appraisals of prototypical contemporary forms of womanhood – *a feminine woman* and *a feminist* – academic women did not fully identify with either of these, but defined their sense of womanhood in their own individualistic terms. Women's and men's empathetic identification modulated according to their domestic or work context, such that both sexes (males being the contemporary 'new men') empathetically identified with *a feminine woman* more closely in their own domestic context and with *a feminist* in their own work context. For women, their choice of academic subject being humanities or sciences, together with being a mother or not, represented different complexes of womanhood and gender identity, for which Wager formulated empirically derived theoretical propositions representing the contemporary socio-historical context of Finnish academia. For women in the humanities motherhood provided a more comfortable nexus of identification than being childless, whereas for those in the sciences being childless – the most 'feminist' – did so more than motherhood.

Saunderson's study in Chapter 7 reports substantial gender variation in the significance of the city-scape of 1990s Belfast, its dwellers and its planners, to identities of both producers (town planners and architects) and consumers (town dwellers) of the built environment. While certain processes of professional development were common to both male and female producers of the urban environment, substantial female alienation from their professional context was witnessed in their low empathetic identification with town planning in general and most town planners. The study demonstrated massive differences in processes of identification between male and female urban dwellers in the city. The urban environment contributed comfortably to male dwellers' identity. However, for female dwellers as users of the built environment it was problematic, as demonstrated by their highly conflicted identifications with amenities such as public transport, children's playgrounds, and the city centre by night, and with those responsible for such amenities such as town planners and city councillors. These findings suggested that an outmoded male-dominated and unaccountable town-planning ethos was particularly detrimental to those who tend to take primary responsibility for raising, and caring for, new generations, namely women.

In Chapter 8 Irvine formulates theoretical postulates about the identity characteristics of adults returning to education, in which a feminist orientation in respect of women's participation is clearly enunciated. Empirical results demonstrated that contemporary developments in gender identity for women returners were particularly salient. These women tended to be dissatisfied with their current identity state, aspiring to social position and power, and to being successful in the public as well as the domestic sphere of life. Their male counterparts tended to be less dissatisfied and less concerned with social mobility, but desiring to enhance self-respect and respect from others.

In Chapter 9 MacNabb presents theoretical postulates concerning the identity manifestations of aspiring entrepreneurs and actual business owners. While gender identification was salient in women's greater idealistic-identification with a successful businesswoman and men's with a successful businessman, expression of female identity varied according to a number of factors. Location within the contemporary socio-historical era was apparent in both aspiring and actual entrepreneurial women's break with more traditional domestic roles, illustrated by their conflicted identifications with their own mothers, and by female business owners' rejection of parental lifestyles. For those females in business who had children, their biographical experience of motherhood was manifested in surprising ways. On the one hand, their higher conflicted identifications with a successful businessman and woman reflected the tension with pursuing standard business practice. On the other hand, aspiring to give priority to the family over business was a highly conflicted stance for those (a majority) who did so, whereas those who aspired to business having priority over family (a formidable minority) countenanced this without such conflict. Those mothers who were business owners, and who aspired to pursuing their business idea without family support, did so more emphatically than childless female owners aspiring likewise. Heightened conflicted identifications characterised the immediate social context of domesticity compared with that of business. In respect of the pursuit of autonomy, businessmen tended to be able to combine this with an aspiration for family support, whereas for women the desire for autonomy entailed conflicted identifications with family members. MacNabb derives empirically grounded theoretical propositions to explicate these entrepreneurial identity processes.

These studies illustrate contemporary women's dilemmas and conflicted identifications in a number of socio-historical contexts: female student (Chapter 5); women pursuing academic careers (Chapter 6); women's experiences as consumers and producers of the urban environment (Chapter 7); mature women returning to tertiary education (Chapter 8); and women as aspiring entrepreneurs and business owners (Chapter 9). Generally, in gender identity studies men provide the necessary comparison – *being the complementary sex* – for establishing psychological processes that differ according to gender and those that are common to both genders. However, equivalently detailed studies of men's identity processes in contemporary society – *pursuing various agendas in society; in relation to others of one's own and the other gender; as parent; as disengaged from the parental role* – are also required to provide complementary explications of their dilemmas and conflicted identifications.

5 Grounding the discursive self: A case study in ISA and discursive psychology

Karyn Stapleton and John Wilson

INTRODUCTION

The nature and development of identity has long formed a focus of inquiry for social scientists. Definitive concepts or conclusions remain elusive, however, with intense debate surrounding even the ontological status of 'the self'. Until recently, such ontological debates took place predominantly outside the psychological domain, with psychologists tacitly accepting the existence of a 'real self', which could be investigated, and ultimately 'known'. Thus, social psychological research on identity has primarily addressed ways of conceptualising and accessing an already assumed entity (Gergen, 1994; Sampson, 1989).

Following the 'crisis in social psychology' (Armistead, 1974), however, such assumptions have been extensively challenged, to the extent that received psychological theories are seen by many as no longer tenable: 'Psychological science now confronts an impasse, a point at which both the knowledge claims of the profession and the individualist view of knowledge sustained by these claims ceases to be compelling' (Gergen, 1994: 3). Consequently, many theorists (notably those from the social constructionist tradition) have called for a reformulation of traditional identity concepts and, in particular, for a refocusing of attention from individual to social processes (Shotter, 1993). In addition, the 'discursive turn', currently manifest across the social sciences (Gill, 1995; Harré, 1998) has foregrounded the role of *language* in the production and maintenance both of individual identity, and of social life more generally.

As a theoretical framework, Identity Structure Analysis (ISA; Weinreich, 1980/86) embodies many of these current strands of psychological thought. Of particular relevance is its explicit formulation of the individual as a social actor, inextricably located within a network of personal relations and identifications. Thus ISA is inherently social in its orientation towards the '. . . individual and societal phenomena within which issues of identity are implicated' (Weinreich, 1991: 75). Furthermore, in its conceptualisation of personal constructs as a resource for self/other definition, ISA accords a central role to the use of language/discourse in the process of identity formation. The framework is hence compatible with, and indeed a useful means of operationalising, some of the most salient concepts within contemporary social psychology. In the present chapter,

we suggest that ISA has a wider applicability to questions arising from engagement with these very concepts. Specifically, we propose that, in addition to
addressing the social and discursive dimensions of identity, ISA may be used to
explore the *ontological status* of 'the self'. In the second part of the chapter, we
demonstrate such an application of ISA, with reference to 'real-life' discursive
data. Prior to this, however, it is necessary to outline the theoretical context and
issues at stake.

Identity: A singular subject?

Current emphasis on the social and collective aspects of identity (e.g. Gergen,
1994), together with postmodernist concepts of 'positioning' and 'subjectivities'
(e.g. Hollway, 1989; Walkerdine, 1996), have led to an ambivalence regarding the
status of personal identity. Within the psychological domain, such ideas have been
popularised by the emergence of Discursive Psychology/Discourse Analysis
(DP/DA; Edwards, 1997; Edwards and Potter, 1992; Potter and Wetherell, 1987);
a paradigm underpinned by the 'interconnected concepts of function, construction,
variation and the analytic unit: the interpretative repertoire' (Wetherell and Potter,
1988: 169). Taken to its logical conclusion, the application of this approach to
identity issues can result in the rejection of individual coherence or unity, as viable
analytic concepts (Burman, 1990; cf. Craig, 1997). Nonetheless, people continue
to perceive themselves, and to behave, as singular and continuous entities (Harré,
1998). Hence, we require a means of identity exploration that not only acknowledges
the social/discursively constituted aspects of self, but also 'grounds' these dimensions within a comprehensible framework of self-knowledge/self-recognition; here,
we suggest that ISA may be uniquely adapted for such an enterprise.

The 'discursive' view of identity

For philosophical reasons, DP shows a general reluctance to distinguish between the
discursive and the extra-discursive (see Edwards *et al.*, 1995) and consequently, pri-
vileges the social/linguistic over the individual, or '. . . what has conventionally
been understood as the psychological' (Wetherell, 1995: 134). Simultaneously
informed by concepts from postmodernism and ethnomethodology, this approach
conceives of *identity* as an ongoing negotiation of available subject positions
(Wetherell, 1998). Thus, speakers are seen as *actively constructing* their identities
in terms of commonly available, but locally negotiated, meanings (e.g. Croghan and
Miell, 1999; Edley and Wetherell, 1999). However, given that language use is seen
as intrinsically *goal-directed* and, further, that these goals are constantly shifting,
then a speaker's linguistic constructions are ultimately *variable* and context-
dependent: '. . . the casting and recasting of events or the creation of different versions is endemic in natural discourse. It is a pervasive and unavoidable feature of
social life' (Marshall and Wetherell, 1989: 110).

From this perspective, a speaker's identity is locally contingent, and open
to continual redefinition, as he/she engages in different interactional situations. This
is partly analogous to the ISA concept of *situated identities* (Weinreich *et al.*, 1988)

whereby individuals experience different identity states, depending on their location within specific social contexts. However, while ISA highlights the essentially continuous nature of overall identity (see later), the DP approach eschews postulations that cannot be evidenced in the immediate discursive data. The suggestion that the self is wholly constituted in discourse replaces traditional notions of singularity, continuity and integration with those of plurality, transience and fragmentation: an identity that is 'reconstructed from moment to moment within specific discursive and rhetorical texts and *distributed* across social contexts' (Edley and Wetherell 1997: 205; emphasis in original).

However, while the introduction of such concepts has been useful in undermining more static versions of identity theory, to adopt them *tout court* could result in an ultimately unproductive form of relativism (Burman and Parker, 1993). Moreover, the DP paradigm leaves a number of theoretical questions unanswered, for example, the process(es) whereby speakers come to repeatedly and predictably occupy particular subject positions (cf. Hall, 1996); the role of identification in this process (e.g. Craig, 1997); and the reflexive experience of the self as qualitatively singular and continuous (cf. Harré, 1998; Jones, 1997).

In light of these issues, it would appear that identity – even when framed as a discursive production – is not constructed entirely afresh, at every moment of speaking. Rather, it seems that speakers produce (albeit modified) versions of themselves in the context of ongoing self-narratives and sets of commitments, through which particular instances of identity production acquire their significance and intelligibility (see e.g. Schrag, 1997; Taylor, 1989). In order to address this simultaneous variability *and* consistency, then, we require a reformulation of 'identity' in a way that encompasses both singularity and multiplicity of self. The second part of this chapter describes how ISA may be used to frame and operationalise these issues, thereby explicating the relationship between particular 'moments of speaking' and the more global processes of identity production.

ISA AND THE DEVELOPMENT OF SELF-NARRATIVES

While 'identity' within the ISA framework is seen as an ongoing process of revision and reformulation, the individual is nonetheless conceived of as retaining a sense of personal continuity across contexts and experiences. Indeed identity *per se* is constituted in such terms; being (at any given time) '. . . the totality of one's self-construal in which how one construes oneself in the present expresses the continuity between how one construes oneself as one was in the past and how one construes oneself as one aspires to be in the future' (Weinreich, 1983: 151).

From this perspective, individuals can be seen to locate themselves as particular types of social actor, within specific socio-biographical contexts. Thus, they perceive and understand themselves in terms of ongoing self-narratives wherein their various (discursive) actions acquire meaning and coherence (cf. Anthony Giddens' [1991] concept of the self as a 'reflexive project' which must be mobilised and sustained in everyday life).

In discursive terms, such self-construals may be seen as 'grounding' the speaker's various constructions of self within a relatively coherent frame of meaning, while simultaneously providing a resource for the presentation of an intelligible identity (cf. Schrag, 1997). However, a crucial feature of the ISA framework is its contention that the individual derives a personal sense of consistency from his/her ongoing self-construal. This extends the process from the domain of discourse and interaction, into the domain of reflexive self-understanding; as in Giddens's notion of '. . . *the self as reflexively understood by the person in terms of her or his biography*' (1991: 53; emphasis in original).

In this way, the ISA framework, as applied to discursive data, provides a powerful elucidation of speakers' persistent and idiosyncratic take-up of subject positions, and their habitual patterns of self/other alignment (cf. Harré and van Langenhove, 1991) – a process that is left unexplored by most 'purely' discursive studies. Furthermore, ISA offers a unique means of discursively conceptualising and demonstrating this process via the process of self-construal; which is itself constituted through the active appropriation and use of particular discourses (see Stapleton, 2000).

Specifically, the notion of 'constructs of appraisal' may be drawn upon in order to explore the use of particular discourses, not only as resources for the linguistic production of identity, but also as a means of self-positioning in the intrapersonal domain (cf. Jones, 1997; Tan and Moghaddam, 1995). In the present study, this latter dimension of discourse use (manifested in the 'structural pressure on constructs' parameter) is taken as central to the notion of identity coherence beyond the 'moment of speaking'. That is, if particular constructs (essentially discourses/fragments of discourse) can be seen to retain evaluative salience *outside* their original context(s) of production, then these may be taken to represent something more enduring than context-contingent identity resources. More specifically, they may be seen as forming 'core' dimensions of the individual's self-narrative, through which he/she constructs a viable public identity, while simultaneously achieving a level of reflexive self-understanding. In addition, it is possible to observe the process of interpersonal identification, on the basis of these constructs, both as a situated discursive achievement and as an aspect of overall self-construal (cf. Craig, 1997).

To summarise, we suggest that the ISA framework may be usefully brought to bear on the discourse–identity relationship, with both 'real-life' linguistic constructions *and* the ISA construal process being viewed as context-specific mobilisations of discourse. However, drawing on ISA analyses, it is possible to demonstrate not only the situated deployment of these resources, but also their relation to the more global narratives and processes of identity production. It is to this end that we propose the integrated analysis of 'construct' usage and real-life talk, as described in the remainder of this chapter.

DATA COLLECTION AND ANALYSIS

The data described here are drawn from a series of idiographic identity analyses, and focus on one woman's discursive negotiation of 'being single'. Zoe (aged 31;

currently undertaking a D.Phil. in psychology) was recorded, as she engaged in a number of informal conversations with friends. Following transcription of these interactions, it was possible to observe Zoe's negotiation of identity categories across a range of local contexts. Then, in order to explore the relationship between these situated constructions, and the more global processes of self-narrative and reflexive understanding (see earlier), an integrated DA/ISA analytic framework was formulated. This comprised three main phases:

1   Discourse analysis of the transcripts (see Potter and Wetherell, 1987), focusing on both the content, and the linguistic organisation of accounts. Particular attention was given to the *variability* evident in Zoe's self-positionings, together with her own orientations towards *consistency* of self-presentation.
2   Construction of an individualised (ISA) identity instrument (drawn directly from Zoe's *own* discursive formulations in the preceding interactions); and the use of IDEX software to analyse her self/other construal, on the basis of these constructs.
3   Integrated analysis of Zoe's use of discourse as a means of self/other-positioning, via the respective process(es) of *in situ*, and ISA, discourse deployment.

Integrated and synthesised in this way, DA and ISA analyses can be seen to provide a dual perspective on Zoe's use of particular discourses; both as resources for (public) self-presentation, and as a means of self-positioning/self-understanding in the intrapersonal domain. Such a synthesised analysis is presented next.

DISCOURSE ANALYSIS

The extracts reproduced here are drawn from Zoe's self-constructions during one discursive episode (i.e. an informal conversation with two female friends). Taken together, these constructions reveal some of the culturally available discourses and ideologies within which she negotiates her identity as a 'single woman', i.e. someone who is not currently involved in a romantic relationship (cf. Lawes' [1999] analysis of the competing discourses surrounding marriage). Space constraints do not allow us to discuss the sequential occasioning of these accounts (see e.g. Edwards, 1997). However, for present purposes, it is sufficient to present the variability of Zoe's self-positioning, as she vacillates between 'positive' and 'negative' discourses, with some (necessarily scant) attention given to the rhetorical organisation of her constructions. Additionally, it is possible to observe her own orientation to the presentation of a 'consistent self'; as evidenced in her attempts to resolve the discursive conflict arising from her use of 'incompatible' discourses (see Billig *et al.*, 1988).

Being single: 'acceptability' vs 'stigma'

Throughout the discussion, Zoe's accounts of being single are frequently constructed through the perceptions of others; alternating between those of social acceptability (or even desirability), and those of social deviance and stigma. These different scenarios make available very different opportunities for self-positioning, as demonstrated in Extracts 1–4 (see Appendix for transcription conventions).

Extract 1
Z: but being single now, has become quite popular and prevalent =
J: = uuh =
Z: = for professionally trained women

Here, Zoe presents a positive account wherein being single is not only socially acceptable ('prevalent'), but also 'popular'. Thus, in her lexical selection, she appeals not only to the notion of *universality* (Edwards and Potter, 1992), but more importantly to that of *choice*. If being single is 'popular', then it must be something that is freely chosen, and therefore desirable. In addition, the temporal context created by the items 'now' and 'become' appears to be one of progression; i.e. a movement towards social acceptance and approbation. Finally, via her characterisation of those people who choose to 'be single', Zoe creates an explicit opportunity for (positive) self-positioning. As a 'professionally trained woman', she can thus present herself as a progressive individual, who is capable of making agentic life-choices and moreover, is totally 'normal' by reference to modern society.

The potential benefits of 'remaining single' are formulated more explicitly at a later point in the discussion, whereby the single life is cast as a list of attractive options.

Extract 2
Z: but what about just (.) re-remaining single (.) I mean I'm not saying not having relationships and not (.) getting involved in encounters of a romantic physical nature (.) I'm just saying you're, basically you're single (0.5) you're free (.) you're independent (.) and you've your own friends

This account overtly invokes the notion of choice; i.e. 'remaining single' is presented in agentic terms, and moreover as an *option* ('what about . . .'). Indeed, given its subsequent formulation, the single life is cast as a particularly discerning option; a 'best of both worlds' scenario, whereby one can choose (when) to engage in romantic/sexual relationships, while simultaneously retaining an independent lifestyle.

It is notable however, that the contrastive element of this scenario (i.e. engaging in romantic/sexual encounters) is formulated as part of a *disclaimer*; i.e. 'a verbal device designed to ward off potentially obnoxious attributions' (Wetherell and Potter, 1988: 176; see also Kleiner, 1998). Thus by prefacing the positive aspects of being single with an exposition of what she is *not* advocating, Zoe displays an orientation towards certain negative perceptions of not having a partner (e.g. emotional isolation and/or forced celibacy). Such (culturally accessible) attributions could be expected to undermine the effectiveness of her account. However, by their very negation, Zoe skilfully builds them into an 'ideal scenario'. Here, romantic/sexual encounters are 'placed in perspective', alongside a *three-part list* (Jefferson, 1990) of freedom, independence and friendship, to convey the potentially positive and holistic experience of single life. Such a scenario could reasonably be expected to appeal to many rational, intelligent people; hence, Zoe can retain her self-positioning as someone who has chosen an unremarkable, but nonetheless discerning, life-option.

However, when 'being single' next arises as a conversational topic (i.e. during an account of a recent visit to her family), Zoe presents a much more negative scenario.

Extract 3
Z: I mean you do get these questions (.) people think that you're making it up you know? (.) but y'know (.) at the start (.) it's funny but (.) as the years go on (.) well it's not funny anymore

In this extract, Zoe is positioned as socially deviant; her not having a partner is so unusual that 'people think [she is] making it up', and therefore subject her to questions (and possibly evaluative comments) regarding her single status. Moreover, as time passes, these questions have changed from amusing banter to something that is no longer funny and, indeed, renders it difficult for Zoe to maintain a positive self-positioning. Thus, as the temporal context shifts, her own reaction to 'these questions' also changes; this is effectively conveyed in the last line by repetition of the main lexical item (i.e. 'funny'), together with a stressed negation particle. Further evidence that social perceptions and expectations negatively affect Zoe's self-positioning, is to be found in the following extract.

Extract 4
Z: I mean the only thing that has given me any (.) kinda space (*laughing*) is the fact that I'm still in study
D: mmm
Z: that's in relation to my mother (.) if I was (.) if anybody was to say anything when we go up town (.) y'know (.) are you seeing anyone or that (.) 'oh she's still in college and she's still' =
D: = right (.) that's an excuse
Z: yeah, but time's running out! (*laughs*)

Here, being single is presented as a tightly constrictive situation wherein there is little 'space', or room for negotiation. (This sense of pressure is intensified by the use of several 'extreme case formulations'; e.g. 'any', 'the only thing'; see Pomerantz, 1986.) Additionally, Zoe's lack of a partner is something for which her mother feels socially accountable; i.e. something that it is necessary to explain/justify, by reference to her 'still' being in college. (Note also Debbie's use of the term 'excuse' in the following turn.)

In this way, Zoe's student status has given her more leeway than would normally be available, in that it offers her mother a means of vindicating her deviation from social norms. However, this leeway/'space' is inescapably finite. That is, through her mother's eyes, she is positioned as a student (and hence *temporarily 'excused'* from fulfilling social expectations), rather than a professional woman who has *actively chosen* to remain single. The notion of urgency and constriction is vividly reinvoked in her final statement that 'time's running out', whereby she suggests (albeit facetiously) that she will ultimately have to conform to others' expectations (i.e. find a partner), or face certain social consequences.

Discursive conflict and resolution

These accounts demonstrate the conflicting social meanings of being single, and consequently, Zoe's differential positioning by various social partners. However, given that she presents herself as personally responsive to these meanings and perceptions (e.g. in Extract 3), then her opportunities for *self-positioning* are also affected. Hence, a degree of discursive tension arises; not only around the discourses themselves (cf. Billig *et al.*, 1988; Smithson, 1999), but also around Zoe's identity as a single woman. In order to maintain a consistent (and positive) self-positioning, she must therefore utilise strategies to resolve this tension. In Extract 5, one such strategy is outlined: A 'chronological milestone' and 'own vs others' perceptions'

> Extract 5
> Z: but it <u>is</u> a pressure (.) y'know when you're single and (.) well I'm in my thirties now and =
> D: = <u>no</u>! =
> J: = I'd get <u>really</u> scared if I were you!
> Z: but there is a thing a<u>bout</u> it right (.) <u>I've</u> no problem with it, well I'd no problem <u>last</u> year with it (.) I mean I was just thinking to myself (.) you know (.) I've reached this far and I'm relatively sane y'know (0.5) it's <u>fine</u> but there is this thing (.) this sharp intake of breath (*inhales loudly*) in relation to it (.) it is a <u>mile</u>stone, you know?

In this extract, Zoe again presents herself as stigmatised, and therefore pressurised to conform to social expectations. Moreover, it is again evident that such factors impinge (and indeed give rise to reflection) upon her own self-positioning. There is an obvious incongruity between this construction and her earlier accounts of normalisation, progression and choice (see Extract 1). Thus, in order to maintain a positive identity, Zoe rationalises her personal response to this social pressure; i.e. the inescapable significance of her thirtieth birthday.

That this represents a chronological 'milestone' is evident in the salience of the category (i.e. 'my thirties'), rather than a precise age. Thus Zoe casts herself in the eyes of society, for whom she has now reached a significant life-stage, after which her single status is increasingly unacceptable. When her interlocutors react humorously to this statement, Zoe re-casts the scenario in more emphatic terms, referring twice to the existence of an amorphous and agentless 'thing' which, by its very lack of definition, assumes an all-pervasive authority (see Edwards and Potter, 1992; Potter, 1996). Her indexing of this 'thing' via sharp inhalation, further underlines the import of being partnerless by the age of thirty.

In the face of such weighty social meanings, it is possible for Zoe to rationalise her own ambivalence about being single. Hence, she can maintain a positive personal alignment, while (understandably) reacting to the more negative perceptions of others. Rhetorically, this balance is achieved via explicit contrasts between (a) personal and social meanings, and (b) her lack of concern 'last year' (i.e. before she turned thirty) and her subsequent acknowledgement of the 'milestone' she has passed. In this way, Zoe's more negative reactions are vindicated (and perhaps rendered inevitable), while her own essentially positive alignment is nonetheless sustainable.

IDENTITY STRUCTURE ANALYSIS

In order to investigate whether/how the preceding patterns of discursive positioning and self/other alignment translate into the intrapersonal domain, it is necessary to extract the discourses in question from their immediate contexts of production. Thus, a custom-designed identity instrument was designed for, and completed by, Zoe. Once obtained, responses were analysed via IDEX-idiographic computer software. This generated a number of identity indices which, together, offer crucial insights into the psycho-discursive processes by which Zoe achieves a reflexively coherent identity.

Constructing the identity instrument

Given the present study's emphasis on 'naturalistic' discourse, it should be noted that the items comprising Zoe's instrument (see Tables 5.1 and 5.2) were drawn solely from the transcripts of her own *in situ* constructions (in contrast to standard psychological sets of 'test items' and researcher-imposed categories). Additionally, although some editing was inevitably necessary, it was sought as far as possible to retain the vocabulary, syntax and idiomatic features of Zoe's linguistic productions.

Using the sets of constructs and entities given in Tables 5.1 and 5.2, the ISA instrument abstracted the discourses that Zoe had drawn upon in the interpersonal domain, and (re)presented these for use in the context of slackened rhetorical and interpersonal requirements. In this way, it was possible to gain a unique perspective on their use in the intrapersonal domain, and specifically on the processes by which a consistent (and positive) self-positioning may be achieved and maintained. For present research purposes, we will be primarily concerned with two such processes; (a) the use of particular discourses as tools of appraisal, and (b) Zoe's self-positioning in relation to other social entities. These dimensions are explored within the ISA framework via two parameters of identity; i.e. structural pressure on constructs and patterns of identification, respectively.

Table 5.1 List of constructs (abbreviated) in Zoe's identity instrument

Number	Construct
1L	believes that double standards of behaviour exist
1R	thinks that behaviour is judged equally by society
2L	sees psychology as a caring profession
2R	sees psychology as primarily scientific
3L	finds gender stereotypes very hard to live up to
3R	finds it easy to fulfil gender expectations
4L	resists change/new situations
4R	welcomes new experiences and changes
5L	thinks that people would generally prefer to be in a relationship
5R	thinks that remaining single has become a popular option
6L	is lazy/wastes time
6R	is industrious and hard-working
7L	promotes rights for minorities/those who can't defend themselves
7R	believes everyone is responsible for their own welfare
8L	enjoys socialising/meeting new people
8R	prefers quiet life/stays at home
9L	believes that getting married is a personal choice
9R	feels that people should get married for family reasons
10L	sees a big difference between rural and city values
10R	thinks that people are much the same everywhere
11L	is intelligent and well-informed
11R	is intellectually limited/ignorant
12L	feels that boxing is too aggressive/male sport
12R	feels that if women want to box, that's their choice
13L	thinks that psychology can produce definite 'answers'
13R	believes there are no clear-cut answers, when you're dealing with people
14L	is serious/'straitlaced'
14R	has a good sense of humour/likes a laugh
15L	believes women are natural care-givers/nurturers
15R	believes that men could 'caregive' as well as women

Structural pressure on constructs

Within the ISA framework, 'structural pressure on constructs' (SP) refers to the degree of stability with which such constructs are used to appraise self and others in the social world (Weinreich, 1980/86). Operationalisation of this parameter hinges on the excess of 'compatibilities' or 'incompatibilities' evident in the respondent's ascription of constructs to particular social entities. Positive SP derives from an excess of such compatibilities, while negative SP is exerted by conflicting evaluative applications. Thus, the 'net' SP on a construct leads to its designation as a 'core', 'secondary', or 'inconsistent'/'unevaluative' identity dimension.

In the present study, the SP parameter may be used to explore the way in which these evaluative dimensions are used to position self and other social entities. Assuming that self–other positioning occurs in the context of an ongoing

Table 5.2 List of entities in Zoe's identity instrument

Me as I am now
Me as I was before I came to University
Me as an undergrad
Me as I would like to be when I finish my Ph.D.
A person I admire
Someone I really can't stand
My closest sibling (Libby)
My mother
My father, when he was alive
My sisters
My brothers
My brother-in-law
Clinical psychologists
University lecturers/academics
My closest friends
High-achieving women
High-achieving men
Research psychologists
Married women
Married men
People who live in the city
Rural/country people
Most media presenters
Psychology undergrads

Table 5.3 Zoe's core constructs

Construct	*No.*	*SP*
thinks that remaining single has become a popular option . . .	5R	85.07
believes that getting married is a personal choice . . .	9L	80.50
believes that men could 'caregive' as well as women . . .	15R	71.63
feels that if women want to box, that's their choice . . .	12R	68.83
finds gender stereotypes very hard to live up to . . .	3L	68.23

SP $= -100$ to $+100$

self-narrative, then the respondent would be expected to display certain patterns of regularity in her reflexive deployment of constructs. Such regularity is evident in Zoe's set of 'core' constructs (i.e. those with SP over 50; see Table 5.3).

On initial inspection, Table 5.3 reveals that Zoe's core constructs have not arisen in a random fashion, but are systematically grouped around two identity dimensions; i.e. a *positive* orientation towards 'being single', and a negative orientation towards 'gender stereotypes'. These issues constituted recurrent themes in Zoe's talk, and were ubiquitous features of her discursive constructions. Additionally, both dimensions can be seen to cohere within a positive self-narrative, whereby she can position herself as a progressive and discerning individual.

With regard to self-positioning, it is particularly telling that the two constructs with the strongest (or most consistently) evaluative connotations are those pertaining to 'being single'. Given her vacillating use of these discourses in the public domain (see earlier 'Discourse analysis' section), a purely situated reading would suggest that Zoe's 'identity' at this site of production is entirely occasioned or context-contingent. The ISA analysis, however, illustrates a much more consistent deployment of these constructs, in that Zoe can be seen to routinely position herself and other social entities on the basis of their (ascribed) orientation towards 'being single'. Moreover, given that such positioning is anchored in a *positive* orientation, then she (as a single woman) can simultaneously maintain a positive identity; both within this constellation of entities (see Table 5.4), and in the context of her ongoing narrative of self.

In this way, Zoe's core constructs can be seen to form salient identity resources, in both the public and private domains – albeit that her favoured self-positioning may be contested in the interpersonal context. The centrality of these dimensions is further evidenced in Zoe's patterns of identification with other entities; as illustrated in Tables 5.4–5.6. (Conversely, it may be inferred that less evaluatively salient constructs do *not* provide such consistent resources for self–other positioning. For example, those constructs pertaining to 'psychology' [see Table 5.1] emerge as *secondary* evaluative dimensions; while the entities comprising Zoe's most salient identifications – such as her mother, siblings and close friends – are unlikely to be delineated/positioned on the basis of these constructs.)

Patterns of identification

In the process of self-positioning, speakers are simultaneously committing themselves to particular types of alignment, vis-à-vis other social entities (Harré and van Langenhove, 1991; cf. Tracy and Anderson, 1999). These alignments then enter into self-narratives, whereby they are deployed both in the construction of a positive identity, and as a basis for reflexive self-knowledge (cf. Holmes, 1997; Linde, 1993). ISA affords a unique perspective on this process via its conceptualisation of social identifications based on discursive constructs; and further, the imbrication of these identifications within the respondent's patterns of self-construal.

Within the ISA approach, there are two basic modes of identification with other social entities; thus, with reference to his/her personal appraisal system, a respondent will variously exhibit *role-model* and *empathetic* identifications with particular others. The crucial distinction here is the degree of aspiration towards, or (perceived) *de facto* commonality with, these entities. Role-model identification may be based on the ascription of (a) positive qualities that the respondent would wish to emulate (i.e. *idealistic-identification*), or (b) negative qualities from which he/she would wish to dissociate (i.e. *contra-identification*). Empathetic identification, on the other hand, derives from the perception of an already existing (*de facto*) commonality with another entity; a commonality that may be construed positively or negatively within the current terms of appraisal (Weinreich, 1980/86). Identification with a given entity depends on the way in which this entity is construed within the existing evaluative system; particularly in relation to the 'core' constructs of appraisal, since these provide an anchor for the respondent's appraisals of self and others. Additionally however, such identifications can give rise to changes within the appraisal system. For example, strong idealistic identification with a particular role-model can increase the salience of constructs ascribed to this entity; thereby modifying the existing terms of self/other construal (see Weinreich, 1983).

From a discursive perspective, then, Zoe's use of particular constructs as tools of appraisal may be seen as a series of dynamic and reciprocal self-alignments within her social milieu. Moreover, given the coherence evident in her use of these constructs (see earlier), then we would expect her patterns of identification to exhibit discernible regularities, commensurate with her particular identity project(s) (cf. Craig, 1997). From Tables 5.4–5.6, it is possible to identify such patterns of self–other alignment within broadly defined discursive spaces. For present purposes, we will focus primarily on Zoe's identifications as they cohere around her core constructs; i.e. those pertaining to 'being single'.

Table 5.4 Zoe's positive role-models

Entity	Idealistic-identification
my closest friends	0.93
my closest sibling (Libby)	0.79
my sisters	0.71
a person I admire	0.64
high-achieving women	0.63

Idealistic-identification = 0.00–1.00

Table 5.5 Zoe's negative role-models

Entity	Contra-identification
my mother	0.50
my brothers	0.36
my brother-in-law	0.36
married men	0.36

Contra-identification = 0.00–1.00

Table 5.6 Perceived similarity with entities

Entity	Empathetic identification
my closest friends	1.00
my closest sibling (Libby)	0.86
a person I admire	0.64
my sisters	0.64
high-achieving women	0.50

Empathetic identification = 0.00–1.00

The patterns of identification illustrated in Tables 5.4–5.6 can be clearly grounded in Zoe's attempts to maintain a positive self-positioning by way of her core constructs. In this way, her consistent use of certain constructs results in a reciprocally located constellation of social entities. While space constraints do not permit a full explication of these processes, certain regularities of identification seem immediately relevant to the present investigation. These are (a) the distinction between idealistic and empathetic identifications on the one hand, and contra-identifications on the other; (b) the gendered dimension of positive/negative role-model construal; and (c) the unique location of Zoe's mother within this (gendered) milieu.

Zoe's positive role-models are generally those who may be expected to have both a positive orientation towards being single, and a negative orientation to gender stereotypical expectations (cf. Table 5.3). Hence, on the basis of these constructs, her strongest positive role-models (Table 5.4) comprise her 'closest friends' (most of whom are engaged in professional or academic careers, and a number of whom are also single); her 'closest sibling' (Libby, who is employed in the financial sector, and is also single); her 'sisters' (of whom two are married and two single); an 'admired person' (unspecified) and 'high-achieving women'.

Alignment with any/all of these entities would provide Zoe with a discursive space wherein 'being single' can be negotiated in positive terms. Moreover, through the high priority that they appear to place on their careers (relative, for example, to romantic relationships), these women can be constructed as challenging traditional concepts of femininity; in particular, the expectation that marriage and family will form pivotal points in a woman's life (cf. Lawes, 1999; Woollett and Phoenix, 1991). In fact, as a group, Zoe's positive role-models may be seen to embody and enact her discursive formulation of a happy and fulfilling single life earlier (see earlier 'Discourse analysis' section). The fact that these entities also constitute Zoe's strongest empathetic identifications (see Table 5.6) reveals her own *de facto* positioning and mode of self-construal. That is, she self-positions in a way that facilitates a positive identity (as a single woman); a positioning that is maintained in the intrapersonal domain, via a coherent set of discourses, and commensurate self–other alignments.

This process is further evidenced in the contrast between Zoe's positive/empathetic identifications, and her set of *negative* role-models (Table 5.5). With the exception of her 'mother' (see later), these entities are generally married males (i.e. her 'brothers', her 'brother-in-law' and 'married men'). Discursively formulated in terms of her core constructs, these entities are relatively conservative with regard to traditional gender ideologies, and particularly to expectations of marriage. (Additional support for this reading is drawn from conversational data, undocumented in the present chapter.) Hence, the way in which she is positioned by these entities could potentially undermine Zoe's self-positioning in the public domain, in that they may be expected to challenge her positive constructions of 'being single' (cf. Harré and van Langenhove, 1991; Jones, 1997). Her reflexive patterns of alignment, however, as evidenced in her ISA responses, allow her to counteract these (other-)positionings, thereby maintaining a positive identity-construal.

Of further interest here, is the gender-specific nature of Zoe's identifications; specifically, her negative role-models are generally male entities, while her positive and empathetic identifications are exclusively with females. On a cursory reading, this would suggest that Zoe almost indiscriminately aligns herself with those of her own gender, thereby displaying a strong sense of femininity/gender identity. It is notable, however, that her mother (who from this perspective could be expected to provide a strong aspirational point) does not feature in Zoe's set of idealistic-identifications. In fact, this entity constitutes her highest degree of *contra*-identification (see Table 5.6), thus indicating that (despite her general alignment with female entities), Zoe draws a clear distinction between her construal of her mother, and her construal of self. This process may be explicated by reference to Zoe's self-positioning within the discourses of 'being single'. In so far as her mother is counter-positioned to Zoe on this issue (see earlier 'Discourse analysis' section) then she may be seen as threatening Zoe's negotiation of a positive 'single' identity. Hence, her mother is discursively aligned with other (generally male) entities who are similarly counter-positioned. Zoe's patterns of identification, then, while displaying clear gender dimensions, appear to be shaped primarily by the location of the relevant entities within particular discursive spaces. This suggests that her own (discursively formulated) gender identity is based on a *specific version*, rather than a general concept, of femininity. Using this version, she is able to maintain a positive identity as a particular type of woman; as pursuing specific goals, within a particular social milieu.

CONCLUSION

The preceding synthesis of DA and ISA provides a holistic perspective on Zoe's use of discourses as identity resources. Specifically, such a synthesised approach allows us to ascertain the *relative salience* of particular discursive constructs which, from analysis of situated discourse alone, appear to be used in a vacillating and entirely contingent manner. This suggests that the philosophy of 'discursive immanence' (which generally characterises DP research) may preclude fundamental aspects of the discourse–identity relationship. Moreover, while offering valuable insights into the processes of *situated/occasioned* identity production, DP's exclusive emphasis on 'the social', and the 'here and now', inevitably obscures the subjective human experience of self-continuity and singularity (cf. Craig, 1997; Hall, 1996; New, 1998). ISA, on the other hand, allows for a unique 'opening up' of such (socially embedded) experiences and subjectivities. Crucially, this approach explicates the constituent psycho-discursive processes (e.g. patterns of identification), as framed within the individual's *own terms of reference*. Hence, we propose that the integration of ISA and DP, as outlined in this chapter, allows for a holistic and innovative approach to the discourse–identity relationship; encompassing both the contingent/socially constituted, *and* the reflexively experienced, aspects of self.

To this end, we suggest that both the (ISA) 'construal' and the (DP) 'construction' processes be seen as contextually variant, but nonetheless active and agentic, appropriations of discursive resources in constituting the social world. However, while discursive analyses explicate the use of these resources only within their immediate context(s) of production, the ISA framework allows us to go beyond situated (interactional) contexts, to consider their use in the intrapersonal domain. Through a consideration of (a) SP on constructs, and (b) the patterns of identification based on these constructs, it is possible to observe how particular discourses are being used in the process of self–other alignment, and hence how these discourses come to acquire evaluative salience for their users. In addition, the ISA concept of ongoing self-construal allows for the location of such processes within a frame of reflexive self-understanding; by reference to which, particular discourses are rendered meaningful, and relatively coherent (see Stapleton, 2000).

Using this integrated approach, then, it is possible to conceptualise/explore the ways in which individuals come to habitually deploy certain discourses, and to occupy certain subject positions; how they come to reflexively 'know' themselves as particular types of social actor; and how they locate themselves in more or less consistent ways within their socio-cultural milieu(s). Thus, the discourse–identity relationship may be reformulated in a way that simultaneously addresses issues of variability *and* consistency; thereby engaging with both the diversity *and* singularity of subjective human experience.

REFERENCES

Armistead, N. (1974) *Reconstructing Social Psychology*. Baltimore: Penguin.

Billig, M., Condor, S., Edwards, D., Gane, M., Middleton, D., and Radley, A. (1988) *Ideological Dilemmas: A Social Psychology of Knowledge*. London: Sage.

Burman, E. (1990) 'Differing with deconstruction: a feminist critique'. In I. Parker and J. Shotter (eds) *Deconstructing Social Psychology*. London: Sage.

Burman, E. and Parker, I. (1993) 'Introduction – Discourse Analysis: the turn to text'. In E. Burman and I. Parker (eds) *Discourse Analytic Research: Repertoires and Readings of Texts in Action*. London: Routledge.

Craig, A. P. (1997) 'Postmodern pluralism and our selves'. *Theory and Psychology*, 7: 505–27.

Croghan, R. and Miell, D. (1999) 'Born to abuse? Negotiating identity within an interpretative repertoire of impairment'. *British Journal of Social Psychology*, 38: 315–35.

Edley, N. and Wetherell, M. (1997) 'Jockeying for position: the construction of masculine identities'. *Discourse and Society*, 8: 203–17.

Edley, N. and Wetherell, M. (1999) 'Imagined futures: young men's talk about fatherhood and domestic life'. *British Journal of Social Psychology*, 38: 181–94.

Edwards, D. (1997) *Discourse and Cognition*. London: Sage.

Edwards, D., Ashmore, M., and Potter, J. (1995) 'Death and furniture: the rhetoric, politics and theology of bottom line arguments against relativism'. *History of the Human Sciences*, 8: 25–49.

Edwards, D. and Potter, J. (1992) *Discursive Psychology*. London: Sage.

Gergen, K. J. (1994) *Realities and Relationships: Soundings in Social Constructionism*. London: Harvard University Press.

Giddens, A. (1991) *Modernity and Self-Identity: Self and Society in the Late Modern Age.* Stanford, CA: Stanford University Press.

Gill, R. (1995) 'Relativism, reflexivity and politics: interrogating Discourse Analysis from a feminist perspective'. In S. Wilkinson and C. Kitzinger (eds) *Feminism and Discourse: Psychological Perspectives.* London: Sage.

Hall, S. (1996) 'Introduction: who needs "identity"?'. In S. Hall and P. du Gay (eds) *Questions of Cultural Identity.* London: Sage.

Harré, R. (1998) *The Singular Self: An Introduction to the Psychology of Personhood.* London: Sage.

Harré, R. and van Langenhove, L. (1991) 'Varieties of positioning'. *Journal for the Theory of Social Behaviour*, 21: 393–407.

Hollway, W. (1989) *Subjectivity and Method in Psychology: Gender, Meaning and Science.* London: Sage.

Holmes, J. (1997) 'Story-telling in New Zealand women's and men's talk'. In R. Wodak (ed.) *Gender and Discourse.* London: Sage.

Jefferson, G. (1990) 'List construction as a task and interactional resource'. In G. Psathas (ed.) *Interactional Competence.* Washington, DC: University Press of America.

Jones, R. A. (1997) 'The presence of self in the person: reflexive positioning and Personal Constructs Psychology'. *Journal for the Theory of Social Behaviour*, 27: 453–71.

Kleiner, B. (1998) 'The modern racist ideology and its reproduction in "pseudo-argument"'. *Discourse and Society*, 9: 187–215.

Lawes, R. (1999) 'Marriage: an analysis of discourse'. *British Journal of Social Psychology*, 38: 1–20.

Linde, C. (1993) *Life Stories: The Creation of Coherence.* New York/Oxford: Oxford University Press.

Marshall, H. and Wetherell, M. (1989) 'Talking about career and gender identities: a discourse analysis perspective'. In S. Skevington and D. Baker (eds) *The Social Identity of Women.* London: Sage.

New, C. (1998) 'Realism, deconstruction and the feminist standpoint'. *Journal for the Theory of Social Behaviour*, 28: 349–72.

Pomerantz, A. (1986) 'Extreme case formulations: a new way of legitimating claims'. *Human Studies*, 9: 219–30.

Potter, J. (1996) *Representing Reality: Discourse, Rhetoric and Social Constructionism.* London: Sage.

Potter, J. and Wetherell, M. (1987) *Discourse and Social Psychology: Beyond Attitudes and Behaviour.* London: Sage.

Sampson, E. E. (1989) 'The deconstruction of the self'. In J. Shotter and K. J. Gergen (eds) *Texts of Identity.* London: Sage.

Schrag, C. O. (1997) *The Self After Postmodernity.* London: Yale University Press.

Shotter, J. (1993) *Conversational Realities.* London: Sage.

Smithson, J. (1999) 'Equal choices: young adults talk about work and family expectations'. *Psychology of Women Section Review*, 1: 43–57.

Stapleton, K. (2000) 'In search of the self: feminism, postmodernism and identity'. *Feminism and Psychology*, 10(4): 483–9.

Tan, S.-L. and Moghaddam, F. M. (1995) 'Reflexive positioning and culture'. *Journal for the Theory of Social Behaviour*, 25: 387–400.

Taylor, C. (1989) *Sources of the Self: The Making of Modern Identity.* Cambridge: Cambridge University Press.

Tracy, K. and Anderson, D. L. (1999) 'Relational positioning strategies in police calls: a dilemma'. *Discourse Studies*, 1: 102–26.

Walkerdine, V. (1996) 'Working class women: psychological and social aspects of survival'. In S. Wilkinson (ed.) *Feminist Social Psychologies: International Perspectives*. Buckingham, UK: Open University Press.

Weinreich, P. (1980/1986) *Manual for Identity Exploration, Using Personal Constructs*. Warwick: Centre for Research in Ethnic Relations, University of Warwick.

Weinreich, P. (1983) 'Emerging from threatened identities: ethnicity and gender in redefinitions of threatened identity'. In G. Breakwell (ed.) *Threatened Identities*. Chichester: Wiley.

Weinreich, P. (1991) 'Ethnic identities and indigenous psychologies in pluralist societies'. *Psychology and Developing Societies*, 3: 73–91.

Weinreich, P., Kelly, A. J. D., and Maya, C. (1988) 'Black youth in South Africa: situated identities and patterns of ethnic identification'. In D. Canter, C. Jesuino, L. Soczka, and G. Stephenson (eds) *Environmental Social Psychology*. Dordrecht, The Netherlands: Kluwer Academic Press.

Wetherell, M. (1995) 'Romantic discourse and feminist analysis: interrogating investment, power and desire'. In S. Wilkinson and C. Kitzinger (eds) *Feminism and Discourse: Psychological Perspectives*. London: Sage.

Wetherell, M. (1998) 'Positioning and interpretative repertoires: Conversation Analysis and post-structuralism in dialogue'. *Discourse and Society*, 9: 387–412.

Wetherell, M. and Potter, J. (1988) 'Discourse Analysis and the identification of interpretative repertoires'. In C. Antaki (ed.) *Analysing Everyday Explanation: A Casebook of Methods*. London: Sage.

Woollett, A. and Phoenix, A. (1991) 'Afterword: issues related to motherhood'. In A. Phoenix, A. Woollett, and E. Lloyd (eds) *Motherhood: Meanings, Practices and Ideologies*. London: Sage.

APPENDIX: TRANSCRIPTION CONVENTIONS

(.)   brief pause (i.e. under 0.5 seconds)

(*n*)   timed pause (in seconds/tenths of a second)

=   no break between two (or more) speakers' utterances

[. . .]   period of overlapping talk

_____   (underlining) emphasis on syllable/word/phrase

?   rising intonation

!   markedly falling intonation

6 Complex identities: The case of academic women

Maaret Wager

INTRODUCTION

What is the connection between the woman researcher's gender identity and her academic work? How does an academic woman perceive herself? How does she construe her femininity? These were the questions I addressed in my research on academic women's identity (Wager, 1993, 1994; see also Wager, 1998a, 1999a). Biographies of women who have devoted their lives to intellectual work often have about them an air of amazement; these women are regarded as 'exceptions' (see Schiebinger, 1987; cf. Wager, 2000a). This indicates that the history of science is regarded as the history of men in science: it contains stories of such men as Aristotle, Einstein, or Freud, who have contributed to the 'great leaps' in our understanding of the universe, society, or the human being. However, since prehistoric times the history of science also includes stories of women who, in spite of their exclusion from educational facilities and the formal and informal fraternities of their male colleagues, have become scientists, often at the expense of their personal lives (see e.g. Alic, 1986; Isaksson, 1987; Schiebinger, 1989.

Women have had access to universities for about a hundred years; yet gender equality in academia has not been reached in any European country, or elsewhere (e.g. Stolte-Heiskanen and Furst-Dilic, 1991; Harding and McGregor, 1995; Fogelberg *et al.*, 1999). This is demonstrated, for example, in the fact that academia is gender-segregated both horizontally and vertically; first, there are fields dominated by men, like the sciences, and those dominated by women, like the humanities (see e.g. Lie and O'Leary, 1990; Husu, 1999). Second, women are concentrated in the lower grades. There is much evidence of discrimination against and marginalisation of women in the academic profession. However, now that the question of equality has become more and more a part of public debate, discriminatory practices in universities have taken increasingly subtle forms. Today the implicit message for women is: *if you don't succeed in academia, it is probably your own fault* (Caplan, 1993). If a woman fails, it is taken as 'proof' that women are inferior, whereas her success is 'proof' that there are no obstacles for women's success in academia (see also Husu, 1998).

It is essential that the research analysing identity in scholars in academia takes into account the well-demonstrated fact that academic organisations are gendered (e.g. Rose, 1994; Morley and Walsh, 1995; cf. Gherardi, 1995; Nicolson, 1996). Gender differentiation can be seen as individuals' activity whereby we 'do' gender (see Lorber and Farrell, 1991; cf. Wager, 1998b). Gendered processes operate at many levels, and in organisations they refer to practices whereby 'advantage and disadvantage, exploitation and control, action and emotion, meaning and identity, are patterned through and in terms of a distinction between male and female, masculine and feminine' (Acker, 1990: 146). My focus is on the gendering of identity. ISA provides an approach to the study of identity that allows its exploration in a way that takes into account as many of its complexities as possible (see Chapter 1 in this volume).

By and large, the aim of the current research is to contribute to a further understanding of gendered identity of women whose importance lies in their intellectual prowess. The basic question is: How does being an academic go together with being a woman? The focus is, in particular, on the women's constructions of themselves in the four categories of women: women in humanities with children and those without; and women in sciences with children and those without.

Rationality is traditionally connected with men's sense of masculine identity (e.g. Seidler, 1989). The image of a woman thinking hard, or asking 'important' questions, does not fit well with the dominant views and stereotypes about traditional femininity in our Western societies – in so far as these stereotypes are associated with emotionality and sexuality. As a consequence, women researchers may find themselves caught between two stereotypes: as professionals we are oddities, and as women we are unusual academics – particularly in male-dominated fields (see Rossiter, 1982). What this can amount to is that women may be faced with a critical problem of identity: we may, for example, try to 'forget' that we are women, or we can try to redefine the familiar notion of 'men of science' (Cole, 1979). It should be noted that male researchers can also be critical of the traditional view of scientific pursuit – as many of them are – but, by contrast to women, their identity does not necessarily require it (Keller, 1985).

The postulates that form the theoretical foundations of the study are based on the notion that the demand for equality between men and women in contemporary Western societies, in terms of equal opportunities in public life (workforce) and shared responsibilities in private life (at home), instigates processes of reappraisal of both femininity and masculininity. It can be argued that the polarisation of the private and public spheres of life into the domains of woman and man in the social organisation of our societies partly dictates the development of gender identity both in girls and in boys – and in women and men. The conceptions of feminine identity in a given society evolve in specific historical and cultural contexts, and acquire differing meanings for women depending on their private or public life spheres. That is, women tend to perceive themselves differently depending on whether they are in their private life or at their work environment (e.g. McBroom, 1986; Marshall and Wetherell, 1989; see also Mackinnon, 1997).

The context of this study is Finland. Finland differs from other Western countries in that the tradition of women's labour-force participation and education is more established than elsewhere, and it is normal for mothers of small children to be part of the labour force, most of them full-time. The percentage of women in paid employment has been for a long time about 80%, and only about 11% of the women work part-time. Nevertheless, the double burden of working women is a reality for most women, irrespective of the state's extensive support system that facilitates the combination of work and parenthood for both women and men. Further, concerning the educational system, the proportion of female undergraduates in Finland was higher at the beginning of the twentieth century than in any other European country (Korppi-Tommola, 1984). In 1927 a woman was appointed to professorship for the first time (Engman, 1989). However, despite the fact that more than half of the graduates nowadays are women, and the proportion of women's doctorates is 40%, the proportion of women holding professorships is 17.9% (Ministry of Education, 1999). Women seem to disappear on their way up the career-ladders.

IDENTITY EXPLORATION IN TERMS OF THE PROTOTYPES OF A WOMAN AND AN ACADEMIC

In ISA gender identity is defined in line with the general definition of identity, that is, as *that part of the totality of one's self-construal made up of those dimensions that express the continuity between one's construal of one's past gender and one's future aspirations in relation to gender* (Weinreich, 1989). Furthermore, professional identity is defined in terms that parallel those of the definition of gender identity. A woman's professional identity *is made up of those dimensions that express the continuity between one's construal of oneself in terms of one's profession in the past and one's future aspirations in relation to one's profession* (Wager, 1994).

In order to investigate academic women's constructions of themselves as women, probably the most common contemporary female prototypes were used in the ISA instrument, namely those of a 'feminine woman' and a 'feminist'. It should be noted that there is no single category, such as 'woman' as opposed to 'man' that would determine a woman's construction of her gender identity, but there are varying construals of aspects of femininity. I intended to investigate some of these aspects by means of these two female prototypes. The prototypes were chosen on the basis of the notion that the reappraisal of the conceptions of femininity in post-World War II Western societies was mainly initiated by the second wave of the feminist movement in the late 1960s. This contributed to the development of the contemporary prototype of a 'feminist' in addition to the conventional prototype of a 'feminine woman' referring generally to the middle-class femininity of Western societies.

As a consequence, these two prototypes appear among the target entities in the ISA instrument (see later section 'Gathering data for the study'). The use of prototypes is justified because they are at the heart of social categories (e.g. Rosch, 1978). In social psychology social categorisations are regarded as the fundamental processes forming a person's social identity (e.g. Turner, 1982). Hence, it can be assumed that a woman's gender identity is partly reflected in her construal of these 'paradigm examples' of woman. Provided that a social category is 'anchored' to the prototype (see Cantor and Mischel, 1979), the use of these two prototypes gives insight into those aspects of a woman's gender identity that she herself associates with these prototypes. The point is that neither a 'feminine woman' nor a 'feminist' is defined externally. In this study they are, in fact, defined individually by each woman in her own terms. The identity exploration then focuses on how the women perceive the relation between themselves and the prototypes as they construe them. For example, a woman's high empathetic identification with a prototype indicates that she construes herself partly in terms of the qualities she attributes to the given prototype. On the other hand, high conflict in identification with the prototype indicates that a woman's associations with some of the qualities she attributes to the prototype are problematic to her.

In order to investigate a woman's professional identity, the entities 'a colleague who has succeeded in his or her academic career' and 'a colleague who has not succeeded in his or her academic career' were used. The assumption behind these entities is that, together with the female prototypes, a woman's identifications with these professional prototypes give information on her construal of herself as a woman in the professional context of self. Of course, one could argue that it is pre-emptive to suggest that women should appraise their professional identity in terms of success. However, the institutional structures of universities provide limited influence and power to both academic women and men. Therefore, in terms of academic competition, success and failure inevitably determine the motivational structure of universities (Keller and Moglen, 1987; Morley, 1995; cf. Wager 1999b). Hence, whatever connotations women attach to particular individuals whom they choose to represent these two entities, their construals of them are most likely related to their perception of themselves as professionals. Furthermore, these two figures are assumed to be not only the 'paradigm examples' of academics, but also crucial targets for role-model identification (either positive or negative) for academic women.

WOMEN IN THE PRIVATE AND PROFESSIONAL CONTEXTS OF SELF: THE POSTULATES

As the contemporary Western views about women have mainly developed along with the division between the private and the public spheres of life characteristic of the industrial societies, this division was used in order to empirically investigate the nature of the women's personal continuity between private and professional identity. It is customary within the ISA framework to present the study's theoretical foundations in the form of postulates. Whereas in this study the first postulate states that the division between the private ('reproductive') sphere of life and the public ('productive') sphere of life may contribute to the association of traditional notions of femininity with private life and traditional notions of masculinity with public life, the second postulate argues that as long as the conventional assumptions about women are associated with the private sphere of life, and those of academic work with the public sphere of life, a professional woman contends with different definitions of women between the private and professional contexts (Wager, 1994: 90).

The point is that within the ISA framework, the changes in a woman's own perception of herself, in terms of her patterns of identification with the female prototypes and the professional prototypes across the life spheres, represent her differing constructions of herself in her private and professional contexts of self. Women in professions often themselves associate notions of femininity with the private sphere of life and perceive themselves as 'persons' or whatever when they are at work. For example, if a woman empathetically identifies with one of the prototypes more in her current self situated either in private life or in professional life compared to her past self-image, it is suggested that this is indicative of an ongoing process where she construes herself in terms of the qualities of that prototype more in that 'situated identity'. Furthermore, whether a woman's empathetic identification with, say, one of the female prototypes is increasing from her past self-image to the current one situated in the private sphere of life, but not to that situated in the work environment, the finding indicates that she construes her gender identity in these two contexts partly differently.

The third postulate suggests that, in so far as a professional woman contends with different definitions for women between the private and professional contexts, she may deal with the dissimilarity either by modulating between the private and professional contexts of self, or by transcending them. The 'modulation process' in this study refers to a person's changing patterns of identification between the two situated selves. For example, a woman's level of empathetic identification, or conflict in identification, with a female prototype may be higher in one context of self compared to the other. This would be indicative of a process whereby she modulates between her private and professional contexts of self in terms of (some of) the qualities attributed to this prototype. She may, for example, attribute to herself more of the qualities of a 'feminine woman' in her private context of self compared to the professional one. An extract from the interview material illustrates the modulation process. A woman explains: 'Feminine for me is something gentle and sensitive. I know I can be gentle, but when I am at work I suppress my femininity. One has to be hard in order to compete in academia.'

On the other hand, as the third postulate states, there is empirical evidence for another strategy that women use to tackle the 'gap' between the two life spheres and the associated societal notions of femininity: they redefine aspects of themselves in order to be able to construe themselves as both women and as professionals in both life spheres. This alternative process is to do with transcending the private and professional contexts of self. It means that a woman's patterns of identification do not change from one context to the other. Overall, the three postulates (postulates 1–3; see Wager, 1994) just explicated establish a theoretical distinction between aspects of a woman's gender identity and aspects of her professional identity in terms of her construal of the female prototypes and the professional prototypes.

A further three postulates (postulates 4–6; see Wager, 1994) lay the groundwork for the exploration of an academic woman's constructions of herself in the private and professional contexts of self in the light of her motherhood or childlessness, on the one hand, and her professional interest governed either by humanities or natural sciences, on the other. It is postulated that the dissimilarity of the societal definitions for professional women between the two contexts varies in relation to these four categories. The assumption is that factors of professional interest and motherhood are differentially incorporated within the women's identities and that these women's differing patterns of identification are underpinned by variations in value and belief systems. The identity exploration concentrates on the extent to which the women's constructions of themselves across the two contexts are linked with the process of modulating between the private and professional contexts of self, and with the process of transcending the two contexts.

GATHERING DATA FOR THE STUDY

In order to devise an appropriate instrument for the identity investigation, I interviewed academic women from different fields to find out which individuals and constructs would be relevant for women both as private persons and as professionals in academia. In addition to these 'brain-storming' sessions with my colleagues, I devised a pilot instrument using the triadic sort method based on grid technique (Kelly, 1955) to elicit the appropriate constructs (cf. Liebkind, 1984; Wager, 1988). The respondents for the pilot study consisted of a random sample of women academics in humanities and in natural sciences. The constructs elicited in this way and the feedback that I received from the respondents on how it 'felt' to complete the instrument, informed me about the selection of the entities and constructs for the final identity instrument. The final instrument consisted of 22 entities and 25 constructs.

The guiding principle in the development of the instrument (and in the research design in general) was what my colleagues and I had discussed on many occasions, namely that there was a tension between our gender identity and profession, such that academic women were often characterised on a 'continuum of outsiderness' (see Aisenberg and Harrington, 1988). In order to explore this 'tension', the chosen entities and constructs for the instrument enabled the respondents to appraise others and also reflect upon themselves both in private and professional contexts. The question was whether the experience of tension was common among women academics in terms of their dissimilar views of themselves in private life and in academia. The facets of self and significant individuals and prototypes in the entity list represented both gender identity and academic profession, on the one hand, and the division between the private and public spheres of life, on the other. The entities are listed in Table 6.1.

Table 6.1 The entities in the academic women's ISA instrument

The facets of self:	*The female and professional prototypes:*
Me as I am now	A feminine woman
Me as I used to be	A feminist
Me as I would like to be	A colleague who has succeeded in his/her career
Me at work	A colleague who has not succeeded in his/her career
Me in my private life	
Me as my partner sees me	
Me as my colleagues see me	

Other significant individuals:	
Partner	A woman that I dislike
Mother	My best female friend
Father	A man that I admire
Ideal mother	A man that I dislike
Ideal father	My best male friend
A woman that I admire	

The parameter 'structural pressure' estimates the centrality or uncertainty of people's values and aspirations as they are represented by the constructs chosen for the instrument. However, eliminating constructs from the abundant set of those elicited is difficult. The constructs were to convey attributes and beliefs associated with academic profession and professional life, on the one hand, and with conventional notions of women and private life, on the other. As a consequence, the areas that the constructs were to touch upon concerned autonomy and self-efficacy, on the one hand, and relations to other people, on the other; the former area is conventionally associated more with traditional masculinity than femininity, whereas the latter is the reverse (see e.g. Gilligan, 1982). However, this division was far from clear: in fact, all of the constructs can be categorised as belonging to both areas. The constructs are listed in Table 6.2.

The data were collected in the early spring of 1989 at the University of Helsinki, Finland. Altogether 104 women participated in this study – a response rate of 31%. I also interviewed 24 of these women for the purpose of providing validity for the ISA findings, and for writing case-studies. On the basis of letters and phone calls from those women who chose not to participate, I concluded that the low response rate was partly due to the nature of the task. The task required quite a lot of thinking and self-reflection. Moreover, some women told me that they felt they were asked to deal with too intimate issues, and they were not prepared for that.

Among the 104 women who participated, there were professors, assistant professors, senior lecturers, lecturers, and full-time researchers from various departments of the Faculties of the Humanities and the Natural Sciences at the University of Helsinki. All except one of the women were Finnish by nationality (other ethnic groups are only gradually entering our universities). The women's backgrounds varied from working class to upper middle class. I was interested in finding out

Table 6.2 The constructs in the academic women's ISA instrument

1. Ambitious/Not at all ambitious
2. Difficult to get on with other people/Gets on well with other people
3. Dependent, looks for support from other people/Can work things out alone
4. Thinks that women and men do not have equal opportunities to advance in their academic career/Thinks that women and men have equal opportunities to advance in their academic career
5. Plays it safe in life, avoids taking risks/Takes new chances in life, ready to take risks
6. Introvert/Extrovert
7. Acts according to emotions/Acts according to rational thinking
8. Acts and thinks independently/Lets other people guide oneself
9. Thinks that for a woman, a desire to both take care of her young children and to advance in her career, creates a contradiction/Thinks that there is no contradiction for a woman to have a desire to both take care of her young children and to advance in her academic career
10. Flexible/Demands more adaptability from others than from self
11. Changeable/Steady
12. Self-sacrificing/Does not make sacrifices
13. Practical/Impractical
14. Traditional/Modern
15. Caring/Mainly takes care of one's own business
16. Inefficient/Gets things done
17. Does not shun disagreements with others/Prefers avoiding disagreements with others
18. Easy-going/Strict
19. Submissive/Dominating
20. Regards sexuality as an important sphere of life/Does not regard sexuality as an important sphere of life
21. Thinks that a relationship requires sexual fidelity/Thinks that sexual fidelity is not a precondition for a relationship
22. Content with one's appearance/Discontent with one's appearance
23. Sexually inhibited/Comfortable with one's sexuality
24. Regards work as the most important thing in life/Regards human relations as the most important
25. Takes care of one's physical well-being/Neglects one's physical well-being

whether the women's conceptions of themselves as female academics varied among the four groups of women: women in the humanities with children (HM) and those without (HN); and women in the sciences with children (SM) and those without (SN) (see Table 6.3). The majority of the women (59%) were born between 1938 and 1951 indicating that they were in their midlife. A small minority (3%) were born between 1930 and 1934, whereas 38% were born between 1952 and 1966. The age factor will be discussed in the results section.

I also contacted a small group of 18 academic men in order to establish the extent to which women's identity processes parallel or differ from those in men. The sample was collected through friends and colleagues in the two faculties. The majority of them were under 38 years of age at the time of the inquiry, and more than half of them had no children. As the male sample was collected through friends, the likelihood of self-selection was great, having some specific ramifications for the particular findings that I will present. These men were, for whatever

Table 6.3 The sample by professional interest and motherhood

	No children	Children	Total
Humanities	40%	60%	100%
Sciences	49%	51%	100%
N	46	58	104

reasons, interested in gender issues in academia and, in that sense, may have represented the so-called 'new man'. Because of this, and also because of the small sample size, the differences and similarities that are found between the group of women and the group of men, are only suggestive. This is no problem, however, as I am not concerned about the generalisability of the findings but about identifying some psychological phenomena related to identity. The differences and similarities that are found between the women and men give valuable information about these phenomena in relation to gender, as they are expressed in this specific group of academics in Finland.

IN SEARCH OF CONTINUITY BETWEEN PRIVATE AND PROFESSIONAL IDENTITY

The overall results indicate that the academic women in this study – both in the humanities and in the sciences, and both mothers and non-mothers – contend with conflicted identifications with most of the female figures that appear in the entity list (see Table 6.1). Unlike the small group of men, who empathetically and idealistically identify with the prototype a 'feminine woman' to a high extent, the women's identification is particularly conflicted with this prototype, as well as with the prototype a 'feminist' – coupled with high ego-involvement with both of them. These women's conflicted identifications indicate that the women are reappraising aspects of their gender identity. That the men of the current study feel close to, and aspire towards 'feminine' qualities – but hold highly conflicted identifications with their primary gender model, that is, their father – suggests that there is an ongoing reappraisal process of masculinity: the 'new man' is more 'feminine' (see Wager, 1994, for details).

There are studies demonstrating that women often think that *it is not possible for a woman to be feminine and also exercise power and authority* (e.g. McBroom, 1986). The interviews with academic women demonstrate that the prototypical 'feminine woman' is associated with the traditional, middle-class femininity that developed after World War II in Europe and the USA (Friedan, 1965; cf. Oakley, 1974). Finnish women after the war were too busy in the labour force to lapse into this suburban 'feminine mystique'. Finland remained an agricultural society until the 1950s, and traditionally men and women worked together in agriculture. Furthermore, the country was poor, which meant that the middle class was not extensive. So perhaps, because of their strict work ethics, women learned to look down on 'feminine' femininity. As one woman said in the interview:

> When I was a child, the prevailing ideology taught me that if a woman was pretty, she couldn't be intelligent. Well, I wanted to be an intelligent girl, not a bimbo.
>
> (Humanities, no children)

The women also contend with conflicted identification with the prototypical 'successful academic' (see Wager, 1994, for details). The interviews demonstrate that these women perceive themselves differently from 'typical successful academics' in that they 'do not take the career so seriously' or that they 'cannot forget things at home while working', whereas they think that academic men are able to compartmentalise their work and their private life and keep them separate (cf. Burris, 1986; Lie, 1990).

There are also studies that indicate that in order to become an academic, a woman needs to combine her 'old' feminine identity and the 'new' professional identity by seeking greater integration between her private and public selves (e.g. Aisenberg and Harrington, 1988). The ISA results indicate that it is problematic for academic women – in both the humanities and in the sciences, and for both mothers and non-mothers – to combine some of their aspirations in relation to success in their profession with certain constructions of femininity. These women feel better about themselves at work both as women and as academics, whereas in their private life they perceive themselves as less positively 'feminine'. This is demonstrated in terms of the women's construals of the prototypes a 'feminine woman', a 'feminist', and a 'successful colleague'. In relation to their identification patterns with these prototypes, the women of the current study modulate between their private and professional contexts of self. The modulation process is linked, as indicated earlier, with their conflicted identifications with these prototypes, and with their more favourable self-evaluation in the professional context of self compared to the private one.

First, this is seen in Tables 6.4 and 6.5, which delineate a process in which both women and men increasingly empathetically identify with a 'feminine woman' from their past self-image to the current one situated in the private sphere of life, but not to that situated at work. With a 'feminist' the process is in reverse: women and men increasingly empathetically identify with this prototype when situated at work but not when situated in the private sphere of life. Within the 'decontextualised self' both groups' empathetic identifications are increasing from the past self-image to the current one significantly in relation to both prototypes. The findings indicate that both women and men do construe themselves (within their 'decontextualised self'), to some extent, as 'feminine' and 'feminist', but at work they construe themselves as 'feminist' to a higher extent than in private life, and in private life as 'feminine' to a higher extent than at work.

Tables 6.4 and 6.5 also indicate that the women empathetically identify with both of these female prototypes less than the men within all three facets of self. The finding suggests that the meaning the men give to these prototypes matches

Table 6.4 Empathetic identification with a 'feminine woman' in women and men

N	Women (104)	Men (18)	M
Past self-image	0.55	0.59	0.57
Current, in private life	0.65	0.73	0.69
M	0.60	0.66	

2-way analysis of variance:
A: $F = 3.99$; df $= 1,236$; $p < 0.05$.
B: $F = 14.37$; df $= 1,236$; $p < 0.0005$.
AB: ns.

Past self-image	0.55	0.59	0.57
Current, at work	0.58	0.66	0.62
M	0.56	0.63	

2-way analysis of variance:
A: $F = 3.99$; df $= 1,235$; $p < 0.05$.
B: ns.
AB: ns.

Past self-image	0.55	0.59	0.57
Current, without context	0.62	0.71	0.67
M	0.58	0.65	

2-way analysis of variance:
A: $F = 4.94$; df $= 1,236$; $p < 0.05$.
B: $F = 8.79$; df $= 1,236$; $p < 0.005$.
AB: ns.

A main effect: gender
B main effect: facets of self (past vs current)

Scale 0.00 to 1.00

their self-conception better than the meaning the women give to the prototypes matches theirs. That men, nevertheless, construct 'feminine' and 'feminist' aspects of themselves across the life spheres in a similar fashion to women indicates that both women and men associate 'feminine' femininity more with the private sphere of life than with the public sphere of life, and 'feminist' femininity more with the public sphere of life than with the private sphere of life. Hence, both women and men make a distinction between their private and professional contexts of self in terms of differing meanings of femininity. Furthermore, the women's identification with a 'feminine woman' to a greater extent in private life compared to professional life is coupled with their less positive self-evaluation in the private context of self compared to the professional one. Overall, women's self-evaluation is less positive than that of men (Table 6.6).

Second, women and men increasingly empathetically identify with their successful colleague from their past self-image to the current one situated in the public

Table 6.5 Empathetic identification with a 'feminist' in women and men

N	Women (104)	Men (18)	M
Past self-image	0.50	0.60	0.55
Current, in private life	0.53	0.60	0.56
M	0.51	0.60	

2-way analysis of variance:
A: $F = 6.16$; df $= 1,236$; $p < 0.025$.
B: ns.
AB: ns.

	Women (104)	Men (18)	M
Past self-image	0.50	0.60	0.55
Current, at work	0.59	0.67	0.63
M	0.55	0.63	

2-way analysis of variance:
A: $F = 8.19$; df $= 1,235$; $p < 0.005$.
B: $F = 7.74$; df $= 1,235$; $p < 0.01$.
AB: ns.

	Women (104)	Men (18)	M
Past self-image	0.50	0.60	0.55
Current, without context	0.59	0.63	0.61
M	0.54	0.61	

2-way analysis of variance:
A: $F = 4.87$; df $= 1,236$; $p < 0.05$.
B: $F = 3.99$; df $= 1,236$; $p < 0.05$.
AB: ns.

A main effect: gender
B main effect: facets of self (past vs current)

Scale 0.00 to 1.00

Table 6.6 Self-evaluation across the life spheres in women and men

N	Women (104)	Men (18)	M
In private life	0.50	0.55	0.52
At work	0.57	0.61	0.59
No context	0.58	0.69	0.64
M	0.55	0.62	

2-way analysis of variance:
A: $F = 3.86$; df $= 1,359$; $p < 0.05$.
B: $F = 3.28$; df $= 2,359$; $p < 0.05$.
AB: ns.

A main effect: gender
B main effect: facets of self (current ones)

Scale -1.00 to $+1.00$

Table 6.7 Empathetic identification with a 'successful colleague' in women and men

N	Women (104)	Men (18)	M
Past self-image	0.57	0.59	0.58
Current, in private life	0.59	0.63	0.61
M	0.58	0.61	

2-way analysis of variance: ns.

Past self-image	0.57	0.59	0.58
Current, at work	0.69	0.68	0.69
M	0.63	0.64	

2-way analysis of variance:
A: ns.
B: $F = 16.46$; df $= 1,239$; $p < 0.00025$.
AB: ns.

Past self-image	0.57	0.59	0.58
Current, without context	0.64	0.65	0.65
M	0.61	0.62	

2-way analysis of variance:
A: ns.
B: $F = 6.48$; df $= 1,240$; $p < 0.025$.
AB: ns.

A main effect: gender
B main effect: facets of self (past vs current)

Scale 0.00 to 1.00

sphere of life, and to that without context, but not to that situated in the private sphere of life (Table 6.7). In other words, both women and men do feel like successful professionals (in their 'decontextualised self') but, parallel to their empathetic identification with a 'feminist', they identify with their 'successful colleague' to a greater extent in the professional context of self. As with the other prototypes, this process is linked with their more positive self-evaluation within these two facets of self compared to the private one. However, in relation to the unsuccessful colleague, women empathetically identify with this person to an equally low level within all three facets of self. Consequently, the prototypical colleague representing 'career unsuccess' does not particularly match the women's self-conceptions (see Wager, 1994, for details).

Overall, the findings support postulates 1–3 that the women may construe aspects of themselves differently across the two life spheres (see earlier). The evidence demonstrates that in their differing constructions of themselves between their private and professional lives, the women feel better about themselves both as women and as professionals in the work environment compared to how they feel about themselves in private life. Furthermore, the overall results indicate that the women are very ambivalent in relation to the values dealing with care for others (Construct 15) and self-sacrifice (Construct 12): values traditionally associated with women (cf. Gilligan, 1982). No matter which pole of the two constructs they choose as positive, they use both constructs inconsistently in their evaluations of self and others. Instead, these women endorse independence as one of their central values. Independence means to them the capacity to work things out efficiently on one's own, both at home and at work (Tables 6.8 and 6.9).

As Tables 6.8 and 6.9 indicate, despite the fact that the group of men also find independence central to their value system, they construe it slightly differently from women. That is, men are far less consistent than women in their appraisal of self and others in terms of these two construct poles. For the men, the construct that contributes as the core evaluative dimension of their identity is 'acts and thinks independently' as opposed to 'lets other people guide oneself' (Construct 8; SP = 70.41).

That there is a difference between the women and the men in their emphasis on their core evaluative dimensions of identity can be interpreted as follows. Historically, women have provided the support for men – both in private life as mothers and wives, and in public life as secretaries or whatever. Women's support, however, has not necessarily intruded upon men's 'independence' because it has been women who have been regarded as lacking independence and, therefore, as being in need of men's support – both financially and intellectually. Consequently, whereas the need for support among men does not necessarily contradict their ideas of independence, among women it does so. Therefore, working things out

Table 6.8 Structural pressure on construct 3, pol. 2 'Can work things out alone'

N	Women (104)	Men (14)
	72.46	55.73

Scale -100 to $+100$
1-way analysis of variance:
$F = 7.30$; df = 1,115; $p < 0.01$

Table 6.9 Structural pressure on construct 16, pol. 2 'Gets things done'

N	Women (104)	Men (14)
	71.18	49.16

Scale -100 to $+00$
1-way analysis of variance:
$F = 21.01$; df = 1,120; $p < 0.00025$

alone – and efficiently – is the guarantee for independence in women, also for independence of 'action and thought'. Furthermore, many of the women that I interviewed said that in order to convince their academic community that they are 'as good as their male colleagues', they need to be, in fact, twice as good as them.

However, in order to 'soften' their intellectual prowess, women tend to attribute their professional success to fate or good fortune. This does not have to do with the 'fear of success' (cf. Horner, 1972). Rather, women's views about success and ambitions may be 'amateurish' (cf. Apter, 1985; Markus, 1986). For example, they may be completely devoted to their subject matter without thinking about a career goal:

> I've never wanted any scientific career, but I have just kept on doing this because it is fun.
>
> (Sciences, no children)

> The subject matter is really very dear to me. In fact, it is so fascinating and versatile that I hardly bear to complete it, let alone handing it over to the world!
>
> (Humanities, children)

Success may also be defined in terms of personal satisfaction with a woman's ability to combine motherhood and career aspirations – not only in everyday life but also on a more symbolic level:

> After I had given birth to my first child I got this defiant attitude and thought that, for god's sake, if I am able to give birth, sure I'm able to complete the PhD!
>
> (Humanities, children)

Finally, the entities that serve as the strongest positive role-models for the women in this study, are the prototypes of the 'ideal mother' and 'ideal father'. These figures represent the women's – as well as the men's – aspirations to the highest extent of all the target entities. The women also maintain their highly increasing empathetic identification with these figures from their past self-image to both their private and professional context of self. In line with postulate 3, the finding suggests that the women – as well as the small group of men – aspire towards transcending the private and professional contexts of self, ideally in such a way that they could construct themselves similarly across the two life spheres, and without restrictions in terms of social, or cultural definitions for women or men.

It is particularly interesting to notice that regardless of whether the women have children or not, all of the women – as well as the men in this study – would like to develop qualities associated with parenting. Clearly, for the women this is something different from the prototypical 'feminine'. Every woman is a potential mother; in order to transcend the private and professional contexts of self both mothers and non-mothers aspire to qualities that enable them to pursue both parenting and academic work. As a consequence, what these women really seem to aspire towards is gendered identity which is not restricted to prototypical 'feminine' or 'feminist' attributes but is compatible with their professional identity – which, for that matter, is not restricted to a prototypical 'successful academic'.

MOTHERS AND CHILDLESS WOMEN IN HUMANITIES AND IN SCIENCES

As stated earlier, the main interest of the current study is in the nature of the continuity between academic women's private and professional identity depending on two factors: first, whether the women are mothers or not and, second, whether their academic interest focuses on natural sciences or on humanities. The findings indicate that the combination of being a woman and an academic is particularly problematic for women with children in the sciences. The results suggest that these women tend to have the greatest need of all the women in the study to redefine aspects of their gender identity, that is, their conflicted identifications with the female others are strong. This has to do, in particular, with ageing: whereas mothers with younger children remain quite comfortable with their perceptions of themselves as women and as professionals, mothers who are over the age of the career peak tend to lack confidence in terms of living up to their goals and ideals of being both academics with authority and being good mothers.[1] Moreover, motherhood in the sciences most likely complicates the women's process of proving to themselves – and to their male colleagues – that they are able to combine a highly demanding profession with motherhood.

Compared to mothers in the sciences, women with children in the humanities turn out to be rather comfortable with what they are. This finding is linked with the women's slight indifference in relation to success in their career: the immediate demands of motherhood seem to be more pertinent to them than their aspirations towards being 'successful academics'. It seems that motherhood in the female-dominated field of humanities serves as a source of strength that helps women to combine aspects of their feminine identity with their professional identity. In the interviews some of these women compared the procedure of doing research to pregnancy, labour, and delivery in childbirth.

What about the childless women? The results demonstrate that the childless women in the sciences, unlike their colleagues who are mothers, have redefined aspects of their gender identity in that, of all the women, they hold the least conflicted identifications, and they identify greatly with their profession. Unlike the other women in this study, they also tend to choose the qualities of a 'feminist' as something to aspire to. These women seem to have gone through a process of proving to themselves – and to their colleagues – that a woman can be a highly successful professional. Family is not necessarily an issue at all. As one of these women explained: 'I would not have time for a family . . . Besides, I think I spend as much time dancing ballet as doing research.'

By contrast, childless women in the humanities do not identify with their profession very strongly at all. Instead, they can regard their work as their 'dear hobby' – as some of the women put it. In particular those under 38 years of age find the concept of 'success' in relation to their career highly problematic. One way of explaining this is to argue that, simultaneously with reaching their career peak (see note), professional women around the age of 38 without children are also approaching the age when the decision about ever having or not having children becomes relevant. As a consequence, some of them might find the tension between their professional and private life so immobilising that they fear choosing either work or family (cf. Aisenberg and Harrington, 1988). Clearly, after having made up their mind, they can find themselves happily child-free (cf. Wager, 2000b).

It can be concluded that whereas among mothers, women in the humanities seem to have dealt with the tension between being a woman and an academic with less ambivalence than women in the sciences, among the women without children, the opposite is the case. The childless women in the sciences are less ambivalent than the childless women in the humanities about combining aspects of their femininity with their profession. However, all of the women in this study aim at resolving the perceived dilemma between their feminine identity and academic work in terms of endorsing, to various extents, the importance of their work, and in terms of aspiring to redefine particular conceptions of femininity. The study demonstrates that feminine identity varies in complex ways and cannot be understood solely in terms of fixed categories such as 'feminist' or 'feminine'. In fact, women's problematic relation with these female prototypes indicates that these categories do not match their self-conceptions very well. Overall, the women of the study define their gender identity in their own terms which differ according to whether they pursue humanities or sciences, and whether or not they are mothers. On the basis of postulates 4–6 (see earlier), four propositions are derived:

Proposition 1. Women with children in the humanities
In so far as motherhood is more 'accepted' in the more female-dominated fields of humanities compared to those of sciences, mothers in humanities do not have a strong need to redefine their gender identity, or identify greatly with their profession.

Proposition 2. Women with children in the sciences
In so far as the fields of sciences are more male-dominated than humanities, ageing has a discouraging effect on women with children in sciences: whereas mothers with younger children remain quite comfortable with their gender identity and academic profession, mothers who are over the age of the career peak in the sciences, lack confidence in terms of attaining their goals related to success in their careers, as well as those related to their ideal of parenting.

Proposition 3. Childless women in the sciences
In so far as the sciences are more of a 'masculine' academic interest than the humanities, childless women in sciences have redefined their gender identity in that they identify greatly with their profession and with a 'feminist', who represents an alternative to the traditional notions of femininity, as their positive role-model.

Proposition 4. Childless women in the humanities
In so far as the humanities are more of a 'feminine' academic interest than the sciences, and a woman's childlessness deviates from the traditional

notions of femininity, childless women in humanities are confronted with redefining their gender identity further in that they do not identify with their profession to a high extent, but also have problems in relation to 'feminine' femininity.

In the current study it is empirically demonstrated that these women are in the process of redefining their constructions of themselves as academic women. Furthermore, depending on the academic field and motherhood, the women of the study have different conceptions of femininity, which do not necessarily coincide, for example, with the given prototypes a 'feminine woman' and a 'feminist' as defined by themselves. Finally, in this condensed account of the study I have demonstrated that ISA conceptualisations in terms of the definitions of concepts and their operationalisation provide unique information about the subtle differences in the redefinition processes of gender identity across the four categories of academic women in the specific cultural and historical context of Finland at the dawn of the 1990s. Perhaps, by now, these women have resolved their conflicted views about being a woman and an academic. Perhaps they have learned to feel equally good about themselves both as private and as professional women; or perhaps not. My hope is that, eventually, we can all be 'women' and 'professional academics' at the same time.

NOTE

1 Note that, in addition to using age as a continuous variable, its effect was explored in terms of the age groups separately for women with children and those without, in order to take into account the notion that life progresses in phases. That is, whether a woman has, or does not have, children phases her life quite differently. Therefore mothers and non-mothers are divided for analytic purposes into two age-groups with different cut-off points. The cut-off point for the age factor for mothers is 44, whereas for non-mothers it is 38. It can be argued that only when women with children are on their way to their 50s, are their children old enough for the women to commit themselves more to their work. On the other hand, women without children may really commit themselves to their work before the age of 40, when they have usually found their place in academia, and are on their way to reaching their occupational goals (see Wager, 1994, for details).

REFERENCES

Acker, J. (1990) 'Hierarchies, jobs, bodies: a theory of gendered organizations.' *Gender and Society*, 4: 139–158.
Aisenberg, N. and Harrington, M. (1988) *Women of Academe. Outsiders in the Sacred Grove*. Amherst: The University of Massachusetts Press.
Alic, M. (1986) *Hypatia's Heritage. A History of Women in Science from Antiquity to the Late Nineteenth Century*. London: The Women's Press.
Apter, T. (1985) *Why Women Don't Have Wives? Professional Success and Motherhood*. London: Macmillan.
Burris, B. H. (1986) 'Working mothers: the impact of occupational status on the family/work nexus.' *The International Journal of Sociology and Social Policy*, 6, 2: 8–21.

Cantor, N. and Mischel, W. (1979) 'Prototypes in person perception.' In L. Berkowitz (ed.) *Advances in Experimental Social Psychology*, Vol. 12. London: Academic Press.

Caplan, P. (1993) *Lifting a Ton of Feathers. A Woman's Guide to Surviving in the Academic World*. Toronto: University of Toronto Press.

Cole, J. R. (1979) *Fair Science. Women in the Scientific Community*. London: The Free Press.

Engman, M. (1989) 'On elettävä täysin yksin. Suomen varhaisimmista naistutkijoista' [One has to live entirely alone. The earliest woman researchers in Finland]. *Naistutkimus* [*Women's Studies Quarterly*], 1: 15–30.

Fogelberg, P., Hearn, J., Husu, L., and Mankkinen, T. (eds.) (1999) *Hard Work in the Academy: Research and Interventions on Gender Inequalities in Higher Education*. Helsinki: Helsinki University Press.

Friedan, B. (1965) *The Feminine Mystique*. Harmondsworth: Penguin.

Gherardi, S. (1995) *Gender, Symbolism and Organizational Cultures*. London: Sage.

Gilligan, C. (1982) *In a Different Voice. Psychological Theory and Women's Development*. Cambridge: Harvard University Press.

Harding, S. and McGregor, E. (1995) *The Gender Dimension of Science and Technology*. London: Unesco.

Horner, M. (1972) 'Toward an understanding of achievement related conflicts in women.' *Journal of Social Issues*, 2, 28:157–175.

Husu, L. (1998) 'Sexism, survival and support in academia: the case of Finland.' Paper presented in the International Conference *Winds of Change – Women and the Culture of Universities*, Sydney 13–17 July.

Husu, L. (1999) 'Gender equality in Finnish academia: contradictions and interventions.' In P. Fogelberg, J. Hearn, L. Husu, and T. Mankkinen (eds.) *Hard Work in the Academy: Research and Interventions on Gender Inequalities in Higher Education*. Helsinki: Helsinki University Press.

Isaksson, E. (1987) *Nainen ja Maailmankaikkeus* [*Woman and the Universe*]. Helsinki: Ursa.

Keller, E. F. (1985) *Reflections on Gender and Science*. New Haven: Yale University Press.

Keller, E. F. and Moglen, H. (1987) 'Competition and feminism: conflicts for academic women.' *Signs*, 12, 3: 493–511.

Kelly, G. A. (1955) *The Psychology of Personal Constructs*, Vols. 1 and 2. New York: Norton.

Korppi-Tommola, A. (1984) 'Naisten kasvatuksen ja koulutuksen tutkimus' [The research on women's education]. In P. Setälä (ed.) *Naiskuvista todellisuuteen* [*From Female Images to Reality*]. Hameenlinna: Gaudeamus.

Lie, S. (1990) 'The juggling act: work and family in Norway.' In S. S. Lie and V. E. O'Leary (eds.) *Storming the Tower. Women in the Academic World*. London: Kogan Page.

Lie, S. S. and O'Leary, V. E. (1990) 'In the same boat? Academic women around the world.' In S. S. Lie and V. E. O'Leary (eds.) *Storming the Tower. Women in the Academic World*. London: Kogan Page.

Liebkind, K. (1984) 'Minority identity and identification processes. A social psychological study.' *Commmentationes Scientiarum Socialium*, 22. Helsinki: The Finnish Society of Sciences and Letters.

Lorber, J. and Farrell S. A. (1991) *The Social Construction of Gender*. Newbury Park: Sage.

Mackinnon, A. (1997) *Love and Freedom. Professional Women and the Reshaping of Personal Life*. Cambridge: Cambridge University Press.

Markus, M. (1986) 'Women, success and civil society. Submission to, or subversion of, the achievement principle.' *Praxis International*, 5, 4: 430–442.

Marshall, H. and Wetherell, M. (1989) 'Talking about career and gender identities: a discourse analysis perspective.' In S. Skevington and D. Baker (eds.) *The Social Identity of Women*. London: Sage.

McBroom, P. A. (1986) *The Third Sex: The New Professional Women*. New York: Morrow.

Ministry of Education, Finland (1999) *KOTA-database on Universities and Higher Education*.

Morley, L. (1995) 'Measuring the muse: feminism, creativity and career development in higher education.' In L. Morley and V. Walsh (eds.) *Feminist Academics: Creative Agents for Change*. London: Taylor & Francis.

Morley, L. and Walsh, V. (1995) (eds.) *Feminist Academics: Creative Agents for Change*. London: Taylor & Francis.

Nicolson, P. (1996) *Gender, Power and Organisation: A Psychological Perspective*. London: Routledge.

Oakley, A. (1974) *Woman's Work: The Housewife Past and Present*. New York: Random House.

Rosch, E. (1978) 'Principles of categorization.' In E. Rosch and B. Lloyd (eds.) *Cognition and Categorization*. New Jersey: Lawrence Erlbaum Associates Inc.

Rose, H. (1994) *Love, Power and Knowledge: Towards a Feminist Transformation of Science*. Cambridge: Polity Press.

Rossiter, M. (1982) *Women Scientists in America*. Baltimore: Johns Hopkins University Press.

Schiebinger, L. (1987) 'The history and philosophy of women in science: a review essay'. *Signs*, 12, 2: 305–332.

Schiebinger, L. (1989) *The Mind Has No Sex? Women in the Origins of Modern Science*. Cambridge, MA: Harvard University Press.

Seidler, V. (1989) *Rediscovering Masculinity: Reason, Language and Sexuality*. London: Routledge.

Stolte-Heiskanen, V. and Furst-Dilic, R. (1991) (eds.) *Women in Science – Token Women or Gender Equality*. Oxford: Berg.

Turner, J. C. (1982) 'Towards a cognitive redefinition of the social group.' In H. Tajfel (ed.) *Social Identity and Intergroup Relations*. Cambridge: Cambridge University Press.

Wager, M. (1988) 'Naiseutta etsimässä. Tutkielma naisen identiteetistä' [In search of femininity: a study on woman's identity]. Ministry of Social Affairs and Health, Finland: *Equality Publications* No 2. Helsinki: Valtionpainatuskeskus.

Wager, M. (1993) 'Constructions of academic women: continuity between private and professional identity', Vols. 1 and 2. D.Phil. Thesis, University of Ulster.

Wager, M. (1994) 'Constructions of femininity in academic women. Continuity between private and professional identity.' *Annales Academiae Scientiarum Fennicae*, Series B 275. Helsinki: The Finnish Academy of Science and Letters.

Wager, M. (1998a) 'Women or researchers? The identities of academic women'. *Feminism & Psychology*, 8, 2: 235–243.

Wager, M. (1998b) 'Arvoituksellinen sukupuoli' [Puzzling gender]. In A.-M. Pirttilä-Backman and A.-L. Lahikainen (eds.) *Sosiaalinen vuorovaikutus* [*Social Interaction*]. Helsinki: Otava.

Wager, M. (1999a) 'Finnish academic women, professionalism and femininities: the question of identity.' In P. Fogelberg, J. Hearn., L. Husu, and T. Mankkinen (eds.) *Hard Work in the Academy: Research and Interventions on Gender Inequalities in Higher Education*. Helsinki: Helsinki University Press.

Wager, M. (1999b) 'Tutkijuus ja tunteet' [Academic identity and emotions]. In S. Näre (ed.) *Tunteiden sosiologiaa* [*The Sociology of Emotions*]. Helsinki: SKS.

Wager, M. (2000a) 'Research practices and relationships: emotions and identity in academic work.' Paper presented in the *16th EGOS (European Group of Organization Studies) Colloquium*, Helsinki School of Economics and Business Administration, 2–4 July.

Wager, M. (2000b) 'Childless by choice? Ambivalence and the female identity.' *Feminism & Psychology*, 10, 3: 381–387.

Weinreich, P. (1989) 'Variations in ethnic identity: Identity Structure Analysis.' In K. Liebkind (ed.) *New Identities in Europe: Immigrant Ancestry and the Ethnic Identity of Youth*. Aldershot: Gower.

7 The city, gender, and identity

Wendy Saunderson

INTRODUCTION

An understanding of the position of gender in the structures, processes and out-comes of urban production and consumption begins with the simple but central questions of 'who plans?' and 'for whom?'. Women comprise only 23% of urban planners and only 12% of urban designers (RIBA, 2001), but 52% of the popula-tion. What does this suggest for urban women, as the majority of city dwellers; and for women architects and planners, as the minority of landed professionals? Do men and women identify differently with city living? What are the core values that shape the identities of the men and women who plan and design our cities? And what lies at the interface between urban production and urban consumption?

A central aspect of the research problem was revealed as the specificity of women's relationship to the built environment, arising from women's social role as the primary carers of dependants (children, elderly, disabled) in our society, and often from women's dual role as mother and worker. Women's gender role-related disadvantage of physical constrictions over time and space is underpinned and 'endorsed' by gendered ideologies embedded in the social, economic and political structures and processes of the city. Such structures and processes, in turn, can enable gender relations which effectively *institutionalise* women's dependency. The implications of such institutionalised dependency are axiomatic to the specificity of women's relationship to the built environment, as both users of cities, and as architects and planners of cities.

THE CONTEXT

The context of this research is Belfast in the 1990s. Belfast is probably best known as a troubled and 'pariah' city: the hotbed of Northern Ireland's political struggles and sectarian violence from 1969 until the first IRA ceasefire in 1994. Its urban area spans sixty square miles and houses around half a million people – almost one-third of the Northern Ireland population. Renowned as a city of contrasts, its status as a contested city is exemplary (Saunderson, 1995b).

However, the 1990s witnessed a revival linked to the 'spatial eugenics' (Greed, 1994) of the Belfast Urban Area Plan (BUAP) 2001: the reflation, reclamation, reinvigoration, and re-imaging of Belfast's urban core via the post-industrial sectors of retailing, leisure and tourism. The old symbolism was replaced by the new values of corporate identity and functional anonymity displayed in built form (Edwards, 1993: 17–18). It is here, in the new 'hyper-reality' (Baudrillard, 1988) that 'post-modern capitalism thrives on the symbolic in the processes surrounding consumption' (Bocock, 1993: 114). And it is here, as demonstrated in the ISA results, that we can 'buy' collective and individual identities: where *ideas* are being consumed as much as objects.

The context of the 1990s literature in this area had moved away from women as the focus of inquiry, through conceptualising unequal gender relations and patriarchy as the root of women's subordination in the city, and firmly towards theorisations of the significance of space and place (as they intersect with gender, class, race, sexuality and culture). These theorisations were used to map out the geographies of women's lives within and between spaces and places, and to explore gendered socio-spatial relations across the life-course (Katz and Monk, 1993; Ardener, 1993; Simonsen, 1996). Explorations of the role of spaces and places in the arenas of gender and sexuality, and the concept of space and place in contextualising gender relations, were *de rigueur* in the late 1990s (Bell and Valentine, 1995; Betsky, 1995; Duncan, 1996; Bondi, 1998; Hubbard, 1998; Nast, 1998; Domosh, 1999). Development of the research area often fractured and fragmented out of disciplinary boundaries, and into a pastiche of 'cultural studies' (Saunderson, 1997: 481). Indeed, in the late 1990s, postmodernism, 'characterised by the crumbling of overarching theories and an unprecedented eclecticism and combination of thought, taste and culture' (Hague, 1995: 211), was often as evident in the literature about the city as it was in the city itself.

THE STUDY

Conceptualising 'urban identity'

The theories, methods and frames of reference used in researching 'the city' have been prolific in quantity and diverse in quality and approach. Since the early, now classic, expositions by Simmel (1903), Park and Burgess (1925) and Wirth (1938), urban sociologists, human geographers and environmental psychologists – from the objective physical determinist schools of thought to the subjective phenomenological schools of thought – have been conceptualising and measuring urban perception and behaviour. While many approaches were commendable efforts at constructing various models or measurements for disentangling specific aspects of the person–environment relationship, few – if any – attempted to simultaneously conceptualise, theorise and 'measure' the person as a whole entity, intimately bound up with his or her environment. As Fransella (1981: vi) believed: 'this might well have led to the study of the person becoming the very basis of the whole discipline of psychology rather than, at present, being only one of its many "areas" of study'. Although possible exceptions do exist in the urban research that uses personal construct psychology to theorise its repertory grid measurements (e.g. Dobbin, 1985; Hanna, 1988), these are essentially cognitive in approach, and therefore leave affective and emotional considerations untapped. Also, because personal construct theory is essentially a self-contained theory, it discourages the exploration and synthesis of other theories and perspectives into its approach.

Alternatively, ISA is an open-ended framework embodying a conceptualisation of identity that contains an operational corpus. ISA attempts to conceptualise and theorise the person as a whole entity with a unique identity, rejecting an atomised view of self, and will empirically 'measure' various aspects of specific 'portions' of such identity. The facility to explore urban identity in this way is the *raison d'être* of ISA in this research on women, cities and identity. Furthermore, ISA transforms almost purely idiographic qualitative information into standardised quantitative indices which allow nomothetic analysis. And importantly, as Lange (1989: 170) points out, analysis is anchored in each individual's value system, and also provides explicit measures of the evaluative consistency of individuals.

In general terms, 'urban identity' is defined here as 'the sense of oneself as a participant in the urban milieu'. It is the 'portion' of self-identity that focuses on relatively conscious, personally held beliefs, interpretations and evaluations of oneself *as a participant* in urban milieux. Using an urban sociopsychological approach (relating psychological perception to social situations within the city) and an urban psychophysical approach (relating subjective perception to objective physical attributes of the city), urban identity is conceptualised, accessed and 'measured' as a type of place-identity (Proshansky *et al.*, 1983), and as a sub-structure of self-identity (Proshansky, 1978), and as such, one that variously subsumes, fuses with, helps to define, and is defined by, other sub-identities like gender identity and professional identity. This conceptualisation of urban identity is couched within, and elaborates, the open-ended framework of Identity Structure Analysis, a formal system of concepts of identity which may be operationalised via ISA's Identity Exploration (IDEX) computer software.

Accessing and measuring 'urban identity'

In order to *access* urban identity, detailed sensitising procedures were needed to ascertain what the nature, parameters, discourse and content of urban identifications might be: personal accounts of city living were collected from male and female architects and town planners at their work places; and from men and women in the cafes, bars, and shops, at the bus stops and on the benches of Belfast. These 'internal, covert and reflective elements of social behaviour and experience' (Denzin, 1978: 252) were used to design an ISA identity instrument containing salient aspects, artefacts and personal constructions of urban life. Following amendments prompted by piloting, the final version of the instrument contained 24 entities (see Table 7.1) and 19 constructs (see Table 7.2).

The urban identity instrument was slightly 'hybrid' in that the version completed by the architects and town planners contained one additional entity to

Table 7.1 Entities in the 'urban identity' instrument

Urban consumers' instrument	Urban producers' instrument
1. Public Transport	Public Transport
2. Children's Public Play Areas	Children's Public Play Areas
3. Me as My Family Sees Me (at home)[#]	Me as My Family Sees Me (at home)[#]
4. Me as My Colleagues See Me (at work)[##]	Me as My Colleagues See Me (at work)[##]
5. Me as I Would Like to Be*	Me as I Would Like to Be*
6. (Most) Town Planners	(Most) Town Planners
7. Leisure Facilities in Belfast (nominate)	Leisure Facilities in Belfast (nominate)
8. Public Housing (new, low-rise)	Public Housing (new, low-rise)
9. Me as I am Now**	Me as I am Now**
10. Me as I Used to Be***	Me as I Used to Be***
11. A Person I Admire (nominate)[†]	A Person I Admire (nominate)[†]
12. Belfast City Centre – Daytime	Belfast City Centre – Daytime
13. Belfast City Centre – Night-time	Belfast City Centre – Night-time
14. (Most) Architects	(Most) Architects
15. Me as 'Producers' See Me[###]	Me as 'Consumers' See Me[###]
16. My Neighbourhood/Locality	My Neighbourhood/Locality
17. Town Parks (e.g. Botanic Park)	Town Parks (e.g. Botanic Park)
18. Most Women I Know	Most Women I Know
19. Most Men I Know	Most Men I Know
20. A Person I Dislike[††]	A Person I Dislike[††]
21. Our Local City Councillors	Our Local City Councillors
22. Castlecourt Shopping Centre	Castlecourt Shopping Centre
23. Town Planning in N Ireland in General	Town Planning in N Ireland in General
24. Me as a User of the Built Environment[¶]	Me as a User of the Built Environment[¶]
25. N/A	Me as a Producer of the Built Environment[¶¶]

Mandatory entities: *ideal or aspirational self; **current self (uncontextualised); ***past self; [†]admired person; [††]disliked person.
Optional entities: [¶]SituatedSelf (as 'user') (consumers and producers); [¶¶]Situated self (as 'producer') (producers only).
Metaperspectives: [#]Me as my family sees me; [##]Me as my colleagues see me; [###]Me as 'producers/consumers' see me (other group)

include their 'urban professional' self ('me as a "producer" of the built environment'). Also, in tracking identifications of each group with the other, one metaperspective (entity no. 15) probed the producers' perception of how the consumers viewed them, and vice versa. Otherwise, for both the producers and the consumers, the instrument contained the five mandatory entities (see Table 7.1) including the uncontextualised self located in the present; a situated self in the present context of 'user of the built environment', and two metaperspectives of self by family and self by colleagues. No past context of situated self was invoked.

The instrument was 'administered' to 120 of Belfast's male and female urban producers and consumers. The 60 architects and town planners (30 women; 30 men) were all involved in some aspect of the planning and design of Belfast; many had

Table 7.2 Constructs in the 'urban identity' instrument

1. Is/Are well designed	Is/Are badly designed
2. Cold, impersonal, distant, discourage/s socialising	Warm, friendly, congenial, encourage/s socialising
3. Welcoming, induce/s a feeling of confidence and belonging	Unwelcoming, make/s me feel like an outsider
4. Not very accessible	Very accessible
5. Feel/s unsafe, make/s me feel a bit insecure	Feel/s safe, allows me to feel very secure
6. Willing to put oneself out for others	Insists on rights for oneself
7. Symbolise/s functional purposes and utility	Symbolise/s power and status
8. Has/Have feminine characteristics	Has/Have no feminine characteristics
9. Pleasant, attractive, aesthetically pleasing	Is/Are 'awkward, unattractive'
10. Not interested in being accepted by and accountable to others	Would like to be accepted by, and accountable to others
11. Facilitate/s and make/s women's day-to-day lives easier	Hamper/s and make/s difficult women's day-to-day lives
12. Difficult with children	Easy with children
13. Has/Have masculine characteristics	Has/Have no or few masculine characteristics
14. Support/s involvement with community-based planning	Do/es not support involvement with community-based planning
15. Effective, show/s professional approach	Ineffective, show/s unprofessional approach
16. Is/Are/Am rigid, closed, rejecting change	Is/Are/Am flexible, open-minded, adaptable
17. Has/Have priorities right	Do/es not have priorities right
18. Believe/s specialised knowledge belongs with the experts/professions	Believe/s the public should have access to, and be able to openly question, urban professional judgements
19. Would like to see things changed	Is/Are/Am satisified with the way things are

major and direct involvement in the BUAP through their employment in Belfast's Divisional Headquarters of the Planning Service. The 60 urban consumers (30 women; 30 men) were all resident in the city for at least 3 years and were frequent users of its built environment. The consumers were randomly sampled from the Electoral Register: from a predominantly 'middle-class' Ward, to roughly accord with the aspirations, educational levels, lifestyles and disposable incomes of the architects and town planners. As regards 'measuring' urban identity, the IDEX software facilitated the transformation of almost purely idiographic, qualitative information about city life into standardised quantitative indices of identity.

Regarding the socio-historical location of the research, Belfast's frequent parallels with Beirut drawn by the international media, and more recent comparisons with the 'urban nightmare' of Detroit (Neill *et al.*, 1995), may render it a curious choice for an investigation of identity, and especially so when there was no particular focus on the city's socially and politically divided context. Possible adverse or intervening effects on empirical data collection did not go unacknowledged, particularly since the data reported here were collected in the early 1990s, during a period of the worst civil unrest for over a decade (several completed identity instruments were lost when the Belfast Divisional Planning Offices were gutted by a 100lb bomb). Issues of, for example, women's personal safety and security feature strongly in the literature, but within the arena of *sexual* politics, not sectarian politics. To avoid ambiguity in interpretation of such personal constructs, non-ISA contingency questions were used during data collection to separate fear of terrorist attack from fear of sexual attack (see Saunderson, 1995a for full account).

THE RESULTS

The overview of empirical findings reported here suggests, in brief, that Belfast's re-imaging has been 'successful'; that (like men) women in Belfast have generally positive urban identities, but that (unlike men) women's urban identity is made *vulnerable* by several particular aspects of urban life when the women construe themselves as *users* of the built environment. Women working as architects and town planners in Belfast appear to have fully absorbed a 'malestream' professional identity. Lastly, incongruities lie at the interface between urban production and consumption in Belfast, particularly regarding the ownership of professional knowledge and the democratisation of urban production.

Women's positive self-image in the city

In so far as the city centre represents the 'essence' of a city, it is possible to discern a general 'orientation' towards the city – i.e. personal, social, spatial and symbolic representations of it – by investigating overall patterns of identification with the city centre. 'Core urban identity', as the organising nexus of the individual in the city, may be pin-pointed by people's levels of ego-involvement, idealistic-identification and empathetic identification with the urban core. In other words, if the qualities one attributes to the city centre are very similar to one's own 'ideal' qualities (high idealistic-identification); and if one perceives similarity between such desirable attributes and those of one's own self-image (moderate to high empathetic identification); and if the urban core is a salient feature of city living (moderate to high ego-involvement), then one may be deemed to have a strong and positive urban identity (which may, of course, be subject to change in different self-contexts). In terms of these criteria, urban women in Belfast possess generally strong and positive urban identities – in other words, women's core urban identity was found to be fairly robust and affirmative. When we compared the urban identity of men living in the city, however, significant differences were revealed (Table 7.3).

While core urban identity is generally strong for both women and men living in Belfast, it is significantly stronger for men – in all three of its

Table 7.3 Core urban identity

Identity index	Men (n = 60)		Women (n = 60)		M
	Prods* *(n = 30)*	*Cons** *(n = 30)*	*Prods** *(n = 30)*	*Cons** *(n = 30)*	
Ego-involvement (scale: 0 to 5)	2.80	3.48	2.52	2.41	2.80
Mean		*3.14*		*2.47*	

2-way Anova:
A: $F = 23.34$; df = 1,115; $p < 0.0001$
B: $F = 4.19$; df = 1,115; $p < 0.05$
AB: $F = 8.06$; df = 1,115; $p < 0.01$

Idealistic-idfn. (scale: 0 to 1)	0.69	0.88	0.65	0.69	0.73
Mean		*0.79*		*0.67*	

2-way Anova:
A: $F = 8.23$: df = 1,115; $p < 0.01$
B: $F = 7.85$; df = 1,115; $p < 0.01$
AB: ns

Empathetic idfn. (CS1) (scale: 0 to 1)	0.71	0.89	0.64	0.70	0.74
Mean		*0.80*		*0.67*	

2-way Anova:
A: $F = 8.94$; df = 1,115; $p < 0.01$
B: $F = 7.40$; df = 1,115; $p < 0.01$
AB: ns

Ego-involvement, idealistic- and current empathetic identification (uncontextualised) with the urban core (Belfast city centre) for men and women as urban producers and consumers
A Main Effect: Gender: Level (i) Men; Level (ii) Women
B Main Effect: Urban Status: Level (i) Producers; Level (ii) Consumers
*Prods – Urban producers (architects and town planners); Cons – Urban Consumers (city dwellers); CS1 – Current uncontextualised self

dimensions: ego-involvement ($p < 0.0001$); idealistic-identification ($p < 0.01$); and empathetic identification ($p < 0.01$). For men as urban dwellers, the city centre comes close to being a truly 'ideal' setting; it is construed as being very agreeable and 'in tune' with their own self-image; and it represents a highly salient feature of their urban lives. Such gender differences are not discernible amongst urban producers. The similar core urban identities of men and women working as architects and town planners is perhaps an important commentary on the socialisation and professionalisation of women into the male-oriented ethos, praxis and pedagogy of the landed professions (a point to be returned to later).

Returning to the generally strong urban identities and identifications of Belfast's women, a particularly prominent and positive feature in the identity structures of urban women (and reinforcing earlier assertions about Belfast's re-imaging) is

Castlecourt Shopping Mall. Often referred to as Belfast's 'heart transplant', Castlecourt was consciously designed as a symbol of a stylish, sophisticated, cosmopolitan consumer culture of a 'new look' Belfast: another Cathedral of Consumerism (Fiske, 1989) in which we are invited to 'buy' or create a social identity for ourselves (Bocock, 1993). Castlecourt is a salient feature in the urban lives of Belfast's women. Not only does it exemplify all they aspire to in terms of aesthetic pleasure, safety, congeniality and accessibility (idealistic-identification = 0.84), urban consumers see themselves as personally 'sharing' the very desirable, sophisticated and thoroughly modern characteristics that Castlecourt epitomises for them (empathetic identification = 0.84). One woman asserted:

> Well, when you walk into it, you just get a buzz [sic]: it's big, modern, trendy, I like Debenhams myself. And you feel really safe, especially with the kids. My friends and I really like it, it's a really good place to be; you could be any-one, in any big city in the world – and you can forget about what's going on outside.

For Belfast's urban consumers, both women and men, Castlecourt clearly rein-forces and enhances a desired self-image in the city (cf. Longhurst, 1998), con-tributing to and supporting a strong and positive urban identity. While other aspects of city living such as city parks and the day-time city centre generally support confident urban identities, certain urban aspects create sharp *vulnerability* in the identity structures of Belfast's urban women.

Women and vulnerable urban identity

When urban women appraised themselves as actually *using* the built environ-ment, certain aspects of the city gave rise to strong conflicts in identification cou-pled with low self-evaluation, contributing to a highly vulnerable identity state. Identification conflicts arise when one perceives similar attributes in oneself and another, while simultaneously wishing to dissociate from the other's attributes, thus creating an 'uncomfortable' psychological state. Figures 7.1 and 7.2 show both men's and women's fairly normal, unremarkable urban identification con-flicts when construing the city in their 'personal' self (i.e. 'me as I am now').

However, while construal in their 'urban-user' self remained unproblematic for men, Figure 7.2 reveals that when women think of themselves in terms of actually *using* the city, vast conflicts in identification arise: 81% have low self-evaluation in this user context, with 64% being classified in a 'crisis' identity state. Urban women appear to experience particularly strong identification conflicts with aspects of the city closely associated with the tasks and demands of their social role as primary carers (e.g. children's public play areas); and with the people responsible for pro-viding such aspects (i.e. town planners and city councillors). The strongest identifi-cation conflicts, contributing to vulnerability in the identity structures of urban women, are in relation to public transport and the night-time city.

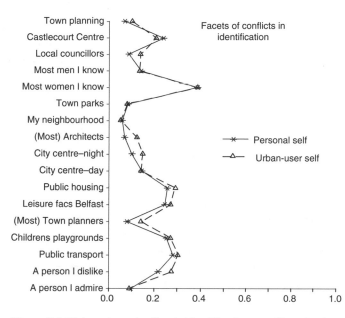
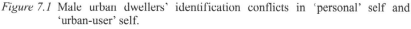

Figure 7.1 Male urban dwellers' identification conflicts in 'personal' self and 'urban-user' self.

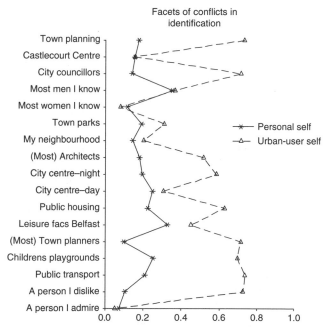
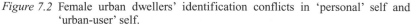

Figure 7.2 Female urban dwellers' identification conflicts in 'personal' self and 'urban-user' self.

Public transport

The specificity of women's relationship to the built environment involves distinctive and demanding spatial activity arising from their social role as the primary carers of children and other dependants, and often their dual role as mother and worker. Such spatial activity gives rise to women's particular mobility needs, often for short, multi-purpose, multi-stage journeys, and always for safe, frequent, accessible, reliable and affordable transport provision. As only 47% of households in the Belfast Urban Area owned a car at the beginning of the 1990s (DOE NI, 1990: 118), many of which will often not be available to women, it is hardly surprising that most urban women either walk or use public transport (RTPI, 1991). Public transport is a highly contested aspect of urban women's lives. That 87% of women are 'not at all satisfied with public transport in Belfast', compared with 3% of men (Saunderson, 1995a), suggests that women's particular mobility needs in the city are *not* being met. Further, Figure 7.2 shows that of all aspects of city life, women's highest identification conflicts (0.74) are associated with public transport, rendering it the strongest contributor to vulnerabilities in the urban identities of women as users of the city. Public transport provision creates no such vulnerability in the urban identities of men, for whom it is not a contested aspect of the city.

The night-time city

Ease of movement in the city is as much psychological as it is physical. If a woman *perceives* personal danger or threat, then fear results. Whether this fear is 'justified' or not, is immaterial with regard to the consequences it will have in influencing subsequent movement, avoidance or encounter. A lack of perceived personal safety and security in the city may create vulnerability in urban identity. And too often, 'women's fear of violence is realised as spatial exclusions' (Koskela, 1999: 111). Table 7.4 demonstrates that the night-time city is unproblematic for women in Belfast when appraised in terms of their uncontextualised self. In this context women's contra-identification is high, and higher than men's ($p < 0.0001$), while their empathetic identification with it is low, and lower than men's ($p < 0.0001$) (This finding shows how two groups can display a similar average identity parameter, but for quite different underlying reasons: i.e. men's low contra-identification and high empathetic identification and women's reverse pattern still result in similarly low conflicts in identification: men = 0.22; women = 0.23.) The women's non-situated self in terms of the night-time city, therefore, is not associated with particular conflicts in identification (0.23), and hence, their urban identity is not rendered vulnerable by it.

However, when these women appraised themselves in the context of *using* the built environment, their identifications with the night-time city immediately paralleled percepts of personal danger and insecurity, and became highly conflicted (see Figure 7.2), unlike those of men in this identity context (compare Figure 7.1). During the open-ended interviews, several women commented that they somehow felt 'uncomfortable in' and really didn't feel 'a part of' Belfast at night.

Table 7.4 Identifications with Belfast city centre by night

Identity index	Men (n = 60)		Women (n = 60)		M
	Prods* (n = 30)	Cons* (n = 30)	Prods* (n = 30)	Cons* (n = 30)	
Contra-identification	0.34	0.10	0.44	0.66	0.39
Mean		0.22		0.55	

2-way Anova:
A: F = 38.26; df = 1,115; p < 0.0001
B: ns
AB: F = 17.88; df = 1,115; p < 0.001

Empathetic identification	0.60	0.82	0.40	0.29	0.53
Mean		0.71		0.35	

2-way Anova:
A: F = 44.61; df = 1,115; p < 0.001
B: ns
AB: F = 9.11; df = 1,115; p < 0.01

Contra-identification and empathetic identification (uncontextualised) with Belfast city centre by night for men and women as urban producers and urban consumers (scale: 0.00 to 1.00)
A Main Effect: Gender: Level (i) Men; Level (ii) Women
B Main Effect: Urban Status: Level (i) Producers; Level (ii) Consumers
*Prods – Urban Producers (architects and Town Planners); Cons – Urban Consumers (urban dwellers)

Many women, particularly urban consumers, said they simply did not go into Belfast at night; some said they would, but only if they were accompanied, were in a car, or had booked a return taxi. One woman submitted:

> You don't go into the city at night if you know what's good for you – it's no place for women late at night. Anyway, I can never be blamed for being caught in 'the wrong place' at 'the wrong time' if I stay at home in my *own* space – at least I can control what goes on here.

Such protestations and indications of an implicit curfew on women using the night-time city reinforced the contention, again and again, of gendered and contested urban space (see also, Koskela, 1997, 1999; Morrell, 1996; Pain, 1997a,b, 2000; Saunderson, 1997). For many urban women in the night-time city, urban space – or rather, 'place' – can act as a structural embodiment of ideals, but in this case, ideals that are challenged by women's *use* of the night-time city (see McLeod and Gordon, 1999). And such challenges are frequently realised as spatial exclusion. Clearly, for women in Belfast, fear for personal security in the night-time city adds a very undesirable dimension – socially, spatially and symbolically – to their urban lives.

But what do urban dwellers in Belfast *mean* by personal safety and security? Safety from *what*? This was a particularly pertinent question in the socio-historical context of the euphemistically termed 'troubles' and the politically distressed 'pre-cease-fire' climate of Belfast. Of urban men, 53% feared personal attack in the city (being robbed/mugged or personally threatened), while 47% felt their personal safety threatened by sectarian violence (being 'caught up' in terrorist bombs or shootings). In contrast, *all* urban women referred to personal safety in terms of being safe from sexual harassment or direct sexual attack (20% of women also fear, among other things, sectarian activity, but only at night). So, it would appear that even in the face of the exceptionally 'troubled' political climate of Belfast, issues of women's personal safety in the city remain very much in the arena of *sexual* politics, not sectarian politics (Saunderson, 2001).

In terms of the meaning of safety and security in the value systems of city dwellers, it would be reasonable to expect that personal safety is a more important evaluative criterion for women than for men, given the foregoing evidence. However, Table 7.5 reveals that 'feeling safe and being allowed to feel very secure' is a comparably core evaluative dimension of both women's and men's identity when judging the desirability of aspects of the city, self and others. Women's particularly high contra-identification with Belfast's night-time city suggests that it falls very short of their aspirations for personal safety and security, and that it actually represents the contrasting pole of the construct: 'feels unsafe, makes me feel a bit insecure', as borne out in the narrative quoted earlier.

What does all this suggest about urban identity, gender, and contested urban space in Belfast? Urban identity, 'the sense of oneself as a participant in the urban milieu', is generally strong and positive for both women and men. However, in so far as urban identity may be conceptualised as an 'indicator' of social, spatial, and symbolic representations of the city, women's user-self construal of *particular aspects* of urban living (such as the night-time city and public transport) renders their urban identity vulnerable and thereby renders Belfast as highly contested space – socially, spatially, and symbolically – along the lines of gender.

Table 7.5 Core values: Safety and security

	Men (n = 60)		Women (n = 60)		M
	Prods* *(n = 30)*	*Cons** *(n = 30)*	*Prods** *(n = 30)*	*Cons** *(n = 30)*	
SP	63.26 (29)	77.48 (29)	65.82 (29)	80.42 (30)	71.75
Mean		70.37		73.12	

2-way Analysis of Variance:
A: ns
B: $F = 20.07$; df = 1,13; $p < 0.001$
AB: ns

Structural pressure on construct: 'feel/s safe, allows me to feel very secure' (scale -100 to $+100$)
A Main Effect: Gender: Level (i) Men; Level (ii) Women
B Main Effect: Urban Status: Level (i) Producers; Level (ii) Consumers
*Prods – Urban Producers (architects and town planners)'; Cons – Urban Consumers (city dwellers);
SP – Structural Pressure on Constructs

Women as urban producers: Contested identities?

Historically and contemporarily, patriarchy and the professions have been seen as largely synonymous. The questions of 'who designs the designers?' and of whether women design differently from men, remain largely rhetorical ones. Women in the urban planning and design professions are interviewed, accepted, trained, examined, judged competent, referred, interviewed again, then employed, and indeed promoted, almost exclusively by men. Certainly, the landed professions of architecture and town planning reflect a male-oriented ethos, praxis and pedagogy. But does women's enculturation into the landed professions affect their identity? Does their identity *modulate* between personal self (me as I am now) and professional self (me as an architect/town planner)? And what effect, if any, does urban-professional training have on women's identifications with the city as 'users' of the built environment?

The components of enculturation may be defined as 'language, beliefs, assumptions and psycho-social history' (Weiner and Marcus, 1994: 213). The processes of enculturation in terms of active (agentic) identification are explicated in Chapter 1 of this volume. The above definition suggests a more passive 'being absorbed by . . .', while the process can in fact be more of an 'active self-investment in . . .' (refer to discussion in Chapter 1). The findings here suggest that women's enculturation into the particular socio-cultural matrix of the landed professions does *not* result in a modulation of urban identity between personal and professional self. Rather, the particular and pervasive processes of professionalisation appear to result in women's identifications in the personal self being *modified* (i.e. tailored) to those of the professional self. Such modification, rather than modulation, of identity between these facets of self reveals that personal and professional self are largely coexistent for urban-professional women in Belfast, just as they are for their male colleagues (both traditionally and contemporarily). This finding would appear to imply enculturation of a more passive 'absorption' nature, but cannot disregard the processes of the women's 'agentic self' and its active identification with the existing design cultures and their continual updating (for example, Castlecourt). Lending graphic illustration to this coexistence or 'merging' of personal and professional identities, Figures 7.3 and 7.4 show the extent to which these women architects and town planners have been 'naturalised' (and to an extent, have 'self-invested') into the particular socio-cultural matrix of the landed professions. These findings may be contrasted to Wager's (1993) study of academic women, which demonstrated a distinct *modulation* between identifications in the personal ('at home') self, and the professional ('at work') self, of female university lecturers in Finland.

However, aside from their enculturation and 'absorption' into a male-dominated urban design culture, for women working as architects and town planners in Belfast, their womanhood – and its attendant social role – remains. Notable though, is that while *all* urban women's identification conflicts increase sharply when they think of actually using the built environment (as already reported), these conflicts are generally much *lower* for the female architects and town planners. It is suggested

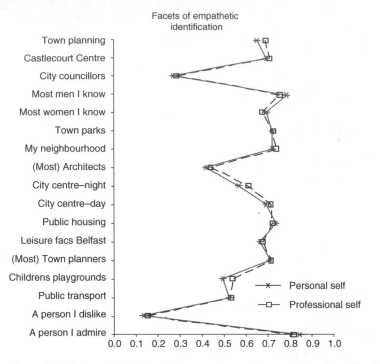

Figure 7.3 Male architects' and town planners' empathetic identification in 'personal' self and 'professional' self.

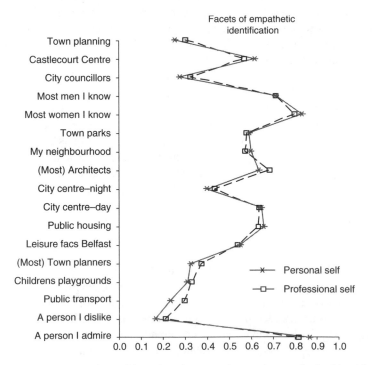

Figure 7.4 Female architects' and town planners' empathetic identification in 'personal' self and 'professional' self.

that female producers' identification conflicts in the 'urban-user' context are *moderated* by their confident orientation towards, and perceived 'control' of, aspects of the city. It is suggested that this is a result of their familiarity and certain 'intimacy' with the urban environment, achieved through being formally educated, trained and experienced in its theory, structure, content, production and development.

Even though women architects and town planners experience a less vulnerable identity state as urban users than do female consumers – and even though their personal and professional identities appear harmonious – this is not to give the impression of satisfaction among the women who plan and design Belfast. On the contrary, the empirical findings (too many to report here) reveal that many women architects and town planners are acutely aware of, and often adversely affected by, both structural inadequacies in city planning and their minority position as women in male-dominated professions.

Tensions at the urban production–consumption interface

Considerable tensions characterise the broad interface between urban production and urban consumption. There is, of course, not just *one* interface between urban production and consumption, but as many interfaces as there are social representations of the systems that regulate the relationships between the production and consumption of the city defined on the basis of gender, age, class, race, sexuality, and culture (Saunderson, 1994a,b, 1995b, 1996). The production–consumption interface to which the following empirical findings respond, is that of the value and belief systems of the women and men who 'produce' and 'consume' Belfast.

Findings reveal that the most central core value of urban designers is 'attractiveness and aesthetic pleasure' (SP = 72.73), and that for urban consumers it is 'being satisfied with the way things are' (SP = 87.59). These core evaluative criteria by which 97% of Belfast's producers and 97% of Belfast's consumers most readily and consistently appraise self, others and the city, underpin the fundamental thrust of the empirical study. Such dominant evaluative dimensions of identity suggest the different 'orientations' and interests of Belfast's urban producers and consumers, which, if *reflected* in the built environment itself, suggest a basic incongruence between the representation of producer and consumer interests and aspirations in the city.

As an extension, perhaps, to their desire for satisfaction with the way things are, urban consumers appear to possess a more 'practical' orientation to the built environment than do urban producers. As evaluative dimensions of identity, issues of assessibility; getting one's priorities right; the facilitation and improvement of women's daily lives in the city; and personal safety, are of significantly more value to the urban consumer culture than to the urban design culture. And somewhat surprisingly, perhaps, attributes of efficiency and a professional approach are more highly valued by urban consumers than by architects and town planners ($F = 7.03$; df $= 1,117$; $p < 0.01$).

Aside from the value of 'practical attributes' to urban consumers, constructs of flexibility, open-mindedness and adaptability – and a willingness to put oneself out for others – occupy a significantly more central place in the value systems of the urban consumer culture than that of the urban design culture ($F = 13.82$; df $= 1,114$; $p < 0.001$). The point being stressed here is that while all these attributes of self and city life are aspired to by both producers and consumers, they are all significantly more central to the value systems of urban consumers – and sufficiently different (more consistently used) to suggest anomalies in the representation of producer–consumer interests in the city. So, regarding questions of 'who plans?' and 'for whom?', incongruities between the perspectives of the sets of beliefs, value systems and symbolic frameworks of urban producers and consumers clearly suggest contested space at the production–consumption interface.

The 'contest' is largely about the ownership of professional knowledge and decision-making power in the city. The key to addressing such a contest is the democratisation of urban planning and design – especially in the Northern Ireland context, where town planners possess the unique status of both 'poacher' and 'gamekeeper' (Saunderson, 1999). With regard to the desire and the potential for participatory planning, urban consumers' *desire* for the demystification of the planning and design professions is greater than that of urban producers ($F = 19.21$; df $= 1,82$; $p < 0.001$). However, the *potential* for realising the demystification of the urban professions, for consumers as a group, is less positive than it might be, due to a split consensus among them regarding the value of such a goal. While 58% of consumers strongly aspire towards (SP $= 52.60$) open access to the urban professions, as many as 42% firmly believe (SP $= 53.07$) that specialised knowledge belongs with the 'experts'. The importance of the public's ability to access and openly question professional judgements about the city is a *core* evaluative dimension of identity for the majority of urban consumers (SP $= 52.60$): it is only a *secondary* evaluative dimension of identity for the majority of architects and town planners (SP $= 30.52$). Clearly, the value of public participatory planning is more central to the urban consumer culture than to the urban design culture.

The concept of who 'owns' urban-professional knowledge is also deeply gendered, especially among urban consumers. Of the urban consumers who aspire towards participatory planning as a core evaluative dimension of identity, 83% are women (with SP of 52.51). However, of the 42% minority of urban consumers who strongly believe that specialised knowledge belongs with the 'experts'/professions, 96% are men (with SP of 52.60). It therefore appears that any impetus from urban consumers to address the contested ownership of professional knowledge at the producer–consumer interface is going to come largely from women. Further, as 93% of female architects and town planners favour the democratisation of urban planning (albeit, as a secondary evaluative dimension of identity: SP $= 37.70$), it also appears that there is considerable support for such an impetus from women within the landed professions. In policy terms, however, and in the particular praxis, ethos and pedagogy of the planning and design professions, *meaningful* support for such an impetus is unlikely in the foreseeable future. Planning and design interventions that recognise *and respond to* the complexities of women's psychology in the city, and the 'symbiotic relationship between urban institutions and urban women's lives', appear equally unlikely.

CONCLUDING COMMENT

The built environment, whether construed as a product or a process, is a function of many complex forces. A polysemantic notion (Mazza, 1995) such as 'design' compounds such complexities. That design problems are multifariously rooted in cultural, social and personal aspects of life, means there exists no objective context for formulating solutions or judging their 'correctness' at any given historical moment or in any given place or space. Indeed, as an attempt to uncover and understand the relationship between gender, social processes, and spatial form in the production and consumption of urban space, this study represents more of a battle report than a victory salute.

However, as an attempt to conceptualise, access and 'measure' the urban identities of men and women who produce and consume the built environment of Belfast – and to uncover the position of gender in the processes of urban production and consumption – this study provides a compelling case for the application of ISA to urban milieux. Its theoretical rigour and empirical detail have provided powerful and sensitive insights into hitherto uncharted depths of the complexities of gender and urban space, and the dynamics, structures and processes of identity in the city.

REFERENCES

Ardener, S. (1993) *Women and Space: Ground Rules and Social Maps.* Oxford: Berg.

Baudrillard, J. (1988) *Selected Writings.* Cambridge: Polity Press.

Bell, D. and Valentine, G. (eds.) (1995) *Mapping Desire: Geographies of Sexuality.* London: Routledge.

Betsky, A. (1995) *Building Sex: Men, Women, Architecture, and the Construction of Sexuality.* New York: William Morrow.

Bocock, R. (1993) *Consumption.* London: Routledge.

Bondi, L. (1998) 'Sexing the city' in R. Fincher and J. Jacobs (eds.) *Cities of Difference.* New York: Guilford Press.

Denzin, N. (1978) *The Research Act* (Second Edition). Chicago: Aldine.

Dobbin, M. (1985) *Women's Environmental Experience in Milton Keynes New Town: A Case Study in Personal Construct Theory.* Unpublished PhD thesis. Milton Keynes: The Open University.

DOE, NI (1990) *Belfast Urban Area Plan 2001.* Belfast: HMSO.

Domosh, M. (1999) 'Sexing feminist geography'. *Progress in Human Geography*, 23, 3: 429–436.

Duncan, N. (1996) 'Renegotiating gender and sexuality in public and private spaces' in N. Duncan (ed.) *Bodyspace: Destabilising Geographies of Gender and Sexuality.* London: Routledge.

Edwards, B. (1993) 'Deconstructing the city: the experience of London Docklands'. *The Planner*, Feb, 16–18.

252   Saunderson

Fiske, J. (1989) *Reading the Popular*. Boston: Unwin Hyman.

Fransella, F. (ed.) (1981) *Personality: Theory, Measurement and Research*. New York: Methuen.

Greed, C. (1994) *Women and Planning: Creating Gendered Realities*. London: Routledge.

Hague, C. (1995) 'Introductory texts on urban and regional planning: a review article'. *Town Planning Review*, 66, 2: 207–212.

Hanna, W. (1988) *Women and the Man-Made Environment: A Study using Personal Construct Theory and Repertory Grid Technique*. Undergraduate dissertation. University of Ulster.

Hubbard, P. (1998) 'Sexuality, immorality and the city: red-light districts and the marginalisation of female street prostitutes'. *Gender, Place and Culture*, 5: 55–76.

Katz, C. and Monk, J. (eds.) (1993) *Full Circles: Geographies of Women over the Life Course*. London: Routledge.

Koskela, H. (1997) 'Bold walk and breakings: women's spatial confidence versus fear of violence'. *Gender, Place and Culture*, 4: 301–19.

Koskela, H. (1999) 'Gendered exclusions: women's fear of violence and changing relations to space'. *Geografiska Annaler*, 81B, 2: 111–124.

Lange, A. L. (1989) 'Identifications, perceived cultural distance stereotypes in Yugoslav and Turkish youth in Stockholm' in K. Leibkind (ed.) *New Identities in Europe: Immigrant Ancestry and the Ethnic Identity of Youth*. London: Gower.

Longhurst, R. (1998) '(Re)presenting shopping centres and bodies: questions of pregnancy' in R. Ainley (ed.) *New Frontiers of Space, Bodies and Gender*. London: Routledge.

Mazza, L. (1995) 'Technical Knowledge, practical reason and the planner's responsibility'. *Town Planning Review*, 66, 4: 389–409.

McLeod, A. and Gordon, K. H. (1999) 'Place and gender'. *European Journal of Women's Studies*, 6, 2: 231–33.

Morrell, H. (1996) 'Women's safety' in C. Booth, J. Darke and S. Yeandle (eds.) *Changing Places: Women's Lives in the City*. London: Paul Chapman.

Nast, H. (1998) 'Unsexy geographies'. *Gender, Place and Culture*, 5: 191–206.

Neill, W., Fitzsimmons, D. and Murtagh, B. (1995) *Reimaging the Pariah City: Urban Development in Belfast and Detroit*. Aldershot: Avebury.

Pain, R. (1997a) 'Social geographies of women's fear of crime'. *Transactions of the Institute of British Geographers*, 22: 231–44.

Pain, R. (1997b) ' "Old age" and ageism in urban research: the case of fear of crime'. *International Journal of Urban and Regional Research*, 21: 117–28.

Pain, R. (2000) Place, social relations and the fear of crime: a review. *Progress in Human Geography*, 24, 3: 365–388.

Park, R. E. and Burgess, E. W. (eds.) (1925) *The City*. Chicago: University of Chicago Press.

Proshansky, H. M. (1978) 'The city and self identity'. *Environment and Behaviour*, 10, 2: 147–169.

Proshansky, H. M., Fabian, A. K. and Kaminoff, R. (1983) 'Place-identity: physical world socialisation of the self'. *Journal of Environmental Psychology*, 3: 57–83.

RIBA (2001) [Personal communication with Angela Brady, Chair of the 'Women in Architecture' group of the Royal Institute of British Architects.]

RTPI (1991) *Traffic Growth and Planning Policy*. London: The Royal Town Planning Institute.

Saunderson, W. (1994a) 'Gender and urban space: Identity Structure Analysis of producers and consumers of the built environment of Belfast'. *Proceedings of the British Psychological Society*, 3, 1: 16.

Saunderson, W. (1994b) *Gendered Narratives in an Irish Urban Milieu: Belfast's Urban Design Culture, Urban Consumption, and Urban Identity*. Paper presented at the 'Gendered Narratives in Ireland' Conference, University of Ulster Magee College, 25–27 March.

Saunderson, W. (1995a) *A Theoretical and Empirical Investigation of Gender and Urban Space: The Production and Consumption of the Built Environment*. PhD thesis. University of Ulster.

Saunderson, W. (1995b) *The Production and Consumption of Gendered Urban Space: Social, Spatial, and Symbolic Representations of the City*. Paper presented at the British Sociological Association's Annual Conference, 'Contested Cities: Social Process and Spatial Form', Leicester, 10–13 April.

Saunderson, W. (1996) *Psychological Aspects of City Living*. Paper presented at the BPS Annual London Conference, University of London, 17–18 December.

Saunderson, W. (1997) 'Women, cities and identity: the production and consumption of gendered urban space in Belfast' in A. Byrne and M. Leonard (eds.) *Women and Irish Society: A Sociological Reader*. Belfast: Beyond the Pale Publications.

Saunderson, W. (1999) 'City, self and identity at the millennium: the town planners and architects of Belfast'. *Proceedings of the British Psychological Society*, 7, 2: 137.

Saunderson, W. (2001) 'Women's fear of urban space in Belfast'. (Special 25th Anniversary Double Issue), *Women and Environments International*, 50/51: 28–31.

Simmel, G. (1903) 'The metropolis and mental life' in K. H. Wolff (ed. & trans.) (1950), *The Sociology of George Simmel*. New York: The Free Press.

Simonsen, K. (1996) 'What kind of space in what kind of social theory?' *Progress in Human Geography*, 20: 494–521.

Wager, M. (1993) *Constructions of Femininity in Academic Women: Continuity Between Private and Professional Identity*. D.Phil. thesis. University of Ulster.

Weiner, M. and Marcus, D. (1994) 'A sociocultural construction of depressions' in T. R. Sarbin and J. I. Kitsuse (eds.) *Constructing the Social*. London: Sage.

Wirth, L. (1938) 'Urbanism as a way of life'. *The American Journal of Sociology*, 44 (July 1938). [Reprinted in P. K. Hatt and A. J. Reiss (eds.) *Cities and Society: The Revised Reader in Urban Sociology*. New York: The Free Press.]

8   Adults returning to education: Gender and identity processes

Helen Irvine

LEARNING SOCIETY/LIFELONG LEARNING

A lifelong learning ethos is recognised as essential for social and economic survival in an increasingly complex and changing society. In the learning society education will not end at 16 or in the early 20s. Individuals of all ages will be constantly engaged in learning processes both informally and through formal structured learning. In his report on higher education, Dearing (1997) envisaged increasing participation by adults from sectors of society that traditionally have been under-represented in higher education.

In view of the current aspirations towards lifelong learning, there is an imperative to develop our understanding of the reciprocal relationship between adult education and adult development. In other words, there is a need for research to explore the interaction between adult identity development and life-stage opportunities with regard to participation in formal education and, conversely, the significance of engagement in educational pursuits for adult identity development.

Theory development in adult education has suffered from problems in achieving generalisation given the diversity of adult education which spans leisure courses, courses in adult literacy, professional development courses and academic courses leading to formal qualifications. The study reported here does not attempt to be all-embracing but focuses specifically on what is considered to be a growth area in education, namely formal academic courses designed to attract adults back to education. These 'widening participation' initiatives, which include Access and Foundation courses, have been developed through partnerships between the further and higher education sectors (Waddington, 1989; Woodrow, 1988). The aim is not only to prepare adults, with few or no formal educational qualifications, for entry to university, but to develop the desire and capacity for learning throughout the lifespan.

The study is concerned with explaining why certain adults decide to pursue formal education, and the reciprocal relationship between adult education and adult development. The research builds upon the prevailing theoretical approach to understanding adult participation in education, the 'motivation-barriers' paradigm. However, it goes beyond psychological perspectives – such as the expectancy theory model incorporated into adult education theory by Rubenson (1977) and Maslow's (1954) 'needs hierarchy' introduced by Miller (1967) – which have dominated adult education theory development (Gooderham, 1993) and which are synthesised in Cross's (1981) chain-of-response model. The study rises to the challenge presented by Courtney (1992) in his extensive review of literature in the area of adult participation in education, urging research to move beyond the existing paradigm and incorporate sociological perspectives. Consideration, therefore, is also given to the structure of society; the educational opportunity structure (particularly in relation to gender); social mobility; and to psychosocial theories of lifespan development. Furthermore, the study investigates the significance of gender, i.e. to what extent the relationship between life issues, internal and external transitions and the return to education is the same for men and women.

IDENTITY STRUCTURE ANALYSIS

The nexus between the adult student, adult life and the formal educational institution is ambiguous. Adults enter the formal education system at different points in their lives and present unique backgrounds and expectations for themselves as learners. The current evolution of adult development theory and adult education theory suggests that the study of adult students should reflect a continuum, as opposed to a dichotomy of categories or characteristics. In attempting to explain participation by asking 'Who is the adult student?' researchers are advised to question the assumptions which have operationally defined the adult student in earlier studies. Given the uniqueness and diversity of adult students, Identity Structure Analysis, incorporating both quantitative and qualitative concerns and acknowledging human agency and the uniqueness of individuals, offers an appropriate and useful research approach.

ISA allows for individuality by anchoring each respondent's identifications in their own value and belief systems, while the nomothetic analysis identifies commonality in adult development experience. The approach also provides profiles of each respondent's own unique identity structure which prove particularly valuable and enlightening when considering individual case studies. Examination of a number of case studies involving idiographic identity structure analysis facilitates the interpretation of nomothetic analysis. The quantitative and qualitative aspects of ISA are complementary and offer rich insights into the reciprocal relationship between adult education and adult development.

As a metatheoretical framework, underpinned by several major theoretical orientations in the social sciences, ISA allows the development of theoretical postulates and empirically derived propositions about the socio-psychological processes of identity development in relation to adult education and the role of education in the adult woman's and adult man's lifespan and ongoing development (the full study is reported in Irvine, 1994).

POSTULATES FOR INVESTIGATION

The postulates for investigation were derived from the key methodological and conceptual issues arising from a synthesis of the extant literature. Although explanations of why adults return to education will probably never be answered by a simple formula, because motives vary across different groups and most individuals are likely to have more than one reason, previous research has identified the major incentives for adult learning. It seems that improving one's status in society by improving one's career prospects is a common major motivation (Cross, 1981).

If, as has been suggested, adult returners tend to express dissatisfaction with their lives, or state that the broad aim in pursuing their education is to improve their position and power in society, then low self-evaluation and high identification conflict with comparative reference groups are likely to be characteristic of these adults on first enrolling for a course. These adults are, in effect, in the process of redefining their identities. A likely consequence of such a process of redefinition will be a tendency towards self-doubt, 'since at the time of incorporating new values and aspirations one will, in most instances, lack the skills for their implementation and therefore downgrade one's self-evaluation in these respects, until such time that one has acquired the relevant mastery' (Weinreich, 1983: 153).

However, there appears to be a dichotomy in the literature. Some commentators propose that many adults who return to education do so because they are dissatisfied with their lives and recognise the need for personal development. In other words, they have low self-esteem (Verner and Newberry, 1965; Miller, 1967; Rubenson, 1977 with respect to those who value and expect to gain improved job prospects). Others (Boshier, 1973; Rubenson, 1977), however, suggest that it is a strong or confident adult who undertakes to complete his or her education. For example, Rubenson proposes that it is those with a high expectation of success who return to education, or that, at least, this confidence in ability is an important contributory factor to their decision to return. Boshier (1973) suggests that participation and non-participation or drop-out are a function of the magnitude of the congruence between self and others in the academic domain.

This dichotomy may be explained by distinguishing between social identity (status and power within the social structure) and academic identity (identifications with academics and attitudes towards education with regard to its value and expectations of success). For example, an adult returner may have low social self-esteem but high academic self-esteem. It could be argued that this might be the case where women returners are concerned. Studies have shown that women returners are likely to have confidence in their ability because, unlike men returners, many of them have had positive experiences at school and in many cases left the school system prematurely due to pressures to fulfil the traditional female role. Thus it is hypothesised that women returners tend to have positive academic identities.

Cross (1981), however, argues that confidence in ability is just one piece in the chain of responses that go into the decision to return to education. She suggests that other factors such as role transition and aspirations may generate sufficiently strong forces to overcome negative forces generated by low confidence. In other words, it may be that identity crisis – a stage in identity development of certain individuals (characterised by high identity diffusion, a wide range of conflicted identifications, and low self-esteem) – may be the driving force in adults with low social and academic self-esteem.

The chain-of-response model developed by Cross serves as a useful framework for organising existing knowledge and focusing further research in the area. This study aims to amplify or develop further some of the ideas proposed by Cross concerning internal psychological factors and participation in adult education by going beyond psychology and considering sociological perspectives (the structure of society, social mobility, the educational opportunity structure) and psychosocial theories of lifespan development.

The study also aims to extend the knowledge base of the field by treating gender as significant. Although women are usually in the majority on 'second chance' or Access courses, outnumbering the men two to one, research studies have not integrated gender into the data analysis or discussed gender-related findings. Many research findings are based on data from women, yet rarely do authors recognise this fact or consider its impact on their results. Furthermore, widespread changes in social conditions and attitudes in this century have affected women more than men. Women are confronting new norms and expectations with regard to social and occupational roles, rendering their social, academic and gender identities of particular interest.

Therefore, in order to further knowledge and understanding of the reciprocal relationship between adult development and adult education, the study should explore academic identity, social identity, and psychological adjustment (self-evaluation and identity diffusion, and incorporate gender into the analysis.

Postulate 1 – Social identity
In so far as improving one's position and power within the social structure is commonly cited as a reason for returning to education, this concern with social status and desire for upward mobility will be reflected in the value systems of adult returners and their patterns of identification with high and low status social groups.

Postulate 2 – Academic identity
It is hypothesised that adults who have positive attitudes towards education and who positively identify with academics are inclined to return to education.

Postulate 3 – Self-evaluation and psychological adjustment
(a) *Postulate concerning self-evaluation.* In so far as returners are concerned with self-improvement and formal education is a challenge which is demanding new skills, their self-evaluation will be low.
(b) *Postulate concerning identity state.* In so far as adults returning to education are dissatisfied with their status and position in society and have extensive identification conflicts with various social groups and individuals, together with low self-evaluation, many of them will be in a vulnerable identity state.

Postulate 4 – Feminist orientation and women's participation
Since the women's movement has influenced society's expectations and norms with regard to women's social and occupational roles, women

returners who are concerned with fulfilling their potential will have adopted a feminist orientation which is reflected in their value systems and patterns of identification.

DISCOURSES AND TEXTS

Preparation and design of the research instruments

Identity Structure Analysis requires two types of information: first, the bipolar constructs which are used to construe oneself, other people and the social world generally; and second, the social groups and individuals who influence one's life.

Several ways of eliciting personal constructs are outlined in Fransella and Bannister (1977). Weinreich (1980) recommends the interview method, which, although time consuming, proves a useful and reliable means of ascertaining both relevant constructs and entities (oneself, significant others and social groups). The semi-structured interview has been used successfully in a number of studies involving ISA to determine the influential people in the individual's life (entities) and the discourses used to construe them (constructs).

However, the longitudinal nature of this study and the time constraints of the project precluded the use of customised interviews in the development of the identity instrument and questionnaire. Instead, the design of the study and the development of the instruments of investigation were informed by the findings from an earlier research project concerning access courses in further education colleges (Irvine, 1991). The earlier project – involving survey questionnaires and semi-structured interviews with mature access students and tutors – provided some insights into the issues and psychological factors involved in adult education and served as useful groundwork for this more focused research.

During interviews and discussions with tutors and mature students, factors relating to identity and self-evaluation were frequently mentioned both with regard to the decision to enrol and with regard to personal development over the duration of the course. In conversation with the mature students about their motives for embarking on the course and what they hoped to get out of it, improvement of job prospects was mentioned and many of the students also expressed dissatisfaction with their lives. Some reported they felt their education was incomplete; some claimed they felt they had to prove something to themselves or others; and several of the women stated explicitly that they were looking for an identity. In other words, the findings from this author's study emphasised that the return to education by adults cannot be explained simply in terms of economics or job prospects, but that psychological factors in relation to adult development across the lifespan, such as self-concept and processes of identity development, are involved.

The intention of this study was to design an identity instrument that can give insights into issues and concerns that mature students are unaware of, or are either unwilling or unable to articulate. The final selection of constructs and entities relevant to this study and its social context resulted from reference to the findings from the author's 1991 study together with analysis of the constructs and entities included in previous ISA studies involving adults; and consideration of the salient questions arising from theoretical research (Cross, 1981) and empirical research (Stephenson and Percy, 1989; Woodley *et al.*, 1987; Osborn *et al.*, 1982) concerning adult education.

The Identity instrument

(i) Entities

An ISA instrument must include a number of mandatory entities: facets of self (past self, current self, ideal self) and also positive and negative role models (an admired person, and a disliked person). In addition to these mandatory entities, an alternate self-image (me when I am in college) was included; this allowed analysis of situational effects on identity parameters.

Review of the literature indicated that dissatisfaction with status and power is often experienced by adults in mid-life (Levinson, 1977; Levinson *et al.*, 1978; Josselson, 1987) and concern about position and power within the social structure is considered to be a motivating factor in adults who return to education (Verner and Newberry, 1965; Miller, 1967). In order to investigate issues and aspects of identity concerning social position and power, entities included social groups representing each end of the social spectrum. 'Unskilled men', 'housewives' and 'the unemployed' were chosen as groups to whom low status is generally accorded in society. Chosen to represent the upper end of the social scale were professionals ('professional men' and 'professional women').

In order to investigate some of the dichotomies in the literature concerning internal psychological factors and the return to education, it was necessary to distinguish between social identity and academic identity, and therefore academics and intellectuals ('teachers', 'university students', 'most intelligent person I know') were included among the entities. These entities representing the educational sphere allowed investigation of the contention held by Boshier (1973) that adult participation in education is a function of the congruence between self and others in the academic domain.

The aims of the study also required investigation of gender issues including the gender identity of women who are concerned with fulfilling their educational and occupational aspirations. With respect to this, the entity 'housewife' represented a traditional woman and the entity 'professional woman' represented a nontraditional woman. A complete list of the entities included in the ISA instrument can be found in Table 8.1.

(ii) Constructs

In the ISA framework the parameter 'structural pressure' estimates the centrality or uncertainty of the respondents' values and beliefs as represented by the constructs chosen for the ISA instrument.

Table 8.1 Entities in the adult returner's identity instrument

1. Current self
2. Ideal self
3. Past self
4. Me as my family sees me
5. Me as my fellow students see me
6. A person I admire
7. A person I dislike
8. Own sex parent
9. Opposite sex parent
10. Partner
11. The unemployed
12. The most intelligent person I know
13. Housewives
14. Lecturers
15. Best friend of the same sex
16. Me when in college
17. Professional women
18. Unskilled men
19. University students
20. Professional men

However, choosing the relevant constructs for a standardised instrument and wording such constructs in a way that avoids misunderstanding is a task that requires careful consideration. The aim was to include constructs that tap the beliefs, attitudes and values pertinent to key issues arising in the study of adult returners. As dissatisfaction with social status and power and the desire for self-improvement and upward mobility are frequently cited as motivational factors in the adult's return to education, the instrument included two constructs that deal with aspiration and personal development:

  1. is happy as they are/would like to change and develop
  12. shies away from competition/is competitive and ambitious

The following constructs deal with social position and recognition:

  10. is respected in the community/is not respected in the community
  16. is unsuccessful/is successful

As some of the literature on adult development points to a mid-life stage in which a desire for personal development and freedom from social pressure and control are salient issues, several constructs deal with autonomy and self-efficacy:

  3. lets people ride over them/is assertive
  4. is lazy/is self-disciplined and hardworking

6. is dependent on others/can work thing out alone
9. takes chances in life/avoids taking risks
14. is knowledgeable/is ignorant
17. believes that life is determined by one's own actions/believes that what happens in life is largely determined by luck
20. is confident/has self-doubts

The following constructs deal with relations to other people:

2. is friendly and mixes easily/has difficulty getting on with people
5. regards work as the most important thing in life/regards human relationships as the most important thing in life
7. is self-sacrificing/doesn't make sacrifices

As education is considered to be the means whereby the adult may achieve his or her occupational and social ambitions, the following construct deals with attitudes towards education:

15. believes that the purpose of education is to prepare for work/believes that the purpose of education is personal enrichment

Investigation of the impact of changing norms and expectations with regard to women's social and occupational roles required the inclusion of constructs which deal with issues concerning gender and gender roles:

11. has no masculine characteristics/has masculine characteristics
19. has no feminine characteristics/has feminine characteristics
8. thinks women have equal educational opportunities/thinks women do not have equal educational opportunities
13. thinks a woman can't pursue a career and care for her family/thinks a woman can have a career and a family
18. is modern/is traditional

A complete list of the constructs in the order presented in the identity instrument is presented in Table 8.2.

Questionnaire

A survey questionnaire was designed to elicit information regarding: (i) demographic characteristics; (ii) educational background, including educational qualifications; (iii) reasons for enrolling on the course. The information given in the questionnaire was used to assign 'group identifiers' to each respondent so that criterion groups could be formed for ISA nomothetic analysis (IDEX-NOMO). This allowed, for example, unemployed students to be compared with employed students with respect to identity structure and development. Information given in

Table 8.2 Constructs in the adult returner's identity instrument

1. happy as they are/would like to change and develop
2. friendly, mixes easily/has difficulty getting on with people
3. lets people ride over them/is assertive
4. lazy/is self-disciplined and hard working
5. regards work as the most important thing in life/regards human relationships as the most important thing in life
6. is dependent on others/can work things out alone
7. is self-sacrificing/doesn't make sacrifices
8. thinks women have equal educational opportunities /thinks women do not have equal educational opportunities
9. takes chances in life/avoids taking risks
10. is respected in the community/is not respected in the community
11. has no masculine characteristics/has masculine characteristics
12. shies away from competition/is ambitious and competitive
13. thinks a woman can't pursue a career and care for a family/thinks a woman can have a career and a family
14. is knowledgeable/is ignorant
15. believes that the purpose of education is to prepare for work/believes that the purpose of education is personal enrichment
16. is unsuccessful/is successful
17. believes that life is determined by one's own actions/believes that what happens in life is largely determined by luck
18. is modern/is traditional
19. has no feminine characteristics/has feminine characteristics
20. is confident/has self-doubts

responses to the questionnaire was also used in addition to idiographic analysis (IDEX-IDIO) in case studies of individual students.

Respondents

A total of 109 adults agreed to participate in the research project. The main study group comprised 72 mature students on University Access courses. Of the 72 mature access students, 52 were female and 20 were male. This ratio of females to males is broadly in line with statistics that indicate that women generally out-number men 2 to 1 on academic courses for adults.

In order to provide a baseline against which to assess or measure the significance of aspects of self-concept and identity with regard to participation in adult education and the development of mature students, a comparison (control) group of 37 adults was included in the study. The comparison group controls for the effects of societal and political influences on adult self-concept and identity over the time period of the study. To control for participation in college activities, adults enrolled on non-vocational (leisure) courses were asked to participate in the study. All adults in the comparison group were required to be 23 years or over (the minimum age for entry to an Access course) and not have had third-level education.

Adults enrolled on Access courses were asked to complete a questionnaire and an identity instrument during the induction period of the course. The adults in the comparison group were contacted around the same time and they completed the same questionnaire and identity instrument as the adults in the main study group.

CONSIDERATION OF THE FINDINGS

Participation – Why do adults return to education?

A major issue arising from consideration of psychosocial theories concerning adult lifespan development in relation to 'second chance education' concerns whether internal transitions (such as dissatisfaction with social identity, or identity crisis) force external changes (e.g. from worker or housewife to student role), or whether external transitions or circumstances allow the adult to take up educational opportunities, and it is the educational experience that facilitates internal transitions such as perspective transformation (Tennent, 1993) and identity development.

The initial task, therefore, was to assess the significance of internal factors and to investigate the nature of identity development issues and possible internal transitions involved in the adult's decision to return to education.

Analysis of the adults' identity structures at the time of enrollment indicates that identity issues and self-evaluation are important aspects of the complex processes involved in the adult's decision to pursue his or her education.

The findings indicate that many adult returners tend to experience dissatisfaction with their social position – they desire upward mobility within the social structure – a psychological state that is reflected by their value systems and patterns of identification with social groups. This finding concurs with Cross (1981) who, in her survey of research on motives for participation in adult education, concludes that 'Learning that will improve one's position in life is a major motivation.' Analysis of the constructs used to evaluate self and others revealed that both men and women returners have internalised values which foster the desire for self-improvement and upward mobility. Compared with others, adults who resume formal education are likely to value (a) personal development; (b)competitiveness, ambition and (c) taking chances in life, and tend to be less concerned with relationships and social aspects of life (see Table 8.3).

Furthermore, analysis of patterns of identification revealed that adult returners have a significantly higher level of identification conflict with low status groups (see Table 8.4). Adult returners see themselves as having characteristics in common with low status groups and individuals (moderate empathetic identification, see Table 8.4) and, simultaneously, have strong inclinations to dissociate from them (high contra identification, see Table 8.4). These patterns of identification, together with low self-evaluation (see Table 8.5), support the contention that adults who decide to pursue their education are experiencing dissatisfaction with their role or position in life which is not experienced by the control group.

Table 8.3 Structural pressure on constructs concerning ambition and drive

(a) Construct 1 – happy as they are/would like to change and develop

		Male (35)	Female (74)
Returners	(72)	23.48 (MJ2, 15)	8.83 (MJ2, 33)
Control	(37)	19.33 (MJ2, 11)	52.50 (MJ1, 11)

Total number in each group – Male returners 20, Male control 15, Female returners 52, Female control 22

The majority of the control females favoured pole 1 of this construct (MJ1) while the majority of the respondents in each of the other three groups favoured pole 2 (MJ2), therefore analysis of variance was precluded.

(b) Construct 12 – avoids competition/is ambitious and competitive
(MJ2 – majority favouring pole 2 of construct)

		Male (35)	Female (74)	All	MJ
Returners	(72)	65.00	59.19	62.09	(67)
Control	(37)	54.27	46.40	50.33	(33)
All		59.64	52.79		

Type effect: $F = 5.58$; df = 1,96; $p < .05$
Gender: ns
Type by gender interaction: ns

(c) Construct 9 – takes chances in life/plays it safe in life
(MJ1 – majority favouring pole 1 of construct)

		Male (35)	Female (74)	All	MJ
Returners	(72)	42.85	32.69	37.77	(54)
Control	(37)	20.19	13.45	16.82	(27)
All		31.52	23.07		

Type effect: $F = 7.55$; df = 1,77; $p < .01$
Gender: ns
Type by gender interaction: ns

Scale -100 to $+100$

High identification conflicts with low status social groups are problematic features of the returner's identity which have a positive influence on the decision to return to education since, in terms of identity dynamics, such conflicts in identification provide impetus for personal development and redefinition of self.

Furthermore, with regard to academic identity (see Table 8.6), the findings indicate that both the men and women returners were responsive to academics (had higher ego-involvement with them) and regarded them as positive role-models (had higher idealistic-identification with them).

Table 8.4 Identifications with low status groups* by type and
gender

(a) Identification conflicts

		Male (35)	Female (74)	All
Returners	(72)	0.34	0.43	0.39
Control	(37)	0.32	0.34	0.33
All		0.33	0.39	

Type effect: $F = 12.09$; df $= 1,290^*$; $p < .001$
Gender: ns
Type by gender interaction trend: $F = 3.53$; df $= 1,290^*$; $p = .057$

(b) Empathetic identification

		Male (35)	Female (74)	All
Returners	(72)	0.44	0.48	0.46
Control	(37)	0.45	0.46	0.46
All		0.44	0.47	

Type: ns
Gender: ns
Type by gender interaction: ns

(c) Contra-identification

		Male (35)	Female (74)	All
Returners	(72)	0.30	0.45	0.38
Control	(37)	0.26	0.33	0.29
All		0.28	0.39	

Type effect: $F = 12.44$; df $= 1,290^*$; $p < .001$
Gender effect: $F = 22.60$; df $= 1,290^*$; $p < .001$
Type by Gender Interaction: ns

Scale 0.00 to 1.00
*Low status groups = housewives, **unemployed, unskilled** men.
Comparison between entities combined as 'Low Status Groups' is not
substantive to the investigation and therefore multiple entities main
and interaction effects are not discussed.

The general conclusion is that internal psychological factors contribute to the
adult's decision to undertake a formal education course and many of the adult
returners are in an important phase of internal transition or identity development
at the time of embarking on the course. In other words, it is generally not a case
of external circumstances (being at a loose end due to unemployment or children
starting school) prompting the adult to enrol on an academic course, and internal
transitions arising during the course (as new identifications are formed and

Table 8.5 Self-evaluation by type and gender

(a) Evaluation of current self

		Male (35)	Female (34)	All
Returners	(72)	0.54	0.44	0.49
Control	(37)	0.66	0.53	0.64
All		0.60	0.53	

Type effect: $F = 9.36$; df $= 1,105$; $p < .01$
Gender: ns
Type by gender: ns

(b) Evaluation of past self

		Male (35)	Female (74)	All
Returners	(72)	0.00	0.10	0.05
Control	(37)	0.30	0.23	0.26
All		0.15	0.16	

Type effect: $F = 7.76$; df $= 1,104$; $p < .01$
Gender: ns
Type by gender interaction: ns

(c) Metaperspectives of self*

		Male (35)	Female (74)	All
Returners	(72)	0.46	0.42	0.44
Control	(37)	0.58	0.56	0.57
All		0.15	0.16	

Type effect: $F = 7.76$; df $= 1,104$; $p < .01$
Gender: ns
Type by gender interaction: ns

Scale -1.00 to $+1.00$
*Metaperspectives of self – 'Me as my family sees me' and 'me as fellow students see me'. Comparison between entities combined as metaperspectives of self is not substantive to the investigation and therefore multiple entities main and interaction effects are not discussed.

beliefs and values change). Instead, identity issues and internal transitions precede and provide impetus for the return to education. The findings, therefore support the conceptualisation of adult participation in education as a function of the interplay of goals or purposes and circumstances (Blair *et al.*, 1995) and also support Gecas and Mortimer's (1987) contention that self-concept and social environment are reciprocally determined; people seek out situations which foster valued identities in a process of spiralling development.

Table 8.6 Identifications with academics* by type and gender

(a) Ego-involvement (scale 0.00 to 5.00)

		Male (35)	Female (74)	All
Returners	(72)	3.62	3.72	3.67
Control	(37)	3.30	3.34	3.32
All		3.46	3.53	

Type effect: $F = 11.95$; df $= 1,299*$; $p < .01$
Gender: ns
Type by gender interaction: ns

(b) Idealistic-identification (scale 0.00 to 1.00)

		Male (35)	Female (74)	All
Returners	(72)	0.75	0.73	0.74
Control	(37)	0.71	0.65	0.68
All		0.73	0.69	

Type effect: $F = 8.68$; df $= 1,299*$; $p < .01$
Gender effect: $F = 4.20$; df $= 1,299*$; $p < .05$
Type by gender interaction: ns

(c) Empathetic identification (scale 0.00 to 1.00)

		Male (35)	Female (74)	All
Returners	(72)	0.67	0.64	0.65
Control	(37)	0.70	0.59	0.64
All		0.69	0.61	

Type: ns
Gender effect: $F = 11.11$; df $= 1,299*$; $p < .01$
Type by gender: ns

*Academics – Lecturers, students, 'most intelligent person I know'. Comparison between entities combined as 'Low Status Groups' is not substantive to the investigation and therefore multiple entities main and interaction effects are not discussed.

Gender issues

However, the findings from this study suggest that the relationships between adult life issues, internal and external transitions, ongoing psychosocial development and the return to education are somewhat different for men and women. The study, recognising the relationship between the dramatic influx of adult women into undergraduate education and changing gender roles, examines the women's psychosocial characteristics.

When gender is taken into consideration in the analysis, it reveals that issues of identity are particularly salient in the case of the women who return to education.

Patterns of identification which are found to be characteristic of adult returners tend to be accentuated in the case of women returners. The women returners' identification conflicts with low status groups are greater than those of the men returners and the adults in the control group (see Table 8.4).

Women returners' strong inclinations to dissociate from low status groups (see Table 8.4) together with low self-evaluation (see Table 8.5) indicate a dissatisfaction with their current position in society that is not apparent among the control women. Compared to men returners a significantly higher proportion of the women returners are in a vulnerable identity state (see Table 8.7). In other words, many of the women who return to education are in an important phase of identity development, reworking and redefining identity in much the same way as might adolescents.

This prompts the question of why these women are in a state of internal transition. Why are aspects of their identities problematic and prompting them to strive for personal development through academic achievement?

Many of the women returning to education left school prematurely, a fact borne out by the high proportion of the women returners who had been to grammar school and had proven academic ability. Many of the women in the current study reached the minimum school leaving age before the resurgence of the women's

Table 8.7 Association of 'well-adjusted'* and 'vulnerable'** identities

(a) Men and women returners

	IDENTITY STATE		
Gender	Well adjusted*	Vulnerable**	Total
Men returners	17	3	20
Women returners	29	23	52

$X^2 = 4.15$, $df = 1$, $p < .05$ $(H_o - X^2 < 3.84$ two tailed$)$

(b) Women returners and control women

	IDENTITY STATE		
TYPE	Well adjusted*	Vulnerable**	Total
Women returners	29	23	52
Control women	16	6	22

$X^2 = 1.21$, $df = 1$, ns $(H_o - X^2 < 3.84$ two-tailed$)$

Well adjusted identity states:
– Confident (moderate diffusion and high self-evaluation)
– Indeterminate (moderate diffusion and self-evaluation)

** Vulnerable identity states:
– Diffusion (high diffusion, moderate self-evaluation)
– Identity crisis (high diffusion, low self-evaluation)
– Diffuse high self regard (high diffusion, high self-evaluation)
– Negative (moderate diffusion, low self-evaluation)
– Defensive high (low diffusion, high self-evaluation)
– Defensive (low diffusion, moderate self-evaluation)
– Defensive negative (low diffusion, low self-evaluation)

movement in the late 1960s and 1970s had made an impact. This was a time when generally girls' educational potential was thwarted by the prevailing socio-cultural expectations and pressure towards traditionally female roles. However, women are currently facing new norms and expectations with regard to social and occupational roles. There has been growing pressure on women to be successful in both the public and private spheres of life and to have ambitions that lie out-side those traditionally prescribed for women.

As the women's movement has influenced society's expectations with regard to women's social and occupational roles, it was postulated that women returners who are concerned with fulfilling their academic and career potential will have adopted a 1980s feminist orientation. Indeed, the value systems and patterns of identification of the women returners do reflect a feminist orientation.

Although the women who are striving for educational achievement cannot be differentiated from the other women with regard to beliefs directly concerning women's rights and roles, they are more likely to value masculinity and traits tra-ditionally associated with masculinity, such as competitiveness and ambition (see Table 8.3), and are less likely to value femininity (see Table 8.8) and also less likely to identify positively with their mothers (see Table 8.9).

In other words, it seems that women who strive for educational achievement have internalised values such as competitiveness and ambition that are tradition-ally associated with masculinity rather than femininity, and generally considered incongruent with the traditional female roles of mother and housewife. The women returners' evaluation of 'mother' and the extent to which they see them-selves as similar to her is significantly less than that of the control women (see Table 8.9). Generally, the findings support the argument that having internalised feminist-orientated values and beliefs, such women, as housewives or in low sta-tus jobs, experience an incongruence between present and preferred roles.

As Eichenbaum and Orbach (1985) point out, the women's movement has helped women make significant gains in their lives (it has become acceptable for

Table 8.8 Structural pressures on constructs concerning masculinity and femininity

(a) Construct 11 – has no masculine characteristics/has masculine characteristics

		Male (35)	Female (74)
Returners	(72)	33.20 (MJ2, 16)	11.85 (MJ1, 28)
Control	(37)	36.48 (MJ2, 15)	32.79 (MJ1, 16)

(b) Construct 19 – Has no feminine characteristics/has feminine characteristics

		Male (35)	Female (74)
Returners	(72)	25.98 (MJ1, 14)	11.85 (MJ2, 28)
Control	(37)	37.25 (MJ1, 13)	36.21 (MJ2, 16)

Scale −100 to +100
MJ1 = majority favoured pole one of construct; MJ2 = majority favoured pole two of construct
Total number in each group: Male returners 20, Male control 15, Female returners 52, Female control 22

Table 8.9 Women's identifications with mother

(a) Ego-involvement (scale 0.00 to 5.00)

Women returners	(52)	3.42
Control women	(22)	3.85

Type (women) trend: $F = 3.23$; df $= 1,54$; $p = .07$

(b) Evaluation (scale −1.00 to +1.00)

Women returners	(52)	0.27
Control women	(22)	0.50

Type (women) effect: $F = 4.77$; df $= 1,54$; $p < .05$

(c) Empathetic identification (scale 0.00 to 1.00)

Women returners	(52)	0.68
Control women	(22)	0.80

Type (women) effect: $F = 5.23$; df $= 1,54$; $p < .05$

(d) Contra-identification (scale 0.00 to 1.00)

Women returners	(52)	0.31
Control women	(22)	0.22

Type (women): ns

(d) Identification conflict (scale 0.00 to 1.00)

Women returners	(52)	0.41
Control women	(22)	0.40

Type (women): ns

women to have a career and a family, a belief favourably endorsed by all the women in the study), but along with new freedoms come new pressures. The new imperative for such women to be self-actualising in terms of education and career means that they may feel inadequate if their concern is solely in the domestic sphere. Increasingly women feel compelled to search for new roles and identities. In other words, changing societal values, norms and expectations have implications for developmental processes in adult women. The findings indicate that for many women, conflicted identifications with traditional females arise from the problem of becoming different from, but maintaining the traditional roles of, and connections with traditional females.

Because women tend to outnumber men two to one on 'second chance' courses, the courses are frequently derided as being designed to occupy the bored housewife. However, the findings from this study emphasise that the issues involve much more for these women than simply occupying their time. It appears that for many women the return to education is part of a plan of action that has been quite consciously and rationally formulated in an attempt to resolve identity issues. Indeed the findings indicate that for many women, internal factors – values and beliefs related to the new social imperative to be career self-actualising, positive academic identity, and low self-evaluation – act together as positive influences towards participation in education. It is the interaction between these internal facilitators (aspects of identity) and external inhibitors and facilitators (personal circumstances such as unemployment or children starting school) that determines the timing of the women's return to education.

The conclusion on the basis of the evidence from this study is that education plays a major role in women's transition from the home to the workplace, as they follow increasing social imperatives to be self-actualising in career terms and seek new roles and identities. The sequence of women's lifespan development that is emerging – partial education, marriage, children, education, career – is a developmental sequence that is uncommon for men but increasingly common for women. This developmental sequence may be explained by the priority women give to relationships in making life decisions (Gilligan, 1982). Indeed, the findings presented here support Gilligan's view that women's morality concerning relationships means that the sequence of life stages is more variable than that for men and may be quite different for different groups of women.

The findings from this study, therefore, contribute to our understanding of women and gender issues in relation to adult education and also to explanations concerning women's psychosocial development, by identifying and explaining the emergence and nature of an additional transitional stage in some women's lifespan development.

Where the men returners are concerned, the findings indicate that social identity issues are less salient. A smaller proportion of the men returners were found to be in a vulnerable identity state at the time of enrolment (see Table 8.6). The men returners' self-evaluation was low in comparison to both men and women in the control group, but not as low as that of women returners (see Table 8.5). Also the men returners do not contra-identify with low status groups and experience the same degree of identification conflict with low status groups as do the women returners (see Table 8.4). In other words, the men returners' identification patterns suggest that they are not facing identity issues related to social position and power to the same extent as the women returners, despite the fact that many of them are unemployed and those who are working are in low status jobs.

Occupational achievement may be implicit in the men returners' desire to enter higher education. However, the findings suggest that social identity and social mobility (which are generally related to occupational status) are not prominent issues involved in the return to education where the men are concerned. These findings bear out Erikson's (1968, 1980) contention that for men, major identity issues focusing on social role are generally addressed and resolved during adolescence. When asked directly about their aim in enrolling on the course, the overwhelming majority of the men returners stated that their main aim was 'to get to university', while 'to prove something to themselves and others' was cited as an important reason for embarking on the course. It therefore appears that for the men returners academic achievement is a means of gaining respect and recognition – a concern which, according to Levinson *et al.* (1978), arises for men in mid-life and constitutes an important internal transitional phase in men's adult development.

For both men and women, therefore, internal factors – more specifically, psychological transitions – are related to their return to education. However, the evidence demonstrates that the nature of these internal forces is somewhat different for men and women. Women returners are concerned about their occupational and social identity. They aspire to social position and power and being successful in the public as well as the private sphere of life. Men, on the other hand, appear to be less concerned with social identity and social mobility. Rather, educational achievement may be seen by them as a means of achieving self-respect, and recognition and respect from others.

In conclusion, analysis of adult returners' identity structure and information about their stated aims at the time of enrolment provides evidence that these gender-specific internal transitions are important motivational forces preceding and providing impetus in the return to education. It seems that it is not so much a triggering or transitional life event that leads to participation, as was premised by Aslanian and Bricknell (1980), but rather more that intrinsic motivators are involved. However, the desire to return to education prompted by internal motivators may, as Sewall (1982) pointed out, be present for some time but be delayed by situational barriers. As Blair *et al.* (1995) suggest, participation is the consequence of the interplay of two phenomena – adults' purposes or goals in returning and their circumstances. Indeed, the evidence from this study suggests that in the case of many of the adult returners, developmental issues act as intrinsic facilitators which interact with extrinsic facilitators and inhibitors to participation in education.

DISCUSSION

The present study using the nomothetic ISA approach has contributed to adult education theory by exploring issues concerning identity and self-concept which the adult student is either unable or unwilling to articulate. Furthermore, by integrating gender into the data analysis and considering the influence of feminist orientation on adult education participation, as suggested by Hayes (1992), the study has enhanced the understanding of women and gender issues in adult education.

Further research involving follow-up studies of those adults who proceed from Access or 'Return to Education' courses into higher education and on to various career paths would provide a fuller picture and understanding of the nature and extent of the psychosocial development experienced by these adult students.

In addition to making a contribution to adult education theory and theory concerning adult identity processes and psychosocial development, the findings from this study and proposed further studies could also have policy implications with regard to adult education practice as follows:

- *Recruitment* – marketing strategies should recognise the developmental needs of adult men and women and should emphasise the role and value of 'second chance' courses for adults with personal development needs.

• *Development* – given the developmental needs of adult students identified in this study, it is suggested that return to education programmes should support the personal commitment to life change and foster career/life planning by aiding the adult student to assume a confident, goal-oriented and critically aware perspective.

Those who have been involved in the education of adults are aware of the benefits to the individual and to society. The notion that education should be the preserve of the young and that adults have had their chance, is rejected by adult educators who generally are fervent in their commitment to the cause of educational opportunities for all. Adult students generally make the most of learning opportunities, having regained an appetite for learning that was lost in their youth after years of compulsory formal education. Increasingly, adults are recognising the value of education for their personal development and are taking up the opportunities that are becoming available to them.

As the adult student becomes a central figure in educational planning and policy making, it is imperative that adult education research – particularly research which considers adult students from lifespan perspectives or theoretical frameworks based in adult development or related psychosocial theories – continues to contribute frameworks that enhance our understanding of the adult's experience in education.

REFERENCES

Aslanian, C. B. and Bricknell, H. M. (1980) 'Americans in transition; Life changes as reasons for adult learning', cited in M. Osborn, A. Charnley and A. Withnall (eds.) *Review of Existing Research in Adult and Continuing Education, Volume XI, Psychology of Adult Learning and Development.* Leicester: NIACE.

Blair, A., McPake, J., and Munn, P. (1995) A new conceptualisation of adult participation in education. *British Educational Research Journal*, 21, 5: 629–644.

Boshier, R. (1973) Educational participation and drop-out: A theoretical model. *Adult Education*, 23, 4: 255–282.

Courtney, S. (1992) *Why Adults Learn: Towards a Theory of Participation in Adult Education.* London: Routledge.

Cross, K. P. (1981) *Adults as Learners.* London: Jossey-Bass.

Dearing Report, The (1997) *Higher Education in the Learning Society.* London: HMSO.

Eichenbaum, L. and Orbach, S. (1985) *Understanding Women.* Harmondsworth: Penguin.

Erikson, E. H. (1968) *Identity: Youth and Crisis.* New York: Norton.

Erikson, E. H. (1980) *Identity and the Life Cycle.* New York: Norton.

Fransella, F. and Bannister, D. (1977) *A Manual for Repertory Grid Technique.* London: Academic Press.

Gecas, V. and Mortimer, J. T. (1987) 'Stability and change in the self-concept from adolescence to adulthood', in T. Honess and K. Yardley (eds.) *Self and Identity: Perspectives Across the Lifespan.* London: Routledge & Kegan Paul.

Gilligan, C. (1982) *In a Different Voice.* Cambridge, MA: Harvard University Press.

Gooderham, P. N. (1993) A conceptual framework of sociological perspectives on the pursuit by adults of access to higher education. *International Journal of Lifelong Education*, 12, 1: 27–39.

Hayes, E. (1992) The impact of feminism on adult education: An analysis of British and American journals. *International Journal of Lifelong Education*, 11: 125–138.

Irvine, H. (1991), *Access Courses in the Further Education Colleges in Northern Ireland*. Unpublished report, DACE, University of Ulster.

Irvine, H. (1994) *Identity Development and Education: A Theoretical and Empirical Investigation of Identity Development in Adults Returning to Education*. Unpublished D.Phil. thesis, University of Ulster, Jordanstown.

Josselson, R. (1987) *Finding Herself*. San Francisco: Jossey-Bass.

Levinson, D. J. (1977) The mid-life transition: A period of adult psychosocial development. *Psychiatry*, 40: 99–112.

Levinson, D. J., Darrow, C. N., Klein, E. B., Levinson, M. H., and McKee, B. (1978) *The Seasons of a Man's Life*. New York: Ballantine.

Maslow, A. H. (1954) *Motivation and Personality*. New York: Harper.

Miller, H. (1967) *Participation of Adults in Education: A Force Field Analysis*. Boston: Boston University Centre for the Study of Liberal Education for Adults.

Osborn, M., Charnley, A., and Withnall, A. (eds.) (1982) Review of existing research in adult and continuing education. *The Psychology of Adult Learning and Development, XI*. Leicester: NIACE.

Rubenson, R. (1977) *Participants in Recurrent Education: A Research Review Paper*. Paper presented at a meeting of national delegates on developments in recurrent Education, Paris. [Cited in K. P. Cross, 1981, *Adults as Learners*. London: Jossey-Bass.]

Sewall, T. J. (1982) *A Study of Factors which Precipitate Adult Enrolment in a College Degree Program*. Green Bay, WI: Wisconson University Assessment Centre.

Stephenson, P. and Percy, K. (1989) The meaning of 'confidence': Student attitudes and experience on an access course. *Journal of Access Studies*, 4, 1–2: 25–42.

Tennent, M. C. (1993) Perspective transformation and adult development. *Adult Education Quarterly*, 44: 34–42.

Verner, C. and Newberry, J. (1965) 'The nature of adult participation', in C. Verner and T. White (eds.) *Participants in Adult Education*. Washington: Adult Education Association.

Waddington, P. (1989) Access: The name of the game. *Education*, 174, 4: 80–82.

Weinreich, P. (1980) *Manual for Identity Exploration Using Personal Constructs*. London: Science Research Council.

Weinreich, P. (1983) 'Psychodynamics of personal identity', in A. Jacobson-Widding (ed.) *Identity: Personal and Sociocultural*. Stockholm: Almquist & Wiksell International.

Williams, H. Y. and Willie, R. (1990) Research on adult development: implications for adult education. *International Journal of Lifelong Education*, 9, 3: 237–243.

Woodley, A., Wagner, L., Slowey, M., Hamilton, M., and Fulton, O. (1987) *Choosing to Learn*. Oxford: SRHE in association with O.U. Press.

Woodrow, M. (1988) The Access course route to higher education. *Higher Eduation Quarterly*, 42, 4: 317–3.

9 Enterprising identities: Gender and family influences

Anita MacNabb

INTRODUCTION

Those who create, develop and expand successful enterprises make a significant contribution to social and economic development. They are often perceived and relied upon by government and society to be 'leaders', 'innovators' and significant job providers. Recent trends such as the downsizing of large business and the contracting-out of services previously provided in-house have given opportunities for existing small businesses and encouraged new business starts. These factors, coupled with the personal motivation of many individuals to take greater control of their own destiny or the impetus to have greater flexibility in their working arrangements, have resulted in a significant increase in the numbers of people becoming self-employed or setting up businesses to employ others. The concept of 'enterprising people' is used in this chapter to describe this heterogeneous mix of people.

Research has shown that only a minority of business owners are 'prototypically entrepreneurial' (Baines & Wheelock, 1998; Chell *et al.*, 1991) when considering their personality characteristics, aspirations, motivations, value systems and behaviours. Four groupings of business owners, differentiated by values and priorities, are identified by Baines and Wheelock (1998): Some, labelled 'survival and security', are motivated primarily to provide an income for their families and are characterised by their long working hours with limited monetary reward; others, known as 'business intrinsic', value the independence of being their own boss and are characterised by the desire to keep control themselves, sometimes at the expense of the growth of the business; third, there are the 'creative', who value their freedom to 'create' through their business; and lastly, there are the 'achievement' orientated, who seek out business challenges and are most likely to grow the business. This typology suggests that the value and belief systems of business owners may be critically important in influencing their approach to decisions about, and probably outcomes of, their business.

However, given the arbitrary nature of these and other such classifications, it is notable that there have been few attempts to empirically *measure* business owners' value and belief systems, based on how they construe self and others. Furthermore, it is now recognised that enterprising people do not operate in isolation from their family circumstances. In Baines and Wheelock's (1998) consideration of the influence of the 'business family' in their categorisation, they found that family support improves the chances of business survival although growth-orientated business owners are more likely to use non-family sources of help. While there is a growing field of research into the 'family business', there has been relatively little research on the 'business family'. This term acknowledges that there are significant interrelationships, formal and informal, between the family and the business (Poutziouris & Chittenden, 1996; Baines & Wheelock, 1998). However, many studies have only questioned the relationship when examining female-owned businesses.

The research presented in this chapter uses Identity Structure Analysis to explore the gender and family influences on the identity characteristics of (1) female, (2) aspiring, and (3) existing business owners. Specifically, it examines the value and belief systems of business owners in relation to family involvement in the business, examining the degree of positive and negative role-model identification with family members, and any conflicts in identification. The influence of other major social roles such as motherhood is also examined. The results are analysed with reference to recent theories regarding gender differences in entrepreneurial roles, and the family/business interface.

IDENTITY STRUCTURE ANALYSIS

Identity Structure Analysis (ISA) as an open-ended framework was chosen to provide empirical evidence on how enterprising individuals construe their identity in the business and the home and family context. A literature review failed to find any empirical studies applying identity theory to entrepreneurship. The ISA metatheoretical framework was appealing because it allows the researcher to examine individuals' construals of themselves and others – based on, and anchored in, their *own* value and belief systems. The approach recognises that identity is not fixed and thus allows for entrepreneurship to be viewed as a developmental process rather than a given state, or an end in itself. Thus, ISA enables the researcher to capture the processes of identity formulation and reformulation of aspiring and existing business owners, as they adopt, adapt, consolidate, and reformulate their entrepreneurial identity over time. Further, entrepreneurial identity can be examined as part of the totality of identity.

Theoretical postulates

It is only relatively recently that theorists have distinguished gender differences in identity development, and even more recently that such differences have been explicated in the business-related literature. A set of four theoretical postulates is formulated to hypothesise possible interactions and effects of gender and family on business practice. These four postulates – used to structure this chapter – are presented under four headings: (1) gender differences, (2) gender roles, (3) motherhood, and (4) family support.

Gender differences

Brush (1992) suggests that when a woman initiates her own enterprise, she 'integrates' a network of business-related relationships into her life. Drawing upon earlier work of Miller (1976) and Gilligan (1982), Brush refers to this as the 'integrated perspective' and offers it as a basis for interpreting unexplained gender differences between male and female business owners. Gilligan (1982) proposed that 'Women's personal reality is "web-like", connecting family, work and community relationships. Men's reality is seen as separate and autonomous, with decision-making being logical and rule based.' The evidence supporting this theory that men's businesses are typically compartmentalised from other aspects of their lives has been described by some as sketchy (cf. Baines & Wheelock, 1998). The first postulate, therefore, seeks to examine whether and to what extent Brush's (1992) assertions are empirically supported:

> *Postulate 1*: In so far as business men and women construe their business and social worlds differently, there will be gender differences in the evaluative connotations or affective associations they draw using the bipolar constructs concerning family support and whether they give priority to family or business.

Gender roles

A notable number of studies of women in business have found that women are 'subjected to ideologies about their place and their obligations to the household and the family' (Allen & Truman, 1993: 2). Many women are believed to set up in business for the independence and flexibility it can offer. Indeed, many women already occupy multiple roles – as mother, daughter, wife or partner – as well as having primary responsibility for household work and management: the business role is often drafted in, and further, 'for women, business is a life strategy rather than a business strategy' (Allen & Truman, 1993). Cowling *et al.* (1997) found that aspirations, occupational choice and job commitments are correlated with child-rearing plans. However, other research evidence warns against such a generalisation, asserting that women are *not* a homogeneous group (Goffee & Scase, 1985; Cowling *et al.*, 1997; Cromie & Hayes 1988). Cowling and his colleagues (1997) discovered that women who employed others (job creators) were more likely to be older, come from dual-income families and have fewer children than women who were self-employed and worked alone. Goffee and Scase (1985) found that business ownership amongst women is influenced by their 'attachment to entrepreneurial ideals' and by the extent to which they are prepared to accept 'conventionally defined male–female relationships'. This finding led them to identify four types of business owners: 'conventionals' and 'domestics' were said to have strong attachment to conventional gender roles, whilst such attachment for 'innovators' and 'radicals' was said to be weak. Goffee and Scase (1985) thus saw business ownership as a means by which some women tackled subordination.

There would also appear to be different types of male business owners, although most categorisations do not distinguish on the basis of gender (cf. Filley, House & Kerr, 1976; Filley & Aldag, 1978; Stanworth & Curran, 1976; Chandler, 1977;

Hornaday, 1990). Neither do they explore the family/business interface. In order to explore attachment to gender roles in more detail, the following effect is postulated:

> *Postulate 2*: In so far as enterprising men and women differ in the degree to which they identify with conventionally defined gender roles, variations in identity structure are likely to emerge.

Motherhood

Following the previous postulate, one might reasonably question whether male–female variations in identity structure and the degree of attachment to conventionally defined gender roles are a consequence of motherhood. The Department of Trade and Industry in the UK reported that 'the greatest factor which affects the economic activity of women is the stage they are in their life cycle and whether or not they have children' (DTI, 1998). Reports such as this have established that childbirth is associated with downward occupational mobility. While some women choose self-employment for the flexibility it offers in allowing them to pursue their aspirations for success in both their business role and their maternal role, others use it as a means of providing some income while devoting most time and effort to child-rearing.

A recent study using ISA revealed that women have problems in combining their desire to be successful at work with 'particular constructions of femininity across both their private and professional contexts of self' (Wager, 1993). Further, the study revealed that not only does motherhood result in a major transition in identity for women (influencing the phases of their lives), but also that having children results in different identity profiles for women. To examine this finding in the context of this research, the following is postulated:

> *Postulate 3*: In so far as motherhood influences identity profiles, aspiring and existing female business owners with children will have higher levels of conflicted identifications with successful business people than those who are childless.

Family support

Research evidence suggests that the degree of support a woman has in coping with her multiple roles is critically important, as a lack of support can lead to increased stress and conflict (Baines & Wheelock, 1998; Shapero & Sokol, 1982; Simpson & Pearson, 1989). In the context of starting or managing a business and balancing its demands with those of family and home, the support of spouses, partners, parents and offspring is particularly important. The degree of such support received by men and women starting up their business has been found to differ significantly (Shapero & Sokol, 1982). Women were less likely than men, for example, to receive encouragement from 'significant others' to pursue self-employment. More specifically, Simpson and Pearson (1989) found that most male partners gave women verbal support and encouragement but the majority did not take more responsibility for practical household or childcare duties nor did they help out in the business.

The study presented here measured the degree to which potential and existing business owners *aspired* to family support and saw it as essential to running their business. By dividing the sample in terms of their orientation towards family support, one might postulate:

> *Postulate 4*: In so far as male and female business owners value family support and integrate business into their family life, they will associate themselves closely with family members when compared with those who aspire to be more autonomous.

THE STUDY AND IDENTITY INSTRUMENT

The chapter is based on a wider ongoing research study that uses Identity Structure Analysis to identify and explore differences amongst small business owners and to generate understanding and theories about why some small businesses grow and others do not. The discourses used to develop the constructs for the ISA instrument (see Table 9.1) emerged from tape-recorded interviews with ten small business owners in Northern Ireland. The discourses concerned business profits, leadership, autonomy and the family/business interface. Many owners identified barriers to the growth of their business.

The entities were selected to include significant people in both the home and business context (see Table 9.2). In addition to ISA's mandatory entities (past, current and aspirational self, admired person, disliked person), the set of entities included mother, father, successful business man, successful business woman, community business person and unsuccessful business person (respondents were asked to nominate people known to them for the latter five entities). The alternate current self entities were 'Me at home' and 'Me as a business person'. Metaperspectives of self were 'Me as my spouse sees me' and 'Me as my employer used to see me'. Alternate past selves were selected as 'Me when I was 18' and 'Me as I was when I worked for someone else and felt unfulfilled': these past selves are not referred to in the present analysis.

The sample consisted of 187 aspiring or current small business owners: 99 men and 88 women. Four phases of business development provided the framework for the sample selection: Pre-start-up, post-start-up, established, and professionally managed. However, for the purpose of this report the latter three phases denoting those in business were considered together.

Table 9.3 shows that 69 respondents (18 males and 51 females) were at the pre-start-up stage. This group was attending business start-up programmes, indicating that they were considering setting up in business. The remainder, 37 females and 81 males, were already in business. The majority of respondents fell into the age range 26–45, the most common age range for starting and establishing small businesses.

Table 9.1 Bipolar constructs (as categorised) for the entrepreneurial identity instrument

Leadership	Prefers to let someone else take the lead/Likes to be in charge or direct others
Expansion/control	Believes that continued expansion is necessary for the success of the business/Believes that expansion should be restricted in the interests of maintaining control oneself
Family/business	Feels that family support for one's business is essential/Would pursue one's business idea without family support
	Would give priority to family interests and commitments/Would give priority to business commitments over family
Team building/ control:	Likes to spread control and responsibility as part of a team/Feels happier to take sole control and responsibility
	Believes that building a strong management team is essential to grow one's business/Believes that a strong leader can grow the business just as effectively alone
Locus of control	Believes that one shapes one's own future/Believes that one's future is chiefly determined by fate
Profit orientation	Would sell/make any goods to make a profit/Would only sell/make goods that reflect good taste
	Would sell a business for profit which one had built from scratch/Would prefer to hold on to the business even if offered a good take-over deal
	Believes some business profits should be used to support and develop the community/Believes business profits should be used to reward individuals
Challenge/security	Would prefer to have a reasonable income in a job one's sure of keeping/Would take a challenging job that offered high remuneration based on performance
Independence and confidence	Would seek the opinion of others before making a decision/Feels comfortable making most decisions without consulting others
Forward planning	Believes planning in advance is essential to achieve success/Believes forward planning is restrictive
Restlessness	Likes to stay with a venture once it is stable and successful/Likes to start a new venture once the current one begins to be stabilised
Creativity	Prefers to respond to, rather than create, opportunities/Prefers to create, rather than respond to, opportunities

This chapter concentrates on the differences between those who were in business and those who were aspiring to start up in business and the differences within these groups of individuals, particularly gender differences.

THE RESULTS

The results of the study are presented here in terms of the four postulates (see earlier) in turn, pertaining to (1) gender differences, (2) gender roles, (3) motherhood, and (4) family support. Independent variables are gender (men or women

Table 9.2 Entities in the entrepreneurial identity instrument

Me at home (Current Self 1)
Me as a business owner (Current Self 2)
Me as I would like to be
Me when I was 18 (Past Self 1)
Me when I worked for someone else and felt unfulfilled (Past Self 2)
Me as my spouse sees me (Metaperspective 1)
Me as my employer used to see me (Metaperspective 2)
Admired person
Disliked person
Father
Mother
Successful business man (nominate someone you know)
Successful business woman (nominate someone you know)
Spouse/partner
Community business person
Unsuccessful business person (nominate someone you know)
Bank clerk

Table 9.3 The sample

	Pre-start (aspiring)	*Post-start-up (existing)*	*Total*
Male	18	81	99
Female	51	37	88
Total	69	118	187

entrepreneurs), and business stage (i.e., aspiring business-owners, 'pre-start-up', or existing business owners, 'post-start-up').

Gender differences

In relation to Postulate 1, Table 9.4 shows how men and women, as aspiring and existing business owners, used the construct 'Would give priority to family interests and commitments/Would give priority to business commitments over family'. Interestingly, the majority of both men and women in established businesses would give priority to family interests and commitments. Amongst men, however, there was only a slight majority preference (53%) for this pole of the construct and it was only a secondary evaluative dimension of their identity, indicating that it was a value that they did not use very consistently when evaluating self and others. The picture for women in business was different: even though the majority (69%) of women owning established businesses aspired towards family commitment, they displayed a very low structural pressure (SP) on this construct, suggesting strong ambivalence – indeed conflict – over whether priority should be given to family commitments over business commitments. This was evidence of the stress and conflict surrounding business women's 'balancing' of their entrepreneurial

Table 9.4 Constructs concerning family where there was a lack of group consensus on the polarity chosen

Construct	Male Pre (n = 18) SP (%choice)	Male Post (n = 81) SP (%choice)	Female Pre (n = 51) SP (%choice)	Female Post (n = 37) SP (%choice)
Feels that family support for one's business is essential	56 (44%)*	43 (76%)+++	46 (65%)+++	55 (51%)*
Would pursue one's business idea without family support	31 (56%)++	46 (24%)+++	37 (35%)++	30 (49%)++
Would give priority to family interest and commitments	49 (38%)+++	24 (53%)+	25 (65%)+	10 (69%)^
Would give priority to business commitments over family	52 (61%)*	45 (47%)+++	26 (35%)+	36 (31%)++

Pre = Pre-start-up (aspiring entrepreneurs)
Post = Post start-up (established entrepreneurs)
'Core' evaluative dimensions ****80+; ***70–79; **60–69; *50–59
'Secondary' evaluative dimensions +++40–49; ++30–39; +20–29
Conflicted dimensions of identity ^−20–+19
Figures in parentheses denote percentage of respondents who selected this pole of the bipolar construct
Structural Pressure Scale ranges from +100 to −100

aspirations and their family commitments. Although the business women's highly conflicted and unstable valuing of prioritising family interests could be interpreted as evidence of trying to 'integrate' both family and business, thus supporting Brush's argument, the psychological effects seemed to be detrimental. Perhaps the degree to which these women felt in control over *whether* and to what extent they could prioritise family vs business was the differentiating factor between themselves and the male business owners. Business men did not seem to be perturbed about it.

Table 9.4 also shows that for the majority (61%) of young males *aspiring* to start their own business, priority would be given to business commitments over family commitments as a fairly core evaluative dimension of their identity (SP 52). In contrast, women wishing to start their own business were more likely to aspire to prioritising family interests and commitments (65%) but only as a secondary evaluative dimension of their identity (SP 25). This could be interpreted, simply, as indicating that the majority of aspiring male entrepreneurs wished to focus on developing their business, while aspiring female entrepreneurs wished to develop their business around their family responsibilities. However, the split consensus on prioritising family vs business interests revealed variations within the groups and therefore neither gender nor stage of business (pre-start/post-start) were found to be sole differentiating factors in entrepreneurial identity.

Gender differences were discernible regarding the issue of whether family support for one's business is essential (see Table 9.4). First, gender differences were notable, particularly among established business owners: the majority of men who were existing business owners (76%) believed that family support is essential for one's business, although the structural pressure (SP 43) denoted that this was only a secondary evaluative dimension of their identity. Women business owners showed an almost totally split consensus on this construct: the 51% of women who believed that family support is essential to one's business held this belief as a fairly core evaluative dimension of their identity, while those 49% of women business owners who 'would pursue their business idea without family support' were rather more ambivalent about this secondary evaluative dimension of their identity (SP = 30). As previously noted, business men were more likely than business women to actually receive support, particularly from their spouses. One might question to what extent the receipt of such support was deemed important to businessmen and women. If – as is thought to be the case – this support were important to women business owners, then its lack or absence would be highly significant in meeting their business goals and aspirations. The issue of family support will be returned to when discussing results in relation to Postulate 4.

Gender roles

In relation to Postulate 2, and given that ISA makes the assumption that 'one's positive and negative role models represent one's positive and negative reference systems', it is appropriate to examine the positive role models (via idealistic-identification) of aspiring and existing small business owners. The results (see Table 9.5) indicated that aspiring and existing business owners used 'successful business people' as their strongest positive role-models.

Table 9.5 Idealistic- and contra-identification with others

	Male pre	*Male post*	*Female pre*	*Female post*
Idealistic-identification				
Successful business man	0.82	0.81	0.77	0.75
Successful business woman	0.78	0.75	0.80	0.78
Father	0.51	0.54	0.58	0.48
Mother	0.37	0.51	0.58	0.47
Spouse/Partner	0.43	0.54	0.67	0.66
Contra-identification				
Successful business man	0.14	0.14	0.20	0.23
Successful business woman	0.14	0.18	0.17	0.20
Father	0.39	0.38	0.39	0.47
Mother	0.42	0.37	0.38	0.48
Spouse/Partner	0.41	0.37	0.31	0.32

Scale: 0–1

However, the results showed that there were gender influences. Irrespective of whether they were in business or not, male respondents idealistically identified to a greater extent with a successful business man while female respondents aspired to be like a successful business woman ($F = 7.59$; df $= 1,183$; $p < 0.01$). This indicates that while potential and existing business owners aspired to business success irrespective of gender, males and females used the same sex as their major business role models.

In the business context, and irrespective of stage of business, women had higher identification conflicts with their parents than men did (Table 9.6). However, aspiring and existing female business owners differed in the way these conflicted identifications came about. Aspiring female business owners empathetically identified with their parents to a greater extent than did female owners of existing businesses. This indicated that they still felt close to their parents and had many characteristics in common with them. In contrast, female owners of existing businesses dissociated from the characteristics they perceived their parents to have, as was evidenced by high levels of contra-identification with both father (0.47) and mother (0.48) (Table 9.5). Their rejection of parental lifestyles may have been necessary in order to meet the demands of their business life.

For women who were already business owners, conflicts in identification with their mothers were also high in the home context, indicating that while they had much in common with their mothers they also wished to dissociate from some characteristics they perceived their mothers as having. These conflicts in identification would often put strain on the relationship. The fact that these women, who for the most part had been in business for quite a few years, had not resolved their identification conflicts with parents would suggest that there was still

Table 9.6 Current empathetic identification and conflicts in identification

	Male pre		Male post		Female pre		Female post	
	CS1	*CS2*	*CS1*	*CS2*	*CS1*	*CS2*	*CS1*	*CS2*
Empathetic identification								
Successful business man	0.75	0.84	0.71	0.79	0.62	0.74	0.61	0.74
Successful business woman	0.69	0.84	0.70	0.77	0.64	0.82	0.67	0.80
Father	0.61	0.53	0.59	0.55	0.59	0.60	0.54	0.52
Mother	0.43	0.37	0.52	0.48	0.57	0.58	0.56	0.49
Spouse/Partner	0.53	0.41	0.56	0.52	0.64	0.68	0.63	0.66
Conflicts in identification								
Successful business man	0.26	0.28	0.26	0.27	0.31	0.34	0.34	0.38
Successful business woman	0.27	0.30	0.29	0.31	0.30	0.34	0.31	0.34
Father	0.43	0.40	0.43	0.40	0.45	0.45	0.47	0.45
Mother	0.39	0.35	0.37	0.35	0.43	0.44	0.49	0.44
Spouse/Partner	0.42	0.37	0.41	0.39	0.40	0.39	0.42	0.43

Scale 0–1
CS1 Me at home; CS2 Me as a business owner

considerable parental influence, and women were torn between their business life and their home life.

This leads us to propose that perceptions of business ownership differ from the reality of it. Conflicted identifications with parents could suggest a rejection of conventional gender roles. However, as the sample contains both mothers and childless women, there is a need to examine the influence of motherhood on their identity profiles.

Motherhood

In relation to Postulate 3 and given the high levels of identity diffusion amongst women, it is worth examining whether this was a factor related to motherhood or whether it is common to all women. First, all 'enterprising women' (pre-start-up and business owners) differed from all 'enterprising men' in respect of their identity diffusion both in home and business contexts ($F = 12.63$; df = 1,183; $p < .0001$), having in general the greater extent (ranging from 0.38 to 0.42 in females compared to 0.32 to 0.37 in men). However, for female business owners these differences did not appear to be primarily related to parenthood as such. In their home context, identity diffusion for both mothers (0.42) and childless women (0.40) was high and greater than for fathers (0.36) and childless men (0.39). In their business context, identity diffusion for both mothers (0.40) and childless women (0.38), though less than in their home context, remained greater than for fathers (0.35) and childless men (0.37). The issue of lower identity diffusion in the business than home context for both females and males, whether parent or not, was of considerable import ($F = 21.88$; df = 1,113; $p < .0001$).

However, the global identity diffusion results mask significant differences in conflicted identifications with significant others. Thus, in their business context both mothers in business and childless women had strongly conflicted identifications with their own mothers and fathers (Table 9.7).

There were 32 women in the sample who had no children, 22 (68%) aspiring to start up in business and 10 (31%) existing business owners. With one exception all were under 35 and 12 were under 25. So this was a group of young women, the majority of whom were setting out on their entrepreneurial career. Given their age profile, all these women were potentially future mothers. As these childless women in business forged their business career, compared with mothers in business ($N = 27$), they empathetically identified with their mothers and also dissociated from their mothers' values. This was evidenced in their significantly higher identification conflict with 'mother' in their business context than held for business mothers ($F = 3.67$; df = 1,79; $p = .05$). Childless women also empathetically identified more closely than did mothers in business with their fathers in their business context ($F = 5.45$; df = 1,66; $p < .05$). The many conflicts in identification with both fathers and mothers in the business context could be indicative of stressful relationships. Childless women had significantly lower identification conflicts than business mothers with the successful business man ($F = 12.42$; df = 1,83; $p < .005$) and with the successful business woman

Table 9.7 Motherhood: current empathetic identification and conflicts in identification

	Mothers pre		Childless pre		Mothers post		Childless post	
	CS1	*CS2*	*CS1*	*CS2*	*CS1*	*CS2*	*CS1*	*CS2*
Empathetic identification								
Successful business man	0.60	0.70	0.65	0.79	0.62	0.74	0.60	0.75
Successful business woman	0.61	0.76	0.69	0.89	0.67	0.80	0.66	0.80
Father	0.56	0.57	0.63	0.65	0.56	0.48	0.51	0.62
Mother	0.57	0.59	0.58	0.57	0.55	0.46	0.60	0.58
Spouse/Partner	0.62	0.67	0.68	0.70	0.60	0.64	0.74	0.69
Conflicts in identification								
Successful business man	0.36	0.39	0.24	0.25	0.36	0.39	0.28	0.33
Successful business woman	0.34	0.37	0.25	0.28	0.33	0.36	0.26	0.29
Father	0.45	0.46	0.46	0.44	0.50	0.45	0.42	0.47
Mother	0.43	0.44	0.43	0.43	0.48	0.42	0.51	0.50
Spouse/Partner	0.39	0.40	0.42	0.38	0.41	0.42	0.48	0.47

Scale 0–1
CS1 Me at home; CS2 Me as a business owner

($F = 7.79$; df $= 1,84$; $p < .05$) in the business context. This indicated that, outside the parental/family context, they had less of a 'struggle' in meeting their aspirations to be successful in business.

Comparing the value and belief systems of mothers and childless women concerning the family/business interface illustrated the stressful situation in which many business mothers found themselves. Even though the majority (60%) of business mothers aspired to give priority to family interests and commitments, very low mean structural pressure (SP 1) indicated strong ambivalence, indeed conflict, over 'balancing' their entrepreneurial aspirations and their family commitments.

However, not all mothers aspired to give priority to family over business. Over a fifth (22%) of mothers in business aspired to 'give priority to business commitments over family'. With a structural pressure of 47, this was a stronger evaluative dimension of identity than that associated with those who aspired to put family first. This gives credence to Goffee and Scase's (1985) and Cromie and Hayes's (1988) assertion that mothers are not a homogeneous grouping, some putting business achievement before family.

For the majority (56%) of business owners who were mothers, the necessity of 'family support for one's business' was a core evaluative dimension of identity. However, a significant number (44%) 'would pursue one's business idea without family support'. The structural pressure was significantly higher for mothers than childless women aspiring to this more autonomous alternative ($F = 5.68$; df $= 1,32$; $p < .05$), indicating that as a 'secondary' evaluative dimension it was a stronger value amongst mothers. For some mothers, therefore, 'going it alone' was the favoured, and perhaps the only, option.

However, this evidence does not wholly support the argument forwarded by Goffee and Scase (1985) and Cromie and Hayes (1988) that 'innovators' can circumvent domestic subordination. Categorisation by way of current identity variants showed that 81% of mothers already in business were 'vulnerable' in the home context (48% identity diffusion, 22% identity crisis, 7% negative, 4% defensive)[1] and 78% were vulnerable in the business context (56% identity diffusion, 7% diffuse high self-regard, 7% defensive high self-regard and 7% negative). This 'vulnerability of identity' was in many cases the result of the aforementioned unresolved identification conflicts, particularly with successful business people, and in several instances of low self-evaluation, particularly in the home context. It would seem therefore that these mothers, who were in business, had difficulty combining family responsibilities with business aspirations.

Childless women in existing businesses did not seem to be a homogeneous group. This lack of consensus was evidenced in their reaction to the need for family support. Of childless women in existing businesses 60% aspired to 'pursue their business idea without family support'. However, very low structural pressure (SP 1) suggested conflict, an indication that family support was an area of contention.

Regarding their overall feelings of contentment in the business role and in their private life, there was a difference between those childless women aspiring to start a business and those already in business. Those aspiring to start a business evaluated themselves highly and anticipated few conflicts in identification in the business role. They had higher levels of identity diffusion and lower self-evaluation in the home context. So, for childless aspiring business owners, the anticipated business role was perceived to allow them to fulfil their aspirations and 'achieve' a business identity.

However, the findings indicated that the reality of business ownership differed from the perception of it, if the sample of childless existing female business owners was representative. Of this group 80% were categorised as vulnerable in the home context (40% identity crisis, 20% identity diffusion, 20% defensive) and 70% in the business context (20% identity crisis, 20% identity diffusion, 10% diffuse high self-regard, 10% defensive high self-regard, 10% defensive). Of these women 50% were vulnerable in the business context because they had high levels of identity diffusion. This was quite an unexpected result as, being in an uncomfortable state, one would have expected this group to have resolved their conflicted identifications over time. One might have expected childless women to have already resolved their identification conflicts, particularly the strong ones with their mothers, and achieved a business identity to a greater degree. However, the reality was that they were just as likely to be in vulnerable identity states and have high levels of identity diffusion as mothers in business.

The evidence showed that it is critically important to examine family influences on identity. Women seemed to be coping with high levels of conflicted identifications with family members, particularly mothers. It would seem important to examine whether there were variations in identity profiles as a result of whether they believed family support to be necessary for the success of the business.

Family support

In relation to Postulate 4, given that the possession of children did not seem to be the single most important differentiating factor, and that there was a lack of consensus between mothers and childless women regarding aspirations towards family support, a new criterion was set, dividing the sample on this issue. The sample was split according to how they evaluated themselves and others in relation to the construct 'Feels that family support for one's business is essential/Would pursue one's business idea without family support' (see Table 9.1). Those who felt family support is essential were labelled 'family-oriented business owners'. Those who chose the alternative polarity were labelled 'independence-orientated business owners'.

The research found evidence of strong family bonds among family-orientated business owners. Irrespective of gender, family-orientated business owners idealistically identified with their mothers more ($F = 6.96$; df = 1,179; $p < .01$) and contra-identified with both their mothers ($F = 19.73$; df = 1,176; $p = .0001$) and their fathers ($F = 4.07$; df = 1,161; $p < .05$) less than those who were independence-orientated.

In the home context, independence-orientated owners of established businesses, irrespective of gender, had generally higher levels of identity diffusion than family-orientated owners of established businesses ($F = 4.05$; df = 1,161; $p < .05$). This was not surprising given their high contra-identification with family members, simultaneously coupled with their close empathetic identification with their parents. However, for this group, contra-identification outweighed empathetic identification, indicating that they were psychologically moving further away from empathetic identifications with their parents. Comparing home with work context these independence-orientated business owners had greatest identity diffusion when at home. It was their business role that allowed them to achieve their identity aspirations to a greater degree. Domestic lifestyles as represented particularly by their mothers were an area of contention, indicated by the finding that independence-orientated business owners had significantly higher identification conflicts with their mothers than did family-orientated business owners ($F = 4.60$; df = 1,176; $p < .05$).

The evidence confirmed that families were most compelling social institutions and family influence extended much deeper than was commonly recognised in the family/business interface. Family support is important for the psychological well-being of males in business. The majority of males believed family support was essential and for the most part this belief tended to bode well for a well-adjusted business identity and contentment in the home context. Men seemed to be able to appeal to family support and yet strive for autonomy.

However, for women the situation was more mixed. At pre-start stage, those who were independence-orientated had less conflicted identities in their business role than those who were family-orientated. Perhaps this was wishful thinking. The reality for the female business owners in the sample was quite different. Over 80% of those who were independence-orientated were categorised in vulnerable identity states. They had identification conflicts with their parents, particularly their mothers and particularly in the home context. Some of these women had family members involved in the business (mostly through partnership arrangements with their spouse, but also in some cases members of their parental family) and perhaps their aspirations towards autonomy were being quashed.

The results presented here show that aspirations for family support versus autonomy had different implications for men and women in business. While family support was important for the psychological well-being of both males and females in business, men tended to be able to *combine* aspirations for family support with autonomy, whereas for women the desire for autonomy could lead to conflicts in identification with family members.

EMPIRICALLY DERIVED THEORETICAL PROPOSITIONS

In the light of the results of the study, the four theoretical postulates (pertaining to gender differences, gender roles, motherhood, and family support) have been developed into a set of empirically based theoretical propositions as follows. Two propositions replace Postulate 1.

Proposition 1a: Given a split consensus in the way in which male and female aspiring and existing business owners construe the need for family support, and whether family or business should be given priority, gender generalisations cannot be made regarding the family–business interface.

This proposition conforms to theories that emphasise categorisation of business owners according to lifestyle values and beliefs.

Proposition 1b: In so far as women in business attempt to 'integrate' family and business, they are more likely than men in business to vacillate between family and business priorities.

This vacillation results in psychologically stressful states and is likely to impair their ability to focus on achieving their aspirations.

Four empirically based propositions were formulated to replace Postulate 2. The research revealed that, as expected, success in business was a major aspiration, with successful business people representing strong positive role models. However, substantial contra-identification with parents was evident.

Proposition 2a: Aspiring and existing small business owners use successful business people as positive role models, which requires dissociation from the lifestyle characteristics of differently orientated parents.

Proposition 2b: Role model identification differs according to gender, such that males aspire to be like successful businessmen while women use successful businesswomen as role models.

By comparing the home and the business context, some interesting differences were found between aspiring and existing business people, and between male and female business people. Furthermore, the results showed that it was not simply the degrees of identification with conventionally defined gender roles that were important, but the combination of such identifications with entrepreneurial aspirations. This was clearly shown when the sample was divided according to orientation to family support. Two further propositions are thus generated:

Proposition 2c: Irrespective of gender, aspired business ownership is a positive context for the development of identity in which, however, the perception of business ownership differs from the reality of it.

Proposition 2d: While business identity cannot be isolated from other social identities such as those of gender and parenthood, additional aspects such as aspirations towards autonomy and family support contribute to variations in identity profiles of aspiring and existing entrepreneurs.

Postulate 3, which postulated that childless women compared with mothers in business would have fewer identification conflicts with successful business people, was supported by the findings. The following three propositions are developed on the basis of these findings.

Proposition 3a: In so far as domestic commitments obtrude for women, women in business have difficulty balancing family and business aspirations.

Proposition 3b: Irrespective of whether or not they have children, women in business contend with higher levels of identity diffusion than men in business as a result of trying to reconcile and balance family and business aspirations.

As already demonstrated in respect of mothers and childless women, women in business do not constitute a homogeneous group.

Proposition 3c: Business women with children have difficulty in prioritising family and business interests, with consequent stress over conflict between business and home, but in so far as mothers in business prioritise business over family they are under less stress.

When the group of aspiring and existing entrepreneurs was divided according to their aspirations towards family support, the evidence supported Postulate 4, but some interesting further findings emerged. Men in business aspired to family support to a greater degree than women in business and had fewer conflicts in identification with family members. Augmenting Postulate 4 then, two further propositions are forwarded:

> *Proposition 4a*: Business men and women's aspirations towards having family support are reflected in strong idealistic and empathetic identification with their family members.

Aspirations for family support versus autonomy have different implications for men and women in business codified as follows:

> *Proposition 4b*: While their endorsement of family support contributes to psychological well-being of both males and females in business, for men an aspiration for autonomy is compatible with the aspiration for family support, whereas for women it generates conflicts in identification with family members.

Women attempt to resolve these identification conflicts through disengaging from their parents and forming new identifications with their spouse and successful business people.

CONCLUSIONS

When investigating business owners and their behaviour, the use of Identity Structure Analysis demonstrates the necessity of placing business enterprise within the context of family, and paying due regard to gender. That women business owners contend with high levels of identity diffusion – an uncomfortable state of affairs – appears to be a result of the 'integrating act' (Brush, 1992) of trying to give parity of priority to both family and business. This presents women entrepreneurs with considerable identity problems: judging by their high levels of identity diffusion, they are not entirely able to find optimal solutions to the complex balancing act of combining aspirations, commitments and expectations across different aspects of their life and involving a broad section of significant people. With their experience of trying to reconcile the complex demands upon them, and their own high aspirations, it is perhaps not surprising that women are often seen as peacemakers, sounding-boards and team-builders.

Entrepreneurial women appear to have difficulty combining their desire for professional success with particular constructions of femininity across their private and professional lives (see Wager, Chapter 6 this volume). High levels of identity diffusion usually cannot be sustained. The findings suggest that resolution of identification conflict involve women in business re-appraising themselves in relation to their mothers in particular. Furthermore, it is likely that female entrepreneurs will form new identifications in the business role, thereby broadening their value system in relation to their business identity and re-appraising how they might combine their private home and familial identity and their business identity.

With particular regard to women in business, in order to facilitate their processes of re-appraisal and resolution of conflicted business identities, societal agencies should reconsider the support systems offered to both aspiring and existing entrepreneurs. For some, family support is a clear need. For others, there is the desire to 'go it alone', and for this group good non-family support is required – practical, moral and financial. This study has shown that there is a particular need to establish a supportive business network that will allow them to form new identifications and resolve identification conflicts with family members. Without adequately improved support systems as mechanisms to reduce the current high levels of conflict in the identities of business women, particularly in their 'balancing' of family commitments and business interests, there is a danger that so-called 'enterprising' identities will be compromised or superseded by 'diffused' identities. Such an outcome would be a highly unpromising prospect for the future development and maintenance of enterprise creation and entrepreneurship.

NOTE

1 For the rationale for the ISA classification of identity variants refer to Chapter 1, and for the actual classification refer to Chapter 2, Table 2.1.

REFERENCES

Allen, S. & Truman, C. (1993) *Women in Business*. London: Routledge.

Baines, S. & Wheelock, J. (1998) 'Working for each other: Gender, the household and micro-business survival and growth', *International Small Business Journal*, 17, 1: 16–35.

Brush, C. G. (1992) 'Research on women business owners: Past trends, a new perspective and future', *Entrepreneurship Theory and Practice*, 16, 4: 5–30.

Chandler, A. D. (1977) *The Visible Hand*. Cambridge, MA: Belknap Press.

Chell, E., Haworth, J. & Brearley, S. (1991) *The Entrepreneurial Personality. Concepts, Cases and Categories*. London: Routledge.

Cowling, M., Taylor, M. P. & Mitchell, P. (1997) *Entrepreneurial Women and Men*. SME Centre Working Paper. Coventry: Warwick Business School.

Cromie, S. & Hayes, J. (1988) 'Towards a typology of female entrepreneurs', *Sociological Review*, 36, 1: 87–113.

DTI (1998) *Small and Medium Enterprise Statistics for the UK*. Sheffield: Department of Trade and Industry.

Filley, A. C. & Aldag, R. J. (1978) 'Characteristics and measurement of an organizational typology', *Academy of Management Journal*, 21, 4: 576–591.

Filley, A. C., House, R. F. & Kerr, S. (1976) *Managerial Process and Organisational Behaviour* (2nd edn). Glenview, IL: Scott, Foresman & Co.

Gilligan, C. (1982) *In a Different Voice*. London: Cambridge.

Goffee, R. & Scase, R. (1985) *Women in Charge: The Experiences of Female Entrepreneurs*. London: George Allen & Unwin.

Hornaday, R. W. (1990) 'Dropping the E-words from small business research: An alternative typology', *Journal of Small Business Management*, 28, 4: 22–23.

Miller, J. B. (1976) *Towards a New Psychology of Women*. Boston: Beacon Press.

Poutziouris, P. & Chittenden, F. (1996) *Family Businesses or Business Families?* Leeds: Institute of Small Business Affairs in association with National Westminster Bank.

Shapero, A. & Sokol, L. (1982) 'The social dimensions of entrepreneurship'. In C. A. Kent, D. L. Sexton & K. H. Vesper (eds) *Encylopedia of Entrepreneurship*. Englewood Cliffs, NJ: Prentice Hall.

Simpson, S. M. & Pearson, E. (1989) *Multiple Roles and Conflict, High Hurdles for Women Entrepreneurs?* Paper presented to the Women in Enterprise/University of Bradford Women Entrepreneurs Conference, University of Bradford, April.

Stanworth, M. J. K. & Curran J. (1976) 'Growth and the small firm – an alternative view', *Journal of Management Studies*, 13, 2: 95–110.

Wager, M. (1993) *Constructions of Femininity in Academic Women: Continuity between Private and Professional Identity*. D.Phil thesis, University of Ulster.

Part IV

Clinical issues

INTRODUCTION

Chapter 10 by Harris considers the utility of applying the ISA conceptual framework to elucidate disturbed states of identity from the perspective of clinical psychology. His approach is exploratory and concerns identifying characteristics of 'mental health' clients, and tracking the efficacy of therapeutic work with a client in a time-series case study with repeated identity structure analyses. ISA can be seen to have diagnostic utility in pinpointing specific representations of problematic identity issues. Harris uses ISA to assist in the therapeutic process by way of providing feedback on the client's progress in dealing with such issues.

The authors of Chapter 11 present a case study of an anorexic client to demonstrate the efficacy of ISA as a 'diagnostic procedure' for:

(1) elucidating the particularities of a client's identity processes rooted in self's biographical experiences of untoward personally threatening happenings;
(2) comprehending the ongoing identity processes that sustain anorexic identity processes peculiar to the client;
(3) elaborating with the client strategies that will facilitate self's agentic reappraisal of biographical experiences, so as to be able to countenance alternative identity processes that diminish anorexic ones.

In the case study, the client's anorexic identity processes appeared to be primarily related to experience of sexual abuse, an idealised view of her mother, but a derogatory maternal metaperspective (*me as my mother sees me*), and a conflicted identification with her father. The particularities of her identity processes included an episode of a very negative past traumatised self. Recall from Chapter 1 Harré's distinction between the agentic singular self (*Self 1*) and self-conception (*Self 2*). In dealing with these ongoing existential issues she (*Self 1*) had adopted procedures that compartmentalised herself (*Self 2*) into two aspects, between which she (*Self 1*) vacillated: her *out of control (bingeing) and depressed 'negative'* state (*Self 2a*), and her *defensive high self-regard* state (*Self 2b*). Her conflicted dimension of identity that represented the arena of her cognitive–affective stress was a contention between dominance by others over moral issues ('the right way to do things') and being allowed her own moral autonomy ('to do things her way and make her own mistakes'). This arena of stress designated an underlying dynamic of vacillation between being out of control and being in control. She attempted to contend with this stress through forming a set of core identity aspirations: wanting to be cherished; not wanting to let go of 'desirable people' she knew, and getting on well with them; not having been sexually abused; doing everything possible to prevent terrible events; and not having experienced or witnessed a terrible tragedy. In her defensive high self-regard state, she appraised herself as having accomplished these 'desirable qualities'. This was a state in which she did not acknowledge the downside of her biographical experience, expressing instead an absurdly idealised view of herself (*Self 2b*) which could not accord with her personal reality. In her out-of-control and depressed state, she was overwhelmed by the negativity of her biographical experience (*Self 2a*). Recalling from Chapter 1 the terminology of compromised intentional expression (*IE*), her expression of self in these two states would be represented by:

Self 1*Q$_a${Self 2a: IE} → Self 1*{cued Self 2a: IE} → Self 1:{pertaining to Self 2a: IE}

for her out-of-control and depressed expression of self, and:

Self 1*Q$_b${Self 2b: IE} → Self 1*{cued Self 2b: IE} → Self 1:{pertaining to Self 2b: IE}

for her defensive high self-regard expression of self, where the cues Q_a and Q_b denote the respective triggers that induce her to switch from the one to the other state.

In assisting anorexic and bulimic clients, a therapeutic climate for optimal autonomy restructuring should be established whereby they have encouraging conditions for trial-and-error social experimentation in which to develop alternative identity processes to their anorexic or bulimic ones.

Black and Weinreich (Chapter 12) used ISA to explore the identity processes of professional counsellors who are prone to experiencing vicarious traumatisation when working intensively with survivors of a major traumatic occurrence. The instance investigated in this study was the detonation in August 1998 of the 'Omagh bomb' in Northern Ireland and its aftermath. Counsellors working with the survivors showed closer empathetic identification and increased conflicted identification with traumatised and difficult clients in respect of self appraised in the short-term aftermath, and facing the long-term consequences, of the bomb. They also tended also to dissociate from both their domestic world and their professional colleagues. Compared with a control group of counsellors not involved with this or similar occurrence, the counsellors who experienced vicarious traumatisation generated conflicted dimensions of identity predominantly based in trauma-specific issues. The ongoing stress accompanying these identity processes may be considered to contribute to 'compassion fatigue'. The counsellors' processes of identity redefinition in the longer term and their manner of coping with vicarious traumatisation are being subjected to two further phases of identity structure analyses, to be reported elsewhere in due course.

10 Identity formulation and reformulation in clinical assessment and therapy

Paul D. G. Harris

PURPOSES OF APPLYING ISA IN CLINICAL SETTINGS

A growing volume of studies attests to the value of applying Identity Structure Analysis in clinical contexts. The research application of ISA with clinical samples spans two decades. Early uses of ISA with clinical groups focused upon individual cases of eating disorders (Harris, 1980, 1988; Weinreich, 1983; Weinreich *et al.*, 1985). An exception was Needham's (1984) study of 'maternity blues'. While continuing to examine anorexic disorders, Connor (1992) extended the remit of ISA from an individual to a family therapy perspective. More recently, the range of client groups sampled has diversified, for example, to include individuals with depression and anxiety (Fox, 1996); those engaged in substance abuse (Allen, 1996); and counsellors dealing with trauma victims (Black and Weinreich, Chapter 12 this volume). At the same time, eating disorders remain highlighted as a clinical presentation for which identity problems have particular relevance (O'Kane and Saunderson, 1997; Saunderson and O'Kane, 1999).

In a study by Harris and Hudson (1996), the mental health sample comprised 33 individuals, 25 female and 8 male cases. The diverse set of presenting problems and clinical features involved spanned obsessive-compulsive disorder, Othello syndrome, childhood sexual abuse, self-harm, post-traumatic stress, serious offending behaviour, bereavement issues, gambling behaviour, and various forms of life transition and relationship difficulties. This overall sample (n = 33) was subdivided into three groups. This allowed a comparison to be made between nine females presenting with eating disorder, eight non-eating disorder female patients, and eight male non-eating disorder patients.

It was found, for example, that diffusion identity variants were relatively common for all three groups (Table 10.1). Current and Past Identity 'Crisis' variants were distinctive to a substantial proportion of both the female and male psychiatric groups (Table 10.2). A trend towards decreasing self-evaluation was characteristic of the female eating disorder patients but not of the other two groups studied (Table 10.3). Also set out in Tables 10.1 to 10.3 are previously published data (Harris, 1988) for four groups. These comprise 10 females characterised as anorexic/bulimic, 11 non-eating disordered psychiatric patients, a 'normal' control group of 11 females, and 22 adolescent females studied by Weinreich.

Table 10.1 Comparison of identity variant types (current and past identity variants combined)

Group	N	Male or female	Diffusion variants	Moderate variants	Foreclosed variants
Non-eating disorder	8	M	12	4	0
Non-eating disorder	16	F	21	11	0
Eating disorder	9	F	11	6	1
Anorexic/bulimic	10	F	12	8	0
Normal control	11	F	3	17	2
Non-eating disorder control	11	F	11	10	1
Adolescent sample	22	F	8	33	3

The adolescent sample is one reported by Weinreich (Harris, 1988).

Table 10.2 Relative evaluation of current and past self

Group	N	Male or female	Increasing self-evaluation	Decreasing self-evaluation
Non-eating disorder	8	M	6	2
Non-eating disorder	16[a]	F	9	6
Eating disorder	9	F	2	7
Anorexic/bulimic	10	F	2	8
Normal control	11	F	7	4
Psychiatric control	11	F	9	2
Adolescent sample[b]	22	F	21	1

a. For the Non-eating disorder female group one individual showed no difference in self-evaluation between current and past self.
b. The adolescent sample is one reported by Weinreich (Harris, 1988).

Table 10.3 Crisis variant compared to other identity variants

Group	N	Male or female	Current crisis variant	Past crisis variant	Other current variants	Other past variants
Non-eating disorder	8	M	5	7	3	1
Non-eating disorder	16	F	12	8	4	8
Eating disorder	9	F	4	6	5	3
Anorexic/bulimic	10	F	7	3	3	7
Normal control	11	F	0	0	11	11
Non-eating disorder control	11	F	4	6	7	5
Adolescent sample	22	F	0	2	22	20

These samples are referred to by Harris (1988) and Harris and Hudson (1996).

Nomothetic comparisons between specific diagnostic groups and both clinical and non-clinical control groups (for example, Weinreich *et al.*, 1985) has been a favoured approach. In addition, detailed case studies illustrating the value of ISA in the initial assessment and evaluation of change during psychotherapy have been recounted (Harris, 1984, 1985; Fox, 1996; Harris, 1997). Harris and Hudson (1996) reported seven clinical cases for whom repeat ISA data were gathered. This included one case for which repeat ISA data were available prior to and following a tragic life event, namely the suicide of a partner. For the seven cases outlined a trend was discerned, marked by stability rather than change in identity variants. Crisis variants tended to eventually resolve into varying degrees of moderate or foreclosed identity variants.

In this chapter the emerging purposes of ISA as both a theoretical framework and a methodology for application in clinical contexts is elaborated. In particular, the process and monitoring of individual formulations and reformulations of identity during the course of therapy will be demonstrated in relation to one of the cases reported by Harris and Hudson (1996).

Theoretical postulates

Much of the published research on therapeutic changes measures alterations in behaviour, cognitions, and symptomatology but neglects to consider correspon-ding changes occurring in self-concept. Fennell's (1997) model encompasses a cognitive perspective on self-esteem and partly addresses this issue. However, this account is limited by the narrowness of a framework which includes the construct of self-esteem but not the broader domain of self-image and identity. Within an approach informed by personal construct therapy, Button (1993: 80) has identi-fied how 'at the heart of therapy in general is the need to reconstrue self and one's relationship with other people'. He outlines how some of the traditional repertory grid methods have been utilised to this end. Their widespread use in application of personal construct theory has yet to be achieved and the resultant theoretical postulates perhaps lack the breadth and cohesion of ISA. In addition, the fact that utilisation of correlation statistics predominates in repertory grid analysis repre-sents a constraint to the scope and interpretation of the data derived.

Time-series methodology

The value and limitations of individual case studies as a form of applied research have been discussed by Barlow *et al.* (1984). These authors noted that if case studies are simply anecdotal case reports they have limited scientific function. When such case studies incorporate repeated systematic measurement, case analysis in the form of time-series methodology becomes feasible. Clinical decision-making informed by repeat ISA data is of particular value when it addresses questions such as the following:

• How can expected variability in repeat scores for ISA indices be distin-guished from trends in data representing significant change in self-image and theoretically significant improvement or deterioration?

- What degree of change in ISA data is necessary to provide adequate evidence that therapeutic intervention is effective?
- At what point can it be concluded that ISA data demonstrate sufficient 'personal recovery' to terminate therapy and discharge a client from psychotherapy, especially in terms of resolution of identity problems?

Barlow *et al.* (1984) have presented guidelines for systematic analysis of retest data for case studies, while also recognising that the task involved is both an art and a science. Without such safeguards a practitioner may perceive and claim clinical improvement when this is not justified on the basis of data analysis.

A CASE SCENARIO

A clinical case scenario will be introduced to illustrate ISA case analysis objectives. Norma (a pseudonym) first presented for psychological assessment and therapy when hospitalised in her mid-twenties with a six-year history of eating disorder. She had been in contact with mental health services for several years, having been hospitalised in her late teens, when a diagnosis of anorexia nervosa was made. She had begun dieting at the age of seventeen and within a year or so her weight had decreased from eight stone twelve pounds to five and a half stone.

A total of five ISA assessments were carried out over a five-year period, the first four within two years. At the point of first assessment using ISA, Norma's clinical presentation was characteristic of bulimia nervosa (Szmukler *et al.*, 1986). She engaged in binge eating and vomiting several times per day, her weight being just over six stone.

During the course of psychotherapy, extending over the subsequent three years, significant life experiences included the sudden illness and death of her father, changes in employment, and fluctuating marital tensions. The form of integrative psychotherapy (Norcross and Goldfried, 1992) followed was primarily cognitive-behavioural in orientation. Therapeutic input included anxiety management, marital therapy, group therapy, and cognitive restructuring (Hawton *et al.*, 1989). Feedback on the five sets of ISA results was cumulatively incorporated into therapy with a view to exploring beliefs about self and others.

Over the course of therapy Norma made significant progress. Occasional setbacks were triggered by life events, in particular the illness and death of her father and marital conflicts. Her weight gradually increased to seven stone and vomiting reduced to being occasional rather than daily. A follow-up assessment, which included a repeat ISA, two years after completion of therapy (baseline plus 53 months) indicated that recovery of functioning had been sustained. Norma had given birth to two children within a much improved marital relationship. At final contact (baseline ISA plus 53 months) Norma reported being symptom-free and presented as having achieved considerable gains in terms of lifestyle and personal adjustment.

ISA DATA ANALYSIS

The form of ISA rating sheet developed for completion by Norma is shown in Table 10.4. Given considerations of confidentiality, some entity designations have been disguised by role terms (for example, names of sisters substituted by role

Table 10.4 Norma: sample rating sheet

	. . . *worries a lot*	. . . *never worries*
	– – – – – – – – –	
	4 3 2 1 0 1 2 3 4	
Mother . . .	– – – – – – – –	
Father . . .	– – – – – – – –	
Sister (1) . . .	– – – – – – – –	
Brother (1) . . .	– – – – – – – –	
Brother (2) . . .	– – – – – – – –	
Sister (2) . . .	– – – – – – – –	
Sister (3) . . .	– – – – – – – –	
Husband . . .	– – – – – – – –	
My family . . .	– – – – – – – –	
Me as father sees me . . .	– – – – – – – –	
Me as mother sees me . . .	– – – – – – – –	
Me as friends see me . . .	– – – – – – – –	
Ex-partner . . .	– – – – – – – –	
Friend . . .	– – – – – – – –	
Mother-in-law . . .	– – – – – – – –	
Father-in-law . . .	– – – – – – – –	
Me as others think I should be . . .	– – – – – – – –	
Me in five years time . . .	– – – – – – – –	
A person I admire . . .	– – – – – – – –	
A bad person . . .	– – – – – – – –	
Me as I am now . . .	– – – – – – – –	
Me as I'd like to be . . .	– – – – – – – –	
Me as others see me . . .	– – – – – – – –	
Me as I used to be . . .	– – – – – – – –	
Friend . . .	– – – – – – – –	

term, Sister). The constructs selected are listed in Table 10.5. These are a mixture of constructs specific to Norma, elicited by interview, and provided constructs drawn from the experience of application of ISA with other eating-disordered patients. For ease of comparison, a decision was made to list the same 30 constructs and 25 entities for repeat ISAs as those administered for the baseline ISA.

Repeat data analysis for current and past identity diffusion, evaluation of self over time, and appraisal of significant others is set out in Table 10.6. The pattern of global identity variants over time is shown in Table 10.7. In terms of Barlow *et al.*'s (1984) distinction between trend and variability around trend, Table 10.6 demonstrates a clear tendency towards decreasing Current Identity Diffusion between the first four data points (spanning a period from baseline to baseline plus 23 months). By the fourth assessment (B + 23M), a relatively low index for Current Identity Diffusion indicates a phase of mild defensiveness, from which she emerges at the final assessment (B + 53M). That is, there is a partial reversal

Table 10.5 Norma: constructs selected

1. . . . outgoing* . . . shy.
2. . . . gets on well with everyone* . . . doesn't get on well with people.
3. . . . always respectful to others* . . . never respectful to others.
4. . . . unhappy within themselves . . . happy within themselves*.
5. . . . tight with money . . . generous with money*.
6. . . . childish . . . mature*.
7. . . . clever* . . . not so bright.
8. . . . honest* . . . dishonest.
9. . . . others decide things for them . . . makes their own decisions*.
10. . . . hopeless when time on hands . . . can handle when has time on their hands*.
11. . . . attractive* . . . not attractive.
12. . . . not bad-tempered* . . . bad-tempered.
13. . . . keeps to themselves . . . open and gets involved*.
14. . . . worries a lot . . . never worries*.
15. . . . is mixed up . . . isn't mixed up*.
16. . . . doesn't suffer from bad nerves* . . . suffers from bad nerves.
17. . . . never boasts* . . . boasts a lot.
18. . . . ambitious* . . . not ambitious.
19. . . . shows it when they care* . . . doesn't show it when they care.
20. . . . dependent . . . independent*.
21. . . . docile . . . dominant*.
22. . . . lacks confidence . . . confident*.
23. . . . emotional* . . . unemotional.
24. . . . always helpful* . . . never helpful.
25. . . . is respected* . . . isn't respected.
26. . . . never talks about sex* . . . is always talking about sex.
27. . . . perfectionist* . . . not perfectionist.
28. . . . relies too much on what others say and think . . . doesn't rely too much on what others say and think*.
29. . . . deep . . . not deep*.
30. . . . complains a lot . . . never complains*.

*denotes Norma's favoured pole of each construct at baseline assessment

Table 10.6 Norma: Repeat ISA indices – identity diffusion and evaluation of entities

	Evaluation of							
	Current identity diffusion	Past identity diffusion	Future self	Current self	Past self	Self to others	Mother	Father
B	0.38	0.41	0.77	0.35	0.15	0.54	0.05	0.07
B + 9M	0.34	0.37	0.71	0.34	0.36	0.58	0.18	0.27
B + 16M	0.30	0.44	0.77	0.60	0.03	0.60	-0.12	0.07
B + 23M	0.21	0.37	0.59	0.58	0.12	0.58	0.03	0.28
B + 53M	0.27	0.39	0.50	0.47	-0.11	0.47	0.16	0.07

B = baseline; M = months

Table 10.7 Norma: Current and past identity variants for repeat ISAs

	Baseline	B + 9M	B + 16M	B + 23M	B + 53M
Current identity variant	Indeterm.	Indeterm.	Indeterm.	Indeterm.	Indeterm.
Past identity variant	Crisis	Indeterm.	Crisis	Negative	Negative

B = baseline; M = months; Indeterm. = indeterminate

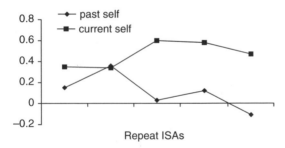

Figure 10.1 Repeat indices for evaluation of current self and past self.

of a trend towards decreasing Current Identity Diffusion at long-term follow-up (B + 53M). In contrast, the data for Past Identity Diffusion display variability rather than a distinct trend over the full span of five data points.

Table 10.6 presents a complex pattern across five data points for discriminating between variability and trend for a comparison of evaluation of Current Self and Past Self. Data abstracted from Table 10.6 for repeat current and past self-evaluation indices are represented in graphic form in Figure 10.1. A trend towards increasing evaluation of Current Self is apparent when comparing data points one and two with data points three, four, and five. There is an additional tendency for this effect to plateau around a mean more typical of non-psychiatric patients, as recorded for nomothetic studies (Harris and Hudson, 1996). This trend of increasing evaluation of Current Self can be viewed as a sign of therapeutically desirable progress in reappraisal of self.

Table 10.6 and Figure 10.1 show that for Past Self, considerable variability is evident but with a resolution towards decreasing evaluation of self in the past when comparing baseline with the final three data points. That is, from the present improved experience of self, self in the past is seen in more negative terms. Thus by the fifth assessment (B + 53M) Norma is able to reappraise her Past Self as having been in a negative state, whilst currently having a moderately positive self-evaluation.

In contrast to the variability indicated for evaluation indices for Current Self and Past Self, comparative stability is the most notable characteristic for the entity Self to Others (Table 10.6), being the metaperspective of self, 'me as others see me'.

Comparing data for evaluation of Current Self and Future Self, the initial two assessments (B and B + 9M) reveal a substantial discrepancy between Norma's hopes for the future and herself currently (Table 10.6). There is a trend towards increasing evaluation of Future Self over the initial three assessments, arriving at what probably represents a more realistic level by the final assessment (B + 53M).

A further aspect of data analysis was to examine structural pressures on constructs for repeat ISA assessments. The aim was to gain an appreciation of Norma's consistency or inconsistency in construing aspects of herself and others. 'Core' or stable evaluative constructs are those used to judge the merits of others with a high degree of evaluative consistency. For each of the five occasions for which ISA profiles were available note was taken of which six constructs had the highest structural pressure scores, that is, the six most stable evaluative dimensions of her identity. One construct appeared in the 'top six' on all five occasions, with structural pressure values which ranged between +86.27 and +98.65. This was the construct No. 2: gets on well with everyone (positive pole); doesn't get on well with people (negative pole).

The values for three other constructs placed them amongst the six highest structural pressure scores for at least three of the five ISA assessments. These were the following constructs (the positive pole was the same in each instance and is shown first):

> *Construct No.17* never boasts . . . boasts a lot,
> *Construct No.3* always respectful to others . . . never respectful to others,
> *Construct No.19* shows it when they care . . . doesn't show it when they care.

In brief, central to Norma's 'thinking' was placing high emphasis upon getting on well with people, being respectful and not boastful, and expressing feelings of care.

In contrast, persistent examples of inconsistently evaluated dimensions of identity were pinpointed. The criteria adopted were of low structural pressure values being apparent for at least three of the five ISA assessments (within the range -20 to $+20$). According to such criteria, just two out of thirty constructs emerged as prominent.

The construct, docile . . . dominant, produced negative structural pressure on three occasions (B + 9 months; B + 16 months; B + 53 months). The scores for these occasions were -1.93, -2.94, and -2.43, 'dominant' being the positive pole each time. This construct therefore represented a conflicted evaluative dimension of Norma's identity. For the other 29 constructs only a single instance of a negative structural pressure was recorded. This was a value of -8.76 on the third ISA profile (B + 16 months) for the construct, never talks about sex . . . is always talking about sex. This construct also yielded low positive scores (below $+20$) on the first and final ISA assessments (B and B + 53 months). For the final ISA evaluation the polarity of the construct changed to 'never talks about sex' as the positive pole. This suggests that even though Norma's use of this construct was still fairly inconsistent, she now favoured construal of self and others in terms of never talking about sex as opposed to always talking about sex. It is clear, however, that any talk of sex represents a considerable arena of stress in Norma's identity structure.

In brief, the data for constructs inconsistently evaluated on repeated occasions indicate that Norma was very ambivalent as to whether or not it is correct to be dominant or docile or to talk openly about sexuality. This corresponds to an observation that issues regarding assertiveness and the discussion of sexuality recurred and were not entirely resolved, during the process of psychotherapy.

CLINICAL RAMIFICATIONS

The versatility of ISA for both idiographic and nomothetic approaches and follow-up studies gives it a special place within the theoretically derived methodologies suitable for use in clinical contexts. A need for individual practitioners to systematically evaluate the outcome of clinical interventions has been increasingly prioritised (Berger, 1996). Given the lack of worthwhile frameworks and measures for monitoring change in self-concept during therapy, the application of ISA for such purposes is welcomed for its flexible and powerful ability to meet this requirement for a variety of clinical case scenarios.

CONCLUSIONS

This chapter has focused upon the value of nomothetic, idiographic and phased ISA studies relevant to clinical samples and settings. In particular, the utility of a phased idiographic approach to understanding stability and change in self-concept and identity during the course of psychotherapy has been explored. It has been proposed that within a scientist-practitioner model of clinical intervention, time-series methodology represents a suitable framework for ISA case analysis. The clinical implications of such an approach have been illustrated for a specific case study highlighting successive reformulations of identity. In general, ISA has been shown to have significant potential for monitoring and interpreting process and outcomes in psychotherapy. Thus the theory and method of Identity Structure Analysis warrants serious and extensive consideration for wide applicability within adult mental health services, building upon the substantial number of preliminary studies now completed.

REFERENCES

Allen, P. (1996) *Identity Structure Analysis for Drug-using and Non Drug-using Groups*. Paper presented at the British Psychological Society London Conference, Institute of Education, London, 17–18 December.

Barlow, D., Hayes, S., and Nelson, R. (1984) *The Scientist Practitioner: Research and Accountability in Clinical And Educational Settings*. New York: Pergamon.

Berger, M. (1996) *Outcomes and Effectiveness in Clinical Psychology Practice*. Leicester: British Psychological Society Division of Clinical Psychology Occasional Paper 1.

Button, E. (1993) *Eating Disorders: Personal Construct Therapy and Change*. Chichester: Wiley.

Connor, T. (1992) *An Identity Exploration of Anorexia Nervosa within a Family Context*. Unpublished D.Phil. thesis, University of Ulster.

Fennell, M. (1997) 'Low self-esteem: a cognitive perspective', *Behavioural and Cognitive Psychotherapy*, 25: 1–25.

Fox, M. (1996) *An Exploration of the Depressed Identity using Identity Structure Analysis*. Unpublished MSc dissertation, University of Ulster.

Harris, P. (1980) *Identity Development in Female Patients Suffering from Anorexia Nervosa and Bulimia Nervosa: An Application of Weinreich's Identity Structure Analysis*. Unpublished M.Psychol. thesis, University of Liverpool.

Harris, P. (1984) *Evaluation of Changes in Self-concept During the Course of Therapy*. Paper presented at the International Conference on Self and Identity, University College, Cardiff, 9–13 July.

Harris, P. (1985) *Towards an Understanding of Changes in Self-concept During the Process of Recovery from Psychiatric Disorders*. Paper presented at British Psychological Society Conference, Clare College, Cambridge, 17–19 September.

Harris, P. (1988) 'Identity development and identification conflict in female anorectic and bulimic patients'. In E. Anthony and C. Chiland (eds.) *The Child in His Family*, vol. 8: 67–78. New York: Wiley.

Harris, P. (1997) *Identity Structure Analysis Applied to Adult Mental Health Case Monitoring*. Paper presented at the Fifth European Congress of Psychology, University College, Dublin, 6–11 July.

Harris, P. and Hudson, A. (1996) *The Utilisation of Identity Structure Analysis in Clinical Psychology Practice*. Paper presented at the British Psychological Society London Conference, Institute of Education, London, 17–18 December.

Hawton, K., Salkovis, P., Kirk, J., and Clark, D. (1989) *Cognitive Behaviour Therapy for Psychiatric Problems: A Practical Guide*. Oxford: Oxford University Press.

Needham, S. (1984) *Maternity Blues and Personal Identity Development in First Time Mothers: An Exploratory Study*. Unpublished research dissertation, Diploma in Clinical Psychology, British Psychological Society, Leicester.

Norcross, J. and Goldfried, M. (eds.) (1992) *Handbook of Psychotherapy Integration*. New York: Basic Books.

O'Kane, M. and Saunderson, W. (1997) *Post Traumatic Stress Disorder and Eating Disorders: Exploring Links in Identity Structure and Development*. Paper presented at Fifth European Congress of Psychology, University College, Dublin, 6–11 July.

Saunderson, W. and O'Kane, M. (1999) 'Self, identity and developmental perspectives in young women with anorexia nervosa', *Proceedings of the British Psychological Society*, 7, 2: 137.

Szmukler, G., Slade, P., Harris, P., Benton, D., and Russell, G. (eds.) (1986) *Anorexia Nervosa and Bulimic Disorders*. Oxford: Pergamon.

Weinreich, P. (1983) 'Psychodynamics of Personal and Social Identity'. In A. Jacobson-Widding (ed.) *Identity: Personal and Societal*. Stockholm: Almqvist & Wiskell/Humanities Press.

Weinreich, P., Harris, P., and Doherty, J. (1985) 'Empirical Assessment of Identity and Bulimia Nervosa', *Journal of Psychiatric Research*, 19: 297–302.

11 Anorexia nervosa: Analysing identity for predisposing, precipitating and perpetuating factors

Wendy Saunderson and Maria O'Kane

ANOREXIA NERVOSA: A BRIEF INTRODUCTION

The history of self-inflicted starvation – variously conceptualised as asceticism, evil, spectacle, martyrdom, insanity, hysteria, self-empowerment and 'beauty' – has been a long, multi-faceted, and largely female one. From the medical curiosity of fasting saints and hysterical women to the post/modern quest towards individuation and self-identity through 'management' of the-body-as-project, anorexia nervosa has inspired and yielded an increasingly detailed and sophisticated understanding of its complex and wide-ranging motivation, meaning and expression (Saunderson and O'Kane, 1999).

A central core of anorexia nervosa is commonly believed to be the struggle for control and a sense of identity. Anorexia is said to reflect the displacement onto the body of young women's struggle for autonomy and selfhood, and is most likely to occur in families and/or circumstances where such autonomy, separation and individuation are difficult to achieve (Benson, 1997). In short, as Wegar (1997: 72) asserts, 'the body has become a prime site of identity'. This chapter presents an idiographic analysis of the identity structure of one young woman diagnosed with anorexia nervosa and, in so doing, demonstrates the use of ISA in a clinical context. As outlined in the Introduction to the clinical section of this volume, ISA is presented here as a 'diagnostic' procedure for:

(i) elucidating the particularities of the anorexic patient's identity processes rooted in self's biographical experiences of untoward personally threatening happenings;

(ii) comprehending the ongoing identity processes that sustain anorexic identity processes peculiar to the patient;

(iii) elaborating with the patient, strategies that will facilitate self's agentic reappraisal of biographical experiences so as to be able to countenance alternative identity processes that diminish anorexic ones.

As such, the value of ISA in extrapolating prognostic features and treatment implications is apparent. By way of contextualising our approach to anorexia nervosa and clarifying it as a clinical idiographic case analysis rooted in the medical model of illness and treatment, we will now outline recent conceptualisations of the 'illness' and key concerns of the medical model from which we drew our analytic framework. This brief background also serves to introduce the reader to salient features of anorexia espoused by the 'assessment–treatment' literature which are relevant to the particularities of the following Identity Structure Analysis of 'Annabel', one young woman with anorexia nervosa.

Conceptualisations of anorexia nervosa

Recent conceptualisations and explanations of anorexia nervosa have been variously rooted in sociological, biological, cultural, feminist, psychosexual, sociopolitical, psychological, and medical frameworks and models. Some suggest that the gender (and age) specificity of anorexia nervosa is context-bound: inextricably enmeshed in the particular sociocultural context (for example, Swartz, 1985; Dolan, 1991; cf. Hoek *et al.*, 1998). Others have argued that it represents a psychobiological maladaptive response to perceived demands of adolescence: a 'distorted biological solution to an existential problem' (Crisp, 1980: v). The conceptualisation of the body as being central to our sense of self-identity has led yet others to assert that the lack of a secure and stable self-concept and sense of self-identity *predisposes* adolescents to focus on 'thinness' as a misguided striving for individuation (Casper, 1983). Many feminist commentators assert that it is no coincidence, since fat connects with fertility and reproduction, that trends of the idealisation of thinness in the 1920s and 1960s paralleled the emancipation of women and sexual liberation in the West (Dolan, 1994).

That each conceptualisation is bound by the parameters of its perspective leads many researchers to view anorexia nervosa as the outcome of a complex interaction of various biological, psychological and social predisposing, precipitating and perpetuating factors – the 'biopsychosocial' model – implying that there is neither a simple explanation nor a standard cure (Vandereycken and van Deth, 1994).

Aside from the popular, lay and tabloid representations as 'the slimmer's disease', current approaches to and debates about anorexia nervosa have been largely dominated by cultural interpretations versus medical formulations. Medical formulations stem from the end of the nineteenth century when the English physician William Gull coined the new term 'anorexia nervosa' to mean 'starvation due to a nervous disorder' (Gull, 1874),[1] and set in motion the quickening medicalisation, categorisation and pathologising of the condition. Current 'official' definitions are provided by the World Health Organisation's International Classification of Mental and Behavioural Disorders (ICD-10) and the American Psychiatric Association's *Diagnostic and Statistical Manual of Mental Disorders* (DSM-IV). Essentially, it is a refusal to maintain body weight at or above a minimally 'normal' body weight, i.e. 15% below that expected for the individual's age and height[2] (Roth and Fonaghy, 1996: 170). The medical model continues to reinforce and reproduce the dominant psychiatric conceptualisation and understanding of anorexia nervosa as a psychopathology.

Cultural interpretations, however, steadfastly resist the pathologising of anorexia nervosa as a disease entity or a 'mental disorder'. The feminist cultural model broadly views the condition as a metaphor for and a manifestation of a multiplicity of sociocultural concerns of the late twentieth century (Turner, 1992, 1994). As Malson (1998: 6) asserts: 'anorexia is saying something about what it means to be a woman in late twentieth century Western culture'. Using a 'post-structuralist discourse analysis' in exploring how subjectivities, events and experiences of anorexia are constituted in language, she offers a convincing argument for the necessity to theorise and research anorexia within a framework that acknowledges the complexities of its multiple sociocultural and gender-specific locations (Malson, 1998; see also, Malson and Ussher, 1996, 1997). In a similar vein, Hepworth (1999) deconstructs psychopathology in the social construction of anorexia nervosa, critically discussing the effects of psychiatry and psychology in simplifying complex social and cultural practices into a particular form of knowledge and practice about psychopathology. She concludes: 'The disciplines of psychology and psychiatry may well be in the last vestiges of reproducing dominant discourses about patients, women and psychopathology, and where these fit within the separation of normality from abnormality' (Hepworth, 1999: 130). This late-1990s work builds on the earlier work of feminist sociologists, for example, MacSween (1993), who examines anorexia as a strategy of resistance (to the construction and control of women's bodies), which ultimately becomes its own prison: the anorexic 'solution' is 'an indirect and individualized response to a social issue. Anorexic women cannot, in their isolation, produce a real or lasting solution to the degraded social construction of the feminine' (MacSween, 1993: 4; see also, Katzman and Lee, 1997).

A more interpretive position deconstructs the debate between the feminist cultural model and the medical model to question the constructions of 'the self' employed in these discourses. One such example is the anthropological work of Lester (1997) who, based on the following assertion, uses Foucault's 'technologies of the self' to bridge the split between the 'inside' and the 'outside', often produced and reified in both the medical and feminist cultural formulations of anorexia:

> While feminist theorising has largely dislodged the current representations of anorexia nervosa from the clamps of myopic medical discourses devoid of detailed cultural analysis, it has in fact produced similar theoretical dichotomies and blind spots that preclude the successful theorising of an embodied self and its particular articulation in anorexia nervosa.
>
> (Lester, 1997: 479)

The approach we adopt in this chapter – as a *clinical* analysis of anorexia nervosa – is rooted in the traditional medical model of illness and treatment. This is part of a larger project, in which the authors are exploring nomothetic representations of the body, sexuality, asceticism and (dis)connection in the identity structures of groups of young women with eating disorders, as well as health policy and practice in their treatment. However, here, in privileging the individual case study, we present an *idiographic* analysis of identity, exploring the *particular* sense of self and identity as expressed by a single young woman with anorexia nervosa. As Harré states, 'in the ontology of the human world the basic particulars are persons' and, to attempt 'to explain the sense of self by borrowing the hypothetico-deductive methods from the physical sciences and postulating unobservable entities, be it the ego or be it generic traits, just populates the ontology of psychology with a class of redundant and mythical beings . . .' (Harré, 1998: 178; cf. Harré, 1993).

The rationale for this chapter, therefore – in focusing solely on the identity structure and processes of 'Annabel'[3] – is to illustrate the value of the idiographic application of ISA in a clinical setting as a diagnostic procedure and a prognostic instrument. We do not use theoretical postulates to 'frame' the analysis. Rather, working within a medical model of illness and treatment, the analytical framework for our ISA identity exploration is structured by (1) predisposing, (2) precipitating and (3) perpetuating factors of anorexia nervosa – all key concerns of the illness and its treatment. A snapshot overview of these factors precedes the study's methodology, the case vignette of Annabel, and the analysis and interpretation of her identity structure and processes.

Key concerns of the medical model

Key concerns in the clinical psychology/psychiatric 'assessment–treatment' literature over the past few decades have been with epidemiology, aetiology, assessment (both physical and psychosocial) and management, and prognosis, treatment and outcome. The core of this body of literature has been steadily produced by a small number of specialist psychiatrists, psychologists and therapists with long-term experience in the field of eating disorders (see for example, Bruch, 1974, 1978, 1988, 1994; Crisp, 1977, 1980, 1996).

To ask what 'causes' anorexia nervosa is as naïve as to ask what 'cures' it. Certainly though – amongst a plethora of possible contributing factors – empirical and clinical evidence suggests a number of predisposing, precipitating and perpetuating factors. Too numerous to rehearse in this chapter, but briefly outlined here, are the main existing theories of the dynamics of anorexia nervosa in terms of predisposing factors, precipitating factors and perpetuating factors which, in turn, serve to 'inform' the idiographic identity structure analysis. Such factors are rarely mutually exclusive and are frequently intertwined (often the perpetuating factors are the very factors that may have strongly predisposed the individual to the anorexia in the first place, and vice versa); and such factors are always complex, often inconclusive and seldom fully explored, theorised or understood.

Predisposing factors

The most obvious predisposing factor of anorexia is being female. While 1.1 million people in the UK are believed to have an eating disorder (EDA, 2000), some estimates of female prevalence maintain that as many as one in twenty-five women under the age of 35 in Britain are suffering with an eating disorder, with at least one in ten cases proving fatal (Cook, 1998: 5). Aside from the persistence of anorexia nervosa as a predominantly female illness (Hsu, 1989; Dolan and

Gitzinger, 1994), claims for predisposing factors in the literature may be broadly categorised into three main areas: dysfunctional families; child abuse (sexual, physical or emotional); and biological/genetic predisposition. Theories of dysfunctional families as antecedents of anorexia largely cluster around issues of failure to convey an adequate sense of self-worth to the child (Bruch, 1974); enmeshment and rigidity as characteristic patterns of transaction (Minuchin *et al.*, 1978); parenting styles being generally over-involved, over-protective, over-critical and over-controlling; and 'high-concern' parenting in childhood (Shoebridge and Gowers, 2000). Theories of child abuse tend to separate into sexual abuse and emotional or physical abuse/harm/loss. Whether an isolated incident or continuous over a period of time, eating-disordered patients who were victims of childhood sexual abuse are noted to have low self-esteem, a negative attitude towards their bodies and sexuality, and a more insecure/unstable self-concept – all deemed to be strong predisposing factors of anorexia (Oppenheimer *et al.*, 1985; Palmer *et al.*, 1990; cf. Pope and Hudson, 1992). A strong genetic predisposition to developing eating disorders is emphasised by psychobiologists, some estimating the heritability of anorexia nervosa to be around 50–60% (Collier, 2000; see also Mitchell and Eckert, 1987; Silver and Morley, 1991; Bryant-Waugh and Lask, 1995). However, Malson (1998: 81) argues that theories of genetically transmitted dispositional traits have been criticised as 'relatively atheoretical and tautological' (Snyder and Ickes, 1985: 892); and that they take little or no account of the way in which people's behaviours may be situationally and temporally specific (Mischel, 1968; McAdams, 1992), as demonstrated in this chapter's ISA study of Annabel.

Precipitating factors

Not unlike nor distinct from the predisposing factors just described, family dysfunction and sexual abuse are strongly implicated as being precipitating factors of anorexia nervosa. Common precipitants are said to include chronic reactivated parental disharmony (Crisp, 1980). Bryant-Waugh and Lask (1995: 19) use the example of 'a teenage girl, who may already be predisposed by virtue of her age, gender, sociocultural status and genetic susceptibility, and who might then develop an eating disorder as a result of having recently been triangulated in a marital conflict'. And even an isolated incident of unwanted sexual contact – or indeed the first intimate/sexual encounter – may be immediately followed by onset of anorexia (Emans, 2000). Aetiological factors are also attributed to a traumatic life event and/or subsequent post-traumatic stress disorder, often merging into comorbidity with the depressive disorders (Tomb, 1994; O'Kane and Saunderson, 1997, 1998b); and other events such as parental separation or divorce (Russell *et al.*, 1990), 'loss' through death or illness, leaving home, onset of puberty, commencing intimate relationships, or even comments about body size/shape or lowered self-esteem leading to dieting. Further, Waller (2000) has recently refined understanding of the link between control issues and sexual abuse in women who had developed eating disorders, reporting that a history of sexual abuse is associated with a lower level of perceived control: the more severe the sexual abuse, the more external was the women's locus of control. Given the centrality of control issues to eating disorders, this theory has powerful implications for early clinical work to focus on cognitions regarding personal control.

Perpetuating factors

Perpetuating factors concern prognosis, treatment and outcome. In prognostic terms, Bryant-Waugh and Lask (1995: 21) state that 'anorexia nervosa can be short-lived, especially if diagnosed and appropriately treated early, but it may run a chronic and unremitting course' (see also, Byely *et al.*, 2000). For anorexia nervosa, the presence of vomiting is a poor prognostic feature; also, factors likely to lead to chronic eating disorders include unresolved interpersonal and family difficulties, and difficulty in giving up 'anorexic' thinking patterns (Wilhelm and Clarke, 1998: 459; O'Kane and Saunderson, 1998a; cf. Bulik *et al.*, 2000). And Wilhelm and Clarke (1998) speculate that lowered mood and feelings of helplessness, which may be associated with depression, are also perpetuating factors. Recent research suggests that hospitalisation, despite a number of short-term benefits, is the major predictor of poor outcome (Gowers *et al.*, 2000). Centrally important in determining the outcome of the illness are intrafamilial relationships (Morgan and Russell, 1975; Connor, 1991; Le Grange *et al.*, 1992; North *et al.*, 1997), and family therapy has long been espoused as an effective treatment for adolescent anorexia nervosa (Minuchin *et al.*, 1978; MacDonald, 1993; Robin *et al.*, 1994; Dare *et al.*, 1995; Lieberman, 1995). Herzog *et al.* (1996) report, however, that most patients remain impaired in physical and social functioning, with continuing disordered eating practices and over-sensitivity to cues about food and weight. Outcome in terms of recovery, morbidity and mortality differs considerably between empirical studies, but it is estimated that about 50% of patients with anorexia make a full recovery; 30% improve; and 20% pursue a chronic course (Steinhausen *et al.*, 1991; cf. Zipfel *et al.*, 2000).

METHODOLOGY FOR AN IDIOGRAPHIC STUDY OF ANOREXIA NERVOSA

Methodology

'The paradox of personal identity – that at any moment we are the same as, yet different from, the persons we once were or ever will be – has inspired many attempts at resolution' (Slugoski and Ginsburg, 1989: 36). This paradox is neatly 'freeze-framed' in the following Identity Structure Analysis of Annabel, a young woman presenting with anorexia nervosa.

Annabel's identity structure and development was accessed and 'measured' using Identity Structure Analysis (ISA). As an approach to the understanding of identity, ISA is presented as a metatheoretical framework (Weinreich, 1989) which draws on several theoretical orientations, namely, personal construct theory (Kelly, 1955); cognitive–affective consistency theories (Festinger, 1957; Rosenberg and Abelson, 1960); psychodynamic theory (Erikson, 1959, 1963, 1968); and self-concept theories (Mead, 1934; Cooley, 1902; James, 1890). From a synthesis of these theoretical orientations, a set of fundamental assumptions and a formal system of concepts of identity have been formulated (see Chapter 1, this volume). When data meet certain requirements of ISA, these concepts of identity may be accessed, operationalised and analysed, idiographically or nomothetically, using ISA's Identity Exploration (IDEX) computer software to provide quantified parameters of identity structure and development (see Chapter 2, this volume). Applications of ISA in clinical, as well as societal and cross-cultural, settings have been many and diverse for over two decades (see Appendix, this volume, for selected bibliography).

Further to uncovering identification patterns and value systems of the singular agentic self (Self 1, as moderated by the cued experienced Self 2s: see Chapter 1), ISA facilitates the investigation of 'situated identities'. In acknowledging our possession of what Schutz called 'multiple realities' (Schutz, 1967a,b), ISA facilitates the explicit singling out from our singular self's overall identity, a selected few of our multiple interconnected facets of self – variously integrated, fragmented or compartmentalised, as situated in different social contexts and situational settings. This facility enables the mapping and plotting of identification patterns with self/s and others in several situated identities within the identity structure of individuals and/or groups. This idiographic investigation explores Annabel's construal of self and significant others in two situated past selves and four situated current contexts of identity (detailed later).

ISA also facilitates the investigation of metaperspectives of self, in other words, how one *construes* the other as seeing oneself (however much or little bearing such a construal has on how the other *actually* sees oneself). Existing studies have shown metaperspectives of self (particularly maternal and/or familial metaperspectives) to be highly salient in the identity structure of eating-disordered females (Weinreich *et al.*, 1985; Harris, 1988; Connor, 1991). Maternal and paternal metaperspectives have therefore been included in the identity instrument (see later). Two months after completing the identity instrument, Annabel took part in an unstructured, face-to-face, in-depth interview at a neutral venue with the first author. It was important for her to be able to identify the interviewer as an 'outsider' and to know that what she said in the interviews would not be divulged to her psychiatrist/therapist, and that it would have no bearing or effect on her ongoing treatment. The interview was tape-recorded and transcribed to be used, where appropriate, to augment the ISA results. Extensive unstructured interview material is used, selectively, in reporting the study.

Identity instrument construction

Towards designing an identity instrument capable of accessing and exploring the 'anorexic' sense of self and identity, detailed and lengthy sensitising procedures were carried out via a series of small focus groups with young anorexic women living in Northern Ireland. Primed by earlier ISA studies of anorexia (see Appendix, this volume), these initial data were used in the preliminary design of an 'identity instrument' containing salient aspects, issues and personal constructions of the young women's selves, lives and experiences. Following a pre-pilot study, where three anorexic women aged between 18 and 22 completed the instrument and provided extensive structured feedback (written and verbal) in a focus group setting, the pilot identity instrument was constructed and prepared for hard-copy administration and further feedback. Considerable changes were made in preparation of the pilot instrument on the basis of the feedback, particularly, the 'softening' of entities and especially constructs dealing with sexuality and sexual activity/abuse. The identity instrument was then successfully piloted with the same three women, and a further two out-patients of a specialist eating disorders unit, each of the entities being rated in terms of each of the bipolar constructs. Following further 'clarifying' changes to the semantics of several constructs, the finalised instrument contained 26 'entities' representing facets of the self, and significant people, groups and institutions of the anorexic women's social worlds (see Table 11.1); and 16 'constructs': personal values, beliefs, feelings and attributes meaningful to the individuals (see Table 11.2).

Table 11.1 Entities in the 'anorectic' identity instrument

Mandatory entities		
Past self (1)	[childhood self]	Me as a child
Current self (1)	['in situ' self]	Me as I am now
Ideal self	[aspired-to self]	Me as I would like to be
Admired person	[+ive anchor]	A person I admire (nominate)
Disliked person	[−ive anchor]	A person I dislike (nominate)
Self-positioning entities		
Past self 2	[past traumatised self]	Myself when I experienced a devasting setback to my person
Current self 2	[depressed self]	Me when I am depressed
Current self 3	['bingeing' self]	Me when I am out of control (i.e. bingeing)
Current self 4	[in-control self]	Me when I am in control of myself (i.e. my eating)
Metaperspective 1	[maternal]	Myself as my mother sees me
Metaperspective 2	[paternal]	Myself as my father sees me
Metaperspective 3	[partner/intimate]	Myself as my boyfriend sees me
Metaperspective 4	[ideal self for others]	Me as others would like or expect me to be
Social world entities		
Familial	My mother	
	My father	
	My sister/brother (the one who is closest to me)	
Intimates	My boyfriend/partner	
	My best friend	
Abstracted others	Ordinary women	
	Ordinary men	
Sexual 'damage'	Someone who has been raped	
	Someone who has been repeatedly sexually abused	
Personal threat/damage	A person who is dangerous to my well-being	
	Someone who has been disfigured	
	Someone who has been tortured/involved in a life-threatening event	
	Someone who has been involved in a terrible mass tragedy	

Table 11.2 Constructs (clustered) in the 'anorectic' identity instrument

Complicity versus resistance
(Dominance/control/dependence vs autonomy/self-actualisation/independence)

6 Believe/s in teaching others 'who rules' (who is boss) and who is in power	Believe/s that only persuasion and consent is meaningful
7 Always want/s to dominate me and tell me the 'right' way to do things	Allow/s me to do things in my own way and to make my own mistakes
9 Intends to get his/her/their own way with me	Respect/s my wishes
13 Let/s me get away with anything	Persuade/s me to be reasonable
14 Has/Have strict views on what is 'right' and 'wrong' for everyone	Believe/s that people should work out what is right and wrong for themselves

Sexual 'damage'/threat

1 Has/Have been sexually abused	Has/Have not been sexually abused
2 Will only have consenting sex with equals/willing participants	Will rape/sexually molest others, making them victims

Personal 'damage'/threat

3 Has/Have experienced a terrible tragedy	Has/Have not experienced, or witnessed first-hand, such a tragedy
4 Do/es everything possible to prevent terrible events	Has/Have responsibility for terrible events
5 Has/Have been tortured and beaten/bullied	Has/Have had no more than the occasional bullying
8 Abuse/s me	Cherish/es me

Attachment/internal locus of control vs dissassociation/external locus of control

12 I don't want to let go of . . .	I really couldn't care less about . . .
15 Always strive/s to reach – and insist upon – perfection in all things	Do/es not mind when things don't work out as perfectly as they might or should
16 Do/es not give up: work/s to the very limits and beyond	Will simply give up when too much effort is demanded

Social connection versus disconnection

10 I get on well with . . .	I cannot get on well with . . .
11 I just make words to . . .	I can really talk to . . .

ISA's facility for the mapping and plotting of identification patterns with self and others in several situated identities was used to explore Annabel's construal of self and significant others in two situated past selves and four situated current contexts of identity. The two explored past contexts of self were: the *childhood self* ('myself as a child'); and the past *'traumatised' self* ('myself when I experienced a devastating setback to my person'). The four explored current situated contexts of identity were: first, *in-situ self* ('me as I am now', i.e. Self 1, not situated in any particular context); second, *depressed self* ('me when I am depressed'); third, *out-of-control self* ('me when I am out of control' [nominate context]), and lastly, *controlled self* ('me when I am in control of myself' [nominate context]).

An interesting twist to this study – and a strong conviction of the authors not to assume, contaminate or 'railroad' the language and the *meanings behind* the language of these personal constructions of self – involved asking the women in the main study to each nominate a specific context for the third and fourth situated selves. In other words, and given the centrality of the concept of control in anorexia, we wanted to know precisely what being 'out of control' and 'in control' represented in the anorexic sense of self. For Annabel, as a binge/purge anorexic, bingeing represented her out of control state; being in control of herself was when she was in control of her eating (although, as the results show, central features of her identity structure suggest ambiguity between what she might call 'normal' controlled eating and her 'anorexic' controlled eating).

The instrument also contained four metaperspectives of self. As discussed earlier, due to the high salience of metaperspectives of self (particularly maternal and/or familial metaperspectives) demonstrated in earlier empirical assessments of identity in eating-disordered females (Weinreich *et al.*, 1985; Harris, 1988), maternal and paternal metaperspectives were included. Several others were also 'tested' in the pre-pilot and pilot stages, resulting in the inclusion of the following four: *maternal metaperspective* ('myself as my mother sees me'); *paternal metaperspective* ('myself as my father sees me'); *partner/intimate metaperspective* ('myself as my boyfriend sees me'); and, *ideal self for others* ('me as others would like or expect me to be'). The latter metaperspective accords with the anorexic's typically high level of attention and importance attached to personal acceptance and approval by others. The finalised 'matrix' of 16 constructs and 26 entities was now ready for administration and was completed by a series of young women presenting with anorexia nervosa – one of whom is analysed and reported here with a particular focus on predisposing, precipitating and perpetuating factors of her diagnosed anorexia nervosa.

'Annabel': A case vignette

Annabel presented as a friendly, cooperative and 'in-control' young woman. She was physically attractive, well-groomed and appeared to take considerable effort, to good effect, over her appearance and demeanour. At the time of interview, she was 20 years of age, was diagnosed with anorexia nervosa almost three years previously, and had since regularly attended a specialist eating disorders clinic for treatment (with one spell of hospitalisation). Diagnosis included associated depressive symptoms, and was of the binge-eating/purging type (defined as 'during the current episode of anorexia nervosa the person has regularly engaged in binge-eating or purging behaviour, i.e. self-induced vomiting or the misuse of laxatives, diuretics, or enemas'. Long, 2000: 21). Lowest weight was five-and-a-half stone. Family relationships and home situation were difficult. She appeared to be showing slow but satisfactory weight-gain and lessening of her anorexia symptoms.

Her face-to-face interview with the first author lasted for almost three hours, during which time she smoked heavily and laughed a lot. Annabel appeared slightly distant ('gazing') and disconnected from the situation at first, but quickly sought/found 'connections' with the interviewer of which she approved and with which she felt comfortable. Unlike many of the other young women with anorexia nervosa who were interviewed as part of the larger project (whose conversation

was often restless and free-associative), Annabel spoke in a series of tightly constructed, but each time deepening, 'A–Zs' of her life (as though she was afraid of
'losing her place' in the story). The general impression was of a whole series of
'layers': at first, a very definite tight-knit 'reality' and account of herself (which
she would periodically return to); ending with a much 'looser', more natural, warm
and 'realistic' account. Parting, she said she 'really enjoyed' the interview and
would be happy if it 'helped' someone else with anorexia nervosa to 'get better'.

ANNABEL: AN IDIOGRAPHIC STUDY OF IDENTITY IN A
YOUNG WOMAN WITH ANOREXIA NERVOSA

Annabel's 'empirically frozen' profile of identity structure and development represented, broadly, the antithesis of Erikson's ego identity achievement when he spoke
of 'a sense of psychosocial well-being', 'a feeling of being at home in one's body'
and 'an inner assuredness of anticipated recognition from those who count' (Erikson,
1956: 74). Annabel's anorexic self personified a deep psychosocial malaise, characterised by remarkably poor self-evaluation when she perceived herself as 'out-of-
control', common to anorexia nervosa patients. Far from feeling 'at home' in her
body, she has consistently and systematically attempted to deny it and negate it
through her anorexic behaviours; and, as for inner assuredness of anticipated recognition from those who count, her parental metaperspectives of self are fearful and
negative. This is, at best, Annabel's anorexia nervosa as psychopathology.

Analysing predisposing factors

Annabel's predisposition to anorexia nervosa was analysed by examining how she
construed her past self (her childhood self and her past 'traumatised' self) in relation to her current self and other entities. A very negatively evaluated childhood
self suggested a childhood that fell substantially short of her aspirations and,
thereby, may indicate possible predisposition to anorexia nervosa. Patterns of past
identifications with significant others prompted examination of specific entities
or constructs which were able to reveal more about the predisposing factors of
Annabel's illness. Table 11.3 immediately reveals that while facets of Annabel's
current self were almost as highly evaluated as her ideal self, her childhood self
and particularly her past 'traumatised' self were extremely negatively evaluated.
Of particular interest was the appraisal of the entities that resulted *between* these
negative evaluations of her two past selves, namely, 'someone who has been
repeatedly sexually abused', 'someone who has been raped' and 'a person who is
dangerous to my well-being'. Clearly, she did *not* remember her childhood fondly,
and displayed particularly negative feelings about her 'traumatised' self, when she
'experienced a devastating setback to her person'.

So who was Annabel empathetically identifying with in her past childhood
self? In other words, with whom did she feel similarities/affinity/associations:
with whom did she share similar characteristics? Her strongest past childhood

Table 11.3 Annabel's most positively and negatively evaluated entities

Entity	Evaluation (scale: −1 to +1)
• Myself as I would like to be	1.00
• Me when I'm in control of myself	0.98
• Myself as I am now	0.98
• Myself as others would like or expect me to be	0.87
• A person I admire	0.83
• **Myself as a child**	**−0.38**
• Someone who has been tortured/ involved in a life-threatening event	−0.50
• Someone who has been repeatedly sexually abused	−0.60
• Someone who has been raped	−0.60
• A person I dislike	−0.69
• A person who is dangerous to my well-being	−0.75
• Myself when I am depressed	−0.77
• Me when I am out of control	−0.80
• **Myself when I experienced a devastating setback to my person**	**−0.95**

empathetic identifications (apart from with her sister) were with 'someone who has been repeatedly sexually abused' (shown in Table 11.5) and 'someone who has been raped'. What may have strongly predisposed Annabel to anorexia nervosa was becoming clearer. The IDEX idiographic software facilitates the extraction of graphs showing appraisal of the set of entities by specific selected constructs. Producing this graph for the construct 'Has been/Has not been sexually abused' revealed that Annabel construed both her childhood self and her past traumatised self at the extreme scale-point of the pole '*Has* been sexually abused'; alongside the entities 'someone who has been repeatedly sexually abused' and 'someone who has been raped' (see Figure 11.1). (Notable, also at the extreme scale-point of the sexual abuse construct, was her similar construal of her current 'depressed' self and 'out-of-control' 'bingeing' self, suggesting strong association of her 'anorexic' sense of self with her past self and these 'sexual abuse' entities.)

This finding then prompted a check on the converse graphs (not shown here), i.e. showing appraisal by the set of bipolar constructs, of specific selected entities (including facets of self). Her appraisal of the 'self-positioning' entity 'myself as a child' and the 'sexual damage' entity 'someone who has been repeatedly sexually abused' simultaneously revealed a striking pattern. Annabel's childhood self *converges* with 'someone who has been repeatedly sexually abused' at the extreme scale-point of two of the constructs: 'has been sexually abused' and 'has experienced a terrible tragedy'. These revelations, in relation to her current construal of self and others, were a compelling indication that sexual abuse – whether an isolated incident or frequent – may have been a predisposing (and perhaps pre-cipitating) factor in Annabel developing anorexia nervosa.

Given the focus of much anorexia research on patient–parent relationships, attention was drawn to parental identification patterns (see Table 11.4). Annabel

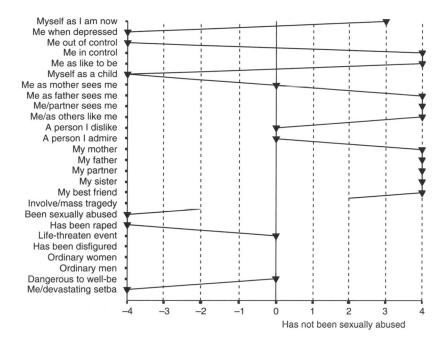

Figure 11.1 Annabel's appraisal by the construct (endorsed pole): 'has not been sexually abused' (see Table 11.1 for full entity titles).

Table 11.4 Annabel's paternal and maternal identifications

		Father	Mother	Paternal metaperspective	Maternal metaperspective
Evaluation (scale: −1 to +1)		0.25	0.58	0.03	−0.27
Idealistic-idfn (scale: 0 to 1)		0.50	0.69	0.25	0.19
Empathetic idfn (scale: 0 to 1)	PS1	0.40	0.40	0.20	0.50
	CS1	0.46	0.62	0.15	0.15
	CS3	0.43	0.14	0.29	0.64
Idfn conflicts (scale: 0 to 1)	PS1	0.39	0.15	0.25	0.50
	CS1	0.42	0.19	0.22	0.27
	CS3	0.40	0.09	0.30	0.57

PS1 past childhood self; CS1 current '*in situ*' self; CS3 current 'in-control' self

appeared to idealise her mother: her childhood maternal identification patterns were unproblematic (even if conflicts in identification with her mother seemed unrealistically low). Annabel's paternal childhood identifications, however, were the source of considerable identification conflict (which has persisted into the present): her father represented a fairly strong negative role model (contra-identification = 0.39), yet she construed him as sharing considerable similarities with herself. But the real problem of Annabel's childhood parental identifications was with her very negative maternal metaperspective, i.e. how she *believes* her mother saw her, reinforcing yet again this common finding in anorexic families (see also, Weinreich *et al.*, 1985; Harris, 1988; Connor, 1991). Because Annabel strongly associated her childhood characteristics with this negative and undesirable metaperspective, her identification with how she feels her mother saw her as a child is highly conflicted, creating considerable psychological 'discomfort' in Annabel's childhood identity (which may well have been to some extent a predisposing factor of her anorexia nervosa).

In summary, Annabel's past self-image, as represented by her construal of this identity instrument, was remarkably negative. Her 'traumatised' self, when she experienced a devastating setback to her person, was evaluated extremely negatively, while she evaluated her general 'childhood' self very negatively. Table 11.5 summarises the identity characteristics of Annabel's past self and shows that she displayed only low to moderate ego involvement with her past self-image (contrasting with her current self, as shown in Figure 11.2); and that she harboured only moderate conflicts in identification, indicated by her generally fairly moderate past identity diffusion. Nonetheless, these conflicts, coupled with her very poor past self-evaluation, classified her past-self identity variant as 'negative'. Annabel's predisposition to anorexia nervosa would appear to lie in a very poor childhood self-concept, with a particular focus on childhood sexual abuse, and more than a partial focus on her mother–daughter relationship, suggesting an unhappy and probably unstable/insecure childhood.

Analysing precipitating factors

It is often difficult to separate out predisposing from precipitating factors. The past 'traumatised' self (when she experienced a devastating setback to her person) that Annabel construed so negatively may or may not have been a (or *the*)

Table 11.5 Identity parameters for facets of Annabel's past self

	Childhood self ('me as a child')	Past traumatised self ('me when I experienced a devastating setback to my person')
Self-evaluation (scale: −1 to +1)	−0.38	−0.95
Ego involvement (scale: 0 to 5)	2.11	2.97
Identity diffusion (scale: 0 to 1)	0.30	0.35
Global identity variant	Negative	Negative
Empathetic idfn (scale: 0 to 1) with 'someone who has been repeatedly sexually abused'	0.50	0.40

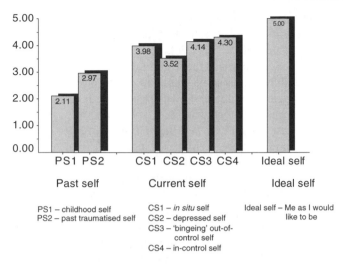

Past self   Current self   Ideal self

PS1 – childhood self   CS1 – *in situ* self   Ideal self – Me as I would
PS2 – past traumatised self   CS2 – depressed self   like to be
                  CS3 – 'bingeing' out-of-
                       control self
                  CS4 – in-control self

Figure 11.2 Annabel's ego involvement with facets of her self-image.

precipitating factor in her anorexia. Further, while we can be fairly sure from these results that her past traumatic experience was of a sexual nature, onset of anorexia may have been due to some other single isolated incident, or comment, perhaps involving her mother, and contributing to her negative maternal meta-perspective. These strands are difficult to extrapolate from this identity instrument. In order to have specifically investigated factors of onset, the instrument might have included a particular 'self-positioning' entity to that effect (e.g. 'me just before I got anorexia nervosa' or 'me at the start of my eating disorder'). Certainly though, the identification patterns presented earlier suggest that in Annabel's case, an uninvited or unpleasant sexual experience (and/or family dynamics) may have been strongly implicated in both predisposing *and* precipitating factors. Towards better understanding of what may have actually 'brought on' the anorexia nervosa, we turn here to narrative (as 'unreliable' as Annabel's account, itself, may be). From this account, it appeared that sexual experience (albeit not uninvited) was indeed implicated as a precipitating factor.

According to Annabel's verbal account, the onset of her anorexia nervosa coincided with, or was an immediate legacy of, her first consenting intimate/sexual encounter, following in the wake of her parents' marital separation. In response to the interviewer's question 'Why do you think it [anorexia] started then, as opposed to sooner or later?', she replied:

No particular reason – I was just FAT and it was about time I did something about it, you know? . . . all the other girls were, like, thin and . . . well I was just *ugly* . . . I *felt* ugly, I couldn't cope with that so I just decided to do something about it, like, you know? And, like, I just felt bad . . .

Interviewer: Why did you feel bad?

Annabel: I just did. It was . . . well I had just, sort of, like gone out with [had a date with] a fella [sic], right? And it was *grand* . . . well, you know . . . it didn't feel right, it kind of . . . I just didn't *like* it . . . all that other stuff, you know, in the past, came back, but like that was *nothing* to do with not eating. It was my mum and Dad. I was seventeen when they split up [sic] . . . it was awful, and I just couldn't let that happen, like, somebody had to *do* something [Annabel's emphases indicated].

But 'the acts by which he [sic] punishes himself are indistinguishable from the acts by which he reveals himself' (Foucault, 1988: 42), so Annabel, in blaming herself for the marital loss of her parents, and in an attempt to control the situation, 'controlled' her eating; and in this strategy of resistance to events, her 'not-eating' became her own prison. Or was she simply seeking attention – whether as wholly self-seeking, or to divert her parents' attention away from their marital disharmony? Or different still, was her assertion that she 'couldn't cope' more to do with her first intimate encounter with a man reawakening fear and loathing of an earlier sexual assault – or perhaps it was just fear, *per se*, of the 'normal' intimacy required to begin/develop a 'grown-up' relationship?

Whether the factor was diet-consciousness, sexual intimacy or parental separation/divorce, Annabel's anorexia nervosa may have been precipitated by any or all such factors, in any combination: as we stated earlier, it is difficult (or misleading) and often not helpful from the clinician's perspective, to separate out predisposing from precipitating factors. And besides, it is perpetuating factors that are of most importance in terms of formulating a strategy of appropriate treatment interventions towards recovery. Since predisposing factors (more so than precipitating factors) are so often the *perpetuating* factors of the psychopathology, it becomes less important (much less, possible) to try to single out and identify an exclusive, definitive precipitating factor.

Analysing perpetuating factors

As discussed earlier, often the perpetuating factors are the very factors that may have strongly predisposed the individual to the anorexia in the first place, and/or vice versa. Assigning such factors to the continuation of anorexia nervosa, exclusively, is impossible; teasing out possible combinations remains complex and difficult. Using ISA to explore Annabel's 'anorexic' identity structure and development, a rewarding starting point was a detailed analysis of her value system. This section discusses the evaluative dimensions of Annabel's identity; and the facets of Annabel's current self – her 'anorexic' self and her 'non-anorexic' self, as she refers to them – before finally analysing the dynamics of her identity via the global classification of her identity variants, and reflecting on how these augur for the perpetuation of her anorexia nervosa or her recovery from it.

Annabel's value and belief system can be ascertained by how centrally and consistently she used her personal constructs (feelings, beliefs, attributes) to appraise herself and others in her social world. In ISA this is indicated by structural pressure on constructs (SP). The most 'core' evaluative dimensions of Annabel's identity – to which she most strongly aspires and by which she most consistently appraises herself and others – are, *being personally cherished* (SP = 83.79: as opposed to 'feeling abused'), and *not wanting to let go of things* (SP = 83.72: as opposed to 'couldn't care less about things') (see Table 11.6). This finding reflects the typical element of rigidity in anorexic psychopathology. From this finding, we can deduce that Annabel's 'anorexic thinking' was still fairly entrenched (although it should be said that recovered anorexic patients often retain/maintain such values, even after their symptoms have subsided/abated). Further, the very high SPs associated with them suggested that these core evaluative dimensions of Annabel's identity were impervious to change. Here we can speculate. The 'imperviousness' to change or revision, of the value of 'being cherished' (i.e. being held, bounded, closed, connected, and 'contained'); and the value of 'not letting go of' (i.e. obstinacy, obduracy, inflexibility, control, and 'keeping a grip on'), suggest that Annabel's very *sense of self* may also be impervious to change. This 'rigidity' would be demonstrated in ISA by a 'foreclosed' identity state, and would not augur well for addressing anorexic behaviours and for developing alternative 'non-anorexic' identity processes.

There was one particularly *in*consistently used, 'conflicted' evaluative dimension of Annabel's identity. The construct, 'always being dominated and told the right way to do things' (SP = 8.55: as opposed to 'being allowed to do things her own way and to make her own mistakes') is a highly confused and inconsistently used value (see Table 11.6). The conflict in Annabel's mind about wanting/needing to be controlled on the one hand, and wanting to take control of herself on the other, reflects a fundamental intertwining of ideas of complicity and resistance. As Benson (1997)

Table 11.6 Evaluative dimensions of Annabel's identity

*Construct (endorsed pole)**	*SP (scale: −100 to +100)*
8 Cherish/es me	83.79
12 I don't want to let go of . . .	83.72
10 I get on well with . . .	79.45
1 Has/Have not been sexually abused	76.97
4 Do/es everything possible to prevent terrible events	76.01
3 Has/Have not experienced, or witnessed first-hand, a terrible tragedy	74.99
7 Always wants to dominate me and tell me the 'right' way to do things/ [Allow/s me to do things in my own way and to make my own mistakes]	8.55

*These are Annabel's endorsed, or aspired-to, values.
(See Table 11.2 for the contra-values, i.e. the opposite poles of the constructs)

believes, these general ideas (and strings of dichotomous associations) about control and indulgence, openness and closure, speak powerfully to the tensions of women's individual lives. Further, they reflect a central contradiction of anorexia nervosa; that of performance/concealment – of bounded body and active self (Benson: 1997: 160). In other words, the carefully concealed control and apparent autonomy of the anorexic in fact demands an audience – as Maud Ellmann (1993: 17) acutely observes: 'Anorexics are *making a spectacle of themselves* . . . Even though the anorexic body seems to represent a radical negation of the other, it still depends upon the other as spectator in order to be read as anything at all' (in Benson, 1997: 135). In this sense, Annabel's highly conflictual values of complicity and resistance – of control and autonomy – may be seen to reflect a core characteristic of her 'anorexic' identity, and may be seen to reflect the 'duality' and endless dichotomous associations personified and embodied by anorexic psychopathology, not least self-absorbtion/actualisation versus self-rejection/anihilation. Of course, tensions between complicity and resistance, as revealed by her core values, must not be detached from Annabel's identity as a young woman faced with the difficult demands, decisions, responsibilities and contradictions of a twenty-first-century postmodern society. Nonetheless, such duality and vacillation between opposite stances of complicity and resistance are found by Benson (1997) to be a particularly enduring feature of anorexia nervosa. And given that Annabel's conflicted identity dimension represented a fundamental duality between domination and autonomy (having control and being controlled), this does not augur well for halting the perpetuation of her anorexic identity processes.

A striking feature of Annabel's value system is a dominant narrative of 'damage'. Of the six most core evaluative dimensions of her identity (all with SPs of >70: see Table 11.6), four relate to either personal 'damage' or sexual 'damage' (shown in Table 11.2). Throughout Annabel's interview, she constantly returned to 'themes of damage': damage by self to others; damage by others to self; and damage by self to self. The impression was of an overarching narrative of damage, underpinned by a constant tension between self-actualisation/production and self-anihilation/destruction, often tempered by varying degrees of 'splitting' (the good mother, good counsellor, good [active] self/the bad father, bad hospital staff, bad [bounded] body). This vacillation, as we will see, was a central feature of her 'anorexic'/'non-anorexic' sense of self.

Moving away from the composition of Annabel's value system to how she *used* it in appraisal of herself, immediately notable were the contrasts between her evaluation of her various facets of self (Figure 11.3). Such stark contrasts characterised not only the four explored contexts of her current self (Table 11.1), but also the dynamics of the temporal dimension of her identity. In these extremely negatively evaluated contexts of self – both past and present – Annabel's most aspired-to values (shown in Table 11.6) were all but negated. In other words, it was the opposite *non*-endorsed/favoured poles of these core values that were at play when she construed her childhood self, her part traumatised self, and her current 'depressed' self and 'out-of-control' (bingeing) self.

In a rather self-absorbed manner, Annabel was highly ego-involved with (responsive to) the four facets of her current self, and her ideal self (refer to

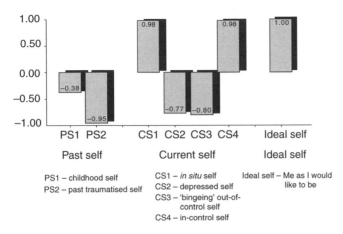

Figure 11.3 Annabel's self-evaluation.

Figure 11.2). The 'splitting' between her 'anorexic' and 'non-anorexic' identity occurred in how she evaluated these self-contexts. Figure 11.3 shows that her *in situ* identity (Self 1: 'me as I am now') and her 'in-control' context of self are evaluated almost as highly (and unrealistically) as her ideal self. Our earlier speculations about Annabel's obduracy, 'closure' and inflexibility return in the light of these highly unrealistic self-evaluations. By stark contrast, she evaluates what she calls her 'anorexic self' (her current 'depressed' self and 'out-of-control' self) extremely negatively. In referring to her anorexia during interview as 'an imposter', Annabel carefully explained that these two 'selves' are interdependent and that they have a particular dynamic: if she's feeling very depressed about something in particular or just generally ('anorexic thinking'), she will go and 'have a binge' to relieve the depression. However, her 'out-of-control' (bingeing) state will always lead to her feeling 'totally depressed and helpless', and so it goes on. In these states, Annabel's exceedingly low self-evaluation had, indeed, a clear association with her poorly evaluated past self (further reinforcing not only the temporal and aetiological link between her childhood and her psychopathology, but also reinforcing the associative link in Annabel's identity).

This associative link in Annabel's identity between her past self and her current 'anorexic' self was further illustrated and consolidated by analysing her global classification of identity variants (Table 11.7). Here, again, the 'splitting' was obvious. Her childhood self, past 'traumatised' self, 'depressed' self and 'out-of-control' (bingeing) self were the 'bad' poorly-evaluated self-contexts of her identity, all globally classified as 'negative', while her current *in situ* self and 'in-control' self were the 'good' highly-evaluated contexts of her identity and, as such, were far removed from this negativity. The 'negative' classification is a function of very low self-evaluation accompanied by moderate levels of identification conflict. For Annabel, this conflict in both her past and her 'anorexic' identity

Table 11.7 ISA global classification of Annabel's identity variants

	Diffused variants		Foreclosed variants
High self-evaluation	*Diffuse high self-regard*	*Confident*	*Defensive high self-regard* CS1, CS4
Moderate self-eval.	*Diffusion*	*Indeterminate*	*Defensive*
High self-evaluation	*Crisis*	*Negative* PS1, PS2 CS2, CS3	*Defensive negative*

PS1 Myself as a child; PS2 Myself when I experienced a devastating setback to my person; CS1 Me as I am now; CS2 Me when I am depressed; CS3 Me when I am out of control (i.e. bingeing); CS4 Me when I am in control of myself (i.e. my eating)

state was largely attributable to her especially significant conflicts in identification with her father, the 'sexual damage' entities and her poorly-evaluated maternal metaperspective (refer to Table 11.4). It was Annabel's identification with these aspects of her social world, more than any others, that may perpetuate her anorexic psychopathology. And clearly, these are the issues that the clinician would focus on and monitor in therapy.

Notwithstanding her very negative past self-image and very negative 'anorexic' self-image, Annabel still faced the task of, as Goffman (1959) put it, 'presentation of self in everyday life'. But the 'good' highly-evaluated contexts of her current identity structure (mentioned earlier) are *vulnerable* identity states, both being globally classified as 'defensive high self-regard' (Table 11.7). In other words, rather than attempting successfully to face up to her conflicted identifications, she had mounted a strong defensive against acknowledging such conflicts, and was operating in a foreclosed identity state paralleled by extremely high self-evaluation. In her adopted idealised view of self, she had shifted to a 'safe' place: an unrealistically optimistic place, where she evaluated her current self almost as highly as her ideal self. In this state, Annabel had few conflicts with her mother (or indeed, with anyone). She remained highly ego-involved with her depressed and out-of-control selves, but currently felt far away from them in her preoccupation with her current and in-control 'infallible' self. So far, her position of foreclosure (defensively 'disowning' and refusing to acknowledge the complexties of her anorexic state) and her very high self-evaluation appear effective as a coping mechanism; as a means of 'managing' herself. However, as the anthropologist Mary Douglas once remarked in her discussion of purity and pollution, 'That which is negated is not thereby removed' (Douglas, 1966: 163). Sadly, since negating is not removing, Annabel's shift to this defensive state leaves little transitional space for admitting, confronting and resolving her considerable parental and 'sexual' conflicts in identification (an advisable strategy for addressing the perpetuation of her anorexia nervosa).

DISCUSSION AND THERAPEUTIC IMPLICATIONS

Emerging from the idiographic ISA analysis, Annabel's predisposition to anorexia nervosa would appear to lie in a very poor childhood self-concept, with a particular focus on childhood sexual abuse, and more than a partial focus on her mother–daughter relationship, suggesting an unhappy and probably insecure childhood. Precipitating factors are difficult to extrapolate, but tentatively point to a first intimate encounter reawakening associations with past sexual abuse and/or parental disharmony. As asserted earlier though, it is perpetuating factors that are of most importance in terms of formulating a strategy of appropriate treatment interventions towards recovery. And since predisposing factors (more so than precipitating factors) are so often the *perpetuating* factors of the psychopathology, it becomes less important (much less, possible) to single out and identify an exclusive, definitive precipitating factor.

Regarding perpetuating factors, in her current 'self-congratulating' (but somehow 'fearful') identity state, Annabel was minimising and defensively neglecting acknowledgement of the significant conflicts in identification related to her past, and those currently associated with her father, the 'sexual entities' and with how she felt her mother saw her. All such past conflicts and negative evaluations were being carried through to and subsumed in/by her self-termed 'anorexic' identity (her depressed self and her 'bingeing' self). And all such current conflicts and negative evaluations were maintaining association with and sustaining these poorly evaluated current self-contexts. In her current unconflicted and positive '*in situ*' and 'in-control' self-worlds, no such negative events and devalued self existed. It would appear that Annabel's 'anorexic' experience (and whatever it connected with in her past) had brought her to a place where she was 'attempting to annihilate the very nature of human existence: *inequality* and *progression* through the life-cycle' [our emphasis] (Birksted-Breen, 1989).

Our earlier speculations about Annabel's obduracy, 'closure' and inflexibility were confirmed by the unrealistic orientation of her self-protective 'foreclosed' identity state. Here, the 'duality' was the vacillation between her tightly compartmentalised current *in situ* and 'in-control' self-absorbed/self-congratulating states; and her past and 'anorexic' self-detached/self-commiserating states. As a short-term coping mechanism, this duality of identity *may* be sustainable, but doubtfully so in the longer term, and certainly only until something shatters this current foreclosed identity state, leaving her plummeting back into her loathed 'anorexic' identity. Clinical intervention would aim to narrow or 'close' the duality.

Interestingly, other researchers using ISA have found an anti-developmental trend in young women with anorexia nervosa: from a favourably evaluated childhood to a negatively evaluated current self, reflecting a wish to reinstate an idealised past and resist the demands of maturation into adulthood (e.g. Harris, 1988). Annabel, however, was not so much 'stuck' in the past as 'stranded' in the present. In other words, rather than wanting to return to the past, she is resisting moving forward. Although Annabel's anorexia symptoms at the time of interview appeared to have weakened, and she was showing signs of weight-gain, the rigidity of her current 'foreclosed' identity (in her *in situ* self and in-control self) was masking considerable conflicts in identification with her past, with 'sexual' issues, and with her father and mother (such conflict was evident during interview, when Annabel's 'tight-knit' self-account fell apart somewhat when she spoke of her past and her 'imposter' [anorexia]). Annabel appeared to be defensively hiding behind a highly evaluated non-conflicted self-concept, leaving little space for forward movement and allowing identity processes that were sustaining her anorexia.

At the same time, and despite the high self-evaluation of her current *in situ* self and in-control self, her childhood self and her 'anorexic' self still represented very negative parts of her identity structure: closely associated with her extremely negative – almost *negating* – beliefs about how her mother sees her in these contexts. Clinical intervention would aim to moderate her unrealistically high self-aspirations, and her very low self-evaluations.

Implications for therapeutic intervention in Annabel's case might be fourfold:

(i) to explore and discuss with her the dynamics of her 'difficult' home-life through her conflicted identifications with her father, and her problematic maternal metaperspective of self (and how these variously feature in different facets of her past, her current and her aspirational self);

(ii) to probe her concept, experience and handling of 'sexual damage' and offer appropriate counselling towards a reformulation of the identifications with her past experiences;

(iii) to focus on the fundamental 'duality' in her identity structure: the nature of the core evaluative dimensions of her identity (and their impermeability to change or revision), and the conflicted 'domination/autonomy' evaluative dimension of her identity, exploring how this 'duality' is operating and explaining to her the effects it may be having on her identity and recovery, and on parental and other relationships;

(iv) to 'moderate' the extremes of her self-evaluation by addressing the 'splitting' between the experiences of her rejected and loathed past and 'anorexic' self and identity, and the unrealistically high and demanding aspirations of her embraced and 'cherished' current *in situ* and 'in-control' self and identity.

All six self-contexts (two past and four current) of Annabel's identity analysed by ISA were classified, for different reasons, as 'vulnerable' identity states. There is potential, however, for Annabel to reformulate her past biographical experiences and institute procedures whereby she may develop alternative identity processes to the anorexic ones, towards what Weinreich terms *optimal autonomy restructuring* (see Chapter 1, this volume, for full explication), in which:

(i) the untoward past experiences (traumas and parental castigating judgements) would be both fully recognised for the damaging activities they were, and reappraised as being one strand of identity among many, which does not need to continue to dominate current identity processes;

(ii) identity aspirations would be moderated to represent realistic, rather than perfectionist, exercises in autonomous behaviour with the freedom to make ordinary mistakes within a supportive rather than chastising milieu.

CONCLUDING COMMENTS

The rationale for this chapter, in focusing on the identity structure and development of one young woman with anorexia nervosa, has been to illustrate the value of the idiographic application of ISA in a clinical setting. As a clinical analysis of anorexia nervosa, the approach adopted in this chapter is rooted in the traditional medical model of illness and treatment. The interpretations made and claims drawn from the idiographic analysis of Annabel's identity structure are, 'typically, cautious, highly detailed and grounded in the data' (Smith *et al.*, 1995: 63). However, Smith also draws together the argument that if 'the particular eternally underlies the general; the general eternally has to comply with the particular' (Goethe, in Hermans, 1988: 785); and, if 'the balance between . . . the particular and the universal is achieved, what will be presented is a unique individual whose knowledge of himself [sic] we can share (Warnock, 1987: 123), then there is value to an idiographic study that taps something not only rich and unique, but also relatively universal or shared (Smith *et al.*, 1995: 60–61).

We are not suggesting that Annabel's 'anorexic story' is every anorexic's story. Nevertheless, it, alongside our other idiographic ISA explorations, represents 'a cautious climb up the ladder of generality' (Harré, 1979: 137). And certainly, from the perspective of the practising clinician specialising in eating disorders, the idiographic application of ISA offers respite from the often myopic medical model of assessment and treatment. In doing so, it provides a wealth of rich, detailed and valuable information about self and identity, towards a better understanding of the ontological world of the single anorexic patient, and towards building a fuller, more three-dimensional picture of anorexia nervosa itself, in turn, facilitating and encouraging more appropriate and sensitive interventions.

ACKNOWLEDGEMENTS

The authors wish to acknowledge Peter Weinreich and Claire Adams for their initial input into this project, and to thank Peter Weinreich for his comments on this chapter.

NOTES

1 Gull changed his earlier-termed 'hysteria' to 'nervosa' since hysteria was deemed a uniquely female condition and he had found occasional occurrences in men. Gull's claim to discovery is hotly debated by some who insist the Frenchman Ernest Lasegue first published the term in 1873.

2 Roth and Fonaghy add that, to meet diagnostic criteria, there must also be an intense fear of becoming fat, even though underweight; a severe restriction of food intake, often with excessive exercising, in order to achieve weight loss; a disturbance in how body weight or shape is experienced, and an undue influence of body weight or shape on self-evaluation; and (in postmenarcheal women) amenorrhea.

3 The patient's name and details have been altered to protect anonymity.

REFERENCES

American Psychiatric Association (1994) *Diagnostic and Statistical Manual of Mental Disorders*, 4th edition (DSM-IV). Washington, DC: American Psychiatric Press.

Benson, S. (1997) 'The body, health and eating disorders' in K. Woodward (ed.) *Identity and Difference*. London: Sage/OUP.

Birksted-Breen, D. (1989) 'Working with an anorexic patient'. *International Journal of Psychoanalysis*, 70: 29–39.

Bruch, H. (1974) *Eating Disorders: Obesity, Anorexia Nervosa and the Person Within*. London: Routledge & Kegan Paul.

Bruch, H. (1978) *The Golden Cage: The Enigma of Anorexia Nervosa*. London: Open Books.

Bruch, H. (1988) *Conversations with Anorexics*. New York: Basic Books.

Bruch, H. (1994) *Conversations with Anorexics* (edited by D. Czyzewski and M. A. Suhr). Northvale, NJ: Jason Aronson.

Bryant-Waugh, R. and Lask, B. (1995) 'Eating disorders: an overview'. *Journal of Family Therapy*, 17, 1: 13–30.

Bulik, C. M., Sullivan, P. F., Fear, J. and Pickering, A. (2000) 'Outcome of anorexia nervosa: eating attitudes, personality, and parental bonding'. *International Journal of Eating Disorders*, 28, 2: 139–47.

Byely, L., Bastiani-Archibald, A., Graber, J. and Brooks-Gunn, J. (2000) 'A prospective study of familial and social influences on girls' body image and dieting'. *International Journal of Eating Disorders*, 28, 2: 155–64.

Casper, R. (1983) 'Some provisional ideas concerning psychological structure in anorexia nervosa and bulimia' in P. Darby, P. Garfinkel, D. Garner and D. Coscina (eds.) *Anorexia Nervosa: Recent Developments in Research*. New York: Alan Liss.

Collier, D. (2000) Paper presented to the British Psychological Society Annual Conference, Winchester, reported by N. Stimpson, 'Eating Disorders'. *The Psychologist*, 13, 7: 344–5.

Connor, T. (1991) *An Identity Exploration of Anorexia Nervosa within a Family Context, Vols. 1 & 2*. Unpublished DPhil theses. Jordanstown: University of Ulster.

Cook, E. (1998) 'Back to life, back to reality'. *The Guardian*, 15 January, 1998: 4–5.

Cooley, C. H. (1902) *Human Nature and the Social Order*. New York: Scribner.

Crisp, A. H. (1977) 'Some psychobiological aspects of adolescent growth and their relevance for the fat/thin syndrome'. *International Journal of Obesity*, 1: 231–8.

Crisp, A. H. (1980) *Anorexia Nervosa: Let Me Be*. London: Academic Press.

Crisp, A. H. (1996) *Anorexia Nervosa – the Wish to Change: Self-Help and Discovery*. Hove, UK: Psychology Press.

Dare, C., Eisler, I., Colahan, M., Crowther, C., Senior, R. and Asen, E. (1995) 'The listening heart and the chi square: clinical and empirical perceptions in the family therapy of anorexia nervosa'. *Journal of Family Therapy*, 1995, 17: 31–57.

Dolan, B. (1991) 'Cross-cultural aspects of anorexia nervosa and bulimia: a review'. *International Journal of Eating Disorders*, 10, 1: 67–78.

Dolan, B. (1994) 'Why women? Gender issues and eating disorders: introduction' in B. Dolan and I. Gitzinger (eds.) *Why Women? Gender Issues and Eating Disorders*. London: Athlone Press.

Dolan, B. and Gitzinger, I. (eds.) (1994) *Why Women? Gender Issues and Eating Disorders*. London: Athlone Press.

Douglas, M. (1966) *Purity and Danger: An Analysis of Concepts of Pollution and Taboo*. London: Routledge.

EDA (Eating Disorders Association) (2000) *Eating Disorders: the Need for Action in 2000 and Beyond*. Norwich: EDA (http://www.edauk.com/action.html).

Ellmann, M. (1993) *The Hunger Artists: Starving, Writing and Imprisonment*. London: Virago.

Emans, S. J. (2000) 'Eating disorders in adolescent girls' (invited paper). *Pediatrics International*, 42: 1–7.

Erikson, E. (1956) 'The problem of ego identity'. *Journal of the American Psychoanalytic Association*, 4: 56–121.

Erikson, E. (1959) *Identity and the Lifecycle*. New York: W.W. Norton.

Erikson, E. (1963) *Childhood and Society*. New York: W.W. Norton.

Erikson, E. (1968) *Identity, Youth and Crisis*. New York: W.W. Norton.

Festinger, L. (1957) *A Theory of Cognitive Dissonance*. Evanston, IL: Row-Peterson.

Foucault, M. (1988) 'The political technology of individuals' in L. H. Martin, H. Gutman and P. H. Hutton (eds.) *Technologies of the Self: A Seminar with Michael Foucault*. Amherst: University of Massachusetts Press.

Goffman, E. (1959) *The Presentation of Self in Everyday Life*. New York: Doubleday-Anchor.

Gowers, S. G., Weetman, J., Shore, A. and Elvins, R. (2000) 'Impact of hospitalisation on the outcome of adolescent anorexia nervosa'. *The British Journal of Psychiatry*, 176: 138–141.

Gull, W. (1874) 'Anorexia Nervosa (apepsia hysterica, anorexia hysterica)' in *Transactions of the Clinical Society of London*, 7: 22–8.

Harré, R. (1979) *Social Being*. Oxford: Basil Blackwell.

Harré, R. (1993) *Social Being* (2nd edition). Oxford: Basil Blackwell.

Harré, R. (1998) *The Singular Self: An Introduction to the Psychology of Personhood*. London: Sage.

Harris, P. (1988) 'Identity development and identification conflict in female anorexic and bulimic patients' in E. J. Anthony and C. Chiland (eds.) *The Child and his Family*. New York: John Wiley & Sons.

Hepworth, J. (1999) *The Social Construction of Anorexia Nervosa*. London: Sage.

Hermans, H. J. (1988) 'On the integration of nomothetic and idiographic research methods in the study of personal meaning'. *Journal of Personality*, 56: 785–812.

Herzog, D. B., Nussbaum, K. M. and Marmor, A. K. (1996) 'Comorbidity and outcome in eating disorders'. *Psychiatric Clinic/Clinicians of North America*, 19: 843–59.

Hoek, H. W., van Harten, P. N., van Hoeken, D. *et al.* (1998) 'Lack of relation between culture and anorexia nervosa: results of an incidence study on Curacao'. *New England Journal of Medicine*, 338: 1231–2.

Hsu, L. K. G. (1989) 'The gender gap in eating disorders: why are the eating disorders more common among women?'. *Clinical Psychology Review*, 9: 393–407.

James, W. (1890) *Principles of Psychology*. New York: Henry Holt.

Katzman, M. A. and Lee, S. (1997) 'Beyond body image: the integration of feminist and transcultural theories in the understanding of self-starvation'. *International Journal of Eating Disorders*, 22, 4: 385–94.

Kelly, G. A. (1955) *The Psychology of Personal Constructs*. New York: Norton.

Le Grange, D., Eisler, I. and Dare, C. (1992) 'Family criticism and self-starvation: a study of expressed emotion'. *Journal of Family Therapy*, 14: 177–92.

Lester, R. J. (1997) The (dis)embodied self in anorexia nervosa. *Social Science and Medicine*, 44, 4: 479–89.

Lieberman, S. (1995) 'Anorexia nervosa: the tyranny of appearances'. *Journal of Family Therapy*, 17: 133–8.

Long, P. W. (2000) 'Anorexia nervosa – American Description: Diagnostic Criteria'. http://www.mentalhealth.com/dis1/p21-et01.html.

McAdams, D. P. (1992) 'The five-factor model in personality: a critical appraisal'. *Journal of Personality*, 60: 329–61.

MacDonald, M. (1993) 'Bewildered, blamed and brokenhearted: parents' views of anorexia nervosa' in B. Lask and R. Bryant-Waugh (eds.) *Childhood Onset Anorexia Nervosa and Related Eating Disorders*. Hove, UK: Lawrence Erlbaum Associates Ltd.

MacSween, M. (1993) *Anorexic Bodies: A Feminist and Sociological Perspective on Anorexia Nervosa*. London: Routledge.

Malson, H. (1998) *The Thin Women: Feminism, Post-Structuralism and the Social Psychology of Anorexia Nervosa*. London: Routledge.

Malson, H. and Ussher, J. (1996) 'Body poly-texts: discourses of the anorexic body'. *Journal of Community and Applied Social Psychology*, 6: 267–80.

Malson, H. and Ussher, J. (1997) 'Beyond this mortal coil: feminity, death and discursive constructions of the anorexic body'. *Mortality*, 2, 1: 43–61.

Mead, G. H. (1934) *Mind, Self and Society: From the Standpoint of a Social Behavourist*. Edited and with an Introduction by Charles W. Morris. Chicago: University of Chicago Press.

Minuchin, S., Rosman, B. and Baher, L. (1978) *Psychosomatic Families: Anorexia Nervosa in Context*. Cambridge, MA: Harvard University Press.

Mischel, W. (1968) *Personality and Assessment*. New York: Wiley.

Mitchell, J. J. and Eckert, E. D. (1987) 'Scope and significance of eating disorders'. *Journal of Consulting and Clinical Psychology*, 55, 5: 628–34.

Morgan, H. G. and Russell, G. F. M. (1975) 'Value of family background and clinical features predictors of long-term outcome in anorexia nervosa: four-year follow-up study of 41 patients'. *Psychological Medicine*, 5: 355–71.

North, C., Gower, S. and Byram, V. (1997) 'Family functioning in adolescent anorexia nervosa'. *British Journal of Psychiatry*, 171: 545–9.

O'Kane, M. and Saunderson, W. (1997) *Post Traumatic Stress Disorder and Eating Disorders: Exploring Links in Identity Structure and Development*. Paper presented at The Fifth European Congress of Psychology, 'Dancing on the Edge', University College, Dublin, 5–11 July.

O'Kane, M. and Saunderson, W. (1998a) *Coping with the 'Female Illness': Anorexia Nervosa, Identity and the Family in Northern Ireland*. Paper presented at the QUB/Irish Journal of Feminist Studies Conference, 'Families in Ireland', Queens University, Belfast, 7–9 January.

O'Kane, M. and Saunderson, W. (1998b) 'Eating disorders and post traumatic stress disorder: exploring links in anorexic identity structure and development'. *Proceedings of the British Psychological Society*, 6, 2: 129.

Oppenheimer, R., Howells, K., Palmer, R. and Chaloner, D. (1985) 'Adverse sexual experiences in childhood and clinical eating disorders'. *Journal of Psychiatric Research*, 19: 357–61.

Palmer, R., Oppenheimer, R., Dignon, A., Chaloner, D. and Howells, K. (1990) 'Childhood sexual experiences with adults reported by women with eating disorders: extended series. *British Journal of Psychiatry*, 156: 699–703.

Pope, H. and Hudson, J. (1992) 'Is childhood sexual abuse a risk factor for bulimia nervosa?' *American Journal of Psychiatry*, 149: 445–63.

Robin, A. L., Siegel, P. T., Koepke, T., Moye, A. W. and Tice, S. (1994) 'Family therapy versus individual therapy for adolescent females with anorexia nervosa'. *Journal of Developmental and Behavioural Pediatrics*, 15: 111–16.

Rosenberg, M. J. and Abelson, R. P. (1960) 'An analysis of cognitive balancing' in M. J. Rosenberg, G. I. Hoyland, W. J. McGuire, R. P. Abelson and J. W. Brehm (eds.) *Attitude Organisation and Change: An Analysis of Consistency Among Attitude Components*. New Haven: Yale University Press.

Roth, A. and Fonaghy, P. (1996) 'Eating disorders' in A. Roth and P. Fonaghy (eds.) *What Works for Whom? A Critical Review of Psychotherapy Research*. London: The Guilford Press.

Russell, J., Halasz, G. and Beaumont, P. (1990) 'Death related themes in anorexia nervosa: a practical exploration'. *Journal of Adolescence*, 13: 311–26.

Saunderson, W. and O'Kane, M. (1999) Self, identity and developmental perspectives in young women with anorexia nervosa'. *Proceedings of the British Psychological Society*, 7, 2: 137.

Schutz, A. (1967a) *Phenomenology of the Social World*. Evanston, IL: Northwestern University Press.

Schutz, A. (1967b) *Collected Papers, Vol I: The Problems of Reality*. The Hague, Netherlands: Nijhoff.

Shoebridge, P. and Gowers, G. (2000) 'Parental high concern and adolescent-onset anorexia nervosa'. *British Journal of Psychiatry*, 176: 132–7.

Silver, A. and Morley, J. (1991) 'Rule of CCK in regulation of food intake'. *Progress in Neurobiology*, 36: 23–34.

Slugoski, B. R. and Ginsburg, G. P. (1989) 'Ego identity and explanatory speech' in J. Shotter and K. J. Gergen (eds.) *Texts of Identity*. London: Sage.

Smith, J. A., Harré, R and van Langenhove, L. (1995) Idiography and the case-study, in J. A. Smith, R. Harré and L. van Langenhove (eds.) *Rethinking Psychology*. London: Sage.

Snyder, M. and Ickes, W. (1985) 'Personality and social behaviour' in G. Lindzet and E. Arenson (eds.) *Handbook of Social Psychology*, Volume 2, 3rd edition. Reading, MA: Addison-Wesley.

Steinhausen, H., Rauss-Mason, C. and Seidel, R. (1991) 'Follow-up studies of anorexia nervosa: a review of four decades of outcome research'. *Psychological Medicine*, 21: 447–51.

Swartz, L. (1985) Anorexia nervosa as a culture-bound syndrome. *Social Science and Medicine*, 20, 7: 725–30.

Tomb, D. A. (1994) 'The phenomenology of post traumatic stress disorder'. *Psychiatric Clinics of North America*, 17, 2: 237–50.

Turner, B. S. (1992) *Regulating Bodies: Essays in Medical Sociology*. London: Routledge.

Turner, T. (1994) 'Bodies and anti-bodies: flesh and fetish in contemporary social theory' in T. J. Csordas (ed.) *Embodiment and Experience*. Cambridge: Cambridge University Press.

Vandereycken, W. and van Deth, R. (1994) 'Food abstinence and emaciation as signs of illness' in W. Vandereycken and R. van Deth, *From Fasting Saints to Anorexic Girls: The History of Self-Starvation*. London: The Athlone Press.

Waller, G. (2000) 'Perceived control in eating disorders: relationship with reported sexual abuse'. *International Journal of Eating Disorders*, 23, 2: 213–16.

Warnock, M. (1987) *Memory*. London: Faber & Faber.

Wegar, K. (1997) 'Cultural representations of women's and men's mental health: an analysis of *Self Magazine* and *Men's Health*' in E. Riska (ed.), *Images of Women's Health: The Social Construction of Gendered Health*. Finland: The Institute of Women's Studies, Abo Akademi University.

Weinreich, P. (1989) 'Variations in ethnic identity: Identity Structure Analysis' (Chapter 3); and 'Conflicted identifications: a commentary on Identity Structure Analysis Concepts' (Chapter 8), in K. Liebkind (ed.) *New Identities in Europe*. Aldershot: Gower.

Weinreich, P., Doherty, J. and Harris, P. (1985) 'Empirical assessment of identity in anorexia and bulimia nervosa'. *Journal of Psychiatric Research*, 19, 2/3: 279–302.

Wilhelm, K. A. and Clarke, S. D. (1998) 'Eating disorders from a primary care perspective'. *Medical Journal of Australia*, 168: 458–63.

World Health Organisation (1992) *International Classification of Diseases (ICD-10) (classification of mental and behavioural disorders: clinical descriptions and diagnostic guidelines)*. Geneva: WHO.

Zipfel, S., Lowe, B., Reas, D. L., Deter, H. C. and Herzog, W. (2000) 'Long-term prognosis in anorexia nervosa: lessons from a 21-year follow-up study'. *The Lancet*, 355, 9205: 721–2.

12 An exploration of counselling identity in counsellors who deal with trauma

Selwyn Black and Peter Weinreich

INTRODUCTION

Counsellors bring the instrument of themselves into the therapeutic setting. 'To every therapy session we bring our human qualities and the experiences that have influenced us most. . . . this human dimension is one of the most powerful determinants of the therapeutic encounter that we have with clients' (Corey, 1996: 15). In bringing the instrument of self before clients, counsellors bring the living models of who they are alongside the continual struggle to live up to their aspirations. Indeed, there is a sense where the counsellor *becomes* the instrument rather than using instruments and counselling techniques. This process has been described as 'the infusing of self' into therapy (Skovholt and Rønnestad, 1995: 81). This research explores some of the ways in which counsellors reconstruct their identity when, in the aftermath of a traumatic event, they are exposed to the trauma of their clients. In the wake of dealing with clients' trauma, counsellors can experience 'disruptions in their schemas about self and world' (McCann and Pearlman, 1990: 138), and through the resultant increased stress, face distancing in both personal and professional relationships (Dutton and Rubinstein, 1995).

There are many definitions in the literature of the terms 'disasters' and 'traumatic events'. For example, Raphael (1986) describes disasters as 'overwhelming events and circumstances that test the adaptational responses of community or individual beyond their capability, and lead, at least temporarily, to massive disruption of function for community or individual'. Similarly, the American Psychiatric Association (1994) describes a 'traumatic event' as

> an event outside the range of usual human experience that would be markedly distressing to almost anyone: a serious threat to his or her life or physical integrity; serious threat or harm to his children, spouse, or other close relatives or friends; sudden destruction of his home or community; or seeing another person seriously injured or killed in an accident or by physical violence.

Gibson (1998: 22) states that, 'any consideration of a personal or major disaster must include the category of civil disturbance or terrorism'. The traumatic event under consideration in this research is the 'Omagh bomb'.

On 15 August 1998, a car bomb exploded in the provincial town of Omagh, County Tyrone, killing twenty eight people immediately – one died subsequently from their injuries. More than 200 people were injured. 'It was the worst single atrocity in the thirty years of violence in Northern Ireland' (Fay *et al.*, 1999a: 18). The first author was granted access to a team of counsellors who were involved in counselling survivors and others affected by the Omagh bomb. Using Identity Structure Analysis (Weinreich, 1980, 1983a,b, 1986, 1989a,b), a research project investigated the impact on counsellors of counselling traumatised victims and the possible resulting experience of 'vicarious traumatisation' on the identity structures of those counsellors. In *The Cost of the Troubles Study*, Fay *et al.* report that 'although there has been some investigation of the impact of the "troubles" on attitudes and moral development, there has been remarkably little consistent interest in the specific mental health or other effects of the "troubles" on the population' (Fay *et al.*, 1999b: 13). While there has been some research conducted on the psychological consequences on various sub-populations, none could be found on the psychological impact on the caring professions, either in the literature or in consultation with professionals working in the field of psychological trauma in Northern Ireland.

'Working with seriously traumatised clients has consequences for the personal functioning of the counsellor' (van der Veer, 1998: 168). Those consequences may range from empathic reactions during the counselling contact in the short term to altering how the counsellor views himself or herself, the world and human nature in the long term. 'A positive value is often placed on "feeling what the other person feels" without considering that such feelings can produce the emotional exhaustion of burnout when experienced over and over, week in and week out, with a variety of people' (Maslach, 1982: 32). Further, it has been recognised more recently amongst counsellors that 'those who have enormous capacity for feeling and expressing empathy tend to be more at risk of compassion stress' (Figley, 1995: 1).

The psychological consequences of working with 'difficult populations' are often discussed under the term 'burnout' (Maslach, 1982). More recently, the term burnout has been superseded by the term 'compassion fatigue' (Joinson, 1992). However, these terms describe the most acute and unfavourable consequences of working with difficult populations in general terms. The psychodynamic concept of counter-transference describes the counsellor's emotional reactions within the therapeutic encounter that may interfere with the counsellor's objectivity. While the concept of counter-transference directs attention to the counsellor's internal world, its major focus has been its operation within the therapeutic setting. It offers little explanation for the affront to the sense of self experienced by the therapists of the traumatised who experience 'a change in their interaction with the world, themselves, and their families' (Cerney, 1995: 137).

Within the context of this research, data were obtained from respondents after the traumatic event. However, respondents were asked to give consideration to how they perceived themselves before their encounter with their clients. In a comparison between the target group and a control group of counsellors of similar professional profiles and experience, who had themselves no direct contact with the traumatic event, the impact of working with trauma survivors is evident in the target group's

sense of identity, beliefs about self and others, world-view and interpersonal relationships. The specific impact of vicarious traumatisation was determined by
exploring the respondents' sense of identity in relation to their social world.

The concept of vicarious traumatisation was first introduced by McCann and
Pearlman (1990) who provided a theoretical framework for understanding the
complex and distressing effects of trauma work on the therapist. 'The concept is
based in constructivist self-development theory, a developmental, interpersonal
theory explicating the impact of trauma on an individual's psychological development, adaptation, and identity' (Pearlman and Saakvitne, 1995: 152).
Constructivist self-development theory describes the aspects of self that are
affected by traumatic events. 'In the face of trauma, each person will adapt and
cope given their current context(s) and early experiences: interpersonal, intrapsy-
chic, familial, cultural, and social' (Saakvitne and Pearlman, 1996: 27). Just as
trauma changes its victims, so counsellors who work with the survivors of traumatic events too may find themselves permanently altered by the experience.
'These alterations include shifts in the therapist's identity and world view'
(Pearlman and Saakvitne, 1995: 152). Munroe *et al.* have described vicarious traumatisation as an 'occupational hazard' for those who work with the traumatised
(Munroe *et al.*, 1995: 211). This research examines the ways in which vicarious
traumatisation disrupts self in terms of (1) global identity states (identity variants), (2) interpersonal relationships (identification processes), (3) the pervasion
of previous traumatic experiences, and (4) belief and value systems.

IDENTITY STRUCTURE ANALYSIS

Within the therapeutic arena Identity Structure Analysis (ISA) has been used previously to explore the notion of identity in relation to depression (Fox, 1996),
anorexia nervosa (Connor, 1991; Harris, 1980), and stress and burnout (Reid,
1990). This is the first occasion that ISA has been used in relation to psychological trauma. Figley notes that ISA is 'a method not well known in traumatology'.
However, it 'offers a paradigm similar but more quantifiable than countertrans-
ference' (Figley, 2000: 2).

Within ISA, the ambiguous concept of identification is clarified by differentiating between two modes of identification: empathetic identification and role-
model identification. 'Empathetic identification with another refers to the degree
of perceived similarity between the characteristics, whether good or bad, of that
other and oneself' (Weinreich, 1989a: 52). On the other hand, 'one's role model
identification refers to the degree to which one might wish to emulate another
when the other is a positive role model (idealistic-identification), or dissociate
from the other when a negative role model (contra-identification)' (Weinreich,
1989a: 52). Weinreich further elaborates the distinction between the two modes:

. . . the role model identification mode refers to one's orientations in terms of
aspirations and dissociations (the mode of wishing to emulate and wishing to

dissociate to varying degrees), and the empathetic identification mode, situated from moment to moment in differing social contexts, refers to the de facto state of affinity with another of the current moment (the mode of being as the one or the other to varying degrees, at this moment now, or in this or that context, or doing this or that activity, and so on).

(Weinreich, 1989b: 224)

Conflicted identifications occur when one simultaneously sees oneself as similar to another and recognises that other as having characteristics from which one wishes to dissociate. In relation to process postulates concerning attempted resolution of identification conflicts and the emergence of new identifications, ISA presents the following postulates (Weinreich, 1989a: 53):

> *Postulate 1* – When one's identifications with others are conflicted, one attempts to resolve the conflicts, thereby inducing re-evaluations of self in relation to the others within the limitations of one's currently existing value system.
>
> *Postulate 2* – When one forms further identifications with newly encountered individuals, one broadens one's value system and establishes a new context for one's self-definition, thereby initiating a reappraisal of self and others which is dependent on fundamental changes in one's value system.

These process postulates are of direct importance in the context of this research where the resolution of past conflicts and the possible generation of new current conflicts are tracked as respondents appraise themselves in relation to the impact of a traumatic incident on their sense of identity. 'Moderate and quite usual levels of identification conflicts are expected to exist in psychologically well-adjusted people' (Weinreich, 1989a: 53). The processes of change and temporal development will inevitably involve the resynthesis of existing identifications and the synthesis of new identifications. However, when counsellors have been impacted by the trauma of their clients, the results show that the extent of some conflicted identifications is particularly high, and may well affect identity change.

In the ISA definition of identity just given, a central place is give to the person's construal of self. Constructs, which are cognitive in form, are used to evaluate the characteristics of self and others. Affective associations are considered in the evaluative connotations of the cognitive constructs both in terms of the positive values (aspirations) and negative values (those from which one wishes to dissociate). Structural pressure is an ISA index that estimates the extent to which individuals consistently attribute favourable and unfavourable characteristics to particular entities. In relation to cognitive–affective consistency and the structural pressure on constructs, ISA presents the following postulates (Weinreich, 1989a: 55–56):

> *Postulate 1* – When the net structural pressure on one of a person's constructs is high and positive, the evaluative connotations associated with it are stably bound.

Postulate 2 – When the net structural pressure on a construct is low, or negative as a result of strong negative pressures counteracting positive ones, the evaluative connotations associated with the constructs are conflicted: the construct in question is an arena of stress.

Postulate 3 – When the net structural pressure on a construct is low as a result of weak positive and negative pressures, the construct in question is without strong evaluative connotations.

In the context of this research, as ISA identifies the strength and intensity of one's core evaluative dimensions of identity, the professional orientation of respondents is examined in relation to both their core and conflicted evaluative dimensions of identity.

METHOD

The target group comprised a team of counsellors who were involved in caring for the survivors of the Omagh bomb. The group represented a range of professional backgrounds, each having substantial training and experience both as counsellors and professionals who had been trained in the techniques of the Mitchell (1983; and Mitchell and Everly, 1997) Critical Incident Stress Debriefing (CISD) process. CISD is a formal, structured protocol developed as 'a direct, action-orientated crisis intervention process designed to prevent or mitigate traumatic stress subsequent to a traumatic event' (Mitchell and Everly, 1997: 4). The target group completed an ISA instrument designed by the first author to be of direct significance to the respondents. The instrument incorporated 'entities' (Table 12.1) from the social world of the self: individuals, groups of people, institutions and emblems that have significance to the respondent; and 'constructs' (Table 12.2) which were based on discourses by means of which the respondent appraised this social world. Both entities and constructs were presented in randomised sequence. A summary of the representative subject areas contained within the instrument's twenty-three constructs is set out in Table 12.3. Each of the ten respondents also took part in a 25–40-minute semi-structured informal interview. The research has been presented as case studies elsewhere (Black, 1999).

In order to explore self as situated in the past (before the traumatic event), a number of 'past selves' are included in the instrument. The past self 'me as I was in childhood' gives a situated self to consider that is unrelated to the arena of trauma. The past selves 'me as I was before the Omagh bomb', 'me as I was in the short-term aftermath of the Omagh bomb' and 'me as I was facing the long-term consequences after the Omagh bomb' explore the impact of the traumatic event on the respondent's sense of identity. The past self 'me as I was as a result of being involved in previous traumatic experiences' explores the possible reverberation between previous traumatic events and the traumatic event under consideration.

Data from the target group were obtained within the period of one calendar month from the beginning of the tenth month after the Omagh bomb. Data obtained

Table 12.1 Entity list – Instrument: Trauma counsellors project

Entities	Categories
1. Me as I would like to be . . .	*IDEAL SELF
2. Me as I am at home . . .	*CURRENT SELF 1
3. Me as I am when counselling currently . . .	CURRENT SELF 2
4. Me as I was in childhood . . .	*PAST SELF 1
5. Me as I was before the Omagh bomb . . .	PAST SELF 2
6. Me as I was in the short-term aftermath of the Omagh bomb . . .	PAST SELF 3
7. Me as I was facing the long-term consequences after the Omagh bomb . . .	PAST SELF 4
8. Me as I was as a result of being involved in previous traumatic experiences . . .	PAST SELF 5
9. Me as my family sees me . . .	METAPERSPECTIVE 1
10. Me as my professional colleagues see me . . .	METAPERSPECTIVE 2
11. Me as my supervisor sees me . . .	METAPERSPECTIVE 3
12. A person I hold in high regard (nominate) . . .	*ADMIRED PERSON
13. A person who offends me (nominate) . . .	*DISLIKED PERSON
14. Father . . .	
15. Mother . . .	
16. Spouse/Partner . . .	
17. My closest friend . . .	
18. Counselling supervisor . . .	
19. A responsive client (nominate) . . .	
20. A difficult client (nominate) . . .	
21. A traumatised client (nominate) . . .	

*Mandatory entities

from completed instruments were analysed using IDEX idiographic for Windows (V3.0) software (Weinreich and Ewart, 1999). The transcribed interviews were analysed using thematic content analysis and narrative analysis techniques.

A control group of counsellors was set up to establish a comparison between the target group of counsellors who had worked within the context of a specific traumatic incident and a group of counsellors who had no direct exposure to that incident. The control group participated in a similar instrument to the target group: the instrument omitted entities and constructs that had any direct connection with the Omagh bomb. It was postulated that, from a comparison between the two groups, the evidence of vicarious traumatisation in the target group could be established. The control group represented counsellors who came from similar professional backgrounds to those of the target group and had similar levels of training supported by substantial therapeutic experience.

RESULTS

The results, presented as case studies, are all idiosyncratic in nature. The case studies exemplify the complex of processes by means of which respondents

Table 12.2 Construct list – instrument: trauma counsellors project

1. . . . can be trusted	. . . can't be trusted
2. . . . attend/s to personal needs first	. . . put/s others needs first
3. . . . like/s me	. . . dislike/s me
4. . . . put/s family before vocation	. . . put/s vocation before family
5. . . . look/s for security in family relationships	. . . has/have loose family ties
6. . . . prefer/s company of known and trusted friends	. . . enjoy/s making new friends
7. . . . adapt/s easily to change	. . . find/s change difficult
8. . . . get/s things done	. . . put/s things off
9. . . . would become quite closely involved with clients	. . . prefer/s to maintain a professional distance
10. . . . see/s themselves as a 'fixer' in helping resolve client's psychological needs	. . . prefer/s to be a 'facilitator' in assisting clients finding their own solutions
11. . . . enjoy/s the intimacy of a close relationship	. . . find/s intimacy in a close relationship difficult
12. . . . look/s to leisure activities as a means of self-care	. . . find/s difficulty breaking away from work issues
13. . . . believe/s that the world is a safe and secure place	. . . believe/s the world is unsafe and threatening
14. . . . prefer/s to 'feel' the client's trauma	. . . seek/s to 'understand' the client's trauma
15. . . . is/are dependent on others in making decisions	. . . prefer/s to work things out alone
16. . . . is/are impervious to others suffering	. . . become/s overwhelmed by others suffering
17. . . . is/are over-sensitive about what others think	. . . is/are able to laugh at themselves
18. . . . take/s themselves seriously	. . . has/have a relaxed attitude to life
19. . . . look/s for support from relevant professional bodies	. . . is/are cynical about relevant professional bodies
20. . . . draw/s upon one's personal trauma experience while counselling clients	. . . is/are concerned to suppress feelings in order to be strong for the clients
21. . . . feel/s aggressive towards the perpetrator of the bomb	. . . feel/s compassion for the perpetrator of the bomb
22. . . . is/are able to disengage from the traumatised client	. . . remain/s engaged with the traumatised client
23. . . . need/s to be up to date with media coverage	. . . feel/s that 'I know all that I want to know'

construct and reconstruct their identities when, in their counselling practice, they are exposed to the traumatised survivors. The case studies are not published here (a) to preserve the anonymity of the respondents and (b) because of the continuing longitudinal study with the respondents. However, 'the nature of ISA indices makes it possible to perform comparisons between individuals, however idiosyncratic the material from which the indices are derived might be' (Lange, 1989: 170).

Table 12.3 Trauma counsellors project – summary of constructs

---

Personal and social constructs
1. . . . can be trusted/ . . . can't be trusted
3. . . . likes me/dislikes me
5. . . . look/s for security in family relationships/. . . has/have loose family ties
18. . . . take/s themselves seriously/. . . has/have a relaxed attitude to life

Self-care constructs
2. . . . attend/s to personal needs first/. . . put/s others needs first
12. . . . look/s to leisure activities as a means of self-care/. . . find/s difficulty in breaking away from work issues

Personal and social/professional constructs
7. . . . adapt/s easily to change/. . . find/s change difficult
8. . . . get/s things done/. . . put/s things off

Professional constructs
4. . . . put/s family before vocation/. . . put/s vocation before family
9. . . . would become quite closely involved with clients/. . . prefer/s to maintain a professional distance
10. . . . see/s themselves as a 'fixer' in helping resolve client's psychological needs/. . . prefer/s to be a 'facilitator' in assisting clients finding their own solutions

Personal and social/trauma related constructs
11. . . . enjoy/s the intimacy of a close relationship/. . . find/s intimacy in a close relationship difficult
15. . . . is/are dependent on others in making decisions/. . . prefer/s to work things out alone
17. . . . is/are over-sensitive about what others think/. . . is/are able to laugh at themselves

Professional/trauma related constructs
14. . . . prefer/s to 'feel' the client's trauma/. . . seek/s to 'understand' the client's trauma
19. . . . look/s for support from relevant professional bodies/. . . is/are cynical about relevant professional bodies
20. . . . draw/s upon one's personal trauma experience while counselling clients/. . . is/are concerned to suppress feelings in order to be strong for the clients

Trauma related constructs
6. . . . prefer/s company of known and trusted friends/. . . enjoy/s making new friends
13. . . . believe/s the world is a safe and secure place/. . . believe/s the world is unsafe and threatening
16. . . . is/are impervious to others suffering/. . . become/s overwhelmed by others suffering
21. . . . feel/s aggressive towards the perpetrator of the bomb/. . . feel/s compassion for the perpetrator of the bomb
22. . . . is/are able to disengage from the traumatised client/. . . remain/s engaged with the traumatised client
23. . . . need/s to be up to date with media coverage/. . . feel/s that 'I know all that I need to know'

The results of comparisons between ten target group counsellors are presented alongside those for ten control group counsellors in terms of (a) identity variants, (b) identification processes, (c) resonance with previous traumatic experiences, and (d) values and beliefs.

Identity variants

The classification of identity variants (Table 12.4) is based exclusively on the underlying parameters of identity diffusion and self-evaluation and is therefore global in nature. The ISA classification of nine identity variants draws on Erikson's states of 'identity' and 'identity diffusion' foreclosure.

Generally, most adults are classified as 'indeterminate' or 'confident' (Weinreich, 1983b, 1985), i.e. they reflect moderate levels of identity diffusion with moderate or high levels of self-evaluation and are considered to be psychologically well-adjusted. Other identity states are regarded as vulnerable.

A comparison between the two groups reveals a higher extent of vulnerable identities in the respondents' appraisals across both past and current selves in the target group (44%) (Table 12.5) than in the control group (26%) (Table 12.6). Considering only current selves the comparison reveals a greater frequency of vulnerable identities in the target group (45%) than in the control group (20%).

Identification processes

Given that professional identification conflicts with a traumatised and a difficult client are in all likelihood going to be the most challenging in the therapeutic context, they are identified specifically in a comparison between the two groups. Respondents in both the control group and the target group are shown to have high conflicted identifications with both traumatised and difficult clients in their currently situated selves. However, there is a higher extent of conflicted identifications with traumatised and difficult clients in the target group (between 70% and 90% taking into account the defended states against identification conflicts) than in the control group (65%) (Tables 12.7 and 12.8). This may be a reflection on the nature of the work with which the target group was involved. Conflicted identifications in the target group show a marked increase in intensity as the respondents appraise themselves in the traumatic setting, that is from their appraisal of self before the Omagh bomb to 'me as I was in the short-term aftermath of the Omagh bomb' and 'me as I was facing the long-term consequences after the Omagh bomb' (Table 12.8).

Table 12.4 Classification of identity variants

Self-evaluation	Identity diffusion		
	High (0.41–1.00)	Moderate (0.26–0.40)	Low (0.00–0.25)
High (0.81–1.00)	Diffuse high self-regard	Confident	Defensive high self-regard
Moderate (0.19–0.80)	Diffusion	Indeterminate	Defensive
Low (−1.00–0.18)	Crisis	Negative	Defensive negative

Table 12.5 Identity variants – trauma counsellors target group

	Current self 1	Current self 2	Past self 1	Past self 2	Past self 3	Past self 4	Past self 5
Respondent 1	Diffusion	Diffusion	Diffusion	Diffusion	Crisis	Diffusion	Diffusion
Respondent 2	Indeterminate	Indeterminate	Indeterminate	Indeterminate	Crisis	Indeterminate	Indeterminate
Respondent 3	Indeterminate	Indeterminate	Negative	Indeterminate	Indeterminate	Indeterminate	Indeterminate
Respondent 4	Indeterminate	Confident	Negative	Indeterminate	Indeterminate	Indeterminate	Indeterminate
Respondent 5	Defensive high self-regard	Defensive high self-regard	Negative	Defensive high self-regard	Indeterminate	Defensive high self-regard	Defensive high self-regard
Respondent 6	Defensive	Defensive high self-regard	Defensive high self-regard	Defensive	Defensive	Defensive	Defensive
Respondent 7	Confident	Defensive high self-regard	Defensive	Indeterminate	Indeterminate	Indeterminate	Confident
Respondent 8	Indeterminate	Indeterminate	Confident	Indeterminate	Indeterminate	Indeterminate	Indeterminate
Respondent 9	Defensive high self-regard	Defensive high self-regard	Indeterminate	Defensive high self-regard	Indeterminate	Indeterminate	Indeterminate
Respondent 10	Indeterminate	Indeterminate	Diffusion	Indeterminate	Crisis	Indeterminate	Diffusion

Situated selves:
Current self 1 – 'me as I am at home'
Current self 2 – 'me as I am when counselling currently'
Past self 1 – 'me as I was in childhood'
Past self 2 – 'me as I was before the Omagh bomb'
Past self 3 – 'me as I was in the short-term aftermath of the Omagh bomb'
Past self 4 – 'me as I was facing the long-term consequences of the Omagh bomb'
Past self 5 – 'me as I was as a result of being involved in previous traumatic experiences'

Table 12.6 Identity variants – trauma counsellors control group

	Current self 1	*Current self 2*	*Past self*
Control 1	Indeterminate	Indeterminate	Indeterminate
Control 2	Indeterminate	Indeterminate	Indeterminate
Control 3	Crisis	Crisis	Crisis
Control 4	Indeterminate	Indeterminate	Indeterminate
Control 5	Indeterminate	Indeterminate	Indeterminate
Control 6	Indeterminate	Indeterminate	Crisis
Control 7	Crisis	Indeterminate	Crisis
Control 8	Diffusion	Indeterminate	Crisis
Control 9	Indeterminate	Indeterminate	Indeterminate
Control 10	Indeterminate	Indeterminate	Indeterminate

Situated selves:
Current self 1 – 'me as I am at home'
Current self 2 – 'me as I am when counselling currently'
Past self – 'me as I was in childhood'

Table 12.7 Conflicted identifications (current selves) – control group

	High identification conflict with a traumatised client	*High identification conflict with a difficult client*
Control 1		
Control 2	✓	✓
Control 3	✓	✓
Control 4	✓	
Control 5	✓	
Control 6	✓	
Control 7	✓	✓
Control 8	✓	✓
Control 9		
Control 10	✓	✓

✓ = Conflicted identifications

Empathetic identification has been described by Weinreich as 'a de facto state of affairs in which ego's recognition and comprehension of the other may refer to a compassionate understanding of shared values, vulnerabilities and eccentricities, as well as of shared aspirations and desired qualities' (Weinreich, 1989b: 223). Empathic concerns, linked to emotional contagion (experiencing the feelings of the sufferer as a function of exposure to the sufferer) are among the components that contribute to compassion stress. For this reason it has been important to track the changes in empathetic identifications with the other in the counsellor's exposure to their client's trauma.

The ability to respond empathically in the therapeutic relationship differs from the notion of empathetic identifications as understood in the context of ISA. Egan (1998: 72) defines empathy as 'an intellectual process that involves understanding

Table 12.8 Conflicted identifications – target group

	High identification conflict with a traumatised client	High identification conflict with a difficult client	Current estimates of conflicted identifications from PS2 to PS3 and PS4
Respondent 1	✓	✓	Increased
Respondent 2	✓	✓	Increased
Respondent 3		✓	Increased
Respondent 4	✓		Increased
Respondent 5	D	D	D
Respondent 6	✓	✓	Increased
Respondent 7	D	D	D
Respondent 8	✓	✓	Increased
Respondent 9	✓	✓	Increased
Respondent 10	✓	✓	Increased

D = Defensiveness against conflicted identifications
✓ = Conflicted identifications
CS1 – 'me as I am at home'
CS2 – 'me as I am when counselling currently'
PS2 – 'me as I was before the Omagh bomb'
PS3 – 'me as I was in the short-term aftermath of the Omagh bomb'
PS4 – 'me as I was facing the long-term consequences after the Omagh bomb'

correctly another person's emotional state and point of view'. Within the context of ISA, 'empathetic identification with another refers to the degree of perceived similarity between the characteristics, whether good or bad, of that other and one-self' (Weinreich, 1989a: 52). In essence, the difference is the contrast between the counsellor having empathy *for* their client and identifying *with* their client.

As a finding of this study (Table 12.9), the commonality of increasing empathetic identifications, as the respondents appraise themselves from before the Omagh bomb to their currently situated selves, may well indicate how 'such experiences can increase the counsellor's capacity to react empathically' (van der Veer, 1998: 166). Those increasing empathetic identifications have both positive and negative outcomes. Respondents show increased empathetic identifications with both professional and domestic entities in their currently situated selves that may be interpreted as a positive outcome (Table 12.9, column 2). However, correspondingly respondents who increasingly empathetically identify with both traumatised and difficult clients, as the respondents appraise themselves from before the Omagh bomb to their currently situated selves (Table 12.9, column 5), may also indicate how the respondents have either become over involved or perhaps even dependent on their clients (Wilson and Lindy, 1994: 25). Increased empathetic identifications come about with their clients because counsellors ascribe to themselves more of the characteristics which their clients are experiencing as a result of being traumatised. These increased empathetic identifications suggest evidence of vicarious traumatisation during the crucial period of counselling the traumatised – a phenomenon that is maintained from past selves through currently situated selves. It is anticipated that ongoing research will

Table 12.9 Empathetic identifications – target group

	Empathetic identifications from PS2 to CS1 and CS2 with both domestic and professional entities	Modulation in empathetic identifications with domestic entities from PS2 to PS3 and PS4	Modulation in empathetic identifications with professional entities from PS2 to PS3 and PS4	Empathetic identifications with traumatised/ difficult clients from PS2 to CS1 and CS2
Respondent 1	Increased	Dissociation	Dissociation	Increased
Respondent 2	Increased	Dissociation	Dissociation	Increased
Respondent 3	Increased	Stable	Closer association	Increased
Respondent 4	Increased	Dissociation	Dissociation	Increased
Respondent 5	Defended	Defended	Defended	Defended
Respondent 6	Defended	Dissociation	Dissociation	Increased
Respondent 7	Increased	Dissociation	Dissociation	Defended
Respondent 8	Increased	Dissociation	Closer association	Increased
Respondent 9	Increased	Dissociation	Dissociation	Increased
Respondent 10	Increased	Dissociation	Closer association	Increased

Increased = Increased empathetic identifications
Defended = Defended orientation
Dissociation = Dissociation from entities
Closer association = Closer association with entities
Stable = Stable empathetic identifications
CS1 – 'me as I am at home'
CS2 – 'me as I am when counselling currently'
PS2 – 'me as I was before the Omagh bomb'
PS3 – 'me as I was in the short-term aftermath of the Omagh bomb'
PS4 – 'me as I was facing the long-term consequences of the Omagh bomb'

clarify both the beneficial and detrimental aspects of increased empathetic identifications.

The majority of respondents (80%) demonstrate dissociation from both domestic and professional entities as they appraise themselves in the 'short-term aftermath' and facing the 'long-term consequences' of the Omagh bomb (Table 12.9, columns 3 and 4). The overall appraised dissociation from both domestic and professional people exhibits the counsellors' temporary alienation and decreased sense of connection. This may be interpreted as a temporary incapacity for social interaction, and subsequent alienation and decreased sense of connection with these significant others in the midst of trauma. The phenomenon of dissociation or distancing is a common response to trauma that takes the form of 'withdrawal from family, friends, or colleagues, perhaps out of the belief that no-one could understand their distressed response to their work' (Dutton and Rubinstein, 1995: 88).

It was postulated that vicarious traumatisation, through exposure to their client's traumatic experiences, would influence how counsellors evaluated self in terms of identifications with significant others. The results show that vicarious traumatisation:

1   has the potential to lead counsellors to over-empathetically identify with their traumatised clients in the short term, and over a prolonged period of time;
2   effects an increase in identification conflicts with traumatised and difficult clients that may be maintained over a prolonged period of time;
3   leads counsellors in the short term to experience a degree of dissociation from others in both the domestic and professional contexts, that is, alienation in their interpersonal relationships;
4   in the long term will enable counsellors to empathetically identify more closely with significant others in both their professional and domestic settings than prior to their traumatic involvement.

Resonance with previous traumatic experiences

Counsellors do not exist in a vacuum – they may well have personal trauma histories that may be intensified by the work in which they are involved (Table 12.10). 'A therapist who has worked through his or her own healing process has a distinct advantage in understanding the client and being able to model healing' (Munroe *et al.*, 1995: 215). Skovholt and Rønnestad (1995) have conducted research that examines how counsellors integrate personal themes into their professional development and practice. Those themes often involve pain in relation to broken relationships, loss, trauma, substance abuse or similar impactful human experience. They warn 'if the process of professional individuation has not occurred through continuous professional reflection, the individual may still be a "wounded healer" who can be harmful to clients in small and large ways' (Skovholt and Rønnestad, 1995: 117).

Table 12.10 Pervasion of previous traumatic experiences – target group

	Previous traumatic experience	Contained/Prolonged influence
Respondent 1	✓	Contained
Respondent 2	✓	Contained
Respondent 3	✓	Prolonged influence
Respondent 4	✓	Prolonged influence
Respondent 5	Defended	Defended
Respondent 6	Defended	Defended
Respondent 7	✓	Contained
Respondent 8	✓	Contained
Respondent 9	✓	Prolonged influence
Respondent 10	No previous trauma history	No previous trauma history

✓ = Evidence of previous traumatic experience based on respondents' semi-structured informal interviews
Contained = Contained in current identity
Prolonged influence = Prolonged influence on current identity
Defended = Defended orientation against revealing any previous traumatic experience

It was postulated that previous traumatic experiences would make an impact on how respondents appraise self in relation to their appraisal of working in the context of the Omagh bomb. The results demonstrate that previous traumatic experiences (whether personal or professional):

- reverberate with new traumatic encounters in the way counsellors construe their identity in both the professional and domestic contexts as evidenced by similar patterns of identifications with significant others;
- have both positive and negative consequences on the way in which counsellors currently construe their identity.

Evidence from the semi-structured informal interviews is supported by the appraised prolonged influence of previous traumatic experiences with three respondents. The literature suggests that such consequences may be determined by training, supervision, work-context variables, external and internal professional individuation in relation to working with trauma survivors, healing processes relating to personal traumatic experiences and the amelioration of such processes into current identity structures (Skovholt and Rønnestad, 1995; Munroe *et al.*, 1995; Dutton and Rubinstein, 1995).

In current, ongoing research, the beneficial and detrimental influences of counsellors' previous traumatic experiences in both their personal and professional dimensions are being explored.

Impact on values and beliefs

A core evaluative dimension of one's identity is a major aspiration (expressed as the endorsed pole of a construct) with cognitive–affective compatibility (indicated by high structural pressure on the construct) in the appraisal of the social world of self and others. A core evaluative dimension of identity is highly evaluative and judgemental in nature, and therefore resistant to change.

Core evaluative dimensions of identity in the target group present a commonality in selection of constructs that represent an overall orientation of how respondents construe their social world whilst appraising themselves and others within the context of this research (Table 12.11). Over half of the respondents reflect a commonality on core evaluative dimensions of identity representing a strong emphasis on trust, support and security within close relationships. The issue of trust is crucial for counsellors involved in trauma work. Vicarious traumatisation can violate trust by disrupted schemas (McCann and Pearlman, 1990), a lost sense of invulnerability (Munroe *et al.*, 1995) and a loss of community (Erikson, 1976). It is not unusual, therefore, to find such a strong emphasis on trust in the respondents' schema. In addition, given the aspiration to be secure in both the familial setting and within the intimacy of a close personal relationship, these core constructs resonate with the dissociation described earlier in relation to the family.

A comparison of core constructs between the target group and the control group reveals that, while there are similarities, there is not quite the same strength

354   *Black and Weinreich*

Table 12.11 Core evaluative dimensions of identity – target group

Construct list		Incidence of high structural pressure within target group on constructs	Preferred polarity	
+	–		+	–
1. . . . can be trusted (p)	. . . can't be trusted	100%	10	0
5. . . . look/s for security in family relationships (p)	. . . has/have loose family ties	80%	8	0
3. . . . like/s me (p)	. . . dislike/s me	60%	6	0
11. . . . enjoy/s the intimacy of a close relationship (p/t)	. . . find/s intimacy in a close relationship difficult	50%	5	0
19. . . . look/s for support from relevant professional bodies (pro/t)	. . . is/are cynical about relevant professional bodies	40%	4	0

(p) = Personal construct; (p/t) = Personal/Trauma related construct; (pro/t) = Professional/Trauma construct

Table 12.12 Core evaluative dimensions of identity – control group

Construct list		Incidence of high structural pressure within control group on constructs	Preferred polarity	
+	–		+	–
1. . . . can be trusted (p)	. . . can't be trusted	60%	6	0
3. . . . like/s me (p)	. . . dislike/s me	60%	6	0
8. . . . get/s things done (p/pro)	. . . put/s things off	60%	6	0
11. . . . enjoy/s the intimacy of a close relationship (p/t)	. . . find/s intimacy in a close relationship difficult	60%	6	0
10. . . . prefer/s to be a 'facilitator' in assisting clients finding their own solutions (pro)	. . . see/s themselves as a 'fixer' in helping resolve client's psychological needs	40%	4	0

(p) = Personal construct; (p/pro) = Personal/Professional construct; (p/t) = Personal/Trauma construct; (pro) = Professional construct

of emphasis on trust or family relationships in the control group as is evidenced in the target group (Table 12.12). The issue of acceptance is equally important to both groups.

Conflicted evaluative dimensions of identity arise when there are inconsistencies between the evaluative connotations of cognitions and the overall evaluations of self and others, resulting in structures of cognitive–affective incompatibilities that are arenas of stress. They are represented by low or negative structural pressures on the constructs in question. When a respondent reflects an overall defensiveness in their identity structure their defensiveness suppresses any indication of identification conflicts. However, it is possible to penetrate that defensiveness by considering the conflicted evaluative dimensions of identity. (Respondents 5, 6 and 9 exemplify this phenomenon, as shown in Table 12.13.)

The incidence of conflicted evaluative dimensions of identity for the target group is presented in Table 12.13. There is a much wider range of constructs (than in the common core evaluative dimensions of identity) representing conflicted dimensions of identity both in the representation of constructs as reflected in the percentage scores and as indicated in the lack of consensus over the preferred polarity of those constructs.

A comparison between the conflicted dimensions of identity common to the target group (Table 12.13) and the control group (Table 12.14) reveals that the target group's incidence of unstable or conflicted evaluative dimensions of identity is associated largely with trauma-specific constructs while the control group reflects much more wide-ranging subject areas.

Table 12.13 Conflicted evaluative dimensions of identity – target group

Construct list		Incidence of low structural pressure within target group on constructs	Preferred polarity	
Left pole	*Right pole*		*Left*	*Right*
13. . . . believe/s that the world is a safe and secure place (t)	. . . believe/s the world is unsafe and threatening	50%	n = 4	n = 1
6. . . . prefer/s company of known and trusted friends (t)	. . . enjoy/s making new friends	30%	n = 2	n = 1
14. . . . prefer/s to 'feel' the client's trauma (pro)	. . . seek/s to 'understand' the client's trauma	30%	n = 2	n = 1
16. . . . is/are impervious to others suffering (t)	. . . become/s overwhelmed by others suffering	30%	n = 0	n = 3
18. . . . take/s themselves seriously (p)	. . . has/have a relaxed attitude to life	30%	n = 0	n = 3
21. . . . feel/s aggressive towards the perpetrator of the bomb (t)	. . . feel/s compassion for the perpetrator of the bomb	30%	n = 1	n = 2
23. . . . need/s to be up to date with media coverage (t)	. . . feel/s that 'I know all that I want to know'	30%	n = 2	n = 1

(t) = Trauma construct; (pro) = Professional/Trauma construct; (p) = Personal construct (Summary of constructs Table 12.3)

Table 12.14 Conflicted evaluative dimensions of identity – control group

Construct list		Incidence of low structural pressure within control group on constructs	Preferred polarity	
Left pole	*Right pole*		*Left*	*Right*
12. . . . find/s difficulty in breaking away from work issues (s/c)	. . . look/s to leisure activities as a means of self-care	50%	n = 1	n = 4
13. . . . believe/s that the world is a safe and secure place (t)	. . . believe/s the world is unsafe and threatening (t)	50%	n = 4	n = 1
14. . . . prefer/s to 'feel' the client's trauma (pro/t)	. . . seek/s to 'understand' the client's trauma	40%	n = 2	n = 2
7. . . . adapt/s easily to change (p/pro)	. . . find/s change difficult	30%	n = 2	n = 1
9. . . . would become quite closely involved with clients (pro)	. . . prefer/s to maintain a professional distance	30%	n = 1	n = 2

(s/c) = Self-care construct; (t) = Trauma construct; (pro/t) = Professional/Trauma construct; (p/pro) = Personal/Professional construct; (pro) = Professional construct

It was postulated that respondents, through exposure to the trauma of their clients, would experience shifts in the way they appraise their social world with regard to self and others. The results show that:

1 Counsellors, upon exposure to the trauma of their clients will, in the first instance, revert to the safety of long-established familial belief and value systems and demonstrate a decreasing sense of trust in their professional belief and value systems.
2 Counsellors subjected to the effects of vicarious traumatisation, will regard the issue of trust as the most important measure by which they appraise their social world.
3 Counsellors, upon exposure to the trauma of their clients, will become pre-occupied with trauma-related issues that represent areas of contradiction and difficulty.

CONCLUSION AND RECOMMENDATIONS

This research has shown that vicarious traumatisation can have deleterious (but also beneficial) cumulative and prolonged effects on the trauma counsellor's identity. These consequences of vicarious traumatisation on counselling identity necessitate further research into understanding the long-term effects of vicarious traumatisation. The research has been limited by its 'in the moment' perspective on the impact on counselling identity of trauma's after-shocks. The first author is presently pursuing a longitudinal study that will give insight into changes in identity processes that were temporary and those that were permanent.

In the light of the findings of this research, the following recommendations are proffered:

At a primary level:

- The caring professions in both the public and voluntary sectors should be made more aware of the consequences of vicarious traumatisation on counselling identity in those who deal with the survivors of trauma.

At a secondary level:

- Those counsellors who deal with the traumatised (whatever the origin of that trauma) should be made more aware of the psychological impact of the aftermath of trauma.
- Counsellors in training, and those from the caring professions who are likely to deal with traumatised patients or clients, should develop a sound theoretical knowledge and understanding of the psychological effects of vicarious traumatisation.

At a tertiary level:

- Managers of any team established to respond to the multiple complex psychosocial needs of traumatised people, including staff, must recognise the danger of using professional identity as a defence against the disrupted self caused by the pain and confusion of vicarious traumatisation.
- Those managers of any team established to respond to the multiple complex psychosocial needs of traumatised people, including staff, must recognise the crucial need to foster collegial identity as a means of preventing isolation and alienation for those who are vulnerable to the affects of vicarious traumatisation.
- Those counsellors recognise the importance of self-care in order to maintain a balance between their personal and professional lives, that is, to insist on time and activities with intimates and friends away from trauma issues.

REFERENCES

American Psychiatric Association (1994) *Diagnostic and Statistical Manual for Mental Disorders* (4th edn) DSM IV. Washington, DC: APA.

Black, W. R. S. (1999) *An Exploration in Counselling Identity in Counsellors who Deal with Trauma*. (Unpublished) MSc thesis: Ulster University.

Cerney, M. S. (1995) 'Treating the heroic treaters'. In C. R. Figley (ed.) *Compassion Fatigue: Coping with Secondary Traumatic Stress in those who Treat the Traumatized*. Bristol, PA: Brunner/Mazel.

Connor, T. (1991) *An Identity Exploration of Anorexia Nervosa within a Family Context*. PhD thesis: University of Ulster, Jordanstown.

Corey, G. (1996) *Theory and Practice of Counseling and Psychotherapy* (5th edn). Pacific Grove, CA: Brooks Cole.

Dutton, M. A. and Rubinstein, F. L. (1995) 'Working with people with PTSD: research implications'. In C. R. Figley (ed.) *Compassion Fatigue: Coping with Secondary Traumatic Stress in Those Who Treat the Traumatized*. Bristol, PA: Brunner/Mazel.

Egan, G. (1998) *The Skilled Helper: A Problem Management Approach to Helping* (6th edn). Pacific Grove, CA: Brooks Cole.

Erikson, K. T. (1976) *Everything in its Path: Destruction of Community in the Buffalo Creek Flood*. New York: Simon and Schuster.

Fay, M., Morrissey, M., and Smyth, M. (1999a) *Northern Ireland's Troubles: The Human Costs*. London: Pluto Press.

Fay, M., Morrissey, M., Smyth, M., and Wong, T. (1999b) *The Cost of the Troubles Study. Report on the Northern Ireland Survey: The Experience and Impact of the Troubles*. Londonderry: INCORE.

Figley, C. R. (1995) *Compassion Fatigue: Coping with Secondary Traumatic Stress in those who Treat the Traumatized*. Bristol, PA: Brunner/Mazel.

Figley, C.R. (2000) 'Editorial'. *Traumatology*, 6(1), 2.

Fox, M. (1996) *An Exploration of Depressed Identity Structure Analysis*. Msc Applied Psychology thesis: University of Ulster, Jordanstown.

Gibson, M. (1998) *Order from Chaos*. Birmingham: Venture Press

Harris, P. D. G. (1980) *Identity Development in Female Patients Suffering from Anorexia Nervosa and Bulimia Nervosa: An Application of Weinreich's Identity Structure Analysis*. M. Psychology thesis: University of Liverpool.

Joinson, C. (1992) 'Coping with compassion fatigue'. *Nursing*, 22(4), 116–122.

Lange, A. (1989) 'Identifications, perceived cultural distance and stereotypes'. In K. Liebkind (ed.) *New Identities in Europe: Immigrant Ancestry and the Ethnic Identity of Youth*. Aldershot: Gower.

Maslach, C. (1982) *Burnout: The Cost of Caring*. Englewood Cliffs, NJ: Prentice Hall.

McCann, L. and Pearlman, L. A. (1990) 'Vicarious traumatisation: a framework for understanding the psychological effects of working with victims'. *Journal of Traumatic Stress*, 3(1), 131–149.

Mitchell, J. (1983) 'Case and situation analysis'. *Sociological Review*, 31, 187–211.

Mitchell, J. and Everly, G. S. (1997) *Critical Incident Stress Debriefing: An Operational Manual for the Prevention of Stress among Emergency Service and Disaster Workers* (2nd edn). Ellicott City, MD: Chevron.

Munroe, J. F., Shay, J., Fisher, L., Makary, C., Rapperport, K., and Zimering, R. (1995) 'Preventing compassion fatigue: a team treatment model'. In C. R. Figley (ed.) *Compassion Fatigue: Coping with Secondary Traumatic Stress in those who Treat the Traumatized*. Bristol, PA: Brunner/Mazel.

Pearlman, L. and Saakvitne, K. W. (1995) 'Treating therapists with vicarious traumatisation and secondary traumatic stress disorders'. In C. R. Figley (ed.) *Compassion Fatigue: Coping with Secondary Traumatic Stress in those who Treat the Traumatized*. Bristol, PA: Brunner/Mazel.

Raphael, B. (1986) *When Disaster Strikes*. London: Hutchinson.

Reid, H. R. (1990) *Theoretical and Empirical Analysis of Occupational Stress: A Study of Residential Social Workers in Child Care*. PhD thesis: University of Ulster, Jordanstown.

Saakvitne, K. W. and Pearlman, L. (1996) *Transforming the Pain: A Workbook on Vicarious Traumatisation*. New York: Norton.

Skovholt, T. M. and Rønnestad, M. H. (1995) *The Evolving Professional Self*. Chichester: Wiley.

van der Veer, G. (1998) *Counselling and Therapy with Refugees and Victims of Trauma*. Chichester: Wiley.

Weinreich, P. (1980, 1986, 1988) *Manual for Identity Exploration using Personal Constructs* (2nd edn). Research paper No. 1, Centre for Research in Ethnic Relations: University of Warwick.

Weinreich, P. (1983a) 'Emerging from threatened identities: ethnicity and gender in redefinitions of ethnic identity'. In G. M. Breakwell (ed.) *Threatened Identities*. Chichester: Wiley.

Weinreich, P. (1983b) 'Psychodynamics of personal and social identity: theoretical concepts and their measurement'. In A. Jacobson-Widding (ed.) *Identity: Personal and Socio-cultural*. Stockholm: Almqvist and Wiksell International.

Weinreich, P. (1985) 'Rationality and irrationality in racial and ethnic relations'. *Ethnic and Racial Studies*, 8, 500–515.

Weinreich, P. (1986) 'The operationalisation of identity theory in racial and ethnic relations'. In J. Rex and D. Mason (eds.) *Theories of Race and Ethnic Relations*. Cambridge: Cambridge University Press.

Weinreich, P. (1989a) 'Variations in ethnic identity'. In K. Liebkind (ed.) *New Identities in Europe: Immigrant Ancestry and the Ethnic Identity of Youth*. Aldershot: Gower.

Weinreich, P. (1989b) 'Conflicted identifications: a commentary on identity structure analysis concepts'. In K. Liebkind (ed.) *New Identities in Europe: Immigrant Ancestry and the Ethnic Identity of Youth*. Aldershot: Gower.

Weinreich, P. and Ewart S. (1999) *IDEX for Windows Version 3.0*. Identity exploration computer software for basic case studies.

Wilson, J. P. and Lindy, J. D. (1994) 'Empathic strain and counter-transference'. In J. P. Wilson and J. D. Lindy (eds.) *Counter-transference and the Treatment of PTSD*. New York: Guilford Press.

Coda

Peter Weinreich

THEORY BUILDING AND PRACTICAL APPLICATION

The literature on self and identity is vast but chaotic. A kaleidoscopic set of conceptualisations, some of which have been outlined in Chapter 1, is in disarray. Methods of assessment of parameters of identity, deriving from disparate conceptualisations of self and identity, are often unrelated. They might, for example, refer to self-labelling, use repertory grid technique, assess social roles, or estimate social identification, but without any consistently conceptualised interrelationship between them. Other studies may concern self-esteem, or notions of identity achievement or failure, or, most common of all, appeal to various ad hoc measures associated with specific parameters such as self-efficacy, introversion, or locus of control. Each tradition proceeds within its own terms with seemingly little awareness of others, giving rise to a plethora of results, the consequences of which are partial findings that cannot readily be related to one another. Further, while experimental approaches can provide powerful means for explicating certain phenomena, for example, the impact of social categorisation on group processes, they cannot substitute for direct assessments of parameters of identity associated with spontaneous expressions of identity in directly experienced everyday social milieus.

The jumbled nature of the literature on self-concept and identity has a paradoxical consequence. In attempting to find some certitude in thought about self and identity processes, many commentators have preferred a mode of thinking that posits an all-encompassing, simple set of propositions. Appeal to more or less self-contained theoretical orientations tends in practice to be the preferred mode for dealing with the highly complex realities of people's identity development, a tendency that favours simplistic explanations over the complex intricacies of biographical development within differing cultural and socio-historical contexts.

ISA attempts to diminish this confusion by integrating significant conceptual strands from extant theorising about self and identity, in which psychological concepts are explicitly defined and their interrelationships made manifest (Chapter 1). All such concepts are operationalised for application in the field, minimising ambiguity as to what is being assessed (as detailed in Chapter 2). The entire conceptual framework is thereby seen to be systematic, interrelated and publicly transparent. It is also an open-ended framework, which invites extension in terms of concepts and process postulates that can be co-ordinated with presently existing ones, as is the case with further postulates shortly to be presented delineating how stress processes in individuals of future eras might be ascertained. It appeals to, and indeed relies on, expertise of an ethnographic kind that investigators in the field have about the myriad issues of self and identity phenomena that characterise the complex individual and social realities of living, successfully or otherwise, in communities the world over.

ISA does not attempt to provide a universal theory of identity formation, maintenance and redefinition. Instead, as demonstrated in this volume, it provides a framework for exploring self and identity processes in areas of interest ranging from the clinical (for instance, anorexia nervosa) to the societal (such as gender identity) and the cross-cultural (for example, ethnic identity and enculturation). Its purpose is to generate theoretical propositions about such processes, in which self and identity are conceived as being inextricably located within biographical and historical contexts. It provides a means by which investigators may incorporate knowledge of their own respective fields that informs the context of identity development and redefinition.

While ISA does not propose common explanatory propositions for all identity phenomena, it does encompass theoretical postulates about certain fundamental identity processes (Chapter 1). It facilitates the investigation of a multitude of identity issues within a common language of explicitly defined concepts. ISA concepts can be operationalised within any linguistic and cultural context for empirical work in field settings. As well as its application to what may be considered mainstream issues, ISA is particularly suited to conceptually problematic cases, such as may be found in transcultural psychiatry and psychotherapy, enculturation of offspring of migrant groups and culturally mixed marriages, and the expression of ethnic identity from alternative subcultural perspectives.

With an entirely practical intention of diminishing confusion and devising an open-ended conceptualisation of direct use to practitioners, the mission of ISA is an avowedly integrative one. Thus, useful notions from different traditions are selectively integrated, thereby undergoing subtle transformations that result in new explicit definitions of crucial concepts. For example, received wisdom about the ubiquitous concept of self-esteem is that many of our social problems are due to poor self-esteem exhibited by distressed individuals or disadvantaged or stigmatised segments of society. Building confidence and enhancing self-esteem are deemed by many commentators to be pathways to solving individual and societal problems. Yet, from the perspective of ISA, although high self-evaluation may be an indication of unproblematic confidence, it could also accompany a defensive (Chapters 4 and 11) or a diffuse (Chapter 9) identity state. High self-esteem accompanying extremes of both defensive and diffuse states of identity tends to be distinctly problematic for both self and others in the community. Therefore, the elucidation of accompanying identity processes associated with high self-evaluation in individuals is an essential requirement prior to making judgements about their state of well-being.

Investigators approaching ISA for the first time will naturally want to assimilate the proffered integrative conceptualisation to their own preferred theoretical orientation, be it experimental social psychological, psychodynamic, symbolic interactionist, social constructionist, personal construct theorist, discourse analyst, or whatever. This is because ISA features elements of these perspectives and therefore has for each orientation a familiar point of departure. But investigators should be wary, because the elements of one perspective tend to be integrated with elements of others, which therefore cannot be ignored. The symbolic interactionist and the personal construct theorist are confronted with psychodynamic concepts, and vice versa, in which significant redefinitions of concepts occur in order to eliminate ambiguities (such as in the concept of *identification*: Chapter 1) and to reorient theoretical perspectives (for example, *primordialism when explaining ethnic identity*: Chapter 3). Experimental social psychological findings and naturalistic discourse analysis also feature as unfamiliar combinations. Qualitative and quantitative aspects are integrated. Culturally specific (emic) viewpoints are integrated within culturally universal (etic) parameters of identity.

The intention of this volume has been to make analysing identity readily accessible in any culture and language. The notion that people subscribe to differing views of the world depending on their cultural backgrounds has a pivotal place in theory and practice presented here. Using well-formulated customised identity instruments, ISA is able to directly incorporate cultural orientations and indigenous psychologies corresponding to nationality, religious affiliation, or ethnic group membership. Each individual's emic interpretation of the social world is ascertained independently, prior to assessing standardised etic parameters of identity.

Given access to computers, the ISA approach is within reach of investigators from any cultural background who have more than a passing interest in processes of development and change in identity, their own and that of others. For reasons of practical efficiency the Identity Exploration (IDEX) computer software (Weinreich & Ewart, 1999a, b)[1] is required for analysing identity in accordance with ISA concepts. Although some useful understanding of identity can be achieved from individual commentaries, a deeper comprehension will emerge from the practical application of ISA using identity instruments customised for individuals whose identities are to be elucidated. Delving beneath the surface requires analytic concepts of a different order from those that can be assessed by direct questioning, as is shown in this volume. A fundamental instance is the conceptual distinction between *aspirational identification* with another, or wishing to emulate characteristics of that other, and *de facto* or *empathetic identification* with another, or being close to that other in the actuality of perceived shared characteristics. Direct questioning or observation, even with considerable analytic skill, is generally insufficient for assessing the individual's pattern of varying identifications, either aspirational or empathetic, with the numerous people and institutions of importance. Conceptually, the notion that identification with another is an absolute (*all* or *none* as commonly conceptualised) can readily be replaced with the more accurate one that the individual identifies to varying degrees and in different ways with many other people. In practice however such identifications are impossibly laborious to assess without using efficient computer-aided procedures.

The exposition presented in this volume is a scientific approach to human existence, without being mechanistic and scientistic. It acknowledges the human agency of the intentional self and with it degrees of individual autonomy varying according to context and mood-state. Rather than mechanistic linear cause–effect determinism, it contends that through agency and innovative thinking humans are capable of creating new world-views, cultures and technologies that in principle cannot be predicted. New scenarios alter earlier established relationships between events and their consequences, thereby resulting in degrees of indeterminism in the longer term. In a scientific enterprise concerned with explanation, ISA directs attention to handling such indeterminism without losing a firm hold on explication (Chapter 2, shown schematically in Figure 2.4).

CONTENDING AND COPING WITH FUTURE STRESS

Consider, for example, the varying significance and meaning of stress for the person according to biographical phases and cultural norms located within socio-historical eras. That which is stressful for a person is to an extent a feature of self's identity, and self's core identity aspirations reflect to some degree self's mode of contending with arenas of stress within that identity consequent upon biographical experience. One's aspirational identifications with a certain set of cultural norms will generate specific manifestations of stress and modes of contending with them. Hence, characteristic manifestations of stress will vary from one culture to another, and from one socio-historical era to another: Witness the evidence of differing female identity vulnerabilities according to professional subcultures in the contemporary era, evidenced in part by women grappling with conflicted identifications with their parents, particularly their mothers, who represent cultural norms of an earlier era (Chapters 6 to 9). For the future, one should expect modes of stress and manners of contending with them that are currently unknown.

The fact that cultural norms in the future are to an extent unknowable can nevertheless be handled for investigations in conjunction with continuing symbolic representations of persisting cultural manifestations. Thus, for each individual, one would establish the personal arenas of cognitive–affective incompatibilities indicated by low structural pressures on constructs, these latter designating the matters as they may be in the future about which the individual is distressed. In the case of the anorexic woman reported in Chapter 11, these distressing matters were ones of control and independent moral worth, engendered as a result of her biographical experiences.

One would continue by revealing the individual's core dimensions of identity, by way of high structural pressures on constructs, that represent both rational identity aspirations and processes with which the individual may in the future engage in an effort to contend with stress. The anorexic woman's mode of contending with her distress over control and moral worth was to attempt to adopt an idealised view of herself – *in a state of defensive high self-regard* – that directly negated her biographical experience. This identity state accorded with her core dimensions of identity, which in their centrally evaluative aspect were themselves reflections of her experience. The process of defensive negation which she adopted was ineffectual and she (agentic *Self 1*) vacillated between this unsustainable fantasy view of herself (*Self 2b*) and her unreconstructed out-of-control, damaged and depressed state (*Self 2a*); together these constituted processes that sustained her anorexia.

This analysis of people's arenas of stress and their processes of contending with stress, when presented as formal theoretical postulates, enables the designation for the future of as yet unknown personally stressed issues. Thus, recall the conceptualisation of cognitive–affective incompatibilities in terms of structural pressures, such that high structural pressure denotes cognitive–affective consonance and low structural pressure indicates substantial cognitive–affective dissonance (Chapter 1, operationalised as indicated in Chapter 2). Instant threats to one's life, integrity and dignity may be short-lived and dealt with by rapid reactions, such as fighting for survival, defending one's moral stance, or fleeing from the threats. Successful implementation of such stratagems contends with the threat, only the unpleasant experience of which remains. However, continuing and habitual appraisals that undermine significant features of one's identity have long-term consequences. Three theoretical postulates attend to personal arenas of distress, the process the person adopts to contend with stress, and the long-term consequences of unresolved stress.

Theoretical postulate 1: Habitual appraisals indicative of long-term arenas of psychological stress
One's constructs associated with cognitive–affective dissonance in respect of habitual appraisals, and discourses used to express them, denote arenas of psychological distress, the forms of which are indicated by the content of these particular discourses.

Theoretical postulate 2: Contending with chronic stress
One's core evaluative dimensions of identity represent preferred modes of contending with such long-term distress, whereby one appeals to one's most stable identity aspirations, attempting to implement one's ideal state.

Theoretical postulate 3: Generation of chronic fatigue
When one's preferred mode of contending with chronic stress does not provide effective resolution of the circumstances of long-term distress, the continuing conflictual pressures will in time induce chronic fatigue.

During one's biographical history one will in all likelihood have developed constructs that characterise psychologically stressed arenas, these being conflicted dimensions of one's identity, and other constructs that represent routes for contending with stress in line with core and stable dimensions of identity. If this analysis is correct, some at least of one's core identity aspirations will represent orientations that one has developed in order to contend and maybe cope with distressing experiences. Cross-culturally and within societal subcultures, both experienced arenas of stress and habitual contending processes will vary according to cultural norms. For the future, people will be likely to experience as yet unknown issues engendering stress, and develop as yet unforeseen processes contending with stress, as hitherto unanticipated scenarios become newly pervasive normative frameworks. Both the unknown issues and individual processes of future scenarios may nevertheless be elucidated using the ISA conceptual framework as outlined here.

Whether or not *contending with stress* translates into *coping with stress* is another matter for analysis. In the anorexic's adoption of a defensive high self-regard state (Chapter 11), she is evidently not coping, this defensive state being itself a feature of her continuing anorexic processes whereby she vacillates between this and her unreconstructed out-of-control state. However, in the case of the ideologically committed Palestinian girl (Chapter 4), her defensive high self-regard in the immediate short-term may well be an effective coping process, albeit signifying a rigid and brittle perspective. ISA enables such distinctions between *contending* and *coping* with stress in future unknown scenarios to be both conceptualised and empirically assessed whatever the then extant contemporary cultural norms. This extension of theorising beyond what has been presented in the body of this volume illustrates the nature of typical theoretical elaborations possible with the open-ended conceptual framework of ISA, and their practical application given its operationalisation whereby emic matters are integrated with etic concepts.

NOTE

1 A fully effective prototype of the IDEX software is currently available from the authors. The dedicated software analyses identity in depth, directly incorporating procedures for assessing parameters of identity in accordance with the definitions of psychological concepts given in Chapter 1, and operationalised for empirical work in Chapter 2. The basic module is essential for generating meaningful identity instruments and obtaining immediate results of identity structure analyses. It is not a statistical package and does not use any statistical concepts. A subsequent module facilitates the aggregation of the ISA parameters across selected individuals and groups to form 'export files' for use with standard statistical packages.

REFERENCES

Weinreich, P. & Ewart, S. (1999a) *IDEXbasic for Windows Version 3.0: Identity Exploration computer software for idiographic, basic case studies*. Jordanstown: University of Ulster School of Psychology.

Weinreich, P. & Ewart, S. (1999b) *IDEXnomo for Windows Version 3.0: Identity Exploration computer software for nomothetic, comparative studies*. Jordanstown: University of Ulster School of Psychology.

Appendix

A BIBLIOGRAPHY OF SELECTED ISA RESEARCH

The editors gratefully acknowledge the assistance of Selwyn Black in assembling this bibliography of ISA research.

Occasional national and international workshops are available to offer 'hands-on' guidance on the practical application of the ISA conceptual framework using the IDEX computer software (see conference press releases for scheduled events).

Ali, N. (1999) *Community and Individual Identity of the Kashmiri Community in the United Kingdom*. DPhil, Luton University.

Bacova, V. (1997) Primordialny versus instrumentalny zaklad etnickej a narodnej identity (Primordial versus instrumental basis of ethnic and national identity). *Ceskoslovenska Psychologie*, 41, 4, 303–313. ISSN 0009-062X.

Bacova, V. (1997) Zvladanie dvojitej socialnej identity jedinca (Coping with double social identity). *Psychologia a Patopsychologia Dietata*, 32, 2, 149–154. ISSN 0555-5574.

Bacova, V. (1998) Moznosti zistovania identity: metodika IDEX (The possibilities of personal identity assessment: the IDEX [Identity Exploration] method). *Ceskoslovenska Psychologie*, 42, 5, 449–461. ISSN 0009-062X.

Bacova, V. (1999) Ethnic/political identity and beliefs about ethnicity among academics in Slovakia. *Studia Psychologica*, 41, 2, 151–166. ISSN 0039-3320.

Bacova, V. (2000) Differences in normative gender beliefs in groups of adolescent boys and girls. *Studia Psychologica*, 42, 3, 261–266. ISSN 0039-3220.

Bacova, V. and Mikulaskova, G. (2000) Rodove presvedcenia a rodove identifikacie adolescentnych chlapcov a dievcat (Gender beliefs and gender identifications in adolescent boys and girls). *Ceskosovenska Psychologie*, 44, 1, 26–44. ISSN 0009-062X.

Bacova, V. and Sutaj, S. (1993) *Re-Slovakization: The Changes of Nationality and Ethnic Identity in Historical Development in Slovak-Hungarian Environment*. In *Small Nations and Ethnic Minorities in an Emerging Europe*. Slavica Verlag dr. Anton Kovac, Munchen 1993, 239–242. ISBN 3-927077-04-6.

Badham, P. (1986) *A Theoretical Base for Investigating Counselling Training*, BPS Counselling Psychology Section Review, Vol. 1, No. 2.

Badham, P. (1995) *Counselling Identity and Personal Development: A Study of Post Graduate Students of Counselling*. MA in Counselling Psychology, Universities of Brighton and Sussex.

Black, W. R. S. (1999) *An Exploration in Counselling Identity in Counsellors who Deal with Trauma*. MSc, University of Ulster.

Black, W. R. S. and Weinreich, P. (2000a) *Exploring the Issue of Identity in Trauma Counsellors*. In *Eisteach: Journal of Counselling and Therapy for the Irish Association for Counselling and Therapy,* Vol. 2(12), 27–32.

Black, W. R. S. and Weinreich, P. (2000b) *An Exploration of Counselling Identity in Counsellors who Deal with Trauma*. In *Traumatology. Online Journal*: *www.fsu.edu/~trauma* Vol. 6(1).

Black, W. R. S., Weinreich, P. and Irving, P. (2000) *Counsellors' Experiences of Working with the Survivors of the Omagh Bomb*. In *Counselling: The Journal of the British Association for Counsellors and Therapists*, November 2000.

Bleakley, E. W. (1985) *An Investigation of the Self Concept and Life Style of Selected Unemployed Males in the South Antrim Area*. MSc Applied Social Research, University of Ulster.

Bloomer, F. and Weinreich, P. (2002) Cross-community relations projects and inter-dependent identities. In, O. Hargie and D. Dickson (eds) *Researching the Troubles: Social Science Perspectives on the Northern Ireland Conflict*. Edinburgh: Mainstream Publishing.

Connor, T. (1991) *An Identity Exploration of Anorexia Nervosa within a Family Context*. DPhil, University of Ulster.

Donnelly, S. (1994) *Ethnic Identity Redefinition During Acquisition of one's Ancestral Language (Irish): An approach based on Identity Structure Analysis*. DPhil, University of Ulster.

Doyle, D. (1999) *The Effects of Retirement on Identity Development*. DPhil, University of Ulster.

Foreman, J. I. (1987) *An Investigation of the Role of Value Systems and Peers in Relation to Day-care Provision for the Under Fives*. MSc Applied Social Research, University of Ulster.

Fox, M. (1996) *An Exploration of the Depressed Identity using Identity Structure Analysis*. MSc Applied Psychology, University of Ulster.

Harris, P. D. G. (1980) *Identity Development in Female Patients Suffering from Anorexia Nervosa and Bulimia Nervosa: An Application of Weinreich's Identity Structure Analysis*. MPsychol, Liverpool: University of Liverpool.

Harris, P. D. G. (1988) *Identity Development and Identification Conflict in Female Anorectic and Bulimic Patients*. In E. J. Anthony & C. Chiland (Eds.) *The Child in his Family. Perilous Development: Child Raising and Identity Formation under Stress*. Volume 8. New York: Wiley.

Harris, P. D. G. (1992) *Développement de l'Identité et Conflit d'Identification chez des Patientes Anorexiques et Boulimiques*. In E. J. Anthony and C. Chiland (Eds.) *Le Développement en Péril: L'enfant dans sa Famille*. Presses Universitaires de France.

Hindmarch, C. J. (1985) *A Study of the Relationship Between Ethnic Action, Perceptions of Aspects of the Socio-Historical Context and Motivation to Becoming Communicatively Competent in English*. MSc (Race Relations), Birmingham: University of Aston.

Irvine, H. (1995) *Identity Development and Adult Education: A Theoretical and Empirical Investigation of Identity Development in Adults Returning to Education*. DPhil, University of Ulster.

Johnston, S. (2000) *Self-Concept and Academic Choice: Stereotypes of Particular Student Groups and Gender Role Stereotypes*. PhD, Queens University Belfast.

Jones, L. (1998) *Identity Structure Analysis with Primary School Children Identified as Experiencing Emotional Difficulty*. MSc Educational Psychology, University of Sheffield.

Kelly, A. J. D. (1983) *Does Unemployment Change Self-Concept? An Exploratory Investigation using Identity Structure Analysis.* MSc Applied Social Research, University of Ulster.

Kelly, A. J. D. (1989) *Ethnic Identification, Association and Redefinition: Muslim Pakistanis and Greek Cypriots in Britain.* In K. Liebkind (Ed.) *New Identities in Europe: Immigrant Ancestry and the Ethnic Identity of Youth*, Volume 3 of the European Science Foundation series: 'Studies in European Migration'. London: Gower.

King, D. (1991) *An Exploratory Study of the Identity Structures of Young Women who were Formerly Foster Children.* MSc Applied Social Research, University of Ulster.

Liebkind, K. (1983) *Dimensions of Identity in Multiple Group Allegiance.* In A. Jacobson-Widding (Ed.) *Identity: Personal and Socio-Cultural.* Stockholm: Almqvist & Wiksell International. Atlantic Highlands: Humanities Press.

Liebkind, K. (1984) *Minority Identity and Identification Processes: A Social Psychological Study. Finnish Society of Sciences and Letters, Commentationes Scientiarum Socialium*, 22, Helsinki. PhD, University of Helsinki.

Liebkind, K. (1989) *New Identities in Europe: Immigrant Ancestry and the Ethnic Identity of Youth.* Volume 3 of the European Science Foundation series: 'Studies in European Migration'. London: Gower.

Louden, E. R. (1988) *Ego and Moral Development in Relation to 16–20-year-olds.* (Unpublished) MSc Applied Social Research, University of Ulster.

Luk, C.-L. (1992) *Multiple Ethnic Identification in Chinese Students.* MSc, Chinese University of Hong Kong.

MacNabb, A., McCoy, J., Northover, M. and Weinreich, P. (1994) *The Entrepreneurial Identity: Application of Identity Structure Analysis to the Study of Entrepreneurship.* In *Frontiers for Entrepreneurship Research 1992*, Vol. 12, 89–103.

MacNabb, A., McCoy, J., Weinreich, P. and Northover, M. (1993) *Using Identity Structure Analysis (ISA) to Investigate Female Entrepreneurship.* In *Entrepreneurship & Regional Development*, Vol. 5, 301–313.

McAtamney, G. (1995) *Comparison of Actors' and Teachers' Identities.* MSc Applied Psychology, University of Ulster.

McCarney, W. (1992) *Changes in Identity Structure of Unemployed School-Leavers Consequent upon a Youth Training Programme.* DPhil, University of Ulster.

McCoy, D. (1986) *Identity Transition in Persons Undergoing Elective Interval Sterilisation and Vasectomy: An Approach Based on Identity Structure Analysis.* DPhil, University of Ulster.

McGarry, M. (2000) *Lone Motherhood, Identity and Psychosocial Health.* MSc thesis, University of Ulster.

McMackin, D. (1993) *Redefinition of Identity Following Surgery for Temporal Lobe Epilepsy.* DPhil, University College Dublin.

Ming, L. (1999) *Under the Two Systems: Comparing the Ethnic Stereotypes and Identification Patterns of Hong Kong and Guang Zhou People.* MSc, Chinese University of Hong Kong.

Needham, S. (1984) *Maternity Blues and Personal Identity Development in First-Time Mother: An Exploratory Study.* Diploma in Clinical Psychology. Leicester: British Psychological Society.

Northover, M. (1988) *A Theoretical and Empirical Investigation of Ethnic Identity and Bilingualism.* DPhil, University of Ulster.

Northover, M. (1988a) *Bilinguals and Linguistic Identities.* In J. N. Jorgensen, E. Hansen, A. Holmen and J. Gimbel (Eds.) *Bilingualism in Society and School.* Copenhagen Studies in Bilingualism, Vol. 5. Clevedon: Multilingual Matters.

Northover, M., Harris, S. and Duffy, M. (1994). *Politicians, Ideological Messages and Voters*. In *Political Psychology*, Vol. 15(4), 713–30.

O'Keeffe, P. (2000) *Suicidology, Counselling and Identity Exploration: An Investigation of Postvention Strategies for Suicide Survivors*. MSc, University of Ulster.

O'Neill, S. (1994) *An Identity Exploration of Children with Special Educational Needs Within the Mainstream Context*. MSc Applied Psychology, University of Ulster.

Phoenix, S. (1994) *Deafness: Identity and Communication*. DPhil, University of Ulster.

Price, L. (1993) *An Analysis of Ethnic and Indigenous Identity Structure in Adolescent Girls*. MEd, West London Institute of Higher Education.

Rampton, B. (1986) *A Methodology for Describing Socio-Linguistic Variability within Multilingual Settings in General, and 'Interactive' and 'Reactive' Ethnic Processes in Language in Particular*. In *York Papers in Linguistics* Vol. 12. York: University of York.

Rampton, B. (1987) *Sociolinguistic Variability in Multilingual Settings*. PhD, University of London Institute of Education.

Reid, H. R. (1990) *Theoretical and Empirical Evaluation of Occupational Stress*. DPhil, University of Ulster.

Rougier, N. (2000) *Ethno-Religious Identities: An Identity Structure Analysis of Clergy in Ireland, North and South*. DPhil, University of Ulster.

Saunders, M. (1975) *Individual Case Study Analysis of Mothers of ESN Children*. MSc, Bradford: University of Bradford.

Saunderson, W. (1995) *A Theoretical and Empirical Investigation of Gender and Urban Space: The Production and Consumption of the Built Environment*. PhD, University of Ulster.

Saunderson, W. (1997) *Women, Cities and Identity: The Production and Consumption of Gendered Urban Space in Belfast*. In A. Byrne and M. Leonard (Eds.) *Women and Irish Society: A Sociological Reader*. Belfast: Beyond the Pale Publications.

Saunderson, W. (2001) *Issues of Women's Fear in Urban Space: The Case of Belfast*. In *Women and Environments International* (Special 25th Anniversary Double Issue), Vol. 50(51), 28–31.

Saunderson, W. (2002) *Women, Academia and Identity: Constructions of Equal Opportunities in the 'New Managerialism' – A Case of 'Lipstick on the Gorilla'?* In *Higher Education Quarterly*, Vol. 56, No. 4.

Saunderson, W. (2002) *Women, Academia and Identity: 'Vulnerable' Identities in the 'New Managerialism' of UK Higher Education*. MSc thesis, University of Ulster.

Sheeran, P. and Abraham, C. (1994) *Unemployment and Self-Conception: A Symbolic Interactionist Analysis*. In *Journal of Community & Applied Psychology* Vol. 4, 115–129.

Stapleton, K. and Northover, M. (1999) *Ethnic Identity in Context: A Comparative Study of Catholicism and Nationalism in Northern and Southern Ireland*. In *Journal of Multilingual and Multicultural Development*, Vol. 20(3), 237–252.

Thornton, M. (2001) *Processes of Gender Identity in a Northern Irish Context*. (Unpublished) DPhil, University of Ulster.

Wager, M. (1993) *Constructions of Femininity in Academic Women: Continuity between Private and Professional Identity*. DPhil, University of Ulster.

Weinreich, P. (1969) *Theoretical and Experimental Evaluation of Dissonance Processes*. PhD, London: University of London.

Weinreich, P. (1976a) *Ethnic Identification and Masculine Identity Formation in a Black Adolescent Boy*. Mimeographed report: *SSRC Research Unit on Ethnic Relations at the University of Bristol*, Bristol, England (currently: Centre for Research in Ethnic Relations, University of Warwick, Coventry, England).

Weinreich, P. (1976b) *A Jamaican Girl's Identity Crisis Involving her Strongly Conflicted Identifications with English Girls.* Mimeographed report: *SSRC Research Unit on Ethnic Relations at the University of Bristol*, Bristol, England (currently: Centre for Research in Ethnic Relations. University of Warwick, Coventry, England).

Weinreich, P. (1976c) *Strong Feminine Sex-Role Identification in a West Indian Girl for whom the School Leaving Transition Results in a Minor Identity Crisis.* Mimeographed report: *SSRC Research Unit on Ethnic Relations at the University of Bristol*, Bristol, England (currently: Centre for Research in Ethnic Relations, University of Warwick, Coventry, England).

Weinreich, P. (1979a) *Cross-Ethnic Identification and Self-Rejection in a Black Adolescent.* In G. Verma and C. Bagley (Eds.) *Race, Education and Identity.* London: Macmillan.

Weinreich, P. (1979b) *Ethnicity and Adolescent Identity Conflict.* In V. Saifullah Khan (Ed.) *Minority Families in Britain.* London: Macmillan.

Weinreich, P. (1980) *Manual for Identity Exploration using Personal Constructs.* London: Social Science Research Council.

Weinreich, P. (1983a) *Emerging from Threatened Identities: Ethnicity and Gender in Redefinitions of Ethnic Identity.* In G. Breakwell (Ed.) *Threatened Identities.* Chichester: Wiley.

Weinreich, P. (1983b) *Psychodynamics of Personal and Social Identity: Theoretical Concepts and their Measurement in Adolescents from Belfast Sectarian and Bristol Minority Groups.* In A. Jacobson-Widding (Ed.) *Identity: Personal and Socio-Cultural.* Stockholm: Almqvist & Wiksell International; Atlantic Highlands: Humanities Press.

Weinreich, P. (1985a) *Rationality and Irrationality in Racial and Ethnic Relations: A Metatheoretical Framework.* In *Ethnic and Racial Studies.* Vol. 8, 500–515.

Weinreich, P. (1985b) *Identity Exploration in Adolescence.* In *International Journal of Adolescent Medicine and Health*, Vol. 1 & 2; 52–71.

Weinreich, P. (1986a) *The Operationalization of Identity Theory in Racial and Ethnic Relations.* In J. Rex and D. Mason (Eds.) *Theories of Race and Ethnic Relations.* Cambridge: Cambridge University Press.

Weinreich, P. (1986) *Manual for Identity Exploration using Personal Constructs.* (Reprint). Coventry: University of Warwick/Economic and Social Research Council. Centre for Research in Ethnic Relations.

Weinreich, P. (1989a) *Variations in Ethnic Identity: Identity Structure Analysis.* In K. Liebkind (Ed.) *New Identities in Europe: Immigrant Ancestry and the Ethnic Identity of Youth.* Volume 3 of the European Science Foundation series: 'Studies in European Migration'. London: Gower.

Weinreich, P. (1989b) *Conflicted Identifications: A Commentary on Identity Structure Analysis Concepts.* In K. Liebkind (Ed.) *New Identities in Europe: Immigrant Ancestry and the Ethnic Identity of Youth.* Volume 3 of the European Science Foundation series: 'Studies in European Migration'. London: Gower.

Weinreich, P. (1991a) *Ethnic Identities and Indigenous Psychologies in Pluralist Societies.* In *Psychology and Developing Societies*, Vol. 3(1), 73–92.

Weinreich, P. (1991b) *National and Ethnic Identities: Theoretical Concepts in Practice.* In *Innovation in Social Science Research*, Vol. 4(1), 9–29.

Weinreich, P. (1992) *Socio-Psychological Maintenance of Ethnicity in Northern Ireland – a Commentary.* In *The Psychologist*, Vol. 5, 345–346.

Weinreich, P. (1998) *Social Exclusion and Multiple Identities.* In *Soundings: A Journal of Politics and Culture.* Vol. 9, 139–144.

Weinreich, P., Doherty, J. and Harris, P. (1985) *Empirical Assessment of Identity in Anorexia and Bulimia Nervosa*. In *Journal of Psychiatric Research*, Vol. 19, 197–303.

Weinreich, P., Doherty, J. and Harris, P. (1986) *Empirical Assessment of Identity in Anorexia and Bulimia Nervosa*. In G. I. Szmukler, P. D. Slade, P. Harris, D. Benton, and G. F. M. Russell (Eds.) *Anorexia Nervosa and Bulimic Disorders: Current Perspectives*. Oxford: Pergamon.

Weinreich, P. and Ewart, S. (1999) *IDEX-Basic for Windows Version. Identity Exploration Computer Software for Basic Case Studies*.

Weinreich, P. and Ewart, S. (1999) *IDEX-NOMO for Windows. Identity Exploration-(Nomothetic) Computer Software*.

Weinreich, P. and Ewart, S. (1999) *IDEX-PHASE for Windows. Identity Exploration (Phase Comparison) Computer Software*.

Weinreich, P., Kelly. A. J. D. and Maja, C. (1988) *Black Youth in South Africa: Situated Identities and Patterns of Ethnic Identification*. In D. Canter, C. Jesuino, L. Soczka, and G. Stephenson (Eds.) *Environmental Social Psychology*. Dordrecht: Kluwer Academic.

Weinreich, P., Luk, C.-L. and Bond, M. (1996) *Ethnic Stereotyping and Identification in a Multicultural Context: 'Acculturation', Self-Esteem and Identity Diffusion in Hong Kong Chinese University Students*. In *Psychology and Developing Societies*. Vol. 8(1), 107–169.

Author Index

Subject Index